Multimedia Systems and Applications

Series editor

Borko Furht, Florida Atlantic University, Boca Raton, USA

More information about this series at http://www.springer.com/series/6298

Shalin Hai-Jew
Editor

Data Analytics in Digital Humanities

 Springer

Editor
Shalin Hai-Jew
Kansas State University
Manhattan, KS, USA

Multimedia Systems and Applications
ISBN 978-3-319-85408-3   ISBN 978-3-319-54499-1   (eBook)
DOI 10.1007/978-3-319-54499-1

Printed on acid-free paper

This Springer imprint is published by Springer Nature
The registered company is Springer International Publishing AG
The registered company address is: Gewerbestrasse 11, 6330 Cham, Switzerland

This book is for R. Max.

Preface

The digital humanities, putatively the intersection between the humanities disciplines and computation, was popularized in the early 1990s. In the intervening decades, the "digital humanities" has not yet settled on a defined self-identity. One indicator of this is that of the dozens of "DH" manifestos on the Web; they all have differing and competing visions for the field. Another indicator is the rich variety of work being done under these auspices that does not fall into simple summaries and descriptions. The Digital Humanities Manifesto 2.0, which originated from nine seminars co-taught by Jeffrey Schnapp and Todd Presner, and was released by the UCLA Mellon Seminar in Digital Humanities, reads in part:

> **Digital Humanities** is not a unified field but an array of convergent practices that explore a universe in which: (a) print is no longer the exclusive or the normative medium in which knowledge is produced and/or disseminated; instead, print finds itself absorbed into new, multimedia configurations; and (b) digital tools, techniques, and media have altered the production and dissemination of knowledge in the arts, human and social sciences. The Digital Humanities seeks to play an inaugural role with respect to a world in which universities—no longer the sole producers, stewards, and disseminators of knowledge or culture—are called upon to shape natively digital models of scholarly discourse for the newly emergent public spheres of the present era (the www, the blogosphere, digital libraries, etc.), to model excellence and innovation in these domains, and to facilitate the formation of networks of knowledge production, exchange, and dissemination that are, at once, global and local" ("The Digital Humanities Manifesto 2.0," 2009).

DH work is additive and contributes to learning and methods in a range of extant fields. It is about hybrid mash-ups that pull from analog and digital sources and that give back digitally. There are combinations of research and analytical methods, drawing from quantitative and qualitative methods, going Web scale and small scale, employing a range of frameworks, and combining various disciplines, often through collaborative and distributed teams.

Deconstructing "DH"

The "digital" part of the "digital humanities" involves a range of technologies: the Web and Internet, mobile devices, social media, databases, digital curation platforms, geographical mapping tools, social mapping tools, linguistic analysis software programs, data analytics tools, and others. The "humanities" focus points to a combination of fields: the classics, literature, philosophy, religious studies, psychology, modern and ancient languages, culture studies, art, history, music, philosophy, theater, film, political science, geography, anthropology, linguistics, social work, communications, and others. For all the technological focuses, the DH work is about people and for people through the ages and for the ages. Every work, no matter how technological, contains the human touch and is conceptualized for human benefit. The works are human-readable, in general, and are packaged as stories and understandings. The works are often aesthetically dazzling: think interactive webscapes, data visualizations, 3D virtual immersive spaces, and network diagrams.

Likewise, one can ask what "data" in the digital humanities is. Well, the general opinion is that everything has some informational value. The world is informatized, and DH researchers themselves are not only researchers and elicitors of insights, but they are in-world participants making the world and information simultaneously. The information is viewed through a subjective and interpretive lens, but that interpretation is backed up by more traditionally quantitative (statistical) and computational (machine learning) methods. The work is not seen as neutral nor theory-free not independent of its contributors.

The challenge is in how to turn a "thing" in the world into something with informational and social value. This data may seem at once a range of contradictions: ephemeral and fragile and yet permanent and perpetual, subjective and objective, created for the local but also the global, inclusive of machine-scale distant reading methods as well as close human reading.

The Spirit of DH

Often, the spirit of the digital humanities is countercultural; it fights against extant power structures and norms. The DH is often value-informed and socially active, in the pursuit of social justice. DH practitioners take a questioning stance because the world is never quite as it seems. There are elusive and latent interpreted truths to be discovered or (co)created.

While its core spirit is of changing the current order, at the same time, DH work requires ever higher levels of expertise in content fields and technological methods. The work is anti-Establishment but requires some of the expertise of Establishment and accrued skills from years of development. Virtuosity in the digital humanities simultaneously requires the fiery rebel spirit and the iciness of acquired expertise. The work is often inclusive of nonexperts and the online crowds, who are sourced for their contributions and voices and concerns in rich ways. It seems fitting that in this hypersocial age that such broadscale collaborations exist.

The spirit of DH is of experimentation along the entire work chain: theorizing and conceptualization, research, data collection, content curation, data processing, data analytics, and often open publishing (of digital corpora and collections, of virtualized experiences, of publications, and of multimedial presentations). The order of the work is not necessarily linear but recursive; for some projects, conceptually and somewhat practically, the work is continuous, ongoing, and perpetual. While some methods and technologies are borrowed from a range of fields, digital humanists have applied experimental means to every step of the process as well, with new technological platforms and tools and fresh methods. Problem-solving is achieved on-the-fly, often with the direct support and help of Web developers, coders, server administrators, data scientists, computer scientists, and librarians. This is about an artist and artisan sensibility with code.

If one asks practitioners what the digital humanities is, there is a range of answers. A common response is to go to the work, to explore it in depth, and to acquire a more inductive sense of the answer. Certainly, as DH rose from a groundswell of practice and self-definition, it may be best to understand it from a bottom-up instead of a top-down way. While practitioners are aware of each other's work, the focus is not on conformance to common practice but rather diversity. The general consensus is that DH is still emerging as an approach. The feeling is that the work is exploratory and provisional and open to re-interpretations and re-visionings.

About This Book

Data Analytics in Digital Humanities was over a year in the making, with various individuals and authoring teams conducting their research and writing it up, going through double-blind peer reviews, revising, and finalizing their work. Here, the respective authors describe their data analytics work in the digital humanities.

The book is comprised of six parts:

Part I: Design of Representational Systems
Part II: Text Capture and Textual Exploration
Part III: Engaging Social Data
Part IV: Applied Technologies for Data Analytics
Part V: Sense-Making in the World
Part VI: Support for Digital Humanities Work

The book is not comprehensive by any means. There are so many live projects and endeavors that each author and team really only have a limited perspective on the whole.

In Part I, "Design of Representational Systems," there are two works that describe data labeling. In "Semantic Web for Cultural Heritage Valorization," a research team proposes a set of ontology modules (Cultural-ON) to model the classification of cultural heritage data, given the heterogeneous nature of cultural artifacts, both analog and digital, tangible and intangible. The authors of Chap. 1 include Dr. Giorgia Lodi, Luigi Asprino, Andrea Giovanni Nuzzolese, Dr. Valentina Presutti, Dr. Aldo Gangemi, Dr. Diego Reforgiato Recupero, Chiara Veninata, and Annarita Orsini.

Dr. Gian Piero Zarri offers an in-depth description of Narrative Knowledge Representation Language (NKRL) and its use to describe narratives as logical associations based on "elementary events." The careful specifications enable its use conceptually and computationally to capture and represent the elements that comprise narratives. Zarri's chapter is titled "Using the Formal Representations of 'Elementary Events' to Set Up Computational Models of Full 'Narratives'" (Chap. 2).

The second part, "Text Capture and Textual Exploration," features two works related to text analytics. Joshua L. Weese, Dr. William H. Hsu, Dr. Jessica C. Murphy, and Dr. Kim Brillante Knight describe a machine learning-based classifier they developed to identify parody, an elusive challenge. Their work is titled "Parody Detection: An Annotation, Feature Construction, and Classification Approach to the Web of Parody" (Chap. 3).

Dr. Michael Percillier, in Chap. 4 "Creating and Analyzing Literary Corpora," describes a methodical process using Python and other tools to collect and process literary corpora based around a particular topic. He includes Python code to demonstrate efficient automated means to build text corpora.

Part III, "Engaging Social Data," offers two works summarizing "social" data. The first is about information from online social networks, and the second about the social aspects of learning.

Davide Di Fatta and Roberto Musotto apply integrated sentiment analysis (iSA) to online social networks in Chap. 5, "Content and Sentiment Analysis on Online Social Networks (OSNs)." They consider various ways to apply their research insights to practical applications, like marketing through social media.

In Chap. 6: "The Role of Data in Evaluating the Effectiveness of Networked Learning: An Auto-Ethnographic Evaluation of Four Experiential Learning Projects," Jonathan Bishop employs a light auto-ethnographic approach to study the role of data in evaluating networked learning across four experiential learning projects. One central question is whether there are more effective designed electronic stand-ins for educator-learner interactions to promote learning.

In the fourth part, "Applied Technologies for Data Analytics," one work focuses on computational linguistic analysis based on psychological features in texts. Another focuses on capturing research insights from related tags networks.

In Chap. 7, "Psychological Text Analysis in the Digital Humanities," Ryan L. Boyd describes insightful uses of the Linguistic Inquiry and Word Count (LIWC) tool for text analysis. His long-term uses of LIWC and direct contributions to the tool's co-development (in LIWC2015) make him a singularly appropriate author for this excellent work. Boyd argues that computational linguistic exploration of psychological aspects in language is an untapped and highly promising area of research.

In "Parsing Related Tags Networks from Flickr to Explore Crowd-Sourced Keyword Associations" (Chap. 8), Dr. Shalin Hai-Jew describes how crowd-based folk tags applied to digital imagery on a content-sharing site may be used for creating collective mental models of large-scale phenomena.

Part V is about "Sense-Making in the World." In this part, Dr. Cobi Smith describes the use of technological methods to harness crowd-sourced imagery during natural disasters. The methods and tools described in this chapter, "A Case Study of Crowdsourcing Imagery Coding in Natural Disasters" (Chap. 9), may have broad applications in the digital humanities.

Dr. Glenda Alicia Leung's "YouTube Comments as Metalanguage Data on Non-standard Languages: The Case of Trinidadian Creole English in Soca Music" (Chap. 10) suggests new analytical applications of interaction comment data related to shared, social videos. This work captures the energy and power of nonstandard lived language in connecting people on Google's global video-sharing platform.

Chapter 11 is about "Creating Inheritable Digital Codebooks for Qualitative Research Data Analysis." Here, Dr. Hai-Jew describes the research importance of sharing digital codebooks, particularly with the popularization of Computer Assisted Qualitative Data AnalysiS (CAQDAS) tools, and she offers firsthand insights on effective processes for developing and sharing such digital codebooks. If researchers are to leave a legacy of their unique coding "fists," then computational means may offer a more convenient and efficient way of transfer.

In Part VI, "Support for Digital Humanities Work," one author highlights supports for DH work. Hannah Lee, in "Is it Worth It? The Library and Information Science Degree in the Digital Humanities" (Chap. 12), argues for the importance of library and information sciences (LIS) to practically support the work in the digital humanities.

So what is the state of data analytics in the digital humanities? Based on these collected works, it is a rich and evolving one, driven by local research needs and some global ones. DH practitioners harness technologies to complement and augment the human abilities of perception, expression, analysis, and memory. The technologies used range from open-source and free to closed-source and proprietary, and these tools are cobbled in creative and complex sequences for understanding and analysis. The skill comes not only in the applied techniques but also in the insights surfaced and the sharing of the applied and innovative techniques. While some data analytics results are "reproducible" and "repeatable" based on computational means, the assumptions underlying the DH research and data analytics are very much drawn from qualitative data analytics:

that all human phenomena have potential informational value, depending on researcher perspective and context (and vision and skill);

that human researchers are wrapped in their own subjectivities, for better and for worse, and benefit from deeper self-understandings through practiced reflection;

that all data are filtered through subjective lenses and self-informed understandings;

that data "measures" are limited, imprecise, conditional, and contested (and yet still are insightful);

that the researchers are part and parcel of the research and inform the research and
  the data findings and their applications;

that the communal context for the humanities is a critical part of the work (as
  research participants, data consumers, and researchers);

that DH research is subsumed to human needs, interests, and values;

and that social justice and practitioner ethics apply to every context.

There are inherent digital humanities truisms about data as well. For example,
writings considered classically "fictional" contain the seeds of truth, and traditionally non-fictional works may not have as much truth as advertised. In this light, there
are critical interrogations to be made, to understand the multihued shades between
truths. Data are extracted in fresh ways, with manuscripts tagged and mapped for
patterns (linguistic, spatial, psychological, cultural, and others), dialogs mined for
insights, genders explored, and cultural practices probed, across and through time.
All human residua contain substance that may be interpreted and informatized for
new ways of seeing, feeling, and being.

DH cartographers describing data analytics in the digital humanities are in the
early phases of defining and mapping this space. In theory and in practice, there are
numerous other potentials that have yet to be explored, applied, and shared.

Data Analytics in Digital Humanities offers an early look at this topic, with hand-
sketched DH data analytics "maps" of fine granular detail for particular defined
needs but which does not yet have the cardinal directions defined or accepted
compass roses.

Manhattan, KS, USA   Shalin Hai-Jew

Acknowledgments

Data Analytics in Digital Humanities would not exist were it not for the work of the respective authors. I owe each one a deep debt of gratitude. Also, thanks to Joelle Pitts, Dr. Brian Rosenblum, Nancy Hays, Dr. Bryan Alexander, Dr. Glenda Alicia Leung, and others for their help in publicizing the original "call for chapters" through their respective professional and social networks. There is a lot to be said for sharing social networks, especially for such a "big ask" as writing a chapter. At Springer, Susan Lagerstrom-Fife was seminal in the acceptance of the initial book proposal, and Jennifer Malat and others on the Springer team were critical in ensuring that this work came together. Thanks to all! Their support has enhanced the quality of the text and ultimately made this work possible. Mr. Dinesh Shanmugam and Ms. Sarumathi Hemachandirane both provided very important support in bringing the book to final published form.

Contents

Authors' Biographies

Luigi Asprino is a Ph.D. student in computer science and engineering at the University of Bologna under the supervision of Prof. Paolo Ciancarini and Dr. Valentina Presutti. He is also a research assistant at the Semantic Technology Laboratory (STLab) of the National Research Council (CNR), in Rome. In October 2014, he earned a master's degree in computer engineering from Sapienza—University of Rome. In January 2015, he joined STLab. During his period in STLab he actively contributed to the following Italian and European projects: FOOD, MARE, MiBACT, MARIO. His research interests include knowledge integration, web service composition, ontology design, and semantic web.

Jonathan Bishop is an information technology executive, researcher, and writer. He founded the Centre for Research into Online Communities and E-Learning Systems in 2005, now part of the Crocels Community Media Group. Bishop's research and development work generally falls within human-computer interaction. He has over 75 publications in this area, including on Internet trolling, cyberstalking, gamification, cyberlaw, multimedia forensics, Classroom 2.0, and Digital Teens. In addition to his B.Sc. (Hons) in Multimedia Studies and various postgraduate degrees, including in law, economics, and computing, Bishop serves in local government as a councilor and has been a school governor and contested numerous elections, including to the UK Parliament and Welsh Assembly. He is a fellow of BCS, CILIP, the InstAM, the RAI, the RSS, and the RSA, senior member of IEEE, and a member of the IMarEST with MarTech. Bishop has won prizes for his literary skills and been a finalist in national and local competitions for his environmental, community, and equality work, which often form part of action research studies. In his spare time, he enjoys listening to music, swimming, and playing chess.

Ryan L. Boyd is a Ph.D. candidate in social/personality psychology at the University of Texas at Austin. His cross-disciplinary research revolves around using computational techniques to explore and understand cognitive-behavioral links, primarily the link between a person's language and their mental worlds. Specifically, Ryan's work on the psychology of language includes high-dimensional personality assessment, values, psychological forensics, motivations, and health, among other topics. Ryan has taught multiple workshops on machine learning, data mining, and language analytics and is considered a leading expert on the psychology of language. He is the chief data scientist at Receptiviti and is the creator of several language analysis programs, including the Meaning Extraction Helper. Ryan is also the co-creator of LIWC2015, one of the most widely used psychological language analysis tools in the field of text analysis.

Davide Di Fatta is a Ph.D. student in economics and management at the University of Messina (Italy). He collaborates with the SEAS Department at the Polytechnic School of the University of Palermo (Italy). His main research fields are, on the one hand, e-commerce, e-marketing, digital marketing, and social media marketing; on the other hand, business systems, systems thinking, and social networks. Davide is editorial assistant for many international journals such as Kybernetes and IJMABS (in systemic field); IJEMR and IJMS (in marketing field). He is also Junior Member Manager for the Business System Laboratory (BS Lab), a nonprofit organization for the promotion of research and collaboration between the universities and the enterprise systems.

Aldo Gangemi is professor at Paris 13 University, and researcher at CNR, Rome. He has founded and directed the Semantic Technology Lab (STLab) of ISTC-CNR. His research focuses on Semantic Technologies as an integration of methods from Knowledge Engineering, the Semantic Web, Linked Data, Natural Language Processing, and Cognitive Science. Publications: https://scholar.google.com/citations?user=-iVGcoAAAAAJ. Software: http://wit.istc.cnr.it/stlab-tools.

Shalin Hai-Jew has worked on a number of digital humanities projects over the years, each harnessing a variety of methods and technologies. She has B.A.s in English and psychology and an M.A. in English from the University of Washington (Seattle), and an Ed.D. from Seattle University (2005). At the University of Washington, she received the Hugh Paradise Scholarship; at Seattle University, she was a Morford Scholar. She worked for The Boeing Company as a Faculty Fellow for two summers. She lived and worked in the People's Republic of China from 1988 to 1990 and 1992 to 1994, the latter 2 years with the United Nations Volunteer Programme of the United Nations Development Programme (UNDP). She works as an instructional designer at Kansas State University. She has published several authored texts and edited a number of technology-related texts. She reviews for a half-dozen academic publishers. Her research interests include online learning, computational research methods, and social media.

William H. Hsu is an associate professor of Computer Science at Kansas State University. He received a B.S. in mathematical sciences and computer science and an M.S. Eng. in computer science from Johns Hopkins University in 1993, and a Ph.D. in computer science from the University of Illinois at Urbana-Champaign in 1998. He has conducted research in digital humanities since 1998, where at the National Center for Supercomputing Applications (NCSA) he was a co-recipient of an Industrial Grand Challenge Award for visual analytics of text corpora and unsupervised learning for topic modeling. His research interests include machine learning, probabilistic reasoning, and information visualization, with applications to digital humanities, cybersecurity, education, geoinformatics, health informatics, and medical informatics. Published applications of his research include spatiotemporal event detection for veterinary epidemiology, crime mapping, and opinion mining; structured information extraction; and analysis of heterogeneous information networks. Current work in his lab deals with geospatial data science and analytics, data mining, and visualization in education research; graphical models of probability and utility for information security; and domain-adaptive models of natural language corpora and social media for text mining, link mining, sentiment analysis, and recommender systems. Dr. Hsu has over 100 publications in conferences, journals, and books.

Kim Brillante Knight is an associate professor of emerging media and communication at the University of Texas at Dallas. Her research focuses on digital culture, negotiations of power and the formation of identity, particularly in relation to marginalized groups. In her book, *Viral Structures in Literature and Digital Media: Networked Counterpublics and Participatory Capitalism* (forthcoming from Routledge), Dr. Knight addresses the role of digital media as it circulates outside of broadcast paradigms and empowers or oppresses subjects in network society. Her latest book, *Fashioning Makers and Counterpublics: Critical Making and Public Humanities*, is under advance contract with the University of Iowa Press. Her public work can be found at kimknight.com, thespiraldance.wordpress.com, and fashioningcircuits.com. More information may be accessed at: https://www.utdallas.edu/ah/events/detail.html?id=1220419626

Hannah Lee is a double alumni of UCLA, obtaining her B.A. in English and MLIS. A doctoral student at Fielding Graduate University in Santa Barbara, the University of California, Los Angeles (UCLA), she is focusing on specializing in the future developments of information systems and technology in the library and information sciences field. Her dissertation examines an organizational approach to the book publishing industry in the United States. She works as a librarian, research analyst, and informationist in the Los Angeles area. Some of her interests include copyright, intellectual property, book arts, mentoring, and volunteering for nonprofit organizations.

Glenda Alicia Leung is an independent researcher and sociolinguist from Trinidad and Tobago. She received her B.A. in English from the University of Florida and her M.A. in applied linguistics from Ball State University before earning her doctorate in English linguistics at the University of Freiburg, Germany, in 2013. Her doctoral thesis "A Synchronic Study of Monophthongs in Trinidadian English" was a quantitative acoustic and sociophonetic study that reported on vowel distribution in contemporary Trinidadian English. Her articles have appeared in *World Englishes*, *Multilingua*, and *Journal of Bilingual Education Research and Instruction*, as well as in the *Varieties of English Around the World Series* from John Benjamins. Her research interests include creole language in performance, English language learning, and language acquisition.

Giorgia Lodi is currently a research assistant at the Institute of Cognitive Sciences and Technologies (ISTC) of the National Council of Research (CNR)—Semantic Technology Laboratory (STLab) and a consultant at "Agenzia per l'Italia Digitale"—AgID. She works in such areas as open government data, Linked Open Data, Semantic Web Technologies, Distributed Systems, Big Data, and smart communities. She received a Ph.D. in computer science from the University of Bologna (Italy) in 2006. Publications: https://scholar.google.com/citations?user=W6gWCGUAAAAJ

Jessica C. Murphy is Associate Professor of Literary Studies at the University of Texas at Dallas. Her research focuses on early modern literature, culture, gender studies, and digital humanities. Murphy's publications include a book, *Virtuous Necessity: Conduct Literature and the Making of the Virtuous Woman in Early Modern England*, published by the University of Michigan Press in 2015; journal articles; solo-authored and co-written book chapters; and a co-edited collection.

Roberto Musotto is an Italian Barrister who works on commercial and property law, trusts, and organized crime. He is a Ph.D. student in economics at the University of Messina and a research and teaching assistant at the University of Palermo in Political Economy. His fields of research interest include spatial and social network analysis, organized crime, commercial law, and game theory.

Andrea Giovanni Nuzzolese is a Postdoctoral Researcher at the Semantic Technology Laboratory (STLab) of the National Research Council (CNR) in Rome, Italy. He received a Ph.D. in computer science in 2014 from the University of Bologna (Italy). His research interests include Knowledge Extraction, Ontology Design Patterns, Linked Data, and Semantic Web. He has been a researcher in the EU-funded project IKS (Interactive Knowledge Stack) and a main developer of Apache Stanbol software stack (reusable components for semantic content management). He has published scientific papers in international journals and conferences.

Annarita Orsini with a master's degree in law, is an employee of the Italian Ministry for Heritage and Cultural Activities and Tourism currently working in the specific domain of the tourism for the definition of common standard data models for key data such as point of interests, accommodations, and tourist guides. In recent years she was head of unit of the Directorate General Organization of the Italian Ministry for Heritage and Cultural Activities and Tourism working in such domains as Open Data, Linked Open Data, technical interoperability for public administrations, to cite a few.

Michael Percillier is a postdoctoral researcher at the University of Mannheim, Germany. His areas of specialization include corpus linguistics, World Englishes, literary linguistics, and historical linguistics. His research has covered the comparative study of institutionalized and learner varieties of English in Southeast Asia, the representation of nonstandardized varieties of English in literary texts, and the contact effects of Old French on Middle English in the medieval period.

Valentina Presutti is a researcher at the Semantic Technology Laboratory of the National Research Council (CNR) in Rome, and she is associated with LIPN (University Paris 13 and CNRS). She received her Ph.D. in computer science in 2006 at the University of Bologna (Italy). She has been the scientific coordinator for CNR in the EU-funded project IKS (Interactive Knowledge Stack—A framework for Semantic CMS that bring semantics at the interaction level), and she has been one of the main researchers in the EU-funded projects NeOn (Networked Ontologies—methods and tool for design of networked ontologies). She has more than 50 publications in international journals/conferences/workshops on topics such as Semantic Web, knowledge extraction, and ontology design.

Diego Reforgiato Recupero has been an Associate Professor at the Department of Mathematics and Computer Science of the University of Cagliari, Italy, since December 2015. He is a programmer, software developer, automation and ICT expert. He holds a double bachelor from the University of Catania in computer science and a doctoral degree from the Department of Computer Science of the University of Naples Federico II. In 2013 he won a Postdoctoral Researcher position within the Semantic Technology Laboratory (STLAB) of the Institute of Cognitive Sciences and Technologies (ISTC) of the National Research Council (CNR) where he worked on Semantic Web and Linked Open Data; he is still an associated researcher at STLAB where he collaborates. He is co-founder of R2M Solution S.R.L. (Italian company), R2M Solution Ltd. (UK company), and Sentimetrix Inc. (US company).

Cobi Smith has a doctorate in science communication at Australian National University. She worked as a UN consultant based inside CERN on the EU-funded Citizen Cyberlab project. She currently works in state government in Australia, in emergency services information management and disaster risk reduction. After a degree in Cultural Heritage Preservation, she took a master's degree for qualified researcher in archival/documental analysis through the use of information technology and formal model (XML, XSL, XSLT, RDF). For more than 10 years she worked at the Rome Research Consortium and she gained expertise in the field of formal languages, markup languages, and ontologies. From 2010 to 2014 she worked at "Archivio Centrale dello Stato" in Rome. Since November 2014 she works at Directorate General Organization of the Italian Ministry for Heritage and Cultural Activities and Tourism.

Chiara Veninata after a degree in Cultural Heritage Preservation, took a master's degree for qualified researcher in archival/documental analysis through the use of information technology and formal model (XML, XSL, XSLT, RDF). For more than 10 years she worked at the Rome Research Consortium, and she gained expertise in the field of formal languages, markup languages, and ontologies. From 2010 to 2014 she worked at "Archivio Centrale dello Stato" in Rome. Since November 2014 she works at Directorate General Organization of the Italian Ministry for Heritage and Cultural Activities and Tourism.

Joshua L. Weese is a Ph.D. candidate focusing on CS education research. His education experience comes from work as a graduate teaching assistant as well as time spent as a NSF GK-12 fellow. Josh's research focuses on operationalizing computational thinking as well as assessing computational thinking, in outreach programs aimed toward enriching K-12 students' experience in STEM. Apart from CS education, Josh is highly active in developing data analytic tools for the physics education research community.

Gian Piero Zarri has been awarded an M.Sc. in electronic engineering (University of Bologna, Italy) and a Ph.D. in computer science (University of Paris XI-Orsay, France). After more than 30 years spent as Research Director at the French National Centre for Scientific Research (CNRS), he cooperates now with the STIH Laboratory of the Paris-Sorbonne University as a senior associated researcher. Professor Zarri is known internationally for having defined and developed NKRL ("Narrative Knowledge Representation Language"), a representation tool used in several EC-funded projects and characterized by the addition of an "ontology of events" to the usual "ontology of concepts." He is the author of about 200 refereed papers concerning Artificial Intelligence, Computational Linguistics, Information Retrieval, Intelligence and Global Security, etc., and is the editor, co-author, and author of several books on Expert Systems, Intelligent Databases, and Representation and Management of Narrative Information. Professor Zarri has co-operated intensively with industry and has worked with international organizations like the European Commission, UNESCO, and Eureka-Eurostar and with national research-funding agencies in France, Italy, Austria, Portugal, the Netherlands, etc.

Part I
Design of Representational Systems

Semantic Web for Cultural Heritage Valorisation

Giorgia Lodi, Luigi Asprino, Andrea Giovanni Nuzzolese, Valentina Presutti, Aldo Gangemi, Diego Reforgiato Recupero, Chiara Veninata, and Annarita Orsini

Abstract Cultural heritage consists of heterogeneous resources: archaeological artefacts, monuments, sites, landscapes, paintings, photos, books and expressions of human creativity, often enjoyed in different forms: tangible, intangible or digital. Each resource is usually documented, conserved and managed by cultural institutes like museums, libraries or holders of archives. These institutes make available a detailed description of the objects as catalog records. In this context, the chapter proposes both a classification of cultural heritage data types and a process for cultural heritage valorisation through the well-known Linked Open Data paradigm. The classification and process have been defined in the context of a collaboration between the Semantic Technology Laboratory of the National Research Council (STLab) and the Italian Ministry of Cultural Heritage and Activities and Tourism (MIBACT) that the chapter describes, although we claim they are sufficiently general to be adopted in every cultural heritage scenario. In particular, the chapter introduces both a suite of ontology modules named Cultural-ON to model the principal elements identified in the cultural heritage data type classification, and the process we employed for data valorisation purposes. To this end, semantic technologies are exploited; that is, technologies that allow us to conceptualise and describe the meaning of data forming the cultural heritage and including such entities as places, institutions, cultural heritage events, availability, etc. These entities have special characteristics and are connected with each other in a profound way. The result is a knowledge base consisting of semantic interconnections with also other data available in the Web to be exploited according to different tasks

G. Lodi (✉) • L. Asprino • A.G. Nuzzolese • D. Reforgiato Recupero
STLab, ISTC-CNR, Via San Martino della Battaglia 44, Rome, Italy
e-mail: giorgia.lodi@istc.cnr.it; giorgia.lodi@gmail.com; luigi.asprino@istc.cnr.it; andrea.nuzzolese@istc.cnr.it; diego.reforgiato@istc.cnr.it

V. Presutti • A. Gangemi
STLab, ISTC-CNR, Via Gaifami 18, Catania, Italy
e-mail: valentina.presutti@cnr.it; aldo.gangemi@cnr.it

C. Veninata • A. Orsini
Ministry of Cultural Heritage and Activities and Tourism, Via del Collegio Romano 27, Rome, Italy
e-mail: chiara.veninata@beniculturali.it; aorsini@beniculturali.it

© Springer International Publishing AG 2017
S. Hai-Jew (ed.), *Data Analytics in Digital Humanities*, Multimedia Systems and Applications, DOI 10.1007/978-3-319-54499-1_1

3

and users preferences. By navigating the semantic relationships between the various objects of the knowledge base, new semantic paths can be revealed and utilised with the aim to develop innovative services and applications. The process is compliant with Linked Open Data and W3C Semantic Web best practices so that to enable a wider promotion of cultural heritage, and of sharing and reuse of cultural heritage data in the Web. The chapter concludes presenting a number of methodological principles and lessons learnt from the STLab/MIBACT collaboration that are applicable to any cultural heritage context and, in some cases, also to other domains.

Introduction and Motivation

Cultural heritage—both tangible and intangible—is a driving force for economic growth and societal development, an irreplaceable means for building a population's identity and culture, an inspiration for creative industry, and a primary reference for the touristic market. It has been formed by a multitude of local cultures and stories determined by the inhabitants of countries and different territories. This entailed that, over time, cultural heritage has been enriched with a highly heterogeneous set of resources that are diverse in their nature and in the way they are managed by each local culture.

Despite this diversity, cultural heritage's elements are semantically interconnected with each other as the result of contaminations of the different cultures. However, these elements are still mostly managed separately like silos, typically by different organisations (e.g., museums, libraries, holders of archives, etc.) that may also use various classifications, definitions and approaches to describe the same elements. An example is the Italian case where, within the same Ministry of Cultural Heritage and Activities and Tourism (MIBACT), two separate institutes define the concept of "cultural site" in two different ways within the data bases they own, respectively. Overall, this led to a scenario of dispersed data, both at national and international level, that cannot be fully and smartly exploited for such an economic growth and development of the touristic market that cultural heritage can potentially boost.

In the last two decades, web technologies and social networks became pervasively present in our daily life, providing a powerful means for sharing personal knowledge and experiences. Potentially, these technologies are the perfect tools for creating a vast interconnected digital cultural heritage that could be open to anyone so as to promote and improve the social cohesion and economic growth. The advent of new paradigms for data management based on these technologies can also support the involvement of citizens for identifying what is relevant as territorial cultural heritage, enhancing its distinctiveness, and cross-border sharing of local traditions and knowledge. This is key for supporting social integration and recognition, and sense of belonging. In particular, in the cultural domain the Open Data movement and the application of Linked Open Data (LOD) as the main data integration paradigm are emerging as new frontiers to valorise a vast amount of public cultural heritage. However, a diversified scenario where isolated islands of data are available on the Web is still observable. This is the case for instance of the Italian scenario: a number of LOD projects carried out by MIBACT were born but they still struggle to be part of an overall strategy that can guide towards a significant valorisation of one of the largest heritage of the cultural sector.

This chapter describes the work conducted in the context of a collaboration between STLab and MIBACT. The work aims at defining an overall framework for cultural data analysis and valorisation, this latter pursued through the construction of an open knowledge base of Italian cultural data. The knowledge base is meant to be publicly available on the Web, using semantic web standards and technologies, for the reuse by anyone willing to exploit it for the development of innovative and creative applications and services. In computer science, the term "semantic web" refers to W3C's vision of an extension of the Web for dealing with interconnected data that is stored, modelled and handled using so-called semantic web standards and technologies (e.g., Resource Description Framework (RDF), SPARQL query language for RDF (SPARQL), Ontology Web Language (OWL), etc.) The framework we present provides a classification of the cultural data landscape, identified within the collaboration, and a common and standard-based data model that can be used as shared interoperability profile for interconnecting different, even available LOD, datasets managed by various institutes of the Ministry. The model consists of a suite of ontology modules for the cultural domain named Cultural-ON, which are defined following a specific methodology. The methodology has been delineated so as to guarantee sustainability, usability and semantic interoperability requirements, with the application of ontology design patterns. The chapter focuses on the module of the suite that represents "cultural institutes and sites" and "cultural events", which are connected to each other. The process we employed to create LOD datasets of the cultural institutes and of the events, aligned with the defined ontology module, is introduced. In particular, we highlight how to integrate it in a real business process and information system managed by the Ministry, and how to link the datasets to others available in the Web of Data. We claim that our model is sufficiently general to be applied in any organisation working in the cultural sector with such data types as cultural sites and events. We then highlight general methodology principles and best practices that can be replicated in other cultural data management processes and, in some cases, also in other domains.

This chapter is structured as follows. Section "State of the Art" provides a state of the art on projects, ontologies and LOD approaches in the cultural heritage domain. Section "A Cultural Heritage Data Framework: The Case of the Italian Ministry of Cultural Heritage" introduces a cultural data landscape analysis and the objectives of the collaboration we carried out with MIBACT. Section "Cultural-ON: The Cultural ONtologies" describes the methodology we followed to define an ontology for cultural institutes and sites and cultural events, detailing the main modelling choices and the design patterns that we reused for supporting semantic interoperability. Section "The Produced Linked Open Data" provides a detailed description of the process we employed for producing LOD datasets, aligned with the ontology and linked to other data in the Web, and a running example with real data coming from an information system available at MIBACT. Additional methodology principles we learnt from this experience are discussed in section "Lesson Learnt (On Methodological Principles)". Finally, section "Concluding Remark" provides concluding remarks and future directions of the work.

State of the Art

Semantic technologies, and in particular Linked Open Data, have been widely and successfully exploited within the cultural heritage field to improve the access to cultural assets, to enhance the experience of citizens in exploring cultural heritage, to facilitate artworks discoverability, to integrate and enrich data about cultural heritage (Isaac and Haslhofer 2013; de Boer et al. 2013; Szekely et al. 2013; Ruotsalo et al. 2013; Aart et al. 2010). Semantic Web technologies have been used to disclose, in a scalable way, the vast amount of interesting and useful information on cultural heritage. In recent years, several institutions put considerable effort into developing and standardising methods and vocabularies for indexing objects. Semantic Web technologies have given the opportunity of easing these processes and achieving results in a collaborative environment. The collaborative development of ontologies [e.g. CIDOC-CRM (Doerr 2003)] has strengthened the collaboration between organisations so that semantic interoperability requirements could be met within their systems. In addition, the use of common ontologies facilitated the data exchange and the creation of huge digital libraries [e.g. (Isaac and Haslhofer 2013)].

In the context of Semantic Web technologies, the Linked Open Data (LOD) paradigm paved the way to the valorisation of cultural assets. In fact, the LOD paradigm has been used to connect data from different cultural institutions, thus increasing the possibility of reaching cultural data available in the Web of Data. The interlinking of contents of collaborating organisations also contributed to enrich the information in a cost effective manner (Hyvönen 2009). The result has been the creation of a knowledge base that can be reused in different applications.

Semantic annotation of cultural objects has been employed to support indexing and searching within large virtual collections (Schreiber et al. 2008). The indexing of collections has benefited of crowdsourcing techniques where large community of users were invited to assist in the selection, cataloguing, contextualisation, and curation of collections (Oomen and Aroyo 2011; Ridge 2013). Furthermore, semantic technologies allowed going beyond traditional free text search (e.g. Google), providing users with "intelligent" facilities based on ontological reasoning such as semantic search, semantic autocompletion or semantic recommendation of contents (Hyvönen 2009; Ruotsalo et al. 2013; Wang et al. 2007).

Ontologies and Other Knowledge Organisation Systems

In the context of cultural heritage and Semantic Web technologies a lot of ontologies and knowledge organisation systems (KOS) have been developed. We describe here a representative sample of them, which have influenced the design and the methodology we propose in this chapter. In general, we noticed that the most important and used ontologies of the cultural sector are principally focused on modelling cultural heritage objects; that is, movable objects hosted/located in cultural sites.

CIDOC-CRM

CIDOC-CRM (Conceptual Reference Model)[1] (Doerr 2003) is a formal and standard ontology intended to enable information integration for cultural heritage data. Its shared usage can contribute to meet semantic interoperability requirements among heterogeneous sources of cultural heritage information. CIDOC-CRM is the result of a long-term interdisciplinary work and an agreement between the International Committee for Documentation (CIDOC) of the International Council of Museums (ICOM) and a non-governmental organism. Since September 2006 it has been considered for standardisation by the ISO standard body that defined the ISO 21127. CIDOC-CRM has a rich taxonomy of classes and properties that describe Space-Time, Events, Material and Immaterial Things for the cultural domain. This makes the model very useful for building query services (queries can be formulated at various granularities) and eases the extension of the model to other domains, reducing the risk of over-generalisation.

The ontology proposed in this paper has points of convergence and divergence with CIDOC-CRM. On the one hand, the convergences between the models can be found in the way of modelling the material things (such as places and physical objects), collections and catalogues (in CIDOC, *E31 Document*). Both the ontologies model information about places, such as place names, addresses, spatial coordinates, geometries. In fact, the classes representing places in our proposal aligned to CIDOC-CRM's (cf. section "Methodology"). Since the intent of CIDOC is to document objects collected and displayed by museums and related institutions, it provides a finer description of individual items and collections than Cultural-ON. However, the *Cultural Heritage Objects* defined in Cultural-ON can be used as a hook to vocabularies more focusing on the description of artworks (such as CIDOC).

On the other hand, CIDOC lacks of a finer conceptualisation of the access to cultural sites (e.g. opening hours specifications, ticketing information, access conditions) and about organisational structures behind a cultural site, which is addressed by Cultural-ON.

---

[1] http://cidoc-crm.org/.

Europeana Data Model (EDM)

The Europeana Data Model (EDM)[2] (Isaac and Haslhofer 2013) is a data model used in the Europeana project[3] for integrating, collecting and enriching data on cultural heritage provided by the different and distributed content providers. EDM reuses and extends a set of well-known vocabularies: OAI ORE (Open Archives Initiative Object Reuse and Exchange) for organising objects' metadata and digital representation(s); Dublin Core for descriptive metadata; SKOS (Simple Knowledge Organisation System) for conceptual vocabulary representation and CIDOC-CRM for the representation of events and relationships between objects. The model distinguishes between cultural heritage objects, web resources and aggregations. Aggregations are used to model a data provider's contribution to Europeana on a cultural heritage object. A contribution, in turn, consists of more web resources (i.e., metadata) provided for the object.

As well as CIDOC-CRM, the main focus of the Europeana Data Model is on the description of Cultural Heritage Objects. The information modelled by EDM is orthogonal to the conceptualisation provided by *Cultural-ON*. Therefore, the data modelled with Cultural-ON enriches the information about Cultural Heritage Objects, collected by Europeana.

Getty Vocabularies

The Getty vocabularies[4] is a suite of KOS developed by the Getty Research Institute, consisting in four controlled vocabularies, i.e. The Art and Architecture Thesaurus (AAT) containing generic terms used for describing items of art, architecture and cultural heritage objects; The Getty Thesaurus of Geographic Names (TGN) including names descriptions of historical cities, empires and archaeological sites; The Cultural Objects Name Authority (CONA) containing titles, attributions, depicted subjects about works of several art, architecture, and other elements of the cultural heritage; The Union List of Artist Names (ULAN) including information about artists. AAT, CONA and ULAN are orthogonal to *Cultural-ON*. They can be exploited by data providers for enriching their datasets with information about authoritative research institutes. Users of *Cultural-ON* can take advantage of TGN by reusing its terms to provide a site with its historical nomenclature. Besides providing coordinates of places (also modelled in *Cultural-ON*), CONA provides a finer conceptualisation of the name attribute by modelling different *name types* (e.g. Official, Vernacular, Provisional, etc.). Cultural-ON models three types of names: institutional, preferred and alternative.

---

[2]http://pro.europeana.eu/edm-documentation.

[3]http://pro.europeana.eu/.

[4]http://www.getty.edu/research/tools/vocabularies/index.html.

Projects

The above mentioned ontologies and KOS were successfully used in a number of projects, carried out by cultural public organisations. In this section we report some of them, which we have reused as guidelines for our work.

Europeana

Europeana[3](Isaac and Haslhofer 2013) is a project co-funded by the European Union with the ambition of "unifying" Europe through culture and making cultural heritage available for all. Europeana Foundation promotes and co-founds within it several projects, such as Europeana Vx, Europeana Creative, Europeana Space, Europeana Food and Drink. Among these, *Europeana Vx* (the last project of the series is Europeana V3.0) aims at both creating and coordinating a network of contributing institutions that act as data providers, and managing the collected data through the development of a service infrastructure that enables an ease data discoverability and access. In October 2012, a subset of the Europeana dataset was released in linked open data, under the license Creative Commons CC0. The dataset was modelled using the earlier mentioned Europeana Data Model (EDM) and then made available in data.europeana.eu. The overall repository currently contains over 40 millions of RDF (Resource Description Framework) cultural data. The data that will be modelled through *Cultural-ON* will be able to enrich the Europeana knowledge base. In fact, Europeana mainly focuses on description and aggregation of metadata about cultural objects, whereas *Cultural-ON* is able to model the information for accessing them.

Smartmuseum

SMARTMUSEUM[5] (Ruotsalo et al. 2013) is a research project funded under the European Commission's 7th Framework Programme. The project aims at developing a mobile ubiquitous recommender system that uses the Web of Data to provide tourists with recommendations for cultural heritage. The system delivers the right content to the users by taking as input users' informational needs and contextual information (such as sensors data captured from mobile devices). Semantic technologies are employed to deal with the heterogeneity of data, which may include content descriptions, sensor inputs and user profiles. For modelling users, the project relies on the General User Model Ontology (GUMO). The content are annotated using the Dublin Core metadata standard which is properly extended for the cultural heritage domain including such metadata as material,

---

[5]http://www.smartmuseum.eu.

object type, and place of creation of the object. The geographical information is modelled using the W3C Geo Vocabulary[6], whereas the objects are indexed with the Getty Vocabularies[7] [i.e., The Art and Architecture Thesaurus (AAT), The Getty Thesaurus of Geographic Names (TGN), The Union List of Artist Names (ULAN)]. The applications developed within *SMARTMUSEUM* can benefit of the data that will be modelled through *Cultural-ON*. In fact, the description and the localisation of the *Cultural Entities* modelled by *Cultural-ON* can help for providing users with more appropriate context information.

Museums and Linked Data

A growing number of museums are relying on semantic technologies for multiple purposes: for providing Internet access to their collections and artworks, for making their assets easily discoverable, for facilitating the integration and enrichment of their data.

In 2011 the *British Museum*[8] released its database of nearly 2 millions of records in linked open data, becoming the first UK art organism to use semantic technologies for making available in the Web its cultural assets. Today the dataset contains over 100 millions of records and is integrated with other data that are present in the Web of Data. The data have been modelled using CIDOC-CRM[1].

In order to make its artworks easily discoverable, in 2014 the *Smithsonian American Art Museum*[9] began to publish authoritative records about American artworks in linked open data. As in the other cases, the records, that have been collected since 1829, are currently modelled using CIDOC-CRM.

To open up and improve the access to its collection of 1 million objects, in 2011 the *Rijksmuseum*[10] in Amsterdam made parts of its collection available online. The Linked Data version of the collection is modelled according to the Europeana Data Model and comprises over 20 millions of RDF data describing almost 600 thousands cultural objects. Furthermore, the collection objects is linked to the *Art and Architecture Thesaurus* of the Getty Vocabularies. The vocabularies provides a structured terminology for art, architecture, decorative arts, archival materials, visual surrogates, conservation, and bibliographic materials.

All these museums can benefit from using *Cultural-ON* for modelling information (such as addresses, contact points, opening hours, ticketing, etc.) for accessing their cultural assets, information about their organisational structure, the services they provide to the public and the events they host.

---

[6]http://www.w3.org/2003/01/geo/.

[7]http://www.getty.edu/research/conducting_research/vocabularies/.

[8]http://collection.britishmuseum.org/.

[9]http://americanart.si.edu/collections/search/lod/about/.

[10]http://rijksmuseum.sealinc.eculture.labs.vu.nl/home.

A Cultural Heritage Data Framework: The Case of the Italian Ministry of Cultural Heritage

The Italian Cultural Heritage is one of the richest in the world, as it is also evidenced by the fact that Italy includes the greatest number of UNESCO World Heritage Sites (i.e., 50, including 46 cultural sites).

The Ministry of Heritage, Cultural Activities and Tourism (referred to as MIBACT from now on) is responsible for supervising, preserving and promoting this huge patrimony. It also produces and manages a vast amount of information regarding the institutions and organisations operating for the promotion of the cultural heritage. In order to understand the characteristics of this large patrimony, a general assessment of the cultural data landscape becomes crucial.

Analysis of the Cultural Heritage Data Landscape

The cultural heritage domain is characterised by a highly heterogeneous data landscape that embraces a variety of resource types. According to the different objectives and priorities in treating those resources, different classification proposals for them are possible. In the context of this chapter, we propose a general classification of data types we encountered when we dealt with the data owned by MIBACT. In particular, we distinguish between the following principal data categories:

- *Cultural property*—this category includes all types of data regarding the cultural heritage and landscape that belong to the State, territorial government bodies, as well as any other public body and institution, and to private non-profit associations.
- *Cultural events and exhibitions*—this category includes events that are related to cultural properties.
- *Restrictions*—this category embodies all those types of data that are related to legal constraints or restrictions defined on cultural properties for conservation and safeguarding purposes.
- *Statistical data*—this category includes statistical data that can be collected about the exploitation of, and access to, cultural properties.

Each category can be further specialised in additional subcategories. In the context of this work we focus on the cultural property and cultural events and exhibitions categories, only, and we provide in the following a more detailed characterisation of them.

Cultural Property Cultural properties can be classified in (1) cultural institutes and sites and (2) cultural heritage collections and objects. The *cultural institutes and sites* are assets that encompass immovable objects and their organisations, these latter referred to as the set of people and procedures governing the immovable objects. A taxonomy for these objects can be identified. In particular, in the Italian context, the legal framework for the cultural heritage domain defines six main types of immovable objects that must be safeguarded and preserved:

1. *Museum*; that is a permanent structure or institution that acquires, conserves and makes available to the public cultural objects (see below) for educational purposes;
2. *Library*; that is a permanent structure or institution that collects and conserves an organised collection of books and any other published and editorial work available on any media type; a library also ensures the consultation of those works for study purposes;
3. *Holder of Archive*; that is a permanent structure or institution that collects, makes an inventory and preserves documents that own an historical value, ensuring the consultation of those documents for research and study purposes;
4. *Archaeological Area*; that is a site (or a group of physical sites) consisting of natural ruins or historical or prehistoric artefacts and structures;
5. *Archaeological Park*; that is an environment characterised by the presence of important archaeological evidence; it can be considered as an outdoor museum;
6. *Monumental Area or Complex*; that is a set of different buildings built in different eras that acquired over time, and as a whole, a relevant and autonomous artistic, religious, historic and ethno-anthropological value.

In addition to the above typologies, *Cinemas* and *Theatres*, *Cultural Landscape Assets*; i.e., buildings and areas which are the expression of historical, cultural, natural, morphological and aesthetic values of the land (e.g., villas, gardens, vantage points, belvederes, etc.) and *Cultural Research and Promotion Center* fall into the cultural institutes and sites category.

The *cultural heritage collections and objects* can be referred to as the movable cultural objects. The objects are created or collected by people and form an important part of a nation's identity. They can be artistic, historical, technological or natural in origin and located within immovable objects. Examples include for instance paintings, sculptures, amphoras, manuscripts, photographs, books, films, and any other tangible or intangible work with a notable public and cultural interest.

Cultural Events and Exhibitions Cultural events and exhibitions are events that may take place within immovable objects and may be related to specific movable objects. They are typically organised by public bodies or institutions or by private organisations operating for the public interest, with the aim to promote the culture and traditions of a nation. There might exist large scale cultural events that consist in turn of smaller events usually held at local level. An example can be the large scale event created to celebrate the first world war centenary that consists of single dispersed events hosted within cultural institutes or sites available on the territory.

Transversal Data All earlier described data are connected to transversal data types; that is, data that are independent of the specific cultural heritage domain. Examples of these data include, among the others, people, organisations (public or private bodies), location and addresses. Although these types of data may appear less important than the previously defined ones when describing the cultural heritage, they however represent important conjunction points towards other data bases and domains.

Objectives

Traditionally, all these data have been managed separately, thus contributing to the creation of isolated data bases that rarely fully interoperate and that include, in some cases, replication of the same data. In the light of this scenario, the following objectives were identified as crucial for the cultural heritage valorisation process.

- *Cultural heritage unique knowledge*—definition of a general methodology for data integration capable of re-establishing the *unicum* nature of the cultural heritage knowledge. The methodology ensures that technical and semantic interoperability requirements are met when data exchanged among data bases on cultural properties is enabled;
- *Openness*—valorisation of the cultural properties by exploiting novel Open Data paradigms. In particular, the Linked Open Data (LOD) approach, based on the use of standards of the Semantic Web, can be used to create a large open and interconnected knowledge base, This can be offered to anyone, without any legal restrictions, in order to enable the development of innovative services and applications. In the Italian context, there already exist LOD initiatives in the cultural heritage domain[11] promoted by different internal institutes of the main Ministry. These initiatives have the merit to use standard ontologies and thesaurus for data definition and classification (see section State of the Art). However, they all still suffer from the dispersed nature of the cultural properties management. The objective is then to use the LOD paradigm for creating interoperable cultural properties data, linkable among each other and with other data available on the Web. These links can facilitate the integration of data in a distributed manner and can be explored so as to reveal unexpected semantic paths.
- *Common data models*—definition of common and standard data models for cultural heritage domain to be re-used by all stakeholders operating at national and local level. In particular, from the assessment of the data landscape as previously introduced, it turns out that the cultural institutes and sites are recurring data with respect to the other data types. Thus, they can be considered as the basis or nucleus of a unique LOD knowledge base of cultural properties that can be used for starting the data integration and valorisation process.

---

[11]http://dati.culturaitalia.it/?locale=en, http://dati.acs.beniculturali.it/, http://san.beniculturali.it/web/san/dati-san-lod.

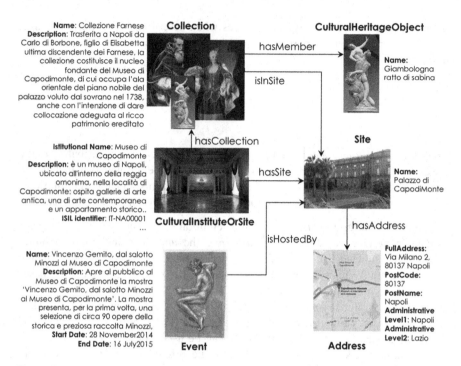

Fig. 1 An example of possible real data on cultural heritage data and their possible relationships

Figure 1 shows an example of real data related to an Italian museum, i.e., "Museo di Capodimonte", which is use as real running example in this chapter, The figure illustrates the real data associated to the principal objects that characterise the museum and the possible relationships among those objects.

Cultural-ON: The Cultural ONtologies

Cultural-ON (Cultural ONtologies)[12] is a suite of ontology modules that provide concepts and relations for modelling knowledge in the cultural heritage domain. At the time of this writing, Cultural-ON embodies one module that allows us to represent cultural institutes and sites and cultural events. In the following sections we provide details about the adopted design methodology (cf. section "Methodology"), the design requirements (cf. section "Design Requirements") and the resulting ontology module (cf. section "Resulting Ontology").

---

[12]The ontology and its documentation can be retrieved on-line at http://stlab.istc.cnr.it/documents/mibact/cultural-ON_xml.owl and http://goo.gl/2lqj0w.

Methodology

Cultural-ON is designed by following best design practices and pattern-based ontology engineering aimed at extensively re-using Ontology Design Patterns (ODPs)[13] (Gangemi and Presutti 2009) for modeling ontologies. According to Gangemi and Presutti (2009), ODPs are modeling solutions that can be re-used in order to solve recurrent ontology design problems. Hence, they enable design *by-reuse* methodologies. For example, ODPs can be reused by means of their specialisation or composition according to their types and to the scope of the new ontology that is going to be modelled. The design methodology that we followed is based on the *eXtreme Design* (XD) (Blomqvist et al. 2010). XD is an agile approach to ontology engineering that adopts competency questions (CQs) (Grüninger and Fox 1995) as a reference source for the requirement analysis. In fact, XD associates ODPs with generic use cases that are used to match the design requirements. Both the generic use cases and the requirements are expressed by means of competency questions.

Based on this methodology, we modelled Cultural-ON by following these steps:

- **Design requirements elicitation**. The result of this step is a set of requirements expressed in terms of CQs;
- **Key entities extraction**. The result of this step is a set of concepts and relations that provide the basic building blocks for dealing with knowledge within the domain of cultural heritage. The key entities are extracted by analysing the CQs;
- **ODPs identification**. This step is aimed at identifying the most appropriate ODPs. The ODPs are identified by applying the XD methodology and come from the on-line repository ontologydesignpatterns.org;
- **ODPs re-use**. The ODPs resulting from the previous step are modelled in Cultural-ON by means of specialisation. However, we do not directly import any specific implementation of ODPs in our ontology, in order to be completely independent of them (see section "Lesson Learnt (On Methodological Principles)" for a detailed discussion on reuse);
- **Ontology alignment**. Finally, the ontology is aligned to other existing ontologies in the Semantic Web that provide similar conceptualisations.

Design Requirements

The design requirements that we identified are expressed as competency questions. These CQs were extracted by analysing a set of scenarios and real use cases provided us by domain experts, i.e., the Italian Ministry of Cultural Heritage and

---

[13]http://www.ontologydesignpatterns.org.

Table 1 Design requirements expressed as CQs and identified target ODPs.

ID	Competency question	ODPs
CQ1	What are the cultural institutes or sites of a given type?	Classification
CQ2	What is the name used in a specific period of time for identifying a certain cultural institute or site?	TimeIndexedSituation
CQ3	What are the contacts that can provide information (e.g., opening hours, ticket fares, etc.) about a cultural institute or site?	–
CQ4	What are the opening schedule of a cultural institute or site?	TimeIndexedSituation
CQ5	When can a person contact a reference agent in order ask her information about a cultural institute or site?	TimeIndexedSituation
CQ6	Who is the agent holding a juridical role in a certain period of time for a cultural institute or site?	TimeIndexedPersonRole
CQ7	What is the physical location of a cultural institute or site?	Place
CQ8	Where is a cultural heritage object preserved ?	Place
CQ9	What is the collection of cultural heritage objects preserved by a cultural institute?	Collection
CQ10	What is the description of a certain entity (e.g., a cultural institute)?	Description
CQ11	What are the events organised by a cultural institute or site?	TimeIndexedSituation
CQ12	What are the events associated with cultural heritage objects	TimeIndexedSituation
CQ13	What is the price of the ticket for entering a cultural institute or an event?	Price
CQ14	What is the validity of a ticket for entering a cultural institute or an event?	TimeIndexedSituation
CQ15	What is the cultural institute that another cultural institute belongs to?	PartOf

Activities and Tourism (MIBACT)[14], the italian Central Institute for Cataloguing and Documentation (ICCD)[15] and other internal institutes of MIBACT. The CQs extracted are reported in Table 1 and are associated with the ODPs that address them by providing a re-usable modelling solution. Thus, Table 1 reports the results of the steps 1 and 3 of our ontology design methodology (cf. section "Methodology").

---

[14]http://www.beniculturali.it/.

[15]http://www.iccd.beniculturali.it.

Resulting Ontology

Cultural-ON is modelled as an OWL ontology. The classes of the ontology that represent the core entities (cf. step 2 of our methodology) are the following:

- `cis:CulturalInstituteOrSite`[16] for representing cultural heritage institutes or sites. An individual of this class is, for example, the Uffizi Gallery or Museum of Capodimonte (see next section);
- `cis:CulturalHeritageObject` for representing cultural heritage movable objects. An individual of this class is any cultural asset (even intangible) of the cultural heritage;
- `cis:Agent` for representing any agentive object, either physical, or social. Individuals of this class can be, for example, people, organisations or any juridical entity;
- `cis:Site` for representing physical places. An individual of this class is, for example, the Uffizi in Florence, Italy. In fact, it is the physical site where the Uffizi Gallery is located in;
- `cis:Collection` for representing collections of cultural heritage objects. For example, the Collections of the Uffizi Gallery are individuals of this class;
- `cis:Event` for representing any kind of event that can be hosted by a cultural institutes and can involve cultural heritage objects;
- `cis:Ticket` for representing tickets. An individual of this class can be any token that grants the entrance to a cultural institute or site or the participation to an event.

These core classes are modelled and organised according to the selected ODPs in order to address the list of requirements presented in Table 1. Figure 2 shows the class diagram of the current version of Cultural-ON represented by using the UML notation.

The requirement CQ1 is addressed by re-using the Classification ODP[17] that in our context allows to represent the category that a certain cultural institute or site belongs to. The category is represented by the class `cis:CISType` whose individuals express actual types of cultural institutes or sites, e.g., museum, library, etc. A `cis:CulturalInstituteOrSite` is related to `cis:CISType` by means of the object property `cis:hasCISType` that in our context plays the role of the object property `classification:isClassifiedBy`[18] as defined in the source Classification ODP.

We did not identify a ODP that could be directly reused for addressing CQ3. However, the class `schema.org:ContactPoint`[19] provides a reference

---

[16]The prefix `cis:` stands for the namespace http://dati.beniculturali.it/cis/.

[17]http://www.ontologydesignpatterns.org/cp/owl/classification.owl.

[18]The prefix `classification:` stands for the namespace http://www.ontologydesignpatterns.org/cp/owl/classification.owl#.

[19]http://schema.org/ContactPoint.

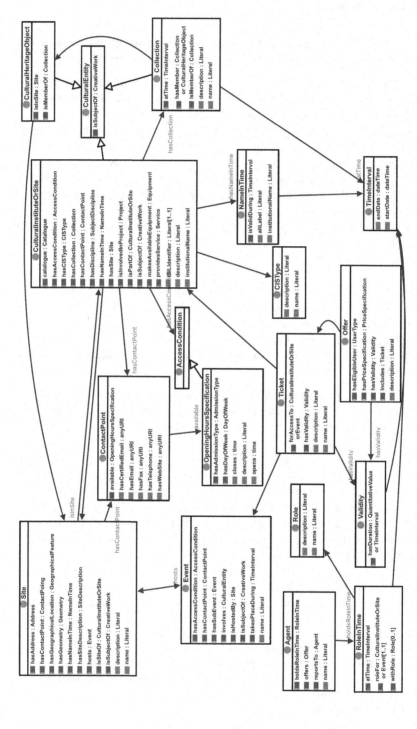

Fig. 2 UML diagram about the core classes and properties defined for modelling Cultural-ON

schema for describing contact points in terms of email addresses, fax numbers, telephone numbers, web sites, opening hours, etc. It is worth mentioning that Schema.org is a collaborative effort aimed at fostering vocabulary sharing over the Web. Hence, Schema.org, similarly to ODP, is a valid source for vocabulary re-use.

The fact the cultural institutes or sites have a name that might change over time (cf. CQ2) is modelled by re-using the TimeIndexedSituation ODP.[20] For example, the Colosseum in Rome was originally known as Amphitheatrum Flavium, while the name further evolved to Coliseum during the Middle Ages. This situations are modelled in Cultural-ON by defining the class `cis:NameInTime` that represents a time indexed situation and allows expressing the temporal validity of the name of a cultural institutes or sites. In fact, a `cis:NameInTime` is associated with (1) a `cis:TimeInterval` by the object property `cis:isValidDuring` and (2) a `cis:CulturalInstituteOrSite` by the object property `cis:hasNameInTime`.[21] The class `cis:TimeInterval` provides the temporal span in terms of a starting and an ending date (i.e., the datatype properties `cis:startDate` and `cis:endDate`, respectively).

The TimeIndexedSituation ODP is also used for addressing the requirements CQ4, CQ5, CQ11, CQ12 and CQ14. For addressing CQ4 and CQ5 we defined the class `cis:OpeningHoursSpecification` that specialises a time indexed situation. Individuals of `cis:OpeningHoursSpecification` can be linked to individuals of `cis:CulturalInstituteOrSite` or `cis:ContactPoint` by the object properties `cis:hasAccessCondtion` and `cis:available`, respectively. In this case the time is represented by an `xsd:time` that is the range of the datatype property `cis:opens`. The property `cis:opens` has the class `cis:OpeningHoursSpecification` as domain. For addressing CQ11 and CQ12 we defined the class `cis:Event` as a time indexed situation. In fact, the temporal dimension is provided by the object property `cis:takesPlaceDuring` whose domain and range are the classes `cis:Event` and `cis:TimeIntervall`, respectively. Instead, the location hosting the event is expressed by the object property `cis:isHostedBy`[22] whose domain and range are the classes `cis:Event` and `cis:Site`, respectively. Finally, in the case of the requirement CQ14, the time indexed situation is represented by the class `cis:Validity`. This class is associated with a `cis:TimeInterval` by means of the object property `cis:hasDuration`. Additionally, it is the range of the object property `cis:hasValidity`. The property `cis:hasValidity` accepts `cis:Ticket` or `cis:Offer` as domain.

---

[20] http://www.ontologydesignpatterns.org/cp/owl/timeindexedsituation.owl.

[21] The object property `cis:hasNameInTime` has `cis:CulturalInstituteOrSite` and `cis:NameInTime` as domain and range, respectively. Thus, the association of a `cis:NameInTime` with a `cis:CulturalInstituteOrSite` is expressed by the inverse of `cis:hasNameInTime`.

[22] Its inverse property is `cis:Hosts`.

The ticket pricing (cf. CQ13) is modelled by re-using the Price ODP.[23] In fact, we defined a class cis:Offer that is associated with (1) a cis:Ticket by the object property cis:includes; (2) a cis:Prices Specification by the object property cis:hasPriceSpecification. The class cis:PricesSpecification specialises the original class price:Price[24] from the Price ODP and allows to describe a price in terms of an amount and a given currency. The amount can be specified by using the datatype property cis:amount whose range is xsd:double, while the currency can be specified by using the object property cis:hasCurrency whose range are individuals of the class cis:Currency.

The approach adopted for modelling the physical site where (1) a cultural institution is located in (cf. CQ7) or (2) a cultural heritage object is preserved in (CQ8), benefits from the re-use of the Place ODP.[25] The physical locations are represented as individuals of cis:Site. The object property cis:hasSite is designed to associate a cis:CulturalInstituteOrSite with a cis:Site. In our domain this representation provides a best practice for disambiguating between a cultural institute and its physical place. For example, it allows to represent the "Uffizi" both as an institution (i.e., the "Uffizi Gallery") and a building.

A cis:Collection allows modelling collections of cultural heritage objects included in a cultural institute or site and to refer to them as cultural heritage entities. A cis:Collection is designed by reusing the Collection Entity ODP.[26] This ODP provides a reference schema for identifying a collection as a whole (i.e., an individual of the class cis:Collection) and for associating such a collection with its members by means of the object property cis:hasMember.[27] The property cis:hasMember has individuals of the class cis:Collection as domain while its range can be any individual of cis:CulturalHeritageObject or cis:Collection. It is worth saying that the class cis:CulturalHeritageObject is designed to identify and provide references to cultural heritage objects. Thus, the description of cultural heritage objects with peculiar properties and classes is out of the scope of this ontology. These properties and classes might be defined in other ontologies and, to this respect, the class cis:CulturalHeritageObject works as a hook to foster data linking from other linked datasets that provide peculiar knowledge about cultural heritage objects.

---

[23] http://www.ontologydesignpatterns.org/cp/owl/price.owl.

[24] The prefix price: stands for the namespace http://www.ontologydesignpatterns.org/cp/owl/price.owl#.

[25] http://www.ontologydesignpatterns.org/cp/owl/place.owl.

[26] http://www.ontologydesignpatterns.org/cp/owl/collectionentity.owl.

[27] The inverse property is cis:isMemberOf.

Cultural-ON reuses the PartOf ODP[28] for describing part-of relations among cultural institutes or sites (cf. CQ15). Namely, the object property `cis:partOf` allows to model an individual of `cis:CulturalInstituteOrSite` to be part of another `cis:CulturalInstituteOrSite`, either administratively or juridically.

The requirement CQ6 is addressed by re-using the TimeIndexedPersonRole ODP.[29] This ODP is a specialisation of the AgentRole ODP. In fact, it allows adding the temporal dimension in order to specify when a given role is held by a certain person. In our ontology this ODP is represented by the class `cis:RoleInTime` that represents an *n*-ary relation whose arguments are a `cis:Role`, a `cis:Agent` and a `cis:TimeInterval`.

The requirement CQ10 is addressed by re-using the Description ODP.[30] This ODP is specialised by defining the datatype property `cis:description` whose range is any value of `xsd:Literal` and can be used for providing textual description about `cis:CulturalInstituteOrSite`.

Finally, the ontology alignment step introduced in section "Methodology" allowed us to map our ontology to other ontologies or vocabularies available in the Semantic Web. The alignments are provided in a separate OWL file[31] by means of `owl:equivalentClass`/ `owl:equivalentProperty` and `rdfs:subClassOf`/`rdfs:subPropertyOf` axioms. In particular, Cultural-ON is aligned with Dublin Core,[32] FOAF, [33] GoodRelations, [34] the Organisation ontology, [35] LODE, [36] DOLCE[37] and PRO.[38] For example, the class `cis:Agent` is declared `owl:equivalentClass` to `foaf:Agent` or `cis:Event` is declared `rdfs:subClassOf lode:Event`. Interested readers can refer to section "Lesson Learnt (On Methodological Principles)" for a detailed description of the methodological principles that guided us in the external ontologies alignment process.

---

[28] http://www.ontologydesignpatterns.org/cp/owl/partof.owl.

[29] http://www.ontologydesignpatterns.org/cp/owl/timeindexedpersonrole.owl.

[30] http://www.ontologydesignpatterns.org/cp/owl/timeindexedpersonrole.owl.

[31] The file containing ontology alignments is available at http://stlab.istc.cnr.it/documents/mibact/alignment_xml.owl.

[32] http://dublincore.org.

[33] http://xmlns.com/foaf/spec/20070524.html.

[34] http://purl.org/goodrelations/v1.

[35] http://www.w3.org/ns/org.

[36] http://linkedevents.org/ontology.

[37] http://www.loa-cnr.it/ontologies/DUL.owl.

[38] http://purl.org/spar/pro.

The Produced Linked Open Data

MiBACT stores records about the Italian cultural institutes or sites (i.e. addresses, opening hours, managing authorities, contacts, etc.) in a database called "DB Unico 2.0".[39] The database also contains information about cultural events[40] (e.g., as exhibitions, seminars, conferences, etc.) hosted in cultural institutes or sites and organised by the MIBACT or by other institutions. A MIBACT's editorial board is responsible for the maintenance of the database.

In the "*Governmental Agenda for the valorisation of the public sector informa-tion*", the Italian Digital Agency (Agenzia per l'Italia Digitale—AgID) classified the data included in *DB Unico 2.0* as high-value data to be released to anyone, and for any reuse, through the Linked Open Data paradigm. It was in fact recognised that publishing data on cultural properties using the LOD paradigm can significantly contribute to valorising cultural assets and promoting cultural events, thanks to the possibility granted to anyone to develop new services and applications using those data. Since cultural institutes or sites can be seen as containers of artworks and events, the cultural institutes or sites dataset can serve as the hub of the Linked Open Data cloud of the Italian cultural heritage: users can start discovering the Italian patrimony by exploring the interlinks that this dataset may enable towards other datasets of the cultural domain.

Figure 3 shows the process we employed in order to produce the Linked Open datasets of cultural institutes or sites and cultural events, by means of an activity diagram. The process in this figure is illustrated by highlighting the flow of the information, the actors and the used tools/technologies. Five types of actors participate in the process; namely, *qualified editors*, an *editorial board*, *Linked Open Data engineers*, *ontology designers* and other *domain experts*.

The process consists of a number of phases. The first phase regards the feeding of the database of cultural institutes or sites and events and it is carried out by qualified editors. This phase is currently foreseen in a specific regulation that confers to MIBACT the obligation to manage and maintain such a traditional relational database. Qualified editors are typically members of a variety of public institutions, national and local, operating in the cultural sector. Although the existence of guidelines for database feeding purposes, they can introduce heterogeneity in the data they document within DB Unico. To address this problem, a data cleansing and data harmonisation phase is executed by MIBACT's editorial board. For this activity, several state of the art tools can be used. In the context of our collaboration with MIBACT, the editorial board decided to take advantage of OpenRefine[41] i.e., a tool for cleaning data and for transforming data from a format into another format.

---

[39] http://goo.gl/srh6op.

[40] http://goo.gl/3C5orD.

[41] http://openrefine.org/.

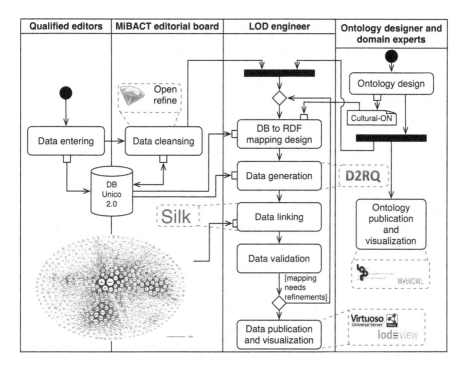

Fig. 3 The process for releasing the information in *DB Unico 2.0* as Linked Open Data

As shown in Fig. 3, in parallel to these activities, the creation of the ontology, following the methodology introduced in the previous section, can be carried out by ontology designers. It is worth noticing that the ontology creation phase requires a strict interaction and collaboration between ontology and domain experts. These latter are the only ones capable of clearly defining the requirements as previously represented, since they know precisely the peculiarities of the data, the legislation that applies, and their everyday working experience.

Once the ontology is defined, it can be published on the Web. To this end, a stable URI for it is selected, human-readable documentation and basic metadata for the ontology are specified, labels and comments are defined in more languages (currently in Italian and English), and the content negotiation is implemented. In this phase, we leveraged LODE (Peroni et al. 2013), i.e., a tool that, used in conjunction with content negotiation, allows us to make available the ontology as a human-readable and browsable HTML page with embedded links. Additional tools such as WebVOWL[42] can be used to graphically visualise on the Web the elements of the ontology.

---

[42]http://vowl.visualdataweb.org/webvowl.html.

Once the data cleansing and ontology creation activities are completed, LOD engineers can be involved in the process phases devoted to the generation, linking and publication of Linked Open datasets. For these phases we used the D2RQ[43] platform; that is, a system for accessing relational databases as RDF graphs. The platform provides two ways of working: *d2r-serv* and *dump-rdf*. The former queries a relational database as a virtual RDF graph; the latter dumps the content of the whole database into a single RDF file. Both ways need a customisable mapping file as input where rules specifying how to transform the relational data in RDF are defined (the activity *DB to RDF mapping design* in Fig. 3). The mapping file can be defined using a declarative mapping language through which describing the relation between an ontology and a relational data model. In this case, LOD engineers need the ontology and database schema as inputs in order to execute this phase of the process.

Once the RDF dump is produced, the data it includes can be linked (data linking in Fig. 3) to other well-known datasets available on the Web of Data (e.g., DBpedia, GeoNames, and any other of the cultural sector). In order to carry out this activity, we used Silk,[44] a linked data integration framework that enables the integration of heterogenous data sources. As D2RQ, Silk requires a mapping configuration for specifying how to discover links between datasets.

A data validation phase is then required in order to verify whether the produced datasets match the desired data quality. If the validation is positive, the datasets can be published: otherwise, the mapping phase has to be re-iterated applying proper mapping refinements.

The final phase of the process involves the Linked Open datasets publication. Data are uploaded in a triple store; that is, a data base capable of storing RDF graphs and enabling SPARQL interrogations on the data. SPARQL is the W3C standard protocol, similar to SQL, that allows to query RDF triples. In our work, we used Virtuoso SPARQL endpoint with its open source version.[45] Finally, in order to favour a better end-users experience, we deployed LodView[46]; that is a Java Web application based on Spring and Jena that implements URI dereferencing and allows users to browse RDF resources in a user-friendly way, as HTML pages.

The described process ensures that the following principles are met: (1) the published information is created and managed within a real business process of a public body; (2) database updates are reflected in the Linked Open datasets by configuring the above process in such a way to be run periodically when changes to the main authoritative sources are applied; (3) the dataset is linked to broadly-known datasets available on the Web, e.g. DBpedia, GeoNames; (4) the data and the ontology are easily accessible through user-friendly interfaces (e.g., LodLive, LODE, WebVOWL) that allow non-expert users to explore the model and the datasets.

---

[43]http://d2rq.org/.

[44]http://silkframework.org/.

[45]https://github.com/openlink/virtuoso-opensource.

[46]http://lodview.it/.

Example of Linked Open Data Aligned to Cultural-ON

In the following we provide an example of usage of the ontology *Cultural-ON* for exporting in RDF the data stored in *DB Unico 2.0*. The example is based on data regarding the National Museum of Capodimonte and an event it hosted. We provide some crucial code snippets; interested readers can refer to the complete example available in TURTLE and in RDF/XML formats at.[47] The example can be explored through LODView by accessing any URI defined in the RDF file, e.g.[48]

Frame 1 provides the definition of the museum as *"Cultural Institute or Site"*. The resource `cissite:Museo_di_Capodimonte` represents the National Museum of Capodimonte. The resource is of type `cis:Museum`, i.e. a Cultural Institute or Site of type Museum. A Cultural Institute or Site has a name `cis:institutionalName` and a description `cis:description`. The values of these properties are also specified in the RDF schema properties `rdfs:label` and `rdfs:comment`, respectively, in order to improve the readability of the data when using semantic web browsers and visualizers. Every Cultural Institute or Site is associated with a unique identifier named ISIL, i.e., International Standard Identifier for Libraries and Related Organizations. In the example of Frame 1 the ISIL identifier is fictive since in Italy it is currently available only for libraries and holders of archives, not for museums (the Ministry is planning to assign an ISIL identifier to all cultural institutes or sites in the near future).

```
cissite:Museo_di_Capodimonte a cis:Museum ;
   rdfs:label "Museo di Capodimonte"@it ;
   rdfs:comment "Nel 1738 Carlo di Borbone ... "@it ;
   cis:institutionalName "Museo di Capodimonte"@it ;
   cis:description "Nel 1738 Carlo di Borbone ... "@it ;
   cis:ISILIdentifier "IT−NA00001" ;
   cis:hasSite site:Sede_del_Museo_di_Capodimonte ;
   cis:hasNameInTime nit:Museo_di_Capodimonte ;
   cis:hasCollection collection:Collezione_Farnese ;
   cis:catalogue cat:Catologo_Collezione_Farnese ;
   ...
```

Frame 1 The code snippet for the definition of the *Cultural Institute or Site* "Museo di Capodimonte"

The 'National Museum of Capodimonte', intended as Cultural Institute, is located in a building commonly known with the name 'National Museum of Capodimonte' represented by the resource `site:Sede_del_Museo_di_Capodimonte`. The definition of the Site is provided by Frame 2.

The separation of `cis:CulturalInstituteOrSite`, i.e. a complex entity that involves an organisation of people and a physical site, from `cis:Site`, i.e. a

---

[47]https://w3id.org/cis/example/.

[48]https://w3id.org/cis/resource/CulturalInstituteOrSite/Museo_di_Capodimonte.

place where a cultural institute or site is physically located, is required to describe situations where multiple institutes or sites are located in the same building or where a single cultural institute or site is dislocated in several buildings. Furthermore, Frame 2 shows an example of usage of the ODPs "*Description*" and "*Place*". The sd:Sede_del_Museo_di_Capodimonte is the description of the building regarding the attribute "Area".

```
site : Sede_del_Museo_di_Capodimonte a cis : Site ;
  cis : name "Sede del 'Museo di Capodimonte '" @it ;
  cis : hasSiteDescription sd : Sede_del_Museo_di_Capodimonte ;
  cis : hosts event : Vincenzo_Gemito_dal_salotto_Minozzi_
    al_Museo_di_Capodimonte ;
  cis : isSiteOf cissite : Museo_di_Capodimonte ;
  ...
sd : Sede_del_Museo_di_Capodimonte a cis : SiteDescription ;
  cis : description "The Museum has an area of 1000
    square meter" @en ;
  cis : hasAttribute attribute : Area .
attribute : Area a cis : Attribute ;
  rdfs : label "Area" @en ;
  cis : description "The extent in square meter of a Site" @en .
```

Frame 2 A code snippet defining the site of the National Museum of Capodimonte

Frame 3 provides an example of usage of the class cis:NameInTime. cis:NameInTime (as well as cis:RoleInTime) implements a specialisation of the ODP called *Time Indexed Situation*. The situation defined by nit:Museo_di_Capodimonte describes the names assigned to the museum since it was founded. Since 1957 the museum has been officially called "*Museo di Capodimonte*"; it also has "*Museo Nazionale di Capodimonte*" as alternative name.

```
nit : Museo_di_Capodimonte a cis : NameInTime ;
  cis : institutionalName "Museo di Capodimonte" @it ;
  cis : altLabel "Museo Nazionale di Capodimonte" @it ;
  cis : isValidDuring ti : Intervallo_di_tempo_per_denominazione_
    nel_tempo_Museo_di_Capodimonte .

ti : Intervallo_di_tempo_per_denominazione_nel_
    tempo_Museo_di_Capodimonte a cis : TimeInterval ;
  cis : startDate "1957" .
```

Frame 3 A code snippet showing an example of usage of the class cis:NameInTime

Frame 4 shows an example of the classes cis:Collection and cis:Catalogue. The resource collection:Collezione_Farnese represents the "Farnese" collection that has been managed by Museum of Capodimonte during a specific time interval ti:Collezione_Farnese_a_Museo_di_Capodimonte. In this example, the collection contains only one *Cultural Heritage Object*; cho:Giambologna_Ratto_di_una_sabina. It is worth noting that the property cis:hasMember of the class Collection allows including in a collection any resource defined in other datasets (e.g. Cultura Italia). In other words, this property allows us to link the dataset generated from the data contained in *DB Unico 2.0* to other datasets related to the descriptions of artworks. The resource `cat:Catologo_Collezione_Farnese` of type `cis:Catalogue` is used to describe collections.

```
collection:Collezione_Farnese a cis:Collection ;
  cis:name "Collezione Farnese"@it ;
  cis:description "Trasferita a Napoli... "@it ;
  cis:atTime ti:Collezione_Farnese_a_Museo_di_Capodimonte ;
  cis:hasMember cho:Giambologna_Ratto_di_una_sabina .

cho:Giambologna_Ratto_di_una_sabina
  a cis:CulturalHeritageObject ;
  cis:name "Giambologna — Ratto di una Sabina" ;
  cis:isMemberOf collection:Collezione_Farnese ;
  cis:isInSite site:Sede_del_Museo_di_Capodimonte .

cat:Catologo_Collezione_Farnese a cis:Catalogue ;
  cis:describes collection:Collezione_Farnese ;
  cis:isCatalogueOf cissite:Museo_di_Capodimonte ;
  ...
```

Frame 4 An example of usage of the classes `cis:Collection` and `cis:Catalogue`

The resource `event:Vincenzo_Gemito_dal_salotto_Minozzi_-al_Museo_di_Capodimonte`, illustrated in Frame 5, defines an event hosted by Museum of Capodimonte. The event was an exhibition of Vincenzo Gemito's artworks. In particular, the event involved the *Cultural Heritage Object* "Il giocatore di carte" represented by the resource `cho:Il_giocatore_di_carte`.

```
event:Vincenzo_Gemito_dal_salotto_Minozzi_al_Museo_di_Capodimonte
  a cis:Event;
  cis:name "Vincenzo Gemito, dal salotto Minozzi
    al Museo di Capodimonte" ;
  cis:description "Apre al pubblico al Museo di ... " ;
  cis:isHostedBy site:Sede_del_Museo_di_Capodimonte;
  cis:involves cho:Il_giocatore_di_carte ;
  ...
```

Frame 5 An example of event hosted by the museum

Lesson Learnt (On Methodological Principles)

Besides the results described in the previous sections, this experience allowed us to reflect on how to improve our ontology development methodology, in particular as far as collaboration with domain experts and ontology reuse are concerned.

Communicating with Domain Experts

Domain experts are always present as one of the main actors in ontology engineering methodologies (Simperl et al. 2010). Their contribution to the process is crucial, especially in defining the domain and task requirements, which drive the ontology design and testing phases. Similarly, in software engineering methodologies, domain experts are the main actor and input source of software and database requirements definition, which determine the corresponding software modelling choices. Nevertheless, there is a difference in how software and databases are perceived by domain experts, as compared to how they perceive ontologies. Software and databases are expected to be black boxes able, respectively, to do what was expressed in form of requirements and to provide, when queried, the data they are expected to store.

Ontologies provide a data model for building knowledge bases, however they are also expected to reflect a shared understanding of a knowledge domain and, in some cases, to be evolved and maintained by domain experts without the help of ontology experts. This important commitment of ontologies is often wrongly interpreted as if the communication between domain experts and ontology experts should be mediated by sharing the ontology implementation (e.g. its OWL representation) and by discussing the modelling choices, applied during its implementation. In other words, the ontology itself is often used as the reference document for discussing domain requirements. Based on our experience, this is a wrong practice.

The good practice, as suggested in most methodological guidelines (Simperl et al. 2010; Suárez-Figueroa et al. 2015; Blomqvist et al. 2010), is to focus the communication on ontological requirements. It is important though to identify a common communication code. In the case of the Cultural-ON project, we used user stories (extracted from normative documents and discussions with domain experts) and competency questions, as shown in section "Cultural-ON: The Cultural ONtologies".

Although we acknowledge that keeping the domain experts focused on requirements is a good practice, we also have to recognise the importance of sharing with them the ontology, at some level of detail. It is important that they have an understanding of the ontology main concepts and usage, in order to facilitate reuse, and favour technological transfer to the domain experts, who may want to maintain and evolve the ontology. This need is not properly addressed, currently: the only way to share ontology details with domain experts is to explain them the OWL representation. Considering that most of them do not have a knowledge representation background, this practice slows down the process significantly and forces ontology and domain experts to perform training sessions in logics and ontology design.

Our experience (not limited to the Cultural-ON project) suggests the need to identify an intermediate ontology representation, able to provide, at the same time, both a clear understanding and a simplified view of the ontology, which shows the essential modelling components, and hides such technical details as complex axiomatisation and *logical sugar*. Ontology design patterns (ODP) may be a practical means for sharing a view of the ontology with domain experts, addressing this idea. A proposal, which we are currently investigating, is to use UML component diagrams as intermediate ontology representation (by defining an appropriate UML profile), where each component represents an ODP, or more in general an ontology module, and its interfaces show the ODP's most important concepts. The interfaces of an ontology module can be either classes or properties. Their role is twofold: (1) to show the points of interaction with the ontology component, and (2) to provide details on the most important concepts covered by the ontology module. Interacting with an ontology component means both communication between two ontology modules, and communication between an ontology module and an external client (for example, a user that wants to instantiate that component).

As a proof of concept, we show in Fig. 4 an example UML component diagram describing Cultural-ON as a set of interconnected ODPs. Grey components represent more general ODPs, which could be omitted depending on the level of detail that one wants to have. The white components show the core parts of the ontology and highlight their main concepts. For example, the component `CulturalInstituteOrSite` shows the class CIS[49] and the fact that one of its main characteristics is the composition (i.e. the `partOf` relation). The component `RoleInTime` shows its three main concepts, providing the intuition of a *n*-ary relation which models the role of an agent during a certain time period. Such component is linked to the component `CulturalInstituteOrSite` by means of the concept `roleAt`, indicating that an agent has a role at a certain CIS. For example, this notation allows to hide the OWL-specific modelling of an *n*-ary relation, which requires reification, while still conveying the conceptual semantics of this part of the ontology.

The choice of what concepts to show as interfaces and which ones to visualise as links between components can change, depending on the intention of the designer. The aim of this example is to show a possible direction of research, more than providing a definitive solution, which is still under analysis.

Practices and Methods for Ontology Reuse

An important reflection that is worth sharing is related to the practice of ontology reuse. The Cultural-ON project was meant to favour the principle of reusing existing resources as much as possible, in order to facilitate interoperability. At the same time the Ministry had the need of having complete control on the evolution and maintenance of Cultural-ON, for ensuring its sustainability. In this section, we

---

[49] Short for `CulturalInstituteOrSite`.

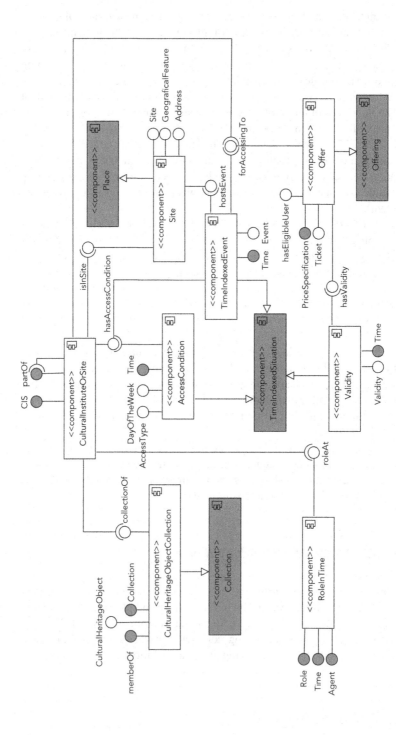

Fig. 4 Example of UML Component Diagram used for sharing the main concept modules of Cultural-ON with domain experts. This example provides the intuition of an ongoing work on defining an intermediate notation for sharing ontology modelling details with domain experts without exposing them to language-specific modelling details

discuss our choices in this respect, by generalising their principles, after a brief survey on the different practices in ontology reuse and their impact on the resulting ontologies.

Ontology reuse is a recommended practice both in scientific (Simperl et al. 2010) and in standardisation (W3C, ISO, ANSI, OASIS) literature. It is considered a good practice as it favours semantic interoperability among diverse knowledge bases, especially in the Semantic Web and Linked Data context. Nevertheless, a standardisation of ontology reuse practices is still missing because ontology design had a non-linear evolution and because modelling requirements may vary significantly depending on the domain, the availability of existing ontologies, the sustainability constraints within a given organisation, the specific requirements of an ontology project, the trends, and finally the personal taste of the ontology developer.

In the light of these considerations, it is possible to highlight a number of ontology reuse models, emerging from the current practices in the Semantic Web and Linked Data community, that can be classified based on the type of ontology that is reused:

- Reuse of foundational ontologies or top-level ontologies, for example when DOLCE[50] or the DBpedia ontology[51] are specialised for modelling events and participation to events, such as the case of the institutes that are involved in an exhibition;
- Reuse of ontology patterns,[52] for example when the "participation" pattern[53] is applied for modelling the participation to events;
- Reuse of domain ontologies, for example when the Music Ontology[54] is reused in another ontology project for modelling musical events.

Reuse models can also be classified based on the type of reused ontology fragments:

- Reuse of individual entities (classes, relations, individuals), for example when an element such as `dolce:hasParticipant` or `dbpedia-owl:Event` is reused as a specific entity;
- Reuse of *groups* of entities (modules, patterns, arbitrary fragments), for example when the pattern "participation", or `dolce:hasParticipant` together with all relevant related entities (`dolce:Object`, `dolce:hasParticipant`, `dolce:Event`, etc.), or the Event Ontology[55] are reused.

---

[50]http://www.ontologydesignpatterns.org/ont/dul/DUL.owl.

[51]http://dbpedia-org/ontology.

[52]http://www.ontologydesignpatterns.org.

[53]http://www.ontologydesignpatterns.org/cp/owl/participation.owl.

[54]http://musicontology.com.

[55]Event Ontology http://motools.sourceforge.net/event/event.html.

or they can be classified based on the amount of reused axioms (an axiom in an ontology is a rule that restricts or extends the possible inferences that can be done on the data):

- Reuse of ontologies by importing all their axioms, for example the whole Music Ontology;
- Reuse of ontologies by importing only the axioms within a given "neighbourhood" of certain entities or fragments, for example `dolce:hasParticipant` with all relevant entities and axioms that link them up to a certain "graph distance" (such neighbourhood is named "module");
- reuse of ontologies without importing axioms, that is by importing only entities (the URI of those entities), for example `dolce:Event`.

Finally, reuse can be classified based on the alignment policy:

- Reuse of ontologies as the source of entities and axioms for the new ontology project, for example when an entity such as `dolce:Event` is directly reused as the type of cultural events;
- Reuse of ontologies through alignments of entities of the ontology under development to the existing ones, for example when the axiom `rdfs:subClassOf` is used for aligning a class of Cultural-On to a class of DOLCE (e.g. `dolce:Event`).

The only characteristic that all reuse models share is to reuse entities with the same logical type as they were defined. For example, an entity defined as `owl:Class` in an ontology, is commonly reused as such, and not as, e.g. `owl:DatatypeProperty`. Besides this shared characteristic, reuse practices can be as diverse as 36 different alternatives (as described above). Possibly, even more than one adopted at the same time in an ontology project. Independently of the personal taste and current trends, a certain choice of reuse practice impacts significantly on the semantics of an ontology, on its sustainability, and on its potential interoperability.

Semantics of Reuse

It spans from *maximum* reuse, when a whole ontology is reused, by importing all axioms and by specialising them for concepts that are not already addressed; to *minimum* reuse, when only some entities are reused, by aligning them to entities defined in the *local* ontology, and without importing their related axioms. The *safest* and most complete semantics is obtained with the maximum reuse approach.

Sustainability of Reuse

In the case of maximum reuse, the usability of the ontology decreases, because the imported ontologies introduce entities and axioms that may be unnecessary (or sometimes undesired) in the local ontology. Furthermore, maximum reuse creates a strong dependency on the reused ontologies; for example, if the local ontology imports the whole Event Ontology, and the latter has some axioms changed, the local ontology might become incoherent with respect to its original requirements.

Interoperability and Reuse

In the case of minimum reuse, interoperability is simplified as there is no constraint caused by the semantics of the reused ontology (its axioms).

In summary, aspects related to the quality of semantics are better addressed by a maximum reuse, while sustainability and interoperability are better satisfied by a minimum reuse. For this reason, the attitude of designers, the scope of the project and the nature of the data to be modelled influence the decision on the reuse approach.

Direct Versus Indirect Reuse of Ontology Elements

Based on the general discussion of the previous sections, we summarise three possible approaches to ontology reuse that have been considered during the development of the Cultural-ON project. Afterwords, we report our choice and the principles and requirements that motivated it.

Minimal Reuse of Individual Entities

This approach seems to be advised by the Linked Data community, however it is a routine, not a good practice, at all. In fact, this practice of reuse is essentially driven by the intuition of the semantics of concepts (which can be relations or classes) based on their names, instead of their defining axioms. In addition to this problem related to the formal semantics of the reused entities, that may be incompatible with the intended semantics to be represented, there is the problem of creating a dependency of the local ontology with all ontologies whose parts are reused. This dependency may put at risk the sustainability and stability of the ontology and its associated knowledge bases.

PROS: Sharing of Linked Data community praxis.
CONS: Semantic ambiguity, difficulty in verifying the consistency among the diverse reused concepts, dependency on external ontologies, risk of instability and unsustainability of the ontology.

Direct Reuse of Ontology Design Patterns and Alignments

Main concepts and relations of the ontology are defined in the local namespace (e.g. `cis:CulturalInsituteOrSite`). They are aligned, when
possible and appropriate, to existing ontologies by means of logical relations
(e.g. `owl:equivalentTo rdfs:subClassOf`). The modelling of some
concepts and relations, which are relevant for the domain but applicable
to more general scopes, is delegated to external ontologies, by means of
ontology design pattern (ODP) reuse. For example, an instance of the class
`cis:CulturalInsituteOrSite` can be involved in an event. Such event
can be modelled as an instance of the class `ex:Event`, defined in an external
ontology. The class `ex:Event` can be directly reused as the range of a property
that expresses such a relation. In this example, the pattern "Event" associated
with the class `ex:Event` in the external ontology, is *directly* reused. When third
parties will reuse the Cultural-ON ontology for modelling their data, they will
represent information about events by using the relations defined in the "Event"
pattern, according to their needs. With this approach, the ontology shows a modular
architecture, with a *core* component that defines the main domain entities and other
components that identify relevant ODPs that model other concepts, needed for
addressing the ontology requirements.

PROS: Stability and sustainability of domain relations and concepts, modularity,
        interoperability.
CONS: Possible heterogeneity in the ODPs usage, risk of instability and unsus-
        tainability limited to external modules.

Indirect Reuse of Ontology Design Patterns and Alignments

ODPs are used in this case as templates. This approach is an extension of the
previous one. It keeps all PROS and decreases the CONS. The ontology is
designed by identifying relevant ODPs from external ontologies to be reused,
and by reproducing them in the local ontology. At the same time, the ontology guarantees interoperability by keeping the appropriate alignments to the
external ODPs, and provides extensions that satisfy more specific requirements.
For example, following this approach the class `cis:Event` and the relation
`cis:isInvolvedInEvent` are locally defined and then aligned to `ex:Event`
and `ex:isInvolvedInEvent` by means of equivalent (or other logical) relations. The alignment axioms may be published separately from the core of the
ontology. If the ontology will need further extensions, the same approach must be
followed, in order to avoid the introduction of dependencies.

PROS: Stability and sustainability of the ontology, modularity, interoperability,
        minimisation of dependencies from external ontologies, identification of external
        ontologies that can be used for more specific and extended requirements.

In all the three approaches described, the alignments must be maintained following the evolution of the reused ontologies. However, in the situation of incoherence raised by a change in an external reused ontology, the third approach guarantees the easiest maintenance, as it will be enough to revise the affected alignment relations.

In the context of the Cultural-ON project, we decided to adopt the third approach, i.e. indirect reuse of ODPs and alignments. This choice is motivated by requirements of the project that can be summarised as follows:

- to favour interoperability;
- to remove and minimise the dependency on external ontologies, in favour of the sustainability of the ontology;
- to provide to potential users of Cultural-ON a "self-contained" ontology, which reuses external ontologies by means of alignments;
- to define a sufficient number of axioms to address both competency questions and the legacy data (i.e. DB Unico);
- to find the best tradeoff in terms of number of reused entities, ODPs and ontology fragments that guarantee coherence among the axioms of the reused ontologies and of the local one. The coherence is tested and checked at design time, by using query engines and reasoners, according to Blomqvist et al. (2012).

Concluding Remark

This Chapter described a work conducted in the context of a collaboration established with the Italian Ministry of Cultural Heritage and Activities and Tourism. The work consisted in two important phases: (1) a cultural data landscape analysis, which allowed us to understand the peculiarities of part of the large Italian cultural patrimony; and (2) the definition of a common and standard-based data model capable of representing cultural property resources, The model has been defined so as to pave the way to the construction of a large open interconnected knowledge base which can, among others, guarantee that different organisations operating in the cultural sector could agree on the precise meaning of common and exchanged information on cultural properties, preserving that meaning throughout the data exchange.

The data model is actually a suite of ontology modules we named Cultural-ON (Cultural ONtologies), where the module related to "cultural institutes and sites" and "cultural events", we presented in this Chapter, is expressed using OWL (Ontology Web Language), a semantic markup language for publishing and sharing ontologies on the Web. The module has been designed by applying a methodology that, starting from a clear definition of requirements to meet, makes extensively reuse of ontology design patterns. Together with ontology design patterns, CulturalON has been structured so as to be linked to other ontologies available on the Web. In doing so, sustainability and semantic interoperability requirements were considered.

Based on the data model, the chapter proposes a process that allows us to produce linked open datasets on cultural institutes and sites and cultural events that can be maintained up-to-date over time. This was realised by integrating the proposed process into the real business process of data management employed by the Ministry.

The chapter also discusses a number of lessons learnt and recommendations that can be sufficiently general to be applied in analogous cultural projects and in other domains.

Future Works

We are planning to extend the Cultural-ON suite with a module for the representation of cultural objects and collections. Currently, the cultural institutes and sites ontology offers a preliminary representation of objects and collections as "hooks" for future extensions, which will capture the peculiarities of those objects and collections. In this sense, standard ontologies such as CIDOC-CRM (as described in the state of the art) can be investigated.

Finally, we are evaluating the reuse of the data model and produced linked open datasets to support the valorisation of less known cultural properties, thus fostering both their fruition by a wide audience of users and the creation of a richer shared culture and a wealthy touristic market.

References

C. Aart, B. Wielinga, W. Robert Hage, Mobile cultural heritage guide: location-aware semantic search, in *Proceedings of the 17th International Conference of Knowledge Engineering and Management by the Masses (EKAW-2010)*. ed. By P. Cimiano, H. Sofia Pinto (Springer, Lisbon, 2010), pp. 257–271

E. Blomqvist et al., Experimenting with eXtreme Design, in *the Proceeding of 17th International Conference of (EKAW-2010)*, ed. By P. Cimiano, H. Sofia Pinto. Lisbon. Lecture Notes in Computer Science, vol. 6317 (Springer Berlin Heidelberg, Lisbon, Portugal, 2010), pp. 120–134. Doi:10.1007/978-3-642-16438-5_9

E. Blomqvist, A. Seil Sepour, V. Presutti, Ontology testing - methodology and tool, in *Knowledge Engineering and Knowledge Management - the Proceeding of 18th International Conference (EKAW-2012)*, ed. By A. ten Teije et al., Galway City. Lecture Notes in Computer Science, vol. 7603 (Springer Berlin Heidelberg, Galway City, Ireland, 2012), pp. 216–226. Doi:10.1007/978-3-642-33876-2_20

V. de Boer et al., Amsterdam museum linked open data. Semantic Web **4**(3), 237–243 (2013)

M. Doerr, The CIDOC conceptual reference module: an ontological approach to semantic interoperability of metadata. AI Magazine **24**(3), 75–92 (2003)

A. Gangemi, V. Presutti, Ontology design patterns, in *Handbook on Ontologies*, 2nd edn., ed. By S. Staab, R. Studer. International Handbooks on Information Systems (Springer, Berlin, 2009), pp. 221–243. Doi:10.1007/978-3-540-92673-3_10

M. Grüninger, M.S. Fox, The role of competency questions in enterprise engineering, in *Benchmarking – Theory and Practice*, ed. by A. Rolstadås. IFIP Advances in Information and Communication Technology (Springer, Boston, MA, 1995), pp. 22–31. Doi:10.1007/978-0-387-34847-6_3

E. Hyvönen, Semantic portals for cultural heritage, in *Handbook on Ontologies*, 2nd edn., ed. By S. Staab, R. Studer (Springer, Berlin, Heidelberg, 2009), pp. 757–778

A. Isaac, B. Haslhofer, Europeana Linked Open Data - data.europeana.eu. Semantic Web **4**(3), 291–297 (2013)

J. Oomen, L. Aroyo, Crowdsourcing in the cultural heritage domain: opportunities and challenges, in *Proceedings of 5th International Conference on Communities & Technologies (C&T-2011)* (ACM, Brisbane, 2011), pp. 138–149

S. Peroni, D. Shotton, F. Vitali, Tools for the automatic generation of ontology documentation: a task-based evaluation. Int. J. Semantic Web Inf. Syst. **9**(1), 21–44 (2013)

M. Ridge, From tagging to theorizing: deepening engagement with cultural heritage through crowdsourcing. Curator: Museum J. **56**(4), 435–450 (2013)

T. Ruotsalo et al., SMARTMUSEUM: a mobile recommender system for the Web of Data. Web Semantics: Sci. Serv. Agents World Wide Web **20**, 50–67 (2013)

G. Schreiber et al., Semantic annotation and search of cultural-heritage collections: the MultimediaN E-Culture demonstrator. Web Semantics: Sci. Serv. Agents World Wide Web **6**(4), 243–249 (2008)

E.P.B. Simperl, M. Mochol, T. Bürger, Achieving maturity: the state of practice in ontology engineering in 2009. Int. J. Comput. Sci. Appl. (IJCSA) **7**(1), 45–65 (2010). ISSN: 0972-9038

M.C. Suárez-Figueroa, A. Gómez-Pérez, M. Fernández-López, The NeOn methodology framework: a scenario-based methodology for ontology development. Appl. Ontol. **10**(2), 107–145 (2015). Doi:10.3233/AO-150145

P. Szekely et al., Connecting the Smithsonian American Art Museum to the linked data cloud, in *Proceedings of the 10th Extended Semantic Web Conference (ESWC-2013)*, ed. By P. Cimiano et al. (Springer, Montpellier, 2013), pp. 593–607

Y. Wang et al., Interactive user modeling for personalized access to museum collections: the Rijksmuseum case study, in *Proceedings of the 11th International Conference of User Modeling (UM-2007)*, ed. By C. Conati, K. McCoy, G. Paliouras (Springer, Corfu, 2007), pp. 385–389

Using the Formal Representations of "Elementary Events" to Set Up Computational Models of Full "Narratives"

Gian Piero Zarri

Abstract In this chapter, we describe the conceptual tools that, in an NKRL context (NKRL = Narrative Knowledge Representation Language), allow us to obtain a (computer-usable) description of full "narratives" as logically structured associations of the constituting (and duly formalized) "elementary events." Dealing with this problem means, in practice, being able to formalize those "connectivity phenomena"—denoted, at "surface level," by logico-semantic coherence links like causality, goal, co-ordination, subordination, indirect speech, etc.—that assure the conceptual unity of a whole narrative. The second-order, unification based solutions adopted by NKRL in this context, "completive construction" and "binding occurrences," allow us to take into account the connectivity phenomena by "reifying" the formal representations used to model the constitutive elementary events. These solutions, which are of interest from a general digital humanities point of view, are explained in some depth making use of several illustrating examples.

Introduction

NKRL, the "Narrative Knowledge Representation Language," is both a *conceptual modeling tool* (Zarri 2009) and a (fully implemented) *computer science environment* (Zarri 2009: Appendix A, 2010), created for dealing with "*narratives*" in an innovative way. In a nutshell a narrative—see, e.g., Bal (1997), Jahn (2005)—is a general unifying framework used for relating real-life or fictional stories involving concrete or imaginary characters and their relationships. A narrative materializes actually as (multimedia) work of speech, writing, song, film, television, video game, photography, theater, etc.

Even if the conceptual structures and the procedures used in NKRL for dealing with narratives are quite general, the concrete applications of this language have concerned mainly *non-fictional narratives*. While fictional narratives have prin-

G.P. Zarri (✉)
Sorbonne University, STIH Laboratory, Maison de la Recherche – 28, rue Serpente,
75006 Paris, France
e-mail: zarri@noos.fr

© Springer International Publishing AG 2017   39
S. Hai-Jew (ed.), *Data Analytics in Digital Humanities*, Multimedia Systems
and Applications, DOI 10.1007/978-3-319-54499-1_2

cipally an entertainment value and represent a narrator's account of a story that happened in an imaginary world (a novel is a typical example of fictional narrative), non-fictional narratives are deeply rooted in the everyday world. They are conveyed, e.g., by NL supports under the form of news stories, corporate memory documents (memos, reports, minutes, etc.), normative and legal texts, medical records, etc. But they can also be represented by multimedia documents like audio and video records, surveillance videos, actuality photos for newspapers and magazines, etc. A photo representing President Obama addressing the Congress, or a short video showing three nice girls on a beach, can be considered as "non-fictional narrative" documents even if they are not, of course, NL documents. We can note immediately the *ubiquitous character* of this sort of (non-fictional) narrative resources and their *general economic importance*.

In agreement with the most recent theoretical developments in the "narratology" domain, NKRL understands a (fictional or non-fictional) "narrative" under the form of a *"coherent" (i.e., logically connected) stream of spatio-temporally constrained "elementary events."* It is then evident that, in an NKRL context, a fundamental step for the modeling of (whole) narratives concerns the possibility of finding a complete, logically correct, and computer-exploitable *formal representation* of the different elementary events that makes up the stream. This topic has been dealt with in-depth in several recent publications, see Zarri (2009, 2010, 2011a, 2015) for example, and will only be alluded to in passing in this paper.[1] This last focuses, instead, on the description of *two specific mechanisms* used in NKRL for formalizing some *relational phenomena* that are particularly relevant in the context of the *logical coherence of the narrative stream* evoked above—and that are of interest, in general, from a cognitive point of view. They are (1) *the need to refer* to an elementary event (or a full narrative) *as an argument of another event* (see, e.g., an event X where someone speaks about Y, where Y is itself an elementary event or a logically coherent set of events), and (2) *the need for associating together through some sort of logico-semantic relationships* elementary events or narratives that could also be regarded as *independent entities* (as an elementary event or full narrative X being linked to another event or narrative Y by causality, goal, coordination,

---

[1] We will only mention that, in an NKRL context, each elementary event is recognized—as usual, see Matsuyoshi et al. (2010) for example—thanks to the detection of "generalized predicates" within the natural language (NL) formulation of the whole stream. These predicates correspond then to the usual tensed/untensed "verbs," but also to "adjectives" ("... worth several dollars ...", "...a dormant volcano ..."), nouns ("...Jane's amble along the park...", "...a possible attack ..."), etc., when they have a predicative function. Let us look, e.g., at two simple narratives proper to a recent NKRL application concerning the conceptual analysis of accident messages in an industrial context, see Zarri (2011b), like: "The control room operator recognizes an alarm" and "The control room operator presses a button to initialize a new start-up sequence." In the first example, the whole narrative is formed of a unique elementary event, detected via the presence of the predicate "recognize." In the second, the narrative is formed of two elementary events, identified thanks to the occurrence of the two predicates "press" and "initialize." The whole narrative is eventually fully formalized by using a "second order operator" in the GOAL style to link together the formal expressions of the two elementary events, see later in this chapter.

alternative, etc. relationships). In an NKRL context, the first relational phenomenon is called "*completive construction*" and the second "*binding occurrences*"; the two are collectively denoted as "*connectivity phenomena*." Passing from the *deep, conceptual level* proper to NKRL to a *surface, linguistic level*, they can then evoke the classical "*textual cohesion*" aspects described, among many others, by Halliday and Hasan (1976) and Morris and Hirst (1991) and the "*contingency phenomena*" recently analyzed, e.g., by Hu et al. (2013) in a film scene descriptions context. At surface level, the presence of connectivity phenomena is recognized through the existence of "*cues*," i.e., *syntactic/semantic features* like causality, goal, co-ordination, subordination, indirect speech, etc.

In the following, we will present first, section "Basic Notions About NKRL", a quick recall of some fundamental principles about NKRL, and the associate terminology. Section "Linking Elementary Events" is the central component of the paper, showing how the basic building blocks corresponding to the elementary events can be associated within wider structures in order to take the "connectivity phenomena" into account. Section "Querying/Inference Procedures" mentions briefly the querying/inference mechanisms of NKRL, referring the reader to other NKRL publications for additional details. Section "Related Work" concerns some comparisons with work related to the specific NKRL's approach; section "Conclusion" supplies, eventually, a short "Conclusion."

Basic Notions About NKRL

NKRL innovates with respect to the current ontological paradigms—e.g., those developed in a Semantic Web (SW) context, see Bechhofer et al. (2004), W3C OWL Working Group (2012)—by adding an "ontology of elementary events" to the usual "ontology of concepts."

The ontology of concepts is called HClass ("hierarchy of classes") in an NKRL context and includes presently (February 2016) more than 7500 "standard" concepts—"standard" meaning here that the "properties" or "attributes" used to define a given concept are simply expressed as *binary (i.e., linking only two arguments) relationships* of the "property/value" type. From a purely "formal" point of view HClass—see Zarri (2009, pp. 43–55, 123–137)—is not fundamentally different, then, from the ontologies that we can build up by using the frame version of Protégé (Noy et al. 2000).

The ontology of elementary events is, by contrast, *a new sort of hierarchical organization* where the nodes correspond to *n*-ary structures called "*templates*," represented schematically according to the syntax of Eq. (1) below. This ontology is then denoted as HTemp (hierarchy of templates) in NKRL. Templates, in opposition to the "*static/basic*" notions (like "human being," "amount," "color," "artefact," "control room," "valve," "level of temperature," etc.) denoted by the HClass concepts, take into account the "*dynamic/structured*" component of the narrative information. They can be conceived, in fact, as *the canonical, formal representation of generic classes of spatio-temporally characterized elementary events* like "move a physical object," "be present in a place," "having a specific attitude towards someone/something," "produce a service," "asking/receiving an advice," etc.

$$\left(L_i \left(P_j \left(R_1 \; a_1\right) \; \left(R_2 \; a_2\right) \ldots \left(R_n \; a_n\right)\right)\right) \tag{1}$$

In Eq. (1), L_i is the *"symbolic label"* identifying (*reifying*) the particular n-ary structure corresponding to a specific template—as we will see in the following, these reification operations are of a fundamental importance in the context of the association of (formalized) elementary events. P_j is a *"conceptual predicate."* R_k is a generic *"functional role"* (Zarri 2011a) used to specify the logico-semantic function of its "filler" a_k with respect to the predicate. a_k is then a *"predicate argument"* introduced by the role R_k.

When a template following the general syntax of Eq. (1) and denoted as Move:TransferMaterialThingsToSomeone in NKRL is *instantiated* to provide the representation of a simple elementary event like "Bill gives a book to Mary," the predicate P_j (MOVE) will introduce its three arguments a_k, JOHN_, MARY_, and BOOK_1 (*"individuals,"* i.e., instances of HClass concepts) through the three functional relationships (R_k roles) SUBJ(ect), BEN(e)F(iciary), and OBJECT. The global n-ary construction is then *reified* through the symbolic label L_i *and necessarily managed as a coherent block at the same time.* The instances of templates are called *"predicative occurrences"* and correspond then to the representation of specific elementary events, see the examples in the following section.

Note that, to avoid the ambiguities of natural language and any possible combinatorial explosion problem—see Zarri (2009, pp. 56–61)—both the conceptual predicate of Eq. (1) and the associated functional roles are *"primitives."* Predicates P_j pertain then to the set {BEHAVE, EXIST, EXPERIENCE, MOVE, OWN, PRODUCE, RECEIVE}, and the roles R_k to the set {SUBJ(ect), OBJ(ect), SOURCE, BEN(e)F(iciary), MODAL(ity), TOPIC, CONTEXT}. Figure 1 reproduces a fragment of the HTemp hierarchy that displays, in particular, the conceptual labels of some off-springs of the Move: (and Produce:) sub-hierarchies. As it appears from this figure, HTemp is structured into *seven branches*, where each branch includes only the templates created—according to the general syntax of Eq. (1)—around one of the seven predicates (P_j) admitted by the NKRL language.

For the sake of clarity, we reproduce in Table 1 the full formalism corresponding to the template Move:TransferMaterialThingsToSomeone (see also Fig. 1) used to produce the predicative occurrence formalizing the elementary event "Bill gives a book to Mary" of the above example. The constituents (as SOURCE, MODAL, (*var2*), etc. in Table 1) included in square brackets are *optional*. HTemp includes presently (February 2016) more than 150 templates, very easy to specialize and customize, see, e.g., Zarri (2009, pp. 137–177, 2014).

As we can see from Table 1, the arguments of the predicate (the a_k terms in Eq. 1) are actually represented by variables (*var$_i$*) with *associated constraints*. These are expressed as *concepts or combinations of concepts*, i.e., using the terms of the NKRL standard ontology of concepts (HClass). When creating a

Fig. 1 Partial image of HTemp, with the Produce: and Move: branches partly unfolded

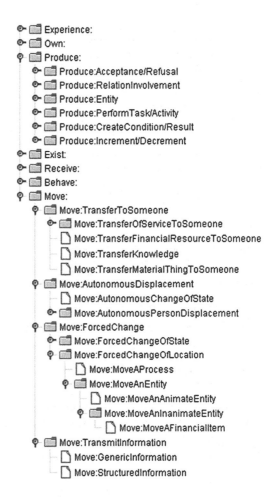

predicative occurrence as an instance of a given template, the constraints linked to the variables are used to specify the *legal sets of HClass terms (concepts or individuals) that can be substituted for these variables within the occurrence*. In the predicative occurrence corresponding to the above example, we must then verify that JOHN_ and MARY_ are real HClass instances of individual_person, a specific term of human_being_or_social_body, see the constraints on the SUBJ and BENF functional roles of the template in Table 1. BOOK_1, as an instance of the HClass concept book_, verifies in turn the constraint artefact_ associated with the filler of the OBJ role. book_ is, in fact, a specific term of artefact_ through intermediate HClass concepts like, e.g., information_support.[2]

---

[2]We can also note that "*determiners*" (or "*attributes*") can be added to templates or predicative occurrences to introduce *further details* about the basic core, "symbolic label/predicate/functional roles/arguments of the predicate," see Eq. (1), of their formal representation (Zarri 2009, pp.

Table 1 A template of the Move: branch of HTemp

---

name: Move:TransferMaterialThingToSomeone
father: Move: TransferToSomeone
position: 4.21
NL description: 'Transfer a Material Thing (e.g., a Product, a Letter...) to Someone'

MOVE	SUBJ	*var1*: [(*var2*)]
	OBJ	*var3*
	[SOURCE	*var4*: [(*var5*)]]
	BENF	*var6*: [(*var7*)]
	[MODAL	*var8*]
	[TOPIC	*var9*]
	[CONTEXT	*var10*]
	{ [modulators], ≠abs }	

var1	=	human_being_or_social_body
var3	=	artefact_
var4	=	human_being_or_social_body
var6	=	human_being_or_social_body
var8	=	sector_specific_activity, service_
var9	=	sortal_concept
var10	=	situation_, symbolic_label
var2, *var5*, *var7*	=	location_

Linking Elementary Events

In section "Introduction", we have mentioned those "*connectivity phenomena*"—signaled, at "*surface linguistic level*," by the presence of NL syntactic/semantic features like causality, goal, indirect speech, co-ordination, subordination, etc.—that assure the logical coherence among the components (elementary events) of a specific narrative.

In NKRL, the connectivity phenomena are dealt with making use of *Higher Order Logic (HOL) structures*—according to HOL, a predicate can take one or more other predicates as arguments—obtained from the *reification* of generic (i.e., not only predicative, see below) occurrences. Concretely, the reification is based on the use of the *symbolic labels* denoted by the L_i terms in Eq. (1) above. "Reification" is intended here—as usual in a Knowledge Representation context—as the possibility

---

70–86). In particular, determiners/attributes of the "*location*" type—represented in general by *lists of instances* of the HClass location_ concept and of its specialization terms—can be associated through the "colon" operator, "*:*", with the *arguments of the predicate* (i.e., the fillers) introduced by the SUBJ, OBJ, SOURCE, and BENF functional roles of a template, see Table 1. Another important category of determiners/attributes associated, in this case, to a *full, well-formed template or predicative occurrence* to particularize its meaning are constants of the "*modulator*" type. Modulators are classed into three categories: *temporal* (begin, end, obs(erve)), *deontic* (oblig(ation), fac(ulty), interd(iction), perm(ission)), and *modal modulators* (for, against, wish, ment(al), etc.). See the examples in the sections below for some additional information about the determiners/attributes.

of creating new objects ("*first class citizens*") out of already existing entities and to "*say something*" about them without making explicit reference to the original entities.

Completive Construction

A first example of HOL connection between elementary events is represented by the "completive construction." This consists in using as *filler* of a functional role in a predicative occurrence pc_i the *symbolic label* L_j of another (*generic*) occurrence c_j. We can note immediately that the c_j (*indirectly*) used as fillers can correspond not only to predicative occurrences pc_i, but also to those "binding occurrences" bc_i we will introduce in the next sub-section. Constraints proper to the "completive construction" category of NKRL HOL constructions are:

- *Only* the OBJ, MODAL, TOPIC, and CONTEXT functional roles of pc_i can accept as filler the symbolic label L_j of a c_j, and *only one of these four roles* can be utilized in the context of a *specific instantiation* of the completive construction mechanism.
- L_j must denote a *single* symbolic label, i.e., any "structured filler" represented under the form of an association of labels *cannot be used* in a completive construction framework.
- For (software) implementation reasons, this *single* label L_j is prefixed, in the "external" NKRL format used in the examples of this chapter, by a "*sharp*," "#", code. The general format of a completive construction filler corresponds then, actually, to #symbolic_label, see the examples below. Note that symbolic_label is a *regular concept* of HClass, the standard NKRL ontology of concepts. This concept has then as *specific instances* all the *actual labels* used to denote (predicative and binding) occurrences in a specific NKRL application.

As a first example, we reproduce in Table 2 a fragment of a scenario concerning a recent Ambient Assisted Living (AAL) application of NKRL. In this fragment, a robot reminds John, an ageing person, of the obligation to lock the front door. The modulator oblig(ation), see Note 2, has been used in aal9.c12 to denote the *absolute necessity* of locking the front door. The "temporal determiners/attributes" date-1/date-2 are used in association with predicative occurrences to introduce the temporal information proper to the original elementary event, see, e.g., Zarri (2009, pp. 80–86, 194–201).[3]

---

[3]With respect to the *(semi-)automatic* synthesis of predicative occurrences like aal9.c11 and aal9.c12 in Table 2 and all the others mentioned in this paper—more in general, with respect to the *(semi-)automatic "translation"* from Natural Language (NL) into NKRL—several prototypes exist. All of them derive, basically, from the algorithms developed in the eighties in the framework of the RESEDA (in French, *Reseau Sémantique Documentaire*) project, an NKRL's ancestor, see Zarri (1983). Very in short, an up-to-date syntactic parser in the style of the well-known Stanford

Table 2 An example of completive construction

---

aal9.c11)   MOVE   SUBJ   ROBOT_1
                     OBJ   #aal9.c12
                     BENF   JOHN_
                     MODAL   audio_warning
                     date-1: 11/4/2011/17:35
                     date-2:

Move:StructuredInformation (4.42)

On 11/4/2011, at 17h35, the robot reminds John through an audio message of what is described in the predicative occurrence aal9.c12.

aal9.c12)   MOVE   SUBJ   JOHN_
                     OBJ   FRONT_DOOR_1: (unlocked_, locked_)
                     { oblig }
                     date-1: 11/4/2011/17:35
                     date-2:

Move:ForcedChangeOfState (4.12)

On 11/4/2011, at 17h35, John must necessarily, modulator "oblig(ation)", lock the front door.

We can note, in the formal encoding of Table 2, the use of predicative occurrences corresponding to *two different types* of Move: templates. The first, Move:StructuredInformation (a specialization of the Move:TransmitInformation template) is necessarily used in NKRL to represent, according to the "completive construction" modalities, the *transmission of some complex information* whose content is described by one or more predicative occurrences. The second, Move:ForcedChangeOfState, a specialization of Move:ForcedChange, is used when an agent (SUBJ) moves an entity (OBJ = physical object, animate entity, process, etc.) from an initial state to a final one. In this case, the *initial state* is represented by the *first position* of the location list associated (through the ":" operator, see again Note 2 above) with the filler of the OBJ role in the predicative occurrence (aal9.c12 in Table 2) that represents the moving. The *final state* is represented by the *second position* of the same list. Possible *intermediary states* can be symbolized as the *ordered sequence* of locations included between the first and last position of the list. Note also that the procedure used in aal9.c12 to denote a forced change of location

---

parser (Klein and Manning 2003) is used for a preliminary syntactic analysis of the NL text corresponding to the NKRL structures to be generated. A set of generalized "if-then" rules is then activated, where the "antecedents" of the rules denote fragments of the syntactic analysis able to "trigger" NKRL template-like structures (represented by the "consequents" of the rules) if some specific lexico-syntactic conditions are recognized. HClass and lexico-semantic resources like WordNet, VerbNet, Roget Thesaurus, etc. are used to complete the "translation" operations. A recent system in this style is described, e.g., in Ayari et al. (2013).

is valid in general, i.e., also when the elements of the vector associated with the OBJ filler correspond to *concrete "physical" locations* and not to "abstract" states.

Binding Occurrences

A second, more general way of linking together NKRL elementary events within the scope of a full narrative consists in making use of *"binding occurrences."* These are lists labelled with specific *"binding operators"* Bn_i whose arguments arg_i are represented (*reification*) by symbolic labels L_j of (*predicative or binding*) c_j occurrences. The general expression of a binding occurrence bc_i is then:

$$(Lb_k \ (Bn_i \ L_1 \ L_2 \ldots L_n)),\qquad\qquad(2)$$

where Lb_k is now the symbolic label identifying the whole (*autonomous*) binding structure. Unlike templates and predicative occurrences, binding occurrences are then characterized by the absence of any predicate or functional role. The eight binding operators are listed (and defined) in Table 3.

The binding occurrences bc_i must necessarily conform to the following mandatory restrictions to be considered as *well formed*:

- Each term (argument) L_j that, in a binding list, is associated with one of the operators of Table 3, denotes exactly a *single* predicative or binding occurrence c_j *described externally to the list*. Therefore, the arguments L_j are always *single terms* and cannot consist of lists of symbolic labels associated in turn with binding operators.
- In the binding occurrences of the ALTERN, COORD, and ENUM type, *no restriction is imposed on the cardinality of the list*, i.e., on the possible number of terms (arguments) L_j.
- In the binding occurrences labelled with CAUSE, REFER, GOAL, MOTIV, and COND, on the contrary, *only two arguments Lm and Ln are admitted*, see Table 3. The binding occurrences labelled with these five binding operators are then simply of the form: $(Lb_k \ (Bn_i \ L_m \ L_n))$. In these lists, the arguments L_m and L_n can denote, in general, *either a predicative or a binding occurrence*: an exception is represented by the COND binding occurrences, where the first argument, L_m, *must correspond necessarily to a predicative occurrence pc_i*, see again Table 3.

To supply now a first idea of the modalities of use of the "binding occurrences" tools let us suppose, see Table 4, we would like to formalize in NKRL terms the following situation: "From the main control room of the GP1Z plant, the production activities leader pushes the SEQ1 button in order to start the auxiliary lubrication pump M202." According to what was explained in Note 1 above, recognizing the presence of two surface predicates like "push" and "start" implies the creation, at *"deep level,"* of two different elementary events (two predicative occurrences). Moreover, the presence of "in order of" denotes the existence of some

Table 3 Binding operators of NKRL

Operator	Acronym	Mnemonic description
Alternative	ALTERN	The *"disjunctive"* operator. *Only a specific elementary event* corresponding to one of the terms included in the list of the associated L_j labels must be taken into account, but this term is not known *a priori*.
Co-ordination	COORD	The *"collective"* operator. *All the elementary events* corresponding to all the L_j terms of the list must *necessarily* be considered *together*.
Enumeration	ENUM	The *"distributive"* operator. *Each elementary event corresponding to each L_j term* of the list must be taken into account, but they are dealt with in a separate way.
Cause	CAUSE	*Only two L_j terms* can appear in a CAUSE binding occurrence (and in all the binding occurrences designated by one of the following binding operators of this Table). CAUSE is the *"strict causality"* operator, introducing a *necessary and sufficient causal relationship between the elementary events denoted by the first, L_m, and the second, L_n, arguments of the list*, the latter event explaining the former.
Reference	REFER	The *"weak causality"* operator, introducing a necessary *but not sufficient* causal relationship between the elementary events denoted by the first, L_m, and the second, L_n, arguments of the list.
Goal	GOAL	The *"strict intentionality"* operator: the elementary event denoted by the first argument L_m is *necessary* to bring about the event denoted by the second argument, L_n, and this second event is *sufficient* to explain the first. The predicative occurrence(s) corresponding to the second argument is/are marked as *"uncertain,"* operator *"*"*, see Zarri (2009, p. 71).
Motivation	MOTIV	The *"weak intentionality"* operator: the event denoted by the first argument L_m is *not necessary* to bring about the event denoted by L_n, but this last is *sufficient* to explain the first. The predicative occurrence(s) denoted by the second argument is/are marked as *"uncertain,"* operator *"*"*.
Condition	COND	The (single) *predicative occurrence pc_i* denoted by L_m represents an event that *could occur* if the predicative or binding occurrence c_j denoted by L_n *should take place*. pc_i is necessarily associated with a modal modulator "poss(ibility)"; the (single or multiple) predicative occurrence(s) corresponding to L_n is/are necessarily marked as "uncertain."

connectivity phenomena that brings together the two events. The first occurrence of Table 4, virt2.c32, corresponds then to the action of "pushing": button_pushing is an HClass concept, specialization of another (high level) concept, activity_, through device_use and other HClass terms. Note that the TOPIC role has the general meaning of "apropos of," "concerning," "with reference to," etc. The second occurrence, virt2.c33, represents the (possible) result of the action of "pushing," i.e., the shift of the auxiliary lubrication pump from an "idle" to a "running" state. Note, in this case, *the assimilation of the two states to "locations,"* with the original state

Table 4 Binding and predicative occurrences

virt2.c32) PRODUCE	SUBJ	INDIVIDUAL_PERSON_102: (GP1Z_MAIN_CONTROL_ROOM)	
	OBJ	button_pushing	
	TOPIC	SEQ1_BUTTON	
	date-1:	16/10/2008/08:26	
	date-2:		

Produce:PerformTask/Activity (6.3)

*virt2.c33) MOVE	SUBJ	AUXILIARY_LUBRICATION_PUMP_M202: (idle_)	
	OBJ	AUXILIARY_LUBRICATION_PUMP_M202: (running_)	
	date-1:	16/10/2008/08:26	
	date-2:		

Move:AutonomousChangeofState (4.32)

virt2.c30)   (GOAL virt2.c32 virt2.c33)

---

occupying the first place of the location list associated with the SUBJ's filler and the final state occupying the second position of this list (see also the location list associated with the OBJ's filler in the occurrence aal9.c12 of Table 2 above).

To encode now the "connectivity phenomena" information, we must introduce a *binding occurrence* virt2.c30 to link together the conceptual labels virt2.c32 (denoting the planning activity) and virt2.c33 (denoting the intended result). This binding occurrence will be labelled using the GOAL operator introduced in Table 3 and involving, as already stated, *only two arguments*. The global meaning of virt2.c30 is then: "The activity described in virt2.c32 is focalized towards (GOAL) the realization of virt2.c33." In agreement with the semantics of the GOAL operator (see Table 3) virt2.c33, the *"result,"* is characterized by the presence of an *uncertainty attribute code*, "*", to indicate that, at the moment of "pushing," the real instantiation of a situation corresponding to "pump running" *cannot be categorically affirmed* (Zarri 2009, p. 71).

Note that, in Table 4, we have used a Move:AutonomousChangeOfState template instead of the template Move:ForcedChangeOfState that appears in Table 2. In NKRL, each elementary event is, in fact, *autonomously modelled*. Should virt2.c33 really take place, we will see the pump starting to move without any apparent human participation. In contrast, in Table 2, John must explicitly step in to carry out the locking of the door.

NKRL Modelling of Full Narratives

The second order (HOL) structures of NKRL, completive construction and binding occurrences, allow us to take correctly into account the connectivity phenomena; accordingly, they play also a crucial role in the modelling of *full narratives* (or scenarios, complex events, knotty circumstances, etc.). As an example, we supply in Table 5 the NKRL representation of a full narrative proper to the context of the "accident messages" application already mentioned: "On November 1st, 2008, at 10h15, the start-up procedure of the GP1Z turbine was stopped by the production activities leader, given that he had been informed by a field operator of the presence of an oil leakage concerning an auxiliary lubrication pump."

The (*mandatory*) starting point for the creation of the NKRL formal representation of any sort of complete narrative consists in the set-up of *a binding occurrence listing the main topics dealt within this narrative*. This "upper level" occurrence corresponds frequently, as in the present case (see virt3.c1), to a binding occurrence of the COORD(ination) type (COORD is one of the "binding operators" listed in Table 3 above). We have then assumed here that the narrative was formed of *three independent but strictly connected items*, relating the first (virt3.c2) the narrative's core, i.e., the specific causes of the turbine's stop, and giving the second (virt3.c3) and the third (virt3.c4) auxiliary information about the jobs of the two involved people. But the upper level binding occurrence could also consist, e.g., of an ENUM(eration) relationship, of a CAUSE binding occurrence, etc.: *all the operators listed in Table 3 can then be used in this role*. Having set-up the top level of the conceptual representation, the different blocks listed in this binding occurrence are *successively expanded* and the corresponding elementary events *separately encoded*.

Let us consider, e.g., the binding occurrence virt3.c6 that illustrates the two (*strictly associated*, COORD) precise reasons of the stop. The first is described in the completive construction formed by the *indirect* inclusion of virt3.c8, the "*message*" signaling the leakage, as *OBJ(ect)* of the *transmission of information* between the two individuals INDIVIDUAL_PERSON_104 and INDIVIDUAL_PERSON_106 represented by the predicative occurrence virt3.c7. Note that, thanks to the completive construction mechanism, the two occurrences virt3.c7/virt3.c8 perform actually as a *unique conceptual unit*. Note also that the insertion of the symbolic label #virt3.c8 within the arguments of the binding occurrence virt3.c6 concerns only, once again, *some coherence controls proper to the NKRL software*, and does not alter at all the *actual cardinality (two)* of the COORD's arguments in virt3.c6. The second reason of the stop is described in virt3.c9: when the leakage is detected we can note, temporal modulator obs(serve), that *the auxiliary pump is linked to the turbine* (coupled_with is an HClass concept, specialization of binary_relational_property). "obs"—see Note 2 and Zarri (2009, pp. 71–75)—is a "*temporal modulator,*" used to indicate that the situation described in the associated predicative occurrence is *certainly true* at the specific date stored in the date-1 temporal attribute of the occurrence (see also the two "status" occurrences virt3.c3 and virt3.c4). We do not care then, for lack of interest, lack of information or for the sake of conformity with the original wording of the narrative, about the *real duration* of this situation, which surely extends in time before and after the given date.

Table 5 NKRL modelling of a full narrative

---

virt3.c1)   (COORD virt3.c2 virt3.c3 virt3.c4)

The conceptual model of the narrative is formed of three components.

virt3.c2)   (CAUSE virt3.c5 virt3.c6)

The first component consists of a CAUSE binding relationship.

virt3.c5)   PRODUCE   SUBJ   INDIVIDUAL_PERSON_102: (GP1Z_MAIN_CONTROL_ROOM)
                          OBJ   activity_stop
                          TOPIC   (SPECIF turbine_startup GP1Z_TURBINE)
                          date-1:   1/11/2008/10:15, (1/11/2008/10:30)
                          date-2:

Produce:PerformTask/Activity (6.3)

On November 1ˢᵗ, 2008, INDIVIDUAL_PERSON_102 *ends the start-up of the* GP1Z_TURBINE.

virt3.c6)   (COORD virt3.c7 #virt3.c8 virt3.c9)

The second term of the CAUSE *relationship consists of a* COORD *binding occurrence.*

virt3.c7)   MOVE   SUBJ   INDIVIDUAL_PERSON_104: (GP1Z_COMPLEX)
                          OBJ   #virt3.c8
                          BENF   INDIVIDUAL_PERSON_102: (GP1Z_MAIN_CONTROL_ROOM)
                          MODAL   vhf_audio_transmitter
                          date-1:   1/11/2008/10:15
                          date-2:

Move:StructuredInformation (4.42)

INDIVIDUAL_PERSON_104 *sends to* INDIVIDUAL_PERSON_102 *the* virt3.c8 *message.*

virt3.c8)   PRODUCE   SUBJ   INDIVIDUAL_PERSON_104: (GP1Z_COMPLEX)
                          OBJ   detection_
                          TOPIC   (SPECIF lubrication_oil_leakage (SPECIF around_
                                                AUXILIARY_LUBRICATION_PUMP_M202))
                          date-1:   1/11/2008/10:02
                          date-2:   1/11/2008/10:15

Produce:PerformTask/Activity (6.3)

INDIVIDUAL_PERSON_104 *has discovered the presence of an oil leakage around the lubrication pump M202.*

virt3.c9)   OWN   SUBJ   AUXILIARY_LUBRICATION_PUMP_M202
                          OBJ   property_
                          TOPIC   (SPECIF coupled_with GP1Z_TURBINE)
                          { obs }
                          date-1:   1/11/2008/10:02
                          date-2:

Own:CompoundProperty (5.42)

On November 1ˢᵗ, 2008, at 10h02, we can observe that the lubrication pump is related to the GP1Z_TURBINE.

virt3.c3)   BEHAVE   SUBJ   INDIVIDUAL_PERSON_102: (GP1Z_MAIN_CONTROL_ROOM)
                          MODAL   production_activities_leader
                          { obs }
                          date-1:   1/11/2008/10:15
                          date-2:

Behave:Role (1.11)

We can remark that INDIVIDUAL_PERSON_102 *fulfils the function of production activities leader.*

virt3.c4)   BEHAVE   SUBJ   INDIVIDUAL_PERSON_104: (GP1Z_COMPLEX)
                          MODAL   field_operator
                          { obs }
                          date-1:   1/11/2008/10:15
                          date-2:

Behave:Role (1.11)

We can remark that INDIVIDUAL_PERSON_104 *fulfils the function of field operator at the GPIZ complex.*

Fig. 2 Tree structure
corresponding to the narrative
of Table 5

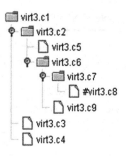

Eventually, we can note that the logical arrangement of a narrative (like that of Table 5) can always be represented as some sort of complex *tree structure*, see Fig. 2. This remark is not new, and can be considered as valid in general independently from the formalization adopted, see, e.g., the "story trees" of Mani and Pustejovsky (2004).

Querying/Inference Procedures

Reasoning in NKRL ranges from the *direct questioning* of a knowledge base of NKRL formal structures to the execution of *high-level inference procedures*. These issues have been dealt with in some detail in Zarri (2005, 2009, pp. 183–243, 2013). We will then limit us, here, to supply some essential information about these topics.

Search Patterns

Direct questioning of NKRL knowledge bases is implemented by means of search patterns p_j (formal queries) that unify information in the base thanks to the use of a Filtering Unification Module (*Fum*).

Formally, search patterns correspond to *specialized/partially instantiated* templates where the "*explicit variables*" that characterize the templates (*var$_i$*, see Table 1 above) have been replaced by concepts/individuals compatible with the constraints imposed on these variables in the original HTemp structures. In a search pattern, the concepts are used then as "*implicit variables*." When trying to unify a search pattern p_j, manually built up from the user or automatically created by an *InferenceEngine* (see below) with the predicative occurrences pc_i of the knowledge base, a p_j concept can match (1) the individuals included in pc_i that represent *its own instances*, and (2) all its pc_i *subsumed concepts* (according to the HClass' structure) *along with their own instances*. This, inheritance-based, way of operating corresponds then to a sort of semantic/conceptual expansion of the original pattern.

"Transformation" Inference Rules

A first class of NKRL high-level inference procedures is implemented through the use of the so-called *transformation* rules. These rules try to "adapt," from a semantic point of view, a search pattern p_j that "failed" (that was unable to find a unification within the knowledge base) to the real contents of this base making use of a sort of *analogical reasoning*. Transformations attempt then to automatically *"transform"* p_j into one or more different $p_1, p_2 \ldots p_n$ that are not strictly *"equivalent"* but only *"semantically close"* (analogical reasoning) to the original one.

A transformation rule is composed of a left-hand side, the *"antecedent,"* and of one or more right-hand sides, the *"consequent(s)."* The antecedent corresponds to the formulation, in search pattern format, of the "query" to be transformed, while the consequent(s) denote(s) the representation(s) of one or more search patterns to be substituted for the given one. Indicating with A the antecedent and with Cs_i all the possible consequents, these rules can be expressed as:

$$A\,(var_i) \Rightarrow Cs_i\,(var_j)\,, \quad var_i \subseteq var_j \tag{3}$$

The restriction $var_i \subseteq var_j$ corresponds to the usual *"safety condition"* constraint that assures the logical congruence of the rules, stating that a transformation rule is *well-formed* when all the variables declared in the antecedent A appear also in the consequent Cs_i accompanied, in case, by additional variables.

Let us now see a concrete example: we want to ask whether, within the particular knowledge base where are stored all the NKRL-encoded events concerning the activation of a gas turbine, we can retrieve the information that a given oil extractor is running. In the absence of a direct answer we can reply by supplying, thanks to a rule like *t11* of Table 6, other related information stating, e.g., that the site leader has heard the working noise of the oil extractor. Expressed in natural language, this last result could be paraphrased as: "The system cannot assert that the oil extractor is running, but it can certify that the site leader has heard the working noise of this extractor."

From Table 6 we can note that the *atoms* of the NKRL rules are expressed using the *usual* NKRL knowledge representation tools, i.e., *as n-ary complex data structures centered on the notion of "functional role"* (Zarri 2011a). This implies the possibility to implement and manage *highly expressive* inference rules whose *atoms* can *directly represent* complex situations, actions, etc. In the context of the NKRL's rule system we are no more restricted, then, to the set-up of rules under the form of ordinary (and *scarcely expressive) binary clauses*. An exhaustive paper on this topic is Zarri (2013).

Table 6 An example of transformation rule

---

t11: "working noise/condition" transformation

antecedent:

```
OWN     SUBJ    var1
        OBJ     property_
        TOPIC   running_
```

var1 = consumer_electronics, hardware_, surgical_tool, diagnostic_tool/system, small_portable_equipment, technical/industrial_tool

first consequent schema (*conseq1*):

```
EXPERIENCE   SUBJ    var2
             OBJ     evidence_
             TOPIC   (SPECIF var3 var1)
```

var2 = individual_person
var3 = working_noise, working_condition

second consequent schema (*conseq2*):

```
BEHAVE   SUBJ    var2
         MODAL   industrial_site_operator
```

Being unable to demonstrate directly that an industrial apparatus is running, the fact that an operator hears its working noise or notes its working aspect can be considered as a proof of its running status.

"Hypothesis" Inference Rules

The "*hypothesis*" rules represent a second important class of NKRL inference rules. They allow us to build up automatically a sort of "*causal explanation*" for an elementary event (a predicative occurrence) retrieved by direct query within an NKRL knowledge base. These rules can be expressed as *biconditionals* of the type:

$$X \text{ iff } Y_1 \text{ and } Y_2 \ \ldots \text{ and } Y_n, \tag{4}$$

where the *head X* of the rule corresponds to a predicative occurrence pc_i to be "explained" and the *reasoning steps* Y_i must all be satisfied; Y_i are called "*condition schemata*" in a hypothesis context. This means that, for each of them, at least a search patterns p_j must be (*automatically* in this case) built up by *InferenceEngine* in order to find, using *Fum* (see section "Search Patterns"), a *successful* unification with some information of the base. In this case, the set of pc_1, pc_2 ... pc_n predicative occurrences retrieved by the condition schemata Y_i, thanks to their conversion into p_j, can be interpreted as a context/causal explanation of the original occurrence pc_i (X). A generalization of the safety condition introduced above is used in a hypothesis rules context.

To mention now a well-known NKRL example, let us suppose we have directly retrieved, in a querying-answering mode, the information: "Pharmacopeia, a USA biotechnology company, has received 64,000,000 dollars from the German company Schering in the context of its R&D activities"; this information corresponds then to pc_i (X). We can then be able to automatically construct, using a "hypothesis" rule, a sort of "causal explanation" for this event by retrieving in the knowledge base information like: (1) "Pharmacopeia and Schering have signed an agreement concerning the production by Pharmacopeia of a new compound," pc_1 (Y_1) and (2) "in the framework of this agreement, Pharmacopeia has actually produced the new compound," pc_2 (Y_2). Of course, as usual in a "hypothesis" context, the explication proposed by this rule *corresponds to only one of all the possible reasons that can be interpreted as the "cause" of the original event.* A particular hypothesis rule must always be conceived as a member of a "family" of possible explication statements.

Note, moreover, that an interesting feature of the NKRL rule system concerns the possibility of making use of "transformations" when working in a "hypothesis" context—i.e., of utilizing these two modalities of inference in an "*integrated*" way. This means in practice that, whenever a search pattern p_j is derived from a condition schema Y_i of a hypothesis to implement a step of the reasoning process, we can use this pattern as it has been *automatically built up by InferenceEngine from its "father" condition schema*, but also in a "*transformed*" form if the appropriate transformation rules exist. In this way, a hypothesis that was deemed to fail because of the impossibility of deriving a "successful" p_j from one of its condition schemata Y_i can now continue if a new p_j, *obtained using a transformation rule*, will find a successful unification within the base, getting then new values for the hypothesis variables. Moreover, this strategy can also be used to discover all the possible *implicit* relationships among the stored data, see Zarri (2005) for further details.

Related Work

In this section, we will mention some approaches to the solution of the "*connectivity phenomena*" problems that have been suggested in an Artificial Intelligence (AI) and Computational Linguistics (CL) context and that have some relationships with the NKRL's procedures described in section "Linking Elementary Events".

Proposals Derived from an "Artificial Intelligence" Context

An *n*-ary knowledge representation model used to encode *narrative-like structures* that was very popular in the seventies is the "Conceptual Dependency" theory of Roger Schank (Schank 1973, Schank and Abelson 1977). In this, the underlying meaning ("*conceptualization*") of a given narrative was expressed as the association of semantic predicates chosen from a set of twelve formal "*primitive actions*" (like INGEST, MOVE, ATRANS, abstract relationship transfer, PTRANS, physical transfer, etc.) with seven *role relationships* ("deep cases") in the Case Grammar style (Fillmore 1968). The seven roles were Object (in a state), Object (of a change of state), Object (of an action), Actor, Recipient/Donor, From/To, and Instrument. Unfortunately, Schank's theory was, on the one hand, *insufficiently specified* and, on the other, *unnecessarily complicated* because of the influence of "psychological" (introspective) considerations according to a characteristic trend of AI in those years. Nevertheless, Schank's work had a particularly strong influence on the development of formalized (and at least partly computerized) systems for the representation and management of *storylines and connectivity phenomena* making use of all sorts of scripts, scenarios, TAUs (Thematic Abstraction Units), MOPs (Memory Organization Packets), etc., see, e.g., (Dyer 1983; Kolodner 1984).

The SnePS (Semantic Network Processing System) proposal of Stuart Shapiro (1979) belongs roughly to the same period and allows us, e.g., to annotate *"narrative"* situations like "Sue thinks that Bob believes that a dog is eating a bone" *by associating labeled graphs* in a way not too different from the NKRL's "completive construction" approach, see section "Completive Construction". Interestingly, solutions of this type have been re-discovered recently in the framework of the "Interoperable Knowledge Representation for Intelligence Support" (IKRIS) project, financed between in 2005–2006 by the US DTO (Disruptive Technology Office). IKRIS' main result is represented by the specifications of IKL, the "IKRIS Knowledge Language" (Hayes 2006; Hayes and Menzel 2006). IKL is an extension of Common Logic (ISO 2007) that, although still dealing with, fundamentally, first-order logic structures, includes *some HOL improvements in the NKRL style*. For example, IKL's formal structures called *"proposition name"* and introduced by the reserved symbol "that" allows us to "reify" the content of a sentence that can then be freely referred to from inside different contexts—the similarity with the *completive construction approach* is then evident. Going back in time to the fifties-sixties we can also note that, among the *"correlators"* introduced by Silvio Ceccato in a Mechanical Translation (MT) context *to represent "narratives" as recursive networks of triadic structures* (Ceccato 1961, 1964), some concerned the representation of *"connectivity phenomena"* like coordination and subordination, apposition, subject–predicate relationships, etc.

Among the recent suggestions for representing phenomena of this kind, we must discuss in particular some mechanisms used in a *Conceptual Graph's environment* for dealing with *"contexts."* John Sowa's Conceptual Graphs (CGs), see (Sowa 1984, 1999), are based on a powerful graph-based representation scheme. A conceptual graph is a finite, connected, bipartite graph that makes use of two kinds of nodes, *"concepts"* and *"conceptual relations"* (these last corresponding to NKRL's functional roles). For example, a CG corresponding to the narrative "John is going to Boston by bus" is represented by a conceptual structure where a *"concept node,"* "Go" (having a function similar to that of an NKRL conceptual predicate, but denoted by an NL term) is associated with three *"relation nodes"* (roles) like Ag(e)nt, Dest(ination), and Instr(ument). These relations introduce the three *arguments of the predicate*, i.e., three new concept nodes representing, respectively, the *constant* John (the "agent") as an instance of the *concept* Person, the *constant* Boston (the "destination") as an instance of the *concept* City, and the *concept* Bus (the "instrument"). The resemblance to HTemp and to the NKRL representation of elementary events is evident. Moreover, for any CGs system, it is assumed that there exists a *pre-defined type hierarchy of "concept-types,"* different according to the domain to formalize and similar then to HClass.

Contexts in CGs are dealt with making use of the second order (nested graphs) extensions that bear some resemblance to NKRL's constructs like completive construction and binding occurrences, as we can see from Sowa's analysis (1999, pp. 485–486) of the complex narrative "Tom believes that Mary wants to marry a sailor." This last is decomposed, as in NKRL, in two parts. In a first one, "Tom believes that . . . " Tom is modeled as an "experiencer" (Expr role) that Believe(s) a "proposition" (an OBJ(ect) filler according to the NKRL's formalism). The second part corresponds to the representation of the proposition/filler " . . . Mary wants to marry . . . ", where the two elementary events signaled by the presence of the two predicates "want" and "marry" are linked together by the fact that the "situation" corresponding to the marriage is the Th(e)me of Mary's wishes. Other similarities between CGs and NKRL concern some specific algorithmic aspects of the querying/inference procedures, see, e.g., (Ellis 1995, Corbett 2003).

We can also find, however, some important differences between the NKRL and the CGs approaches. They are related, e.g., to the organization of the "standard" hierarchy of concepts (quite simple in a CGs context with respect to the sophistication of the HClass hierarchy in NKRL), the choice of the deep cases (functional roles in NKRL terms) or the *general theoretical background* proper to the inference procedures. But the central point of any discussion about the relationships between CGs and NKRL concerns John Sowa's choice of leaving *completely free*, for the sake of generality, the selection of those *"predicates"* that, in CGs as in NKRL, represents the focal element of the formal representation of an elementary event. In the CGs representation of the "John is going to Boston . . . " event, see above, the predicate can then be *simply represented by the surface element "Go"*—it would be a primitive like MOVE in NKRL. Note that Sowa emphasizes (1984, p. 14) that a CGs' predicate can be either a primitive or an NL term, but it is normally the second (simpler) solution that is chosen. As a consequence, *it is practically impossible to create an exhaustive and authoritative list of CGs "canonical graphs,"* roughly equivalent to NKRL's "templates," *for evident reasons of combinatorial explosion* (e.g., 3100 English verbs are included in the well-known Levin's classification (1993), which is notoriously incomplete). A tool like HTemp—extremely important for the set-up of concrete NKRL applications and, in practice, part and parcel of the definition of the NKRL language—is not really conceivable, then, in a CGs context.

Other general knowledge representation systems that share with CGs some ambitions of "universality" are CYC (Lenat and Guha 1990; Lenat et al. 1990) and Topic Maps (Pepper 2000).

CYC concerns one of the most controversial endeavors in the history of Artificial Intelligence. Started in the early 1980, the project ended about 15 years later with the set-up of an enormous knowledge base containing *about a million of hand-*

entered "logical assertions" including both simple statements of facts and rules about what conclusions could be inferred if certain statements of facts were satisfied. The "upper level" of the CYC ontology is now freely accessible on the Web, see http://www.cyc.com/cyc/opencyc. A criticism often addressed to CycL—the *n*-ary knowledge representation language of CYC—concerns its uniform use of the same representation model (substantially, a frame system rewritten in logical form) to represent phenomena *conceptually very different* (the "*one and only syndrome*"). In NKRL, on the contrary, concepts are represented in the (usual) binary way, elementary events/situations (and general classes of events/situations) like *n*-ary predicate/roles-based structures, connectivity phenomena as labelled lists with reified arguments, special conceptual structures have been conceived to take the temporal phenomena into account, etc.

With respect now to Topic Maps (TMs), a TMs "*topic*" is used to represent *any possible specific notion that could be interesting to speak about*, like the play Hamlet, the playwright William Shakespeare, or the "authorship" relationship. A topic *reifies* then a subject, making it "real" for a computer system. Topics can have "*names*," and each individual topic is an instance of one or more classes of topics ("*topic types*"). They can also have "*occurrences*," that is, information resources, specified as a text string that is part of the Topic Map itself, or as a link to an external resource, which are considered as relevant to the subjects the topic reify. Topics can participate in relationships with other topics, called "*associations*": an association consists in a number of "*association roles*" each of which has a topic attached as a "*role player*." In spite of the introduction of *associations*, Topic Maps do not seem to present really new insights into the connectivity phenomena issues. More in general, it must be noticed that TMs have been often considered as a downgraded version of other (more structured and powerful) conceptual proposals, like Semantic Networks (Lehmann 1992), Conceptual Graphs, or NKRL.

Eventually, we can note that the now popular "Semantic Web" (SW) tools and languages (see http://semanticweb.org/wiki/Tools for an overview) *cannot represent* a viable alternative for an effective management of the "connectivity phenomena" and the related, *high-level knowledge representation problems*. This is linked to the difficulties that concern the set-up of *complete and effective formal description of complex information structures* like spatio-temporal data, contexts, reified situations, human intentions and behaviors, etc. making use only of the *quite limited "binary" knowledge representation tools* proper to the SW languages. As already stated, properties in the binary model are simply expressed, in fact, as a *binary (i.e., accepting only two arguments) relationship linking two individuals or an individual and a value*. The resulting, well-known lack of expressiveness of the SW languages is described, to give only few examples, in papers like Mizoguchi et al. (2007), Salguero et al. (2009), and Liu et al. (2010). Dealing with the above high-level representation problems requires, on the contrary, to make use of *high-level knowledge representation tools* in the NKRL, CGs, CycL, etc. style, able then too take care of *higher arity relations*. Note also, in this context, some perplexities in the knowledge representation milieus about recent proposals of SW origin suggesting to deal with all sort of very complex problems—from the representation of temporal data (Scherp et al. 2009) to the modelling of the user context—by exploiting *fragments of existing SW ontologies* under the form of *"Ontology Design Patterns"* (ODPs) that, at least in principle, we could freely compose, specialize, and reutilize. Unfortunately, existing ODPs—see, e.g., those collected within the ODP portal (http://ontologydesignpatterns.org/wiki/Ontology_Design_Patterns_._ org_%28ODP%29)—are characterized by a *high level of heterogeneity and the lack of shared theoretical principles for their construction and use*. They are not without evoking, then, those *"idiosyncratic patterns"* whose development, according to Kozaki et al. (2007), can lead " . . . to a decrease of the semantic interoperability of ontologies because . . . such patterns will lack compatibility with others."

Proposals Derived from a "Linguistics/Computational Linguistics" Context

Looking now at a broad Computational Linguistics/Natural Language Processing (NLP) context, we can note immediately that *interesting similarities* can be found between the use of NKRL for the *modelling of the inner meaning of narrative documents* and the use of tools as VerbNet, PropBank, and FrameNet for the *surface semantic/thematic role labeling of NL texts* in a "post-case grammars" framework (Palmer et al. 2010).

However, the main objectives of any possible kind of NLP procedures concern, firstly, the implementation of *linguistically motivated*, surface analyses of NL documents aiming at discovering *syntactic/semantic relationships between NL items expressed in a specific language*. Therefore, these objectives coincide only in part with those concerning the execution of *deep "conceptual" procedures* in an NKRL' style. Look, e.g., at the NKRL's *"functional roles"*: even if they are labelled with terms borrowed from research on case grammar (Fillmore 1968) and thematic roles, they are in fact *"deep cases,"* used to link together *"conceptual entities"* (concepts, concept instances, semantic predicates, spatio-temporal abstractions, etc.) instead of *"words."* Pure *surface phenomena* like the idiosyncrasies in the lexical choices, the active/passive alternation, the morphology, etc. *are then totally ignored.* This means that the *formal expressions* dealt with in an NKRL context *are independent from any particular natural language formulation*—even if they are drafted in a sort of "basic English" for human understanding in their "external" formulation, a choice shared with other conceptual approaches like CGs, Schank's Conceptual Dependency, etc.—and that NKRL follows then a sort of *"interlingua"* (i.e., language independent) approach. All the above can be summed up by saying that NKRL, as all the formal systems mentioned in the previous sub-section, addresses the problem of encoding the *"meaning"* of generic (not only NL) multimedia documents through the development of an *a priori* formal notation for expressing conceptual contents that is *independent* from the search for an optimal *form of correspondence*—see Jackendoff's (1990) "θ-Criterion"—with the *"surface"* (syntactic) form these contents can assume. Obviously, in an NKRL, etc. approach, the *correspondence problem still exists*, but can be tackled *a posteriori* in a very pragmatic way, see, e.g., Note 3 above.

We briefly mention below, nevertheless, some linguistic/NLP systems/theories that can be considered as *particularly significant* from a *"semantic/conceptual"* point of view.

Episodic Logic (EL) (Schubert and Hwang 2000) is an *NL-like*, highly formalized logical representation for narrative understanding allowing, among other things, the expression of sentence and predicate reification, of intensional predicates (corresponding to wanting, believing, making, etc.) of episodes, events, states of affairs, etc. "Episodes" can be *explicitly related* in terms of part-whole, temporal, and causal relations. Interesting solutions for the connectivity phenomena management can also be found in the *Discourse Representation Theory*, DRT (Kamp and Reyle 1993), a semantic theory developed for representing and computing *trans-sentential anaphora and other forms of text cohesion*. See, for example, the specific DRT procedures—that make use, among other things, of "embedding functions" similar, at the surface level, to the context solutions proposed by Sowa, etc., see above—that have been suggested for managing all sort of context-related problems. The *Text Meaning Representation* model (TRM) is part of the OntoSem environment (Nirenburg and Raskin 2004). It consists of an (at least partially) implemented theory of *natural language processing* that aims at automatically deriving *structured meaning* (in TMR terms) *from unstructured texts*. The central piece of TMR is a language-independent *single* ontology structured as a DAG (Direct Acyclic Graph) where the arcs represent IsA relationships. The ontology includes about 8500 concepts represented according to a plain frame-like format. Detailed analyses of the advantages and weaknesses of TRM are presented in Sowa (2005) and Zarri (2009, pp. 146–149).

Conclusion

This chapter focuses on the problem of finding a *complete and coherent way* of representing the *"global meaning"* of complex (multimedia) *"narratives"* by properly associating its constituent basic entities represented as a set of formalized *"elementary events."* Solving this problem means, in practice, being able to formalize those *"connectivity phenomena"*—denoted, at *linguistic surface level*, by logico-semantic cohesion links like causality, goal, co-ordination, subordination, indirect speech, etc.—that assure the conceptual unity of the narratives, scenarios, situations, etc. Note that the problem of finding *reasonable solutions* for dealing with this sort of phenomena is, at the same time, far from being trivial from a Computer Science point of view (see also the "State of the Art" in the previous section) and of a strong interest from a general *Cognitive Science/Digital Humanities* perspective. It is part, in fact, of a wider problem that concerns finding *reasonable solutions* for dealing with *"contexts"*; representing contexts in full is still a largely unsettled problem. See

McCarthy (1993) for the most cited formal theory about representing contexts as abstract mathematical, first class objects,[4] a theory that goes back to more than 20 years ago.

Specifically, the solutions adopted by NKRL, *"completive construction"* and *"binding occurrences,"* allow us to model the connectivity phenomena by *"reifying"* the formal representations associated with the constitutive elementary events; these solutions have been explained making use of several illustrating examples. In particular, the NKRL representation of a complex, structured narrative that involves the occurrence of several elementary events has been presented in full and commented in some detail.

We can conclude the chapter by noticing that, apart from being a knowledge representation language, NKRL is also a *fully operational computer science environment*, implemented in Java and built up, thanks, at least partly, to the support of several European projects; a detailed description of the NKRL software can be found in Zarri (2009: Appendix A). The environment exists in two versions, a (standard) SQL-based version and a (lighter) file-oriented one, to be used mainly as a "demonstration" version. The environment includes also powerful "inference engines" able to carry out complex inference procedures based, e.g., on "analogical" and "causal" reasoning principles, see again Zarri (2005, 2013) in this context.

References

N. Ayari, A. Chibani, Y. Amirat, in *Proceedings of the 2013 IEEE International Conference on Robotics and Automation (ICRA)*. Semantic Management of Human-Robot Interaction in Ambient Intelligence Environments Using N-Ary Ontologies (IEEEXplore, Piscataway, 2013), pp. 1164–1171

M. Bal, *Narratology: Introduction to the Theory of Narrative*, 2nd edn. (University Press, Toronto, 1997)

S. Bechhofer, F. van Harmelen, J. Hendler, I. Horrocks, D.L. McGuinness, P.F. Patel-Schneider, L.A. Stein (eds.), *OWL Web Ontology Language Reference* (W3C Recommendation 10 February 2004). W3C (2004), http://www.w3.org/TR/owl-ref/. Accessed 28 Feb 2016

S. Ceccato (ed.), *Linguistic Analysis and Programming for Mechanical Translation* (Technical Report RADC-TR-60-18) (Feltrinelli, Milano, 1961)

S. Ceccato, Automatic translation of languages. Inf. Storage Retr. **2**, 105–158 (1964)

D. Corbett, *Reasoning and Unification Over Conceptual Graphs* (Kluwer Academic/Plenum Publishers, New York, 2003)

M.G. Dyer, *In-Depth Understanding* (The MIT Press, Cambridge, 1983)

G. Ellis, Compiling conceptual graph. IEEE Trans. Knowl. Data Eng. **7**, 68–81 (1995)

---

[4]In McCarthy's theory, the main formulas are sentences of the form $ist(c, p)$, which are to be taken as assertions that the proposition p *is true in (ist) the context* c, itself asserted in an outer context c'. A well-known concrete implementation of McCarthy's theory is represented by the "microtheories," introduced by Ramanathan V. Guha and largely used in a CYC framework (Guha and Lenat 1994); a recent re-interpretation of McCarthy's ideas in Description Logics terms is (Klarman and Gutiérrez-Basulto 2011).

C.J. Fillmore, in *Universals in Linguistic Theory*, ed. by E. Bach, R.T. Harms. The Case for Case (Holt, Rinehart and Winston, New York, 1968), pp. 1–88

R.V. Guha, D.B. Lenat, Enabling agents to work together. Commun. ACM **37**(7), 127–142 (1994)

M.A.K. Halliday, R. Hasan, *Cohesion in English* (Longman, London, 1976)

P. Hayes, *IKL Guide* (Florida Institute for Human & Machine Cognition (IHMC), Pensacola, 2006), http://www.ihmc.us/users/phayes/IKL/GUIDE/GUIDE.html. Accessed 28 Feb 2016

P. Hayes, C. Menzel, *IKL Specification Document* (Florida Institute for Human & Machine Cognition (IHMC), Pensacola, 2006), http://www.ihmc.us/users/phayes/IKL/SPEC/SPEC.html. Accessed 28 Feb 2016

Z. Hu, E. Rahimtoroghi, L. Munishkina, R. Swanson, M.A. Walker, in *Proceedings of the Conference on Empirical Methods in Natural Language Processing (EMNLP '13)*, ed. by T. Baldwin, A. Korhonen. Unsupervised Induction of Contingent Event Pairs from Film Scenes (ACL, Stroudsburg, 2013), pp. 369–379

International Organization for Standardization, ISO, *Information Technology-Common Logic (CL): A Framework for a Family of Logic-based Languages* (ISO/IEC 24707:2007) (ISO, Geneva, 2007)

R. Jackendoff, *Semantic Structures* (The MIT Press, Cambridge, 1990)

M. Jahn, *Narratology: A Guide to the Theory of Narrative* (version 1.8) (English Department of the University, Cologne, 2005), http://www.uni-koeln.de/~ame02/pppn.htm. Accessed 28 Feb 2016

H. Kamp, U. Reyle, *From Discourse to Logic. Introduction to Modeltheoretic Semantics of Natural Language, Formal Logic and Discourse Representation* (Kluwer, Dordrecht, 1993)

S. Klarman, V. Gutiérrez-Basulto, in *Proceedings of the Twenty-Fifth AAAI Conference on Artificial Intelligence*, ed. by W. Burgard, D. Roth. Two-Dimensional Description Logics for Context-Based Semantic Interoperability (AAAI Press, Menlo Park, 2011), pp. 215–220

D. Klein, C.D. Manning, in *Proceedings of the 41st Annual Meeting of the Association for Computational Linguistics*, ed. by E. W. Hinrichs, D. Roth. Accurate Unlexicalized Parsing (ACL, Stroudsburg, 2003), pp. 423–430

J.L. Kolodner, *Retrieval and Organizational Strategies in Conceptual Memory: A Computer Model* (Lawrence Erlbaum Associates, Hillsdale, 1984)

K. Kozaki, E. Sunagawa, Y. Kitamura, R. Mizoguchi, in *Proceedings of the 2nd Workshop on Roles and Relationships in Object Oriented Programming, Multiagent Systems and Ontologies, co-located with ECOOP 2007 (Technical Report 2007-9)*, ed. by G. Boella, S. Goebel, F. Steimann, S. Zschaler, M. Cebulla. Role Representation Model Using OWL and SWRL (Technische Universität Berlin, Berlin, 2007), pp. 39–46

F. Lehmann (ed.), *Semantic Networks in Artificial Intelligence* (Pergamon Press, Oxford, 1992)

D.B. Lenat, R.V. Guha, *Building Large Knowledge Based Systems* (Addison-Wesley, Reading, 1990)

D.B. Lenat, R.V. Guha, K. Pittman, D. Pratt, M. Shepherd, CYC: toward programs with common sense. Commun. ACM **33**(8), 30–49 (1990)

B. Levin, *English Verb Classes and Alternation, A Preliminary Investigation* (University Press, Chicago, 1993)

W. Liu, Z. Liu, J. Fu, R. Hu, Z. Zhong, in *Proceedings of the 2010 International Conference on Complex, Intelligent and Software Intensive Systems*, ed. by L. Barolli, F. Xhafa, S. Vitabile, H.-H. Hsu. Extending OWL for Modeling Event-Oriented Ontology (IEEE Computer Society Press, Los Alamitos, 2010), pp. 581–586

I. Mani, J. Pustejovsky, in *Proceedings of the ACL Workshop on Discourse Annotation*, ed. by B. Webber, D. Byron. Temporal Discourse Models for Narrative Structure (Stroudsburg, ACL, 2004), pp. 57–64

S. Matsuyoshi, M. Eguchi, C. Sao, K. Murakami, K. Inui, Y. Matsumoto, in *Proceedings of the International Conference on Language Resources and Evaluation, LREC 2010*, ed. by N. Calzolari, K. Choukri, B. Maegaard, J. Mariani, J. Odijk, S. Piperidis, M. Rosner, D. Tapias. Annotating Event Mentions in Text with Modality, Focus, and Source Information (European Language Resources Association (ELRA), Paris, 2010), pp. 1456–1463

J. McCarthy, in *Proceedings of the Thirteenth International Joint Conference on Artificial Intelligence – IJCAI/93*, ed. by R. Bajcsy. Notes on Formalizing Context (Morgan Kaufmann, San Francisco, 1993), pp. 555–562

R. Mizoguchi, E. Sunagawa, K. Kozaki, Y. Kitamura, A model of roles within an ontology development tool: Hozo. J. Appl. Ontol. **2**, 159–179 (2007)

Morris, J. and G. Hirst, G. (1991). Lexical cohesion computed by Thesaural relations as an indicator of the structure of text. Comput. Linguist. 17: 21-48.

S. Nirenburg, V. Raskin, *Ontological Semantics* (The MIT Press, Cambridge, 2004)

N.F. Noy, R.W. Fergerson, M.A. Musen, in *Knowledge Acquisition, Modeling, and Management – Proceedings of EKAW 2000*, ed. by R. Dieng, O. Corby. The Knowledge Model of Protégé-2000: Combining Interoperability and Flexibility, vol 1937 (Springer LNCS, Berlin, 2000), pp. 17–32

M. Palmer, G. Gildea, N. Xue, *Semantic Role Labeling* (Morgan and Claypool Publishers, San Rafael, 2010)

S. Pepper, *The TAO of Topic Maps: Finding the Way in the Age of Infoglut* (Ontopia AS, Oslo, 2000), http://www.ontopia.net/topicmaps/materials/tao.html. Accessed 28 Feb 2016

A.G. Salguero, C. Delgado, F. Araque, in *Computer Aided Systems Theory, 12th International Conference, EUROCAST 2009*, ed. by R. Moreno Díaz, F. Pichler, A. Quesada Arencibia. Easing the Definition of N-Ary Relations for Supporting Spatio-Temporal Models in OWL, vol 5717 (Springer LNCS, Berlin, 2009), pp. 271–278

R.C. Schank, in *Computer Models of Thought and Language*, ed. by R. C. Schank, K. M. Colby. Identification of Conceptualizations Underlying Natural Language (W.H. Freeman and Co., San Francisco, 1973), pp. 187–247

R.C. Schank, R.P. Abelson, *Scripts, Plans, Goals and Understanding: An Inquiry into Human Knowledge Structures* (Lawrence Erlbaum, Oxford, 1977)

A. Scherp, T. Franz, C. Saathoff, S. Staab, in *Proceedings of the Fifth International Conference on Knowledge Capture, K-CAP '09*, ed. by Y. Gil, N. Noy. F – A Model of Events Based on the Foundational Ontology DOLCE+DnS Ultralite (ACM, New York, 2009), pp. 137–144

L.K. Schubert, C.H. Hwang, in *Natural Language Processing and Knowledge Representation: Language for Knowledge and Knowledge for Language*, ed. by L. Iwanska, S. C. Shapiro. Episodic Logic Meets Little Red Riding Hood: A Comprehensive, Natural Representation for Language Understanding (MIT/AAAI Press, Cambridge & Menlo Park, 2000), pp. 111–174

S.C. Shapiro, in *Associative Networks: Representation and Use of Knowledge by Computers*, ed. by N. V. Findler. The SNePS Semantic Network Processing System (Academic Press, New York, 1979), pp. 179–203

J.F. Sowa, *Conceptual Structures: Information Processing in Mind and Machine* (Addison-Wesley, Reading, 1984)

J.F. Sowa, *Knowledge Representation: Logical, Philosophical, and Computational Foundations* (Brooks Cole Publishing Co., Pacific Grove, 1999)

J.F. Sowa, Review of "Computational Semantics" by Sergei Niremburg and Victor Raskin. Comput. Linguist. **31**, 147–152 (2005)

W3C OWL Working Group (eds.), *OWL 2 Web Ontology Language Document Overview*, 2nd edn (W3C Recommendation 11 December 2012). W3C (2012), http://www.w3.org/TR/owl2-overview/. Accessed 28 Feb 2016

G.P. Zarri, in *Proceedings of the First International Conference on Applied Natural Language Processing*, ed. by I. M. Kameny, B. T. Oshika. Automatic Representation of the Semantic Relationships Corresponding to a French Surface Expression (ACL, Stroudsburg, 1983), pp. 143–147

G.P. Zarri, Integrating the two main inference modes of NKRL, transformations and hypotheses. J. Data Semant. (JoDS) **4**, 304–340 (2005)

G.P. Zarri, *Representation and Management of Narrative Information, Theoretical Principles and Implementation* (Springer, London, 2009)

G.P. Zarri, in *Computational Models of Narratives – Papers from the AAAI 2010 Fall Symposium (Technical Report FS-10-04)*, ed. by M. A. Finlayson, P. Gervás, E. Mueller, S. Narayanan, P. Winston. Representing and Managing Narratives in a Computer-Suitable Form (AAAI Press, Menlo Park, 2010), pp. 73–80

G.P. Zarri, in *Proceedings of the 24th International Florida AI Research Society Conference, FLAIRS-24*, ed. by R. C. Murray, P. M. McCarthy. Differentiating Between "Functional" and "Semantic" Roles in a High-Level Conceptual Data Modeling Language (AAAI Press, Menlo Park, 2011a), pp. 75–80

G.P. Zarri, Knowledge representation and inference techniques to improve the management of gas and oil facilities. Knowl.-Based Syst. (KNOSYS) **24**, 989–1003 (2011b)

G.P. Zarri, Advanced computational reasoning based on the NKRL conceptual model. Expert Syst. Appl. (ESWA) **40**, 2872–2888 (2013)

G.P. Zarri, in *Special Issue on Affective Neural Networks and Cognitive Learning Systems for Big Data Analysis*, ed. by A. Hussain, E. Cambria, B. Schuller, N. Howard. Sentiments Analysis at Conceptual Level Making Use of the Narrative Knowledge Representation Language, vol 58 (Neural Networks (NEUNET), 2014), pp. 82–97

G.P. Zarri, in *Proceedings of the Twenty-Eighth International Florida Artificial Intelligence Research Society Conference, FLAIRS-28*, ed. by I. Russell, W. Eberle. The "Qua-Entities" Paradigm versus the Notion of "Role" in NKRL (Narrative Knowledge Representation Language) (AAAI Press, Menlo Park, 2015), pp. 97–102

Part II
Text Capture and Textual Exploration

Parody Detection: An Annotation, Feature Construction, and Classification Approach to the Web of Parody

Joshua L. Weese, William H. Hsu, Jessica C. Murphy, and Kim Brillante Knight

Abstract In this chapter, we discuss the problem of how to discover when works in a social media site are related to one another by artistic appropriation, particularly parodies. The goal of this work is to discover concrete link information from texts expressing how this may entail derivative relationships between works, authors, and topics. In the domain of music video parodies, this has general applicability to titles, lyrics, musical style, and content features, but the emphasis in this work is on descriptive text, comments, and quantitative features of songs. We first derive a classification task for discovering the "Web of Parody." Furthermore, we describe the problems of how to generate song/parody candidates, collect user annotations, and apply machine learning approaches comprising of feature analysis, construction, and selection for this classification task. Finally, we report results from applying this framework to data collected from *YouTube* and explore how the basic classification task relates to the general problem of reconstructing the web of parody and other networks of influence. This points toward further empirical study of how social media collections can statistically reflect derivative relationships and what can be understood about the propagation of concepts across texts that are deemed interrelated.

J.L. Weese • W.H. Hsu (✉)
Department of Computer Science, Kansas State University, Manhattan, KS 66506, USA
e-mail: weeser@k-state.edu; bhsu@k-state.edu; banazir@gmail.com

J.C. Murphy
School of Arts and Humanities, University of Texas at Dallas, Richardson, TX 75080, USA
e-mail: jessica.c.murphy@utdallas.edu

K.B. Knight
School of Arts, Technology, and Emerging Communication, University of Texas at Dallas, Richardson, TX 75080, USA

© Springer International Publishing AG 2017
S. Hai-Jew (ed.), *Data Analytics in Digital Humanities*, Multimedia Systems and Applications, DOI 10.1007/978-3-319-54499-1_3

Toward a Web of Derivative Works

We consider the problem of reconstructing networks of influence in creative works—specifically, those consisting of sources, derivative works, and topics that are interrelated by relations that represent different modes of influence. In the domain of artistic appropriation, these include such relationships as "B is a parody of A." Other examples of "derivative work" relationships include expanding a short story into a novel, novelization of a screenplay, or the inverse (adapting a novel into a screenplay). Still more general forms of appropriation include quotations, mashups from one medium into another (e.g., song videos), and artistic imitations. In general, *derivative work* refers to any expressive creation that includes major elements of an original, previously created (*underlying*) work.

The task studied in this paper is detection of source/parody pairs among pairs of candidate videos on *YouTube*, where the parody is a derivative work of the source. Classifying an arbitrary pair of candidate videos as a source and its parody is a straightforward task for a human annotator, given a concrete and sufficiently detailed specification of the criteria for being a parody. However, solving the same problem by automated analysis of content is much more challenging, due to the complexity of finding applicable features. These are multimodal in origin (i.e., may come from the video, audio, metadata, comments, etc.); admit a combinatorially large number of feature extraction mechanisms, some of which have an unrestricted range of parameters; and may be irrelevant, necessitating some feature selection criteria.

Our preliminary work shows that by analyzing only video information and statistics, identifying correct source/parody pairs can be done with an ROC area of 65–75%. This can be improved by doing analysis directly on the video itself, such as Fourier analysis and extraction of lyrics (from closed captioning, or from audio when this is not available). However, this analysis is computationally intensive and introduces error at every stage. Other information can be gained by studying the social aspect of *YouTube*, particularly how users interact by commenting on videos. By introducing social responses to videos, we are able to identify source/parody pairs with an f-measure upwards to 93%.

The novel contribution of this research is that, to our knowledge, parody detection has not been applied in the *YouTube* domain, nor by analyzing user comments. The central hypothesis of this study is that by extracting features from *YouTube* comments, performance in identifying correct source/parody pairs will improve over using only information about the video itself. Our experimental approach is to gather source/parody pairs from *YouTube*, annotating the data, and constructing features using analytical component libraries, especially natural language toolkits. This demonstrates the feasibility of detecting source/parody video pairs from enumerated candidates.

Context: Digital Humanities and Derivative Works

The framing contexts for the problem of parody detection are the *web of influence* as defined by Koller (2001): graph-based models of relationships, particularly first-order relational extensions of probabilistic graphical models that include a representation for universal quantification. In the domain of digital humanities, a *network of influence* consists of creative works, authors, and topics that are interrelated by relations that represent different modes of influence. The term "creative works" includes texts and also products of other creative domains, and includes musical compositions and videos as discussed in this chapter. In the domain of artistic appropriation, these include such relationships as "B is a parody of A." Other examples of "derivative work" relationships include expanding a short story into a novel, novelization of a screenplay, or the inverse (adapting a novel into a screenplay). Still more general forms of appropriation include quotations, mashups from one medium into another (e.g., song videos), and artistic imitations.

The technical objectives of this line of research are to establish representations for learning and reasoning about the following tasks:

1. how to discover when works are related to one another by artistic appropriation
2. how this may entail relationships between works, authors, and topics
3. how large collections (including text corpora) can statistically reflect these relationships
4. what can be understood about the propagation of concepts across works that are deemed interrelated.

The above open-ended questions in the humanities pose the following methodological research challenges in informatics: specifically, how to use machine learning, information extraction, data science, and visualization techniques to reveal the network of influence for a text collection.

1. **(Problem)** How can relationships between documents be detected? For example, does one document extend another in the sense of textual entailment? If statement A *extends* statement B, then B entails A. For example, if A is the assertion "F is a flower" and B is the assertion "F is a rose," then A extends B. Such extension (or appropriation) relationships serve as building blocks for constructing a web of influence.
2. **(Problem)** What entities and features of text are relevant to the extension relationship, and which of these features transfer to other domains?
3. **(Technology)** What are algorithms that support relationship extraction from text and how do these fit into information extraction (IE) tools for reconstructing entity-relational models of documents, authors, and inspirational topics?
4. **(Technology)** How can information extraction be integrated with search tasks in the domain of derivative works? How can creative works, and their supporting data and metadata, support free-text user queries in portals for accessing collections of these works?

5. **(Technology)** How can newly captured relationships be incorporated and accounted for using ontologies and systems of reasoning that can capture semantic entailment in the above domain.
6. **(System)** How can a system be developed that maps out the spatiotemporal trajectory of an entity from the web of influence? For example, how can the propagation of an epithet, meme, or individual writing style from a domain of origin (geographic, time-dependent, or memetic) be visualized?

The central thesis of this work is that this combined approach will enable link identification toward discovering networks of influence in the digital humanities, such as among song parody videos and their authors and original songs. The need for such information extraction tools arises from the following present issues in text analytics for relationship extraction, which we seek to generalize beyond text. System components are needed for:

1. expanding the set of known entities
2. predicting the existence of a link between two entities
3. inferring which of two similar works is primary and which is derivative
4. classifying relationships by type
5. identifying features and examples that are relevant to a specified relationship extraction task.

These are general challenges for information extraction, not limited to the domain of modern English text, contemporary media studies, or even digital humanities.

Problem Statement: The Web of Parody

Goal: To automatically analyze the metadata and comments of music videos on a social video site (*YouTube*) and extract features to develop a machine learning-based classification system that can identify source/parody music videos from a set of arbitrary pairs of candidates.

The metadata we collected consists of quantitative features (descriptive statistics of videos, such as playing time) and natural language features. In addition to this metadata, the video contents can be analyzed using acoustical analysis to recognize song lyrics (Mesaros and Virtanen 2010) or image recognition to recognize human actions in music videos (Liu et al. 2008). Such sophisticated multimedia processing is, however, computationally intensive, meaning data analysis takes orders of magnitude longer and requires sophisticated hardware. Moreover, while the residual error is in generally excess of 25%, the potential reduction using natural language features is hypothesized to be significant. As our experiments show, this is indeed the case, using topic modeling features derived from descriptor text and comments had far lower computational costs than those of extracting audiovisual features from video. The remaining residual error makes any achievable marginal improvement from multimedia analyses too small to be cost effective, and so we deem them to be beyond the scope of this work.

Fig. 1 Literary devices used
in derivative works

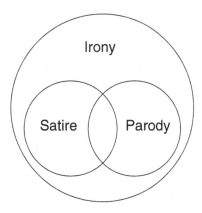

The Need for Natural Language Features

The relative tractability of natural language analyses makes the language of derivative works the focus of this research. More importantly, we narrow the scope to discover whether the social response to a derivative work reflects its unique linguistic features. Derivative works employ different literary devices, such as irony, satire, and parody. As seen in Fig. 1, irony, satire, and parody are interrelated. Irony can be described as appearance versus reality. In other words, the intended meaning is different from the actual definition of the words (LiteraryDevices Editor 2014). For example, the sentence "We named our new Great Dane 'Tiny'" is ironic because Great Dane dogs are quite large. Satire is generally used to expose and criticize weakness, foolishness, corruption, etc., of a work, individual, or society by using irony, exaggeration, or ridicule. Parody has the core concepts of satire; however, parodies are direct imitations of a particular work, usually to produce a comic effect.

Background and Related Work: Detecting Appropriated Works

Irony, Satire, and Parody Detection

Detecting derivative works can be a technically challenging task and is relatively novel beyond the older problems of plagiarism detection and authorship attribution. Burfoot and Baldwin (2009) introduce methodology in classifying satirical news articles as being either true (the real or original news article) or satirical. In a variety of cases, satire can be subtle and difficult to detect. Features focused on were mainly lexical, for example, the use of profanity and slang and similarity in article titles. In most cases, the headlines are good indications of satires, but so are profanity and slang since satires are meant for ridicule. Semantic validity was also introduced by using named entity recognition. This refers to detecting whether or not a named entity is out of place or used in the correct context.

Similar features can also be found in parodies. Bull (2010) focused on an empirical analysis on non-serious news, which includes sarcastic and parody news articles. Semantic validity was studied by calculating the edit distance of common sayings. This expands beyond just parody as many writings use "common phrases with new spins." Unusual juxtapositions and out of place language were also shown to be common in parody text, for example, "Pedophile of the Year" is phrase that is not uttered often in a serious context. This also leads to a comparison of the type of language used in parody and satirical articles. Non-serious text tends to use informal language with frequent use of adjectives, adverbs, contractions, slang, and profanity, where serious text has more professional qualities of style, diction, tone, and voice. In contrast to serious text, parodies can also be personalized (use of personal pronouns). Punctuation was also seen an indicator as serious text rarely use punctuation like exclamation marks (Tsur et al. 2010; Bull 2010).

As seen in Fig. 1, irony encompasses both satire and parody, but can also be more problematic to detect without a tonal reference or situational awareness. It is "unrealistic to seek a computational silver bullet for irony" (Reyes et al. 2012). In an effort to detect verbal irony in text, Reyes et al. (2012) focus on four main properties: signatures (typographical elements), unexpectedness, style (textual sequences), and emotional scenarios. Properties of irony detection clearly cascade down to the subdomains of parody and satire.

Music Video Domain

YouTube as a Data Source

YouTube has become one of the most popular user driven-video sharing platforms on the Web. In a study on the impact of social network structure on content propagation, Yoganarasimhan (2012) measured how YouTube propagated based on the social network to which a video was connected (i.e., subscribers). He shed light on the traffic YouTube receives such that "In April 2010 alone, YouTube received 97 million unique visitors and streamed 4.9 billion videos" (Yoganarasimhan 2012). Per recent reports from the popular video streaming service, YouTube's traffic and content has exploded. YouTube, in 2016, had over a billion users, streamed hundreds of millions of hours of video each day, and spanned over 88 countries (Google 2016). YouTube videos are also finding their way to social sites like Facebook (500 years of YouTube video watched every day) and Twitter (over 700 YouTube videos shared each minute). This leads to many research opportunities such as the goal of reconstructing a web of derivative works. With over 100 million people that like/dislike, favorite, rate, comment, and share YouTube videos, YouTube is a perfect platform to study social networks and relations.

The *YouTube* Social Network

YouTube is a large, content-driven social network, interfacing with many social networking giants like *Facebook* and *Twitter* (Wattenhofer et al. 2012). Considering the size of the *YouTube* network, there are numerous research areas, such as content propagation, virality, sentiment analysis, and content tagging. Recently, Google published work on classifying *YouTube* channels based on *Freebase* topics (Simmonet 2013). Their classification system worked on mapping *Freebase* topics to various categories for the *YouTube* channel browser. Other works focus on categorizing videos with a series of tags using computer vision (Yang and Toderici 2011). However, analyzing video content can be computationally intensive.

To expand from classifying videos based on content, this study looks at classifying *YouTube* videos based on social aspects like user comments. Wattenhofer et al. (2012) performed large scale experiments on the *YouTube* social network to study popularity in *YouTube*, how users interact, and how *YouTube*'s social network relates to other social networks. By looking at user comments, subscriptions, ratings, and other related features, they found that *YouTube* differs from other social networks in terms of user interaction (Wattenhofer et al. 2012). This shows that methodology in analyzing social networks such as *Twitter* may not be directly transferable to the *YouTube* platform. Diving further into the *YouTube* social network, Siersdorfer (2010) studied the community acceptance of user comments by looking at comment ratings and sentiment (Murphy et al. 2014; Trindade et al. 2014). Further analysis of user comments can be made over the life of the video by discovering polarity trends (Krishna et al. 2013).

Machine Learning Task: Classification

Machine learning, the problem of improving problem solving ability at a specified task given some experience (Mitchell 1997), is divided by practitioners into several broad categories: *supervised learning*, which involves data for which a target prediction or classification is already provided by past observation or by a human annotator, and *unsupervised learning*, where the aim is to formulate categories or descriptors based on measures of similarity between objects, and these categories are not provided as part of input data (Mitchell 1997; Murphy 2012; Alpaydin 2014). Classifying previously unseen items based on known categories by training them on labeled texts is an instance of supervised learning (Mitchell 1997), while *topic modeling*, the problem of forming as-yet unnamed categories by comparing members of a collection of items based on their similarities and differences, is a typical application of unsupervised learning (McCallum 2002; Blei and Ng 2003; Elshamy and Hsu 2014). In text analytics, the items are text documents; however, we seek in this work and future work to extend the items being classified and categorized as derivative of others. That is, we seek to generalize to a broader range of creative works, including musical instruments or singers (Weese 2014), musical compositions, videos, viral images and other memes, social media posts, users, and communities (Yang et al. 2014), etc.

Over the last decade, researchers have focused on the use of the formulation of kernel-based methods with the purpose of determining similarity and indexing documents for such machine learning tasks as classification (Trindade et al. 2011) and clustering (Bloehdorn and Moschitti 2007). The use of kernels allows a complex data space to be mapped to a compact feature space, where the level of similarity between documents can be easily and efficiently calculated using dynamic programming methods based on a kernel function (Doddington et al. 2004; Shawe-Taylor and Cristianini 2004). Such a kernel function forms the basis to a kernel machine such as support vector machine or online perception that can be applied for classification. The approach has been demonstrated to be effective for various representations of documents in NLP from sequence kernels for POS tagging (Bunescu and Mooney 2005; Lodhi et al. 2002) to tree kernels based on parse trees (Cancedda et al. 2003). Moschitti has explored on the use of kernels for a number a specialized NLP tasks such as relation extraction (Nguyen et al. 2009), semantic role labelling (Moschitti 2006; Moschitti et al. 2008), and question and answer classification (Moschitti 2008).

Relation extraction (RE), as defined by the Automatic Context Extraction (ACE) evaluation (Doddington et al. 2004), is the task of finding semantic relations between pairs of named entities in text, e.g., organization, location, part, role, etc. ACE systems use a wide range of lexical, syntactic, and semantic features to determine the relation mention between two entities. Supervised, semi-supervised, and unsupervised machine learning methods have been applied to relation extraction. Supervised methods are generally the most accurate, however, with the proviso that there are only few relationship identified types and the corpus is domain-specific (Mintz et al. 2009). There has been extensive work in the latter direction with regard to the use of kernel methods. A number of kernel-based approaches have been derived either through the use of one or more the following structural representations for a sentence: its constituent parse tree and its dependency-based representation which encode the grammatical dependencies between words. The approach of kernels over parse trees was pioneered by Collins and Duffy (2002), where the kernel function counts the number of common subtrees with appropriate weighting as the measure of similarity between two parse trees. Zelenko et al. (2003) considered such use of parse trees for the purpose of relation extraction. Culotta and Sorensen (2004) extended this work to consider kernels between augmented dependency trees. Zhang et al. (2006) proposed the use of convolution kernels which provide a recursive definition over the structure (Moschitti 2004). Nguyen et al. (2009) consider the use of a novel composite convolution kernels not just based on constituent parse trees but also for dependency and sequential structure for RE. A relation is represented by using the path-enclosed tree (which is the smallest subtree containing both entities) of the constituent parse tree or the path linking two entities of the dependency tree. Bunescu and Mooney (2005) proposed shortest path dependency kernel by stipulating that the only information to model a relationship between two entities can be captured by the shortest path between them in the dependency structure.

The latter is represented as a form of subsequence kernel (Doddington et al. 2004). Wang (2008) evaluated the latter structure in comparison to other subsequence kernels.

Kernels have been applied not only for relation extraction between named entities but also more complex relationship learning discovery tasks between whole sentences such as question and answering and textual entailment. Moschitti et al. (2008) propose a kernel mechanism for text fragment similarity based on the syntactic parse trees.

Methodology: Using Machine Learning to Detect Parody

Feature Analysis and Selection

We treat the problem of parody detection over candidate source video pairs as a classification task given computable ground features. Similar task definitions are used for prediction of friends in social networks: e.g., classification of a proposed direct friendship link as extant or not (Hsu et al. 2007; Caragea et al. 2009). This supervised inductive learning thus presents a simultaneous feature analysis (extraction) and selection task.

Finding quantitative ground features is in many instances a straightforward matter of interrogating the *YouTube* data model (API Overview Guide 2014) to extract fields of interest. In some social media analytics domains, this produces attributes that are irrelevant to some inductive learning algorithms (Hsu et al. 2007); in this domain, however, we found the effects of feature selection wrappers to be relatively negligible. By contrast, natural language features generally require crawling and parsing free text to extract sentiment, keywords of interest (including suppressed stop words), and ultimately named entities.

Annotation for Supervised Learning

Ground truth for the supervised learning task is obtained by developing a user interface that presents candidate pairs of videos to an annotator, renders the metadata as it appears in *YouTube*, allows the annotator to view the video, and having him or her provide a Boolean-valued judgment as to whether the pair consists of a source and parody. No special expertise is required; no explanations are elicited; and this approach admits validation via annotator agreement (*cf.* Hovy and Lavid 2010).

Addressing the Class Imbalance Problem

Class imbalance occurs when there is a significantly large number of examples of a certain class (such as positive or negative) over another. Drummond and Holte

(2012) discuss the class imbalance problem as cost in misclassification. As the imbalance increases, algorithms like Naïve Bayes that are somewhat resistant to the class imbalance problem suffer performance. Instead of using different algorithms to overcome class imbalance, the authors suggest generalizing the data to create a more uniform distribution to help overcome class imbalance. There are various methods to create a more uniform distribution of classes in a dataset. *YouTube* has millions of videos with a fraction of those being source/parody pairs. In order to keep the dataset in this study from becoming imbalanced, candidate source/parody pairs were filtered to give improved representation.

Data Acquisition and Preparation

Data Collection and Preprocessing

Criteria for Generation of Candidates

One challenge to overcome was that there is no parody dataset for *YouTube* and no concrete way of collecting such data. Our initial dataset included only information about the *YouTube* video (video statistics), rather than the video itself. The search for videos was quite limited (search bias in which videos were chosen). Given a well-known or popular parody video, the corresponding known source was found. The problem of multiple renditions of the same source arose and to solve it, only those deemed "official" sources were collected (another search bias). The term "official" refers to the video being published (uploaded) by the artistic work's artist or sponsor *YouTube* channel or account. The collection of known sources and parodies (28 of each) were retrieved using Google's *YouTube* API and stored into an XML file format for easy access.

The final experimentation greatly expanded the preliminary dataset. Kimono Labs, an API for generating crawling templates, was used to generate seeds for crawling *YouTube* for source and parody videos (Kimono Labs 2014). The Kimono API allowed quick and easy access to the top 100 songs from billboard.com (the week of November 3rd was used). The song titles were collected and used to retrieve the top two hits from *YouTube* using the *YouTube* Data API (API Overview Guide 2014). Parodies were retrieved in a similar fashion, except the keyword "parody" was added to the *YouTube* query which was limited to the top five search results. This helped reduce the class imbalance problem. Pairs were generated by taking the cross product of the two source videos and the five parody videos, making 1474 videos after filtering invalid videos and videos that were not in English. The cross product was used to generate candidate pairs since source videos spawn multiple parodies as well as other fan made source videos. Information retrieved with the videos included the video statistics (view count, likes, etc.) and up to 2000 comments.

Annotation

A custom annotator was built to allow users to label candidate source/parody pairs as valid or invalid. This was a crucial step in removing pairs that were not true parodies (false positive hits in the YouTube search results) of source videos. Naively, videos could be tagged based on whether the candidate parody video title contains parody keywords like "parody" or "spoof," but this generates several incorrect matches with sources. Likewise, if a parody video is popular enough, it also appears in the search results for the corresponding source video. It is also important to note that source lyric videos and other fan made videos were included in the dataset, so as to extend preliminary data beyond "official" videos. Having only two annotators available, pairs that were marked as valid by both annotators were considered to be valid source/parody pairs. In future works, more annotators will be needed and as such, inter-annotator agreement can be verified by kappa statistics and other means. Annotation left only 571 valid pairs (38.74%), which shows the importance of annotating the data versus taking the naïve approach to class labels. The number of pairs used in the final dataset was reduced to 162 valid pairs (about 11%) and 353 invalid pairs (23.95%) after removing videos that did not have a minimum of 100 comments available for crawling.

Feature Analysis

Preliminary experiments included four different feature sets:

1. The first used only ratios of video statistics (rating, number of times favorited, number of likes/dislikes, etc.) between the candidate source and parody.
2. The second used video statistic ratios plus a feature which indicated whether or not the second video in the pair was published after the first.
3. The third experiment used only the raw data collected (no ratios) plus the "published after" feature; this experiment was used as the baseline and used for comparison.
4. The fourth experiment included all features from the first three experiment designs.

The best performance was achieved as a result of the fourth feature set. The dataset was also oversampled to reduce the class imbalance. This gave a 98% ROC area; however, using the raw data as features, along with the oversampling caused overfitting. A better representative of the preliminary results was an average ROC area of 65–75%. Note that this is only with features generated from the video statistics.

Table 1 Features of the final experiment

Feature	Description
SentenceCount	Number of sentences from comments
Stanford NLP sentiment	Sentiment of comment sentences which range from very negative to very positive (a five value system)
AvgCommentSentiment	Average word sentiment from TwitIE
BadWordCount	Percentage of words that are profanity
Penn treebank NLP	The parts of speech tags in the penn treebank (Liberman 2003) as generated by stanford NLP
Penn treebank TwitIE	The parts of speech tags in the penn treebank generated by TwitIE
Punctuation	Punctuation marks
WordCount	Number of words in comments
AverageWordLength	Average length of words in comments
Top 20 mallet topics	The top 20 topics generated by mallet for source videos and for parody videos
Views	Number of views the video received
Likes	Number of likes for the video
Dislikes	Number of dislikes for the video
FavCount	Number of times the video was favorited
CommentCount	Number of comments the video has
TitleSimilarity	The edit distance of the parody and source video titles

Note that each is unique to the source video and the parody video except TitleSimilarity which is for both

Feature Extraction from Text

Extracting features from video content can come with a high computational overhead. Even though some natural language processing (NLP) tasks can be costly (depending on the size of text), this study focuses on using only features extracted from video information, statistics, and comments as shown in Table 1. One area of focus were lexical features extracted from user comments per video. Parts of speech tags were generated by two different toolkits: Stanford NLP (Manning et al. 2014) and GATE's TwitIE (Bontcheva et al. 2013). This allows the evaluation of a short-text tagger (TwitIE) and a multipurpose tagger (Stanford NLP). Both were also used to analyze sentiment of user comments. TwitIE was used to produce an average word sentiment, where Stanford NLP was used for sentence level sentiment. Other features include statistical lexical and structural features like punctuation, average word length, and number of sentences. A profanity filter was used to calculate the number of bad words in each set of comments. The number of unrecognizable tokens by the parts of speech taggers was also added as a feature. This hints at the unique language of the user comments where nontraditional English spelling and internet slang is used. All counts (sentiment, parts of speech, etc.) were normalized to percentages to take into account the difference in the number of comments

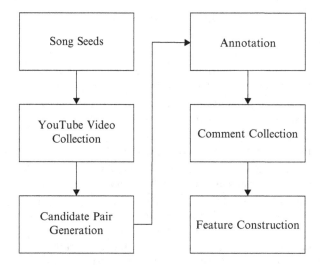

Fig. 2 Workflow model of a system for collecting and classifying YouTube video source/parody pairs

available between videos. Another large portion of features generated were by using Mallet (McCallum 2002), a machine learning toolkit for natural language. The built in stop word removal and stemming was used before collecting the top 20 topics for all parodies and sources for each training dataset. The summary of the process described in this section can be seen in Fig. 2.

Experimental Results

Statistical Validation Approach

Experiments were conducted using a ten fold cross validation with 90% of the data used for training and 10% used for testing. All features were generated per video automatically with the exception of a few features like title similarity, which requires both videos to construct the feature. Topic features were constructed by training the topic model in Mallet using the training datasets, and then using that model to infer the topics for the test datasets. Two data configurations were used to test whether or not the occurrence of the word "parody" would introduce a bias to classification. A synset was created for removing these occurrences: {parody, parodies, spoof, spoofs}. The data configurations were then combined with different feature arraignments to test the impact of using Stanford NLP, TwitIE, and video statistics.

Results Using Different Feature Sets

This section describes results on the parody-or-not classification task: learning the concept of a parody/original song pair by classifying a candidate pair (*Song*1, *Song*2) as being a parody paired with the original song it is based on. All classification tasks were done using the machine learning tool WEKA (Hall et al. 2009a, b). The supervised inductive learning algorithms (inducers) used included: Naïve Bayesian (NaiveBayes), instance-based (IB1), rule-based (JRip), decision tree (J48), artificial neural network (MLP), and logistic regression (Logistic).

Results were averaged across all ten folds. The f-measure (Powers 2011), standard deviation, and standard error can be found for each feature configuration in Tables 2, 3, 4, 5, 6, and 7. On average, the best performing inducers were MLP and IB1 at 90–93% f-measure. J48 performed well, but after looking at the pruned tree, the model tended to overfit. With the addition of features from user comments, performance increased significantly when compared to the preliminary work which used only video statistics. Stanford NLP (Tables 4 and 5) is shown to overall produce more relevant features than the TwitIE parts of speech tagger (Tables 2 and 3). When the TwitIE features were removed, performance was relatively unaffected (1–2% at most). Logistic is an exception to this analysis as it dropped 6.59%; however, this is taken as an intrinsic property of the inducer and requires further investigation. The removal of the video statistic features, however, did reduce performance for most

Table 2 Results for the stanford NLP, TwitIE, and video statistics feature set that include parody synsets

Average F-measure: Stanford NLP, TwitIE, and video statistics with parody synsets			
Inducers	AVG F measure (%)	STD (%)	STD-ERR (%)
IB1	91.01	2.87	0.91
J48	90.78	4.11	1.30
JRip	86.60	5.06	1.60
Logistic	87.95	2.87	0.91
MLP	91.35	3.36	1.06
NaiveBayes	82.37	4.21	1.33

Table 3 Results for the stanford NLP, TwitIE, and video statistics feature set that exclude parody synsets

Average F-measure: Stanford NLP, TwitIE, and video statistics without parody synset			
Inducer	AVG F measure (%)	STD (%)	STD-ERR (%)
IB1	91.39	3.17	1.00
J48	85.67	5.99	1.89
JRip	82.14	5.58	1.76
Logistic	88.29	3.72	1.18
MLP	90.44	2.64	0.83
NaiveBayes	80.18	3.87	1.22

Table 4 Results for the stanford NLP and video statistics feature set that include parody synsets

Average F-measure: Stanford NLP and video statistics with parody synset			
Inducer	AVG F measure (%)	STD (%)	STD-ERR (%)
IB1	92.59	2.96	0.94
J48	90.70	4.21	1.33
JRip	85.80	4.57	1.45
Logistic	86.80	4.65	1.47
MLP	90.28	3.65	1.16
NaiveBayes	82.55	4.50	1.42

Table 5 Results for the stanford NLP and video statistics feature set that exclude parody synsets

Average F-measure: Stanford NLP and video statistics without parody synset			
Inducer	AVG F measure (%)	STD (%)	STD-ERR (%)
IB1	93.15	3.19	1.01
J48	85.05	4.88	1.54
JRip	86.16	4.96	1.57
Logistic	81.73	5.10	1.61
MLP	90.09	3.06	0.97
NaiveBayes	78.50	3.69	1.17

Table 6 Results for the stanford NLP feature set that include parody synsets

Average F-measure: Stanford NLP with parody synset			
Inducer	AVG F measure (%)	STD (%)	STD-ERR (%)
IB1	92.39	2.87	0.91
J48	88.50	3.41	1.08
JRip	84.06	3.83	1.21
Logistic	82.94	6.41	2.03
MLP	88.73	2.87	0.91
NaiveBayes	78.51	4.70	1.48

Table 7 Results for the stanford NLP feature set that exclude parody synsets

Average F-measure: Stanford NLP without parody synset			
Inducer	AVG F measure (%)	STD (%)	STD-ERR (%)
IB1	92.94	3.19	1.01
J48	86.87	4.25	1.34
JRip	81.63	4.80	1.52
Logistic	81.73	5.03	1.59
MLP	87.71	3.08	0.97
NaiveBayes	75.14	4.11	1.30

inducers, showing that the popularity of a video helps indicate the relation between a parody and its source. Removing the parody synset did not have a heavy impact on performance. This is an important find, such that the word "parody" does not degrade classification of source/parody pairs.

Interpretation of Results: Topic and Feature Analysis

The most influential features were seen by using feature subset selection within *WEKA*. This showed that source and parody topics were most influential in the classification task. However, some topics clusters tend to overfit to popular videos or artist, especially for source videos. Generic clusters were also formed for things like music, humor, appraisal (users liked the song), and hate. A few unexpected topics also appeared, which show that current events also make it into the trending topics of the videos, for example: Obama, Ebola, and religion. Other feature analysis concluded that personal nouns were not relevant. This contradicts related work. Lexical features that were relevant included verbs, symbols, periods, adjectives, average word length in parody comments, and undefined or unrecognized tokens. Sentiment also showed promise during feature selection, though further experiments and dataset expansion will be needed to achieve more insightful feature selection.

The original hypothesis of this study is supported by the results. After introducing features extracted from comments, classification of source/parody pairs improved. The hypothesis also held after removing the parody synset. This generalizes the approach and makes it applicable to other domains, such as improving search, classifying news articles, plagiarism, and other derivative work domains. The proof of concept in this study leaves many possible directions for future research, including domain adaptation and feature expansion. Features left for future work include named entity recognition (this can help detect original authors of works), unusual juxtapositions and out of place language (Bull 2010), sentence structure beyond punctuation (Reyes et al. 2012), and community acceptance of comments to supplement sentiment analysis (Siersdorfer 2010).

Summary and Future Work

The results reported in Tables 2, 3, 4, 5, 6, and 7 of this paper support the original hypothesis of this study: after introducing features extracted from comments, classification of source/parody pairs improved. More significantly, results obtained with the parody synset removed also support the hypothesis. This generalizes the approach and makes it applicable to other domains, such as improving search, classifying news articles, plagiarism, and other derivative work domains. The proof of concept in this study leaves many possible directions for future research, including domain adaptation, feature expansion, and community detection. Features left for future work include named entity recognition (this can help detect original authors of works), unusual juxtapositions and out of place language (Bull 2010), sentence structure beyond punctuation (Reyes et al. 2012), and community acceptance of comments to supplement sentiment analysis (Siersdorfer 2010).

As mentioned in the introduction, a central goal of this work is to develop techniques and representations for heterogeneous information network analysis (HINA) to better support the discovery of webs of influence in derivation of creative works and the recognition of these and other instances of cultural appropriation. Figure 3 illustrates one such use case using early modern English ballads from the English Broadside Ballad Archive (EBBA); Fig. 4 illustrates another based on the meme *Sí, se puede* ("Yes, one can," popularly rendered "Yes, we can"). These are hand-constructed examples of the types of "network of influence" diagrams that we aim to produce in continuing research.

Figure 5 depicts the data flow and workflow model for our system for *Extracting the Network of Influence in the Digital Humanities (ENIDH)*, as a block diagram. The system described in this book chapter implements a simplified variant of this workflow. On the left side, the input consists of candidate items to be compared—in this case, digital documents such as song videos bearing metadata. Named entity (NE) recognition and discovery plus terminology discovery are preliminary steps to relation discovery. As described in Section "Results using Different Feature Sets", supervised learning to predict parody/original song pairs was conducted using a variety of inducers, but not using support vector machines (SVM) and other kernel-based methods. The desired web of influence (Koller 2001) is represented by a heterogeneous information network (containing multiple types of entities such as "original song" and "parody video" or "original video" and "parody lyrics") as illustrated in Figs. 3 and 4.

Entity: Works

Source
Author: Martin Parker
Title: "A proverbe olde"
Date: 1625
Genre: Ballad
Summary: argues forwidows remarrying
Source: EBBA
Link: http://ebba.english.ucsb.edu/ballad/20179/citation

Derivation
Author: Martin Parker
Title: "The wiving age"
Date: 1627
Genre: Ballad
Summary: argues against widows remarrying
Relationship: Response; contrary
Source: EBBA
Link: http://ebba.english.ucsb.edu/ballad/20178/citation

Entity: Authors

Source
Author: Martin Parker
Title: "The wiving age"
Date: 1627
Genre: Ballad
Summary: argues against widows remarrying
Source: EBBA
Link: http://ebba.english.ucsb.edu/ballad/20178/citation

Derivation
Author: Unknown
Title: "The maiden lottery"
Date: 1672-1696
Genre: Ballad
Summary: men would rather marry young women than
        sleep with widows
Relationship: Similar themes
Source: EBBA
Link: http://ebba.english.ucsb.edu/ballad/22342/citation

Entity: Topic/Occasion

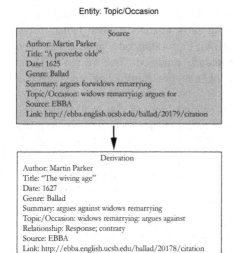

Source
Author: Martin Parker
Title: "A proverbe olde"
Date: 1625
Genre: Ballad
Summary: argues forwidows remarrying
Topic/Occasion: widows remarrying: argues for
Source: EBBA
Link: http://ebba.english.ucsb.edu/ballad/20179/citation

Derivation
Author: Martin Parker
Title: "The wiving age"
Date: 1627
Genre: Ballad
Summary: argues against widows remarrying
Topic/Occasion: widows remarrying: argues against
Relationship: Response; contrary
Source: EBBA
Link: http://ebba.english.ucsb.edu/ballad/20178/citation

Fig. 3 Example of a network of derivative works based on the English Broadside Ballad Archive
(EBBA)

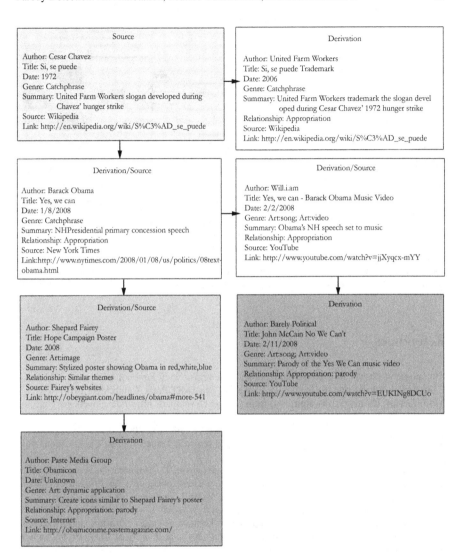

Fig. 4 Example of a heterogeneous information network of derivative works based on the meme *Sí, se puede*/Yes, We Can

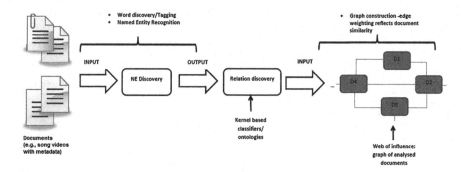

Fig. 5 System block diagram: Extracting the Network of Influence in the Digital Humanities (ENIDH)

Acknowledgements We thank the anonymous reviewers for helpful comments, and Hui Wang and Niall Rooney for the survey of kernel methods for clustering and classification of text documents in Section "Machine Learning Task: Classification".

References

Kimono Labs, (2014). Retrieved from Kimono Labs: https://www.kimonolabs.com/

E. Alpaydin, *Introduction to Machine Learning*, 3rd edn. (MIT Press, Cambridge, 2014)

API Overview Guide, (2014). Retrieved from Google Developers: https://developers.google.com/youtube/

D.M. Blei, A.Y. Ng, Latent dirichlet allocation. J. Mach. Learn. Res. **2003**(3), 993–1022 (2003)

S. Bloehdorn, A. Moschitti, Combined syntactic and semantic kernels for text classification. Adv. Inf. Retr. **4425**, 307–318 (2007)

K. Bontcheva, L. Derczynski, A. Funk, M. A. Greenwood, D. Maynard, N. Aswani, TwitIE: an open-source information extraction pipeline for microblog text, in *Proceedings of the International Conference on Recent Advances in Natural Language Processing* (2013)

S. Bull, *Automatic Parody Detection in Sentiment Analysis* (2010)

R. Bunescu, R. Mooney, A shortest path dependency kernel for relation extraction. in *Proceedings of the Conference on Human Language Technology and Empirical Methods in Natural Language Processing*(2005), pp. 724–731

C. Burfoot, T. Baldwin, in *ACL-IJCNLP, Automatic Satire Detection: Are You Having A Laugh?* (Suntec, Singapore, 2009), pp. 161–164

I. Cadez, D. Heckerman, C. Meek, P. Smyth, S. White, Visualization of Navigation Patterns on a Web Site Using Model-Based Clustering, in *Proceedings of the 6th ACM SIGKDD International Conference on Knowledge Discovery and Data Mining (KDD 2000)*, ed. by R. Ramakrishnan, S. J. Stolfo, R. J. Bayardo, I. Parsa (Boston 2000), pp. 280–284

N. Cancedda, E. Gaussier, C. Goutte, J. Renders, Word sequence kernels. J. Mach. Learn. Res. **3**, 1059–1082 (2003)

D. Caragea, V. Bahirwani, W. Aljandal, W. H. Hsu, Ontology-Based Link Prediction in the Livejournal Social Network, in *Proceedings of the 8th Symposium on Abstraction, Reformulation and Approximation (SARA 2009)*, ed. by V. Bulitko, J. C. Beck, (Lake Arrowhead, CA, 2009)

S. Choudury, J. G. Breslin, *User Sentiment Detection: A Youtube Use Case*, (2010)

M. Collins, N. Duffy, Convolution kernels for natural language. Adv. Neural Inf. Proces. Syst. **1**, 625–632 (2002)

A. Culotta, J. Sorensen, Dependency tree kernels for relation extraction, in *Proceedings of the 42nd Annual Meeting on Association for Computational Linguistics*, (2004), p. 423-es

A. Cuzzocrea, I.-Y. Song, K. C. Davis, Analytics over large-scale multidimensional data: the big data revolution!, in *Proceedings of the ACM 14th International Workshop on Data Warehousing and On-Line Analytical Processing (DOLAP 2011)*, ed. by A. Cuzzocrea, I.-Y. Song, K. C. Davis, (ACM Press, Glasgow, 2011) pp. 101–104

R. Dawkins, in *The Meme Machine*, ed. by S. Blackmore, Foreword, (Oxford: Oxford University Press, 2000). pp. i–xvii

R. Dawkins, *The Selfiish Gene*, 30th edn. (Oxford University Press, Oxford, 2006)

G. Doddington, A. Mitchell, M. Przybocki, L. Ramshaw, S. Strassel, R. Weischedel, The automatic content extraction (ace) program–tasks, data, and evaluation. Proc. LREC **4**, 837–840 (2004)

C. Drummond, R. E. Holte, *Severe Class Imbalance: Why Better Algorithms aren't the Answer* (2012). Retrieved from http://www.csi.uottawa.ca/~cdrummon/pubs/ECML05.pdf

C.E. Elger, K. Lehnertz, Seizure prediction by non-linear time series analysis of brain electrical activity. Eur. J. Neurosci. **10**(2), 786–789 (1998)

W. Elshamy, W. H. Hsu, in Continuous-time infinite dynamic topic models: the dim sum process for simultaneous topic enumeration and formation, ed. by W. H. Hsu, Emerging Methods in Predictive Analytics: Risk Management and Decision-Making (Hershey, IGI Global, 2014), pp. 187–222

U. Gargi, W. Lu, V. Mirrokni, S. Yoon, Large-scale community detection on youtube for topic discovery and exploration, in *Proceedings of the 5th International Conference on Weblogs and Social Media*, ed. by L. A. Adamic, R. A. Baeza-Yates, S. Counts (Barcelona, Catalonia, 17–21 July 2011)

P. Gill, M. Arlitt, Z. Li, A. Mahanti, YouTube traffic characterization: a view from the edge, in *IMC'07: Proceedings of the 7th ACM SIGCOMM Conference on Internet Measurement* (ACM, New York, 2007), pp. 15–28

J. Gleick, *The Information: A History, a Theory, a Flood* (Pantheon Books, New York, 2011)

J. Goldstein, S. F. Roth, Using aggregation and dynamic queries for exploring large data sets, in *Proceedings of the SIGCHI Conference on Human Factors in Computing Systems (CHI 2004)*, ed. by E. Dykstra-Erickson, M. Tscheligi (ACM Press, Boston, MA, 1994), pp. 23–29

Google. Statistics. (2012). Retrieved from YouTube: http://www.youtube.com/t/press_statistics

M. Hall, E. Frank, G. Holmes, B. Pfahringer, The WEKA Data Mining Software: An Update. ACM SIGKDD Explorations Newsletter **11**(1), 10–18 (2009b)

M. Hall, E. Frank, G. Holmes, B. Pfahringer, P. Reutemann, I.H. Witten, The WEKA Data Mining Software: An Update. SIGKDD Explorations **11**(1), 10–18 (2009a)

J. Heer, N. Kong, M. Agrawala, Sizing the horizon: the effects of chart size and layering on the graphical perception of time series visualizations, in *Proceedings of the 27th International Conference on Human Factors in Computing Systems (CHI 2009)* (ACM Press, Boston, 2009), pp. 1303–1312

E. Hovy, J. Lavid, Towards a 'Science' of corpus annotation: a new methodological challenge for corpus linguistics. Int. J. Translat. **22**(1), 13–36 (2010). doi:10.1075/target.22.1

W. H. Hsu, J. P. Lancaster, M. S. Paradesi, T. Weninger, Structural link analysis from user profiles and friends networks: a feature construction approach, in *Proceedings of the 1st International Conference on Weblogs and Social Media (ICWSM 2007)*, ed. by N. S. Glance, N. Nicolov, E. Adar, M. Hurst, M. Liberman, F. Salvetti (Boulder, CO, 2007), pp. 75–80

H. Jenkins. *If it Doesn't Spread, it's Dead*. (2009). Retrieved 06 16, 2011, from Confessions of an Aca-Fan: The Official Weblog of Henry Jenkins: http://www.henryjenkins.org/2009/02/if_it_doesnt_spread_its_dead_p.html

D. A. Keim, Challenges in visual data analysis, in *10th International Conference on Information Visualisation (IV 2006)*, ed. by E. Banissi, K. Börner, C. Chen, G. Clapworthy, C. Maple, A. Lobben, . . . J. Zhang (IEEE Press, London, 2006), pp. 9–16

D. Koller (2001). Representation, reasoning, learning: IJCAI 2001 computers and thought award lecture. Retrieved from Daphne Koller: http://stanford.io/TFV7qH

A. Krishna, J. Zambreno, S. Krishnan, Polarity trend analysis of public sentiment on Youtube, in *The 19Tth International Conference on Management of Data* (Ahmedabad, 2013)

N. Kumar, E. Keogh, S. Lonardi, C. A. Ratanamahatana, Time-series bitmaps: a practical visualization tool for working with large time series databases, in *Proceedings of the 5th SIAM International Conference on Data Mining (SDM 2005)* (Newport Beach, CA, 2005), pp. 531–535

M. Liberman. *Penn Treebank POS*, (2003). Retrieved 2014, from Penn Arts and Sciences: https://www.ling.upenn.edu/courses/Fall_2003/ling001/penn_treebank_pos.html

LiteraryDevices Editors, (2014). Retrieved from Literary Devices: http://literarydevices.net

J. Liu, S. Ali, M. Shah, Recognizing human actions using multiple features, in *IEEE Computer Society Conference on Computer Vision and Pattern Recognition (CVPR 2008)* (2008), pp. 1–8. doi: 10.1109/CVPR.2008.4587527

H. Lodhi, C. Saunders, J. Shawe-Taylor, N. Cristianini, C. Watkins, Text classification using string kernels. J. Mach. Learn. Res. **2**, 419–444 (2002)

C. D. Manning, M. Surdeanu, J. Bauer, J. Finkel, S. J. Bethard, D. McClosky, The Stanford CoreNLP Natural Language Processing Toolkit, in *Proceedings of 52nd Annual Meeting of the Association for Computational Linguistics: System Demonstrations* (2014), pp. 55–60

C. Mario, D. Talia, The knowledge grid. Commun. ACM **46**(1), 89–93 (2003)

A. K. McCallum (2002). Retrieved from MALLET: A Machine Learning for Language Toolkit: http://mallet.cs.umass.edu

A. Mesaros, T. Virtanen, Automatic recognition of lyrics in singing. EURASIP J. Audio, Speech, and Music Processing **2010** (2010). doi:10.1155/2010/546047

M. Mintz, S. Bills, R. Snow, D. Jurafsky, Distant supervision for relation extraction without labeled data, in *Proceedings of the Joint Conference of the 47th Annual Meeting of the ACL and the 4th International Joint Conference on Natural Language Processing of the AFNLP: Volume 2* (2009), pp. 1003–1011

T.M. Mitchell, *Machine learning* (McGraw Hill, New York, 1997)

M. Monmonier, Strategies for the visualization of geographic time-series data. Cartographica: Int. J. Geogr. Inf. Geovisualization **27**(1), 30–45 (1990)

A. Moschitti, A study on convolution kernels for shallow semantic parsing, in *Proceedings of the 42nd Annual Meeting on Association for Computational Linguistics* (2004), p. 335-es

A. Moschitti, Syntactic kernels for natural language learning: the semantic role labeling case, in *Proceedings of the Human Language Technology Conference of the NAACL, Companion Volume: Short Papers on XX* (2006). (pp. 97–100)

A. Moschitti, Kernel methods, syntax and semantics for relational text categorization, in *Proceeding of the 17th ACM Conference on Information and Knowledge Management* (2008), pp. 253–262

A. Moschitti, D. Pighin, R. Basili, Tree kernels for semantic role labeling. Comput. Linguist. **34**(2), 193–224 (2008)

J. C. Murphy, W. H. Hsu, W. Elshamy, S. Kallumadi, S. Volkova, Greensickness and HPV: a comparative analysis?, in *New Technologies in Renaissance Studies II*, ed. by T. Gniady, K. McAbee, J. C. Murphy, vol. 4 (Toronto and Tempe, AZ, USA: Iter and Arizona Center for Medieval and Renaissance Studies, 2014), pp. 171–197

K.P. Murphy, *Machine Learning: A Probabilistic Perspective* (MIT Press, Cambridge, 2012)

T. Nguyen, A. Moschitti, G. Riccardi, Convolution kernels on constituent, dependency and sequential structures for relation extraction, in *Proceedings of the 2009 Conference on Empirical Methods in Natural Language Processing: volume 3* (2009), pp. 1378–1387

T. O'reilly, *What Is Web 2.0* (O'Reilly Media, Sebastopol, 2009)

A. Reyes, P. Rosso, T. Veale, A multidemensional approach for detecting irony in twitter. Lang. Resour. Eval. **47**(1), 239–268 (2012)

J. Selden, *Table Talk: Being the Discourses of John Selden*. London: Printed for E. Smith (1689)

J. Shawe-Taylor, N. Cristianini, *An Introduction to Support Vector Machines: And Other Kernel-Based Learning Methods* (Cambridge University Press, Cambridge, 2004)

S. C. Siersdorfer, How useful are your comments?-Analyzing and predicting Youtube comments and comment ratings, in *Proceedings of the 19th International Conference on World Wide Web*, vol. 15 (2010), pp. 897–900

V. Simmonet, Classifying Youtube channels: a practical system, in *Proceedings of the 22nd International Conference on World Wibe Web Companion* (2013), pp. 1295–1303

J. Steele, N. Iliinsky (eds.), *Beautiful Visualization: Looking at Data Through the Eyes of Experts* (O'Reilly Media, Cambridge, 2010)

L. A. Trindade, H. Wang, W. Blackburn, N. Rooney, Text classification using word sequence kernel methods, in *Proceedings of the International Conference on Machine Learning and Cybernetics (ICMLC 2011)* (Guilin, 2011), pp. 1532–1537

L. A. Trindade, H. Wang, W. Blackburn, P. S. Taylor, Enhanced factored sequence kernel for sentiment classification, in *Proceedings of the 2014 IEEE/WIC/ACM International Joint Conferences on Web Intelligence and Intelligent Agent Technologies (WI-IAT 2014)* (2014), pp. 519–525

O. Tsur, D. Davidov, A. Rappoport, in *ICWSN—A Great Catchy Name: Semi-Supervised Recognition of Sarcastic Sentences in Online Product Reviews,* AAAI (2010)

M. Wang, A re-examination of dependency path kernels for relation extraction, in *Proceedings of IJCNLP* (2008), 8

H.J. Watson, B.H. Wixom, The current state of business intelligence. IEEE Comput. **40**(9), 96–99 (2007)

T. Watt, *Cheap Print and Popular Piety, 1550–1640* (Cambridge University Press, Cambridge, 1991)

M. Wattenhofer, R. Wattenhofer, Z. Zhu, The YouTube Social Network, in *Sixth International AAAI Conference on Weblogs and Social Media* (2012), pp. 354–361

J. L. Weese, in Emerging Methods in Predictive Analytics: Risk Management and Decision-Making, ed. by W. H. Hsu, Predictive analytics in digital signal processing: a convolutive model for polyphonic instrument identification and pitch detection using combined classification. (Hershey: IGI Global, 2014), pp. 223–253

M. Yang, W. H. Hsu, S. Kallumadi, in Emerging Methods in Predictive Analytics: Risk Management and Decision-Making, ed. by W. H. Hsu, Predictive analytics of social networks: a survey of tasks and techniques (Hershey: IGI Global, 2014), pp. 297–333

W. Yang, G. Toderici, Discriminative tag learning on Youtube videos with latent sub-tags. *CVPR*, (2011), pp. 3217–3224

H. Yoganarasimhan. (2012). *Impact of Social Network Structure on Content Propagation: A Study Using Youtube Data.* Retrieved from: http://faculty.gsm.ucdavis.edu/~hema/youtube.pdf

D. Zelenko, C. Aone, A. Richardella, Kernel methods for relation extraction. J. Mach. Learn. Res. **3**, 1083–1106 (2003)

M. Zhang, J. Zhang, J. Su, G. Zhou, A composite kernel to extract relations between entities with both flat and structured features, in *Proceedings of the 21st International Conference on Computational Linguistics and the 44th Annual Meeting of the Association for Computational Linguistics* (2006), pp. 825–832

Creating and Analyzing Literary Corpora

Michael Percillier

Abstract Using a study of non-standardized linguistic features in literary texts as a working example, the chapter describes the creation of a digital corpus from printed source texts, as well as its subsequent annotation and analysis. The sections detailing the process of corpus creation take readers through the steps of document scanning, Optical Character Recognition, proofreading, and conversion of plain text to XML, while offering advice on best practices and overviews of existing tools. The presented corpus annotation method introduces the programming language *Python* as a tool for automated basic annotation, and showcases methods for facilitating thorough manual annotation. The data analysis covers both qualitative analysis, facilitated by CSS styling of XML data, and quantitative analysis, performed with the statistical software package *R* and showcasing a number of sample analyses.

Introduction

The present chapter provides a detailed description of the methodology used in the research project *Representations of oral varieties of language in the literature of the English-speaking world* (Paulin and Percillier 2015; Percillier and Paulin 2016). The aim of the project is to compile and subsequently analyze a corpus of literary prose texts, placing an emphasis on non-standardized linguistic features. The chapter addresses three topics of interest to the field of Digital Humanities:

1. The creation of a digital corpus from printed source texts
2. Corpus annotation
3. Qualitative and quantitative data analysis.

Using the project's corpus of literary texts as a working example, the three aforementioned topics are explained in turn. Section "Corpus Creation" describes the process of creating a corpus from a printed text to a digital corpus, providing details on scanning practices (Scanning), methods for converting images of scanned

M. Percillier (✉)
University of Mannheim, Mannheim, Germany
e-mail: percillier@uni-mannheim.de

© Springer International Publishing AG 2017
S. Hai-Jew (ed.), *Data Analytics in Digital Humanities*, Multimedia Systems
and Applications, DOI 10.1007/978-3-319-54499-1_4

text into digital text (Optical Character Recognition), and advice on proofreading said digital text (Proofreading). Section "Basic Corpus Annotation" deals with basic annotation of the corpus, which is performed automatically using *Python*. After harmonizing quotation marks throughout the corpus (Harmonizing Quotation Marks), the plain text files are converted to the XML format (From Plain Text to XML), and basic automatic annotation such as paragraph numbering and character passage recognition is added (Applying Automatic Basic Annotation). Section "Applying Manual Annotation" describes the method used to apply the actual linguistic annotation to the corpus. The annotation can then be used to facilitate a qualitative analysis of the data, as described in section "Enabling Qualitative Analysis," as well as a quantitative analysis, described in section "Quantitative Analysis," which outlines a number of sample analyses using *R*.

Corpus Creation

A corpus is defined as a large collection of texts. The definition also implies that said texts should be in a digital format in order to be analyzed by computers in automatic and interactive ways (Biber et al. 1998, p.4). For this reason, any research project aiming to effectively analyze texts not readily available in a digital format should first convert them from a printed medium to a digital medium. The present section describes best scanning practices, the use of *Optical Character Recognition* (henceforth OCR) to render the scanned text machine-readable, and provides recommendations for proofreading the OCR output.

An ever increasing number of texts, including literary texts, are available in digital format as so-called *e-books*. This applies to older texts, which enter the public domain 70 or 100 years after their author(s)'s death (depending on the local jurisdiction) and can be made freely available on platforms such as the *Project Gutenberg* (Project Gutenberg Literary Archive Foundation 2015), as well as recent texts sold as digital versions and readable on computers, mobile devices, and dedicated *e-book* devices. Readers intending to create a corpus based on digitally available texts may skip sections "Scanning," "Optical Character Recognition," and "Proofreading," and proceed directly to section "Basic Corpus Annotation," while readers planning to base their corpus on printed texts are advised to follow the recommendations offered in sections "Scanning," "Optical Character Recognition," and "Proofreading."

Scanning

The process of scanning refers to the conversion of a physical object, in our context a printed page, to a digital image. Ordinary flatbed scanners are usually sufficient for the scanning of book excerpts on a moderate scale. When scanning, a minimum resolution of 300 pixels per inch (PPI) should be selected to ensure that the OCR process [cf. section "Optical Character Recognition"] is as reliable as possible. As long as this minimum resolution is set, the file format under which the scan is saved can be chosen by the user, e.g., PDF, TIFF, JPEG, etc.

Optical Character Recognition

A scanned page is not yet a digital text, but merely a digital image, a picture of the text. While it can be read on screen by a user, its contents cannot be searched for specific character sequences, copied, transformed, or undergo any other operations that can be done with a digital text. OCR is a process that analyzes the picture of a text and converts it to a digital text.

There are a multitude of software titles capable of OCR, consisting of commercial as well as free titles, as summarized in Table 1.

The OCR output is usually saved as a plain text file (with a .txt file ending). It is recommended to choose Unicode, specifically UTF-8, as the text encoding, as this will avoid encoding problems due to the presence of accented characters on Latin characters (e.g., in the word *fiancée*) or non-Latin characters.

Proofreading

While OCR software can be quite accurate, even commercial titles rarely achieve 100% accuracy. OCR output should therefore be proofread whenever possible. As the digitization process described aims to create a corpus and not an e-book similar to the original printed version, the main interest when proofreading the OCR output lies in the "pure" text, i.e., the content, and not on the formatting of the original print edition. For this reason, the use of a text editor (cf. suggestions in Table 2) rather than a word processor is strongly recommended. The only formatting unit to be maintained is the paragraph. A paragraph in the printed volume corresponds to a line in the digitized text. To clarify, one should not hit the *Enter* key at each line break

Table 1 Selection of OCR software titles

Title	License
Acrobat (Adobe 2016)	Commercial
FineReader (ABBYY 2016)	Commercial
OneNote (Microsoft 2016)	Proprietary freeware
ReadIris (IRIS 2015)	Commercial
Tesseract (Smith 2015)	Open source (Apache)
VueScan Professional Edition (Hamrick and Hamrick 2016)	Commercial

Table 2 Selection of suitable text editors

Title	Operating system	License
gedit (Maggi et al. 2015)	Linux/Mac OS X/Windows	Open source (GNU GPL)
Notepad++ (Ho 2016)	Windows	Open source (GNU GPL)
TextWrangler (Bare Bones Software 2015)	Mac OS X	Proprietary freeware

Table 3 Comparison of typefaces

Preview	Typeface family	Typeface name
rnm cld 0O 1lI	Roman/serif	Times New Roman
rnm cld 0O 1lI	Sans serif	Helvetica
rnm cld 0O 1lI	Monospaced	Courier

found in the printed edition, but only at paragraph breaks. A blank line between paragraphs is recommended for maximum clarity, as well as for later automatic processing (cf. section "Applying Automatic Basic Annotation").

Typefaces for Proofreading

Many errors in OCR are due to the fact that many print editions use roman/ serif typefaces, which means that some characters are narrower than others, and adjacent character combinations may look like a different character altogether. A contrast of various typefaces showing characters or character combinations that can be easily confused is given in Table 3. Character sequences such as <rn> and <cl> look like <m> and <d>, respectively, in serif typefaces, but are easier to distinguish in monospaced typefaces. Additionally, individual characters may be hard to distinguish in serif typefaces, e.g., <0, O> (zero, uppercase o) and <1, l, I> (one, lowercase l, uppercase i). Specialized proofreading typefaces featuring even more distinctive character shapes than monospaced typefaces are also available, e.g. DPCustomMono2 (Distributed Proofreaders Foundation 2015).

Additional Measures in the Proofreading Process

OCR software is generally unable to discern italics, or distinguish hyphens from dashes. As such, these aspects should be verified and marked during the proofreading process should they be relevant for the project. Further issues such as obvious errors in the print edition can also be addressed at this stage. Suggestions on how to handle such cases are shown in Table 4. The structure used for marking print errors will be explained when the XML data format is discussed in section "From Plain Text to XML." The digital files, once proofread, actually meet the requirements of a corpus, albeit not a very useful one, given that it consists of nothing but plain text. While simple queries for specific keywords could be performed, the potential of a digital corpus greatly increases with annotation.

Table 4 Suggestions for handling special cases in the proofreading process

Case	Print appearance	Proofread digitized text
Italics	Text in *italics*	Text in _italics_
Hyphens and dashes	- Hyphen – Dash	- Hyphen -- Dash
Print errors	to he reminded	to <correction orig='he'>be</correction>reminded

Basic Corpus Annotation

The present section will describe a way to automatically add basic annotation to the corpus. Specifically, paragraphs will be numbered, italics will be marked as such, as will direct discourse. This will result in a new version of the corpus in the XML (Extensible Markup Language) format annotated with the aforementioned information. The automatic annotation will be performed using *Python* (Python Software Foundation 2015), a general purpose programming language with a comparatively simple syntax. The *Python* code used is displayed and commented in the Appendix section and on the companion website.

Installing and Running Python

Although *Python* comes pre-installed with most versions of Mac OS X and Linux, it is recommended for all users to install the newest available version from the official *Python* website.[1] The present chapter uses Version 2.7.11. Once installed, *Python* scripts can be entered in a text editor and saved with the file extension .py. To run a script, open the operating system's command-line interface (*Terminal* on Mac OS X and Linux, *Command Prompt* on Windows). Within the command-line interface, use the cd command to change to the directory in which the *Python* script is located, e.g.: cd Home/Documents/Scripts, and hit the Enter key (Windows users will need to use backslashes rather than regular slashes between folder names). To run a *Python* script, type python followed by the name of the script file, e.g., python test.py, then hit Enter.[2]

Additional functionality can be added to *Python* by external modules. Most modules used in the present chapter are included in the standard *Python* installation, with the exception of *Beautiful Soup* (Richardson 2015), an HTML and XML parser. The simplest way to install *Beautiful Soup* is to enter the following command in the command-line interface: pip install beautifulsoup4, then hit Enter. As *Beautiful Soup* relies on *lxml* (Behnel 2015) for parsing XML, this module should be installed as well using the following command: pip install lxml.

---

[1] https://www.python.org.

[2] Windows users may have to add *Python* to the *Environment Variables*, see https://docs.python.org/2/using/windows.html.

Harmonizing Quotation Marks

One of the aims of the basic annotation process is to automatically detect text passages in direct discourse and mark them as such. However, this task is made difficult by the fact that printed texts may use different sets of quotation marks to indicate direct discourse. For English, this is usually either "double quotation marks" or 'single quotation marks.' A preliminary task is to harmonize the texts to use "double quotation marks" only, not only for consistency, but first and foremost to enable the automatic detection of direct character discourse later on (cf. section "Applying Automatic Basic Annotation"). Double quotation marks are reliable, whereas single quotation marks use the same character as the apostrophe.

The first *Python* script performs the task of harmonizing all quotation marks to double quotation marks. Needless to say, it only has to be used on texts with single quotation marks. The strategy used to differentiate between quotation marks and apostrophes is to consider their usual position in relation to other characters: opening quotation marks usually precede capital letters (as they contain a new sentence), and closing quotation marks usually follow punctuation marks (as the sentence ends when the quotation does). These two principles are used in the short *Python* script given in Appendix 1.

However, the substitution rule described does not capture all cases. For example, direct discourse after inserted quotatives, as shown in example (1), are not detected by the script.

(1)   "You can thank your stars that I am not a wicked man," he continued as though I had said nothing, "otherwise I would have told him..." (Achebe 1966, p. 17)

The character's quote in example (1) is interrupted by a quotative construction. The resumption of the quote is therefore not a new sentence, and does not begin with a capital letter. Because of such cases, it is recommended to run the script before the proofreading process, so that such exceptions can be corrected manually.

From Plain Text to XML

The preferred format for a corpus is XML, as it is a standard that allows for a clear distinction between data and metadata. The main feature of XML is the use of tags in angle brackets. XML distinguishes three types of tags:

1. start-tags, e.g., `<tag>` or `<tag attribute="value">`
2. end-tags, e.g., `</tag>`
3. empty-element-tags, e.g., `<tag/>` or `<tag attribute="value"/>`

Start-tags and end-tags operate in concord and mark the beginning and end of an annotated stretch of data. Empty-set tags appear on their own and do not mark a stretch of data, but rather a specific point in the data. Start-tags and empty-set tags may also contain attributes, which specify additional information.

The benefits of XML lie in its flexibility and consistency. Readers familiar with HTML may have noticed similarities in the tag structure of both formats. The main differences between them is that XML allows the creation of new tags, while HTML is limited to a fixed set of tags with predetermined functions, e.g., <h1> for a main heading. XML is also stricter, as any start-tag needs to be closed by a corresponding end-tag. The leniency of HTML allowing start-tags with no closing equivalent, leading to so-called *tag soup*, does not exist in XML.

To convert the plain text version into XML, the content of the plain text file can be pasted into an XML template file, e.g. as shown below.

```
<?xml version="1.0" encoding="UTF-8"?>
<?xml-stylesheet type="text/css" href="./corpus_style.css"?>
<text>
  <header>
    <region></region>
    <country></country>
    <author></author>
    <title></title>
    <year></year>
    <source></source>
  </header>
  <body>

  </body>
</text>
```

The first line specifies the XML version and the encoding, while the second line links to a stylesheet file (cf. section "Enabling Qualitative Analysis").[3] The remainder of the template is enclosed in a set of start-tag and end-tag named <text>.[4] The content of this block is divided into two sections: a header, meant to contain metadata about the text, such as author, title, etc., and a body, where the content of the plain text file should be pasted. The sets of tags within the header are meant to surround information about the text, e.g., the author's name can be entered between the tags <author> and </author>. Once the template is filled out, it can be saved under a file with the ending .xml.

---

[3]The link ./corpus_style.css refers to a file named corpus_style.css located in the same folder as the XML file. The sequence ./ refers to the current folder. It may occasionally be useful to link to a stylesheet file in the parent folder, so that a common style may apply to files in multiple folders. For such a case, the reference to the parent folder can be specified with the ../ sequence.

[4]NB: The indentation used is not mandatory, but highly recommended to make the tag hierarchy clearly visible.

Applying Automatic Basic Annotation

At the current stage, the corpus file is in a valid XML format, but apart from the metadata in the header and the markers for errors found in the printed editions, it contains no annotation whatsoever. The aim of the current section is to automatically annotate the text with the following:

1. Paragraph numbering
2. Marking of passages in italics
3. Marking of direct character discourse

The *Python* script used to perform this annotation is shown in Appendix 2.

Following this preliminary annotation process, the actual annotation process can take place, which depending on the project goals and the features to be marked can be undertaken automatically or manually. Automatic annotation can be grammatical, such as part-of-speech tagging and syntactic parsing, or semantic, such as named-entity recognition or sentiment analysis. An overview of tools for automatic annotation, by no means exhaustive, is shown in Table 5. The research project for which the methodology described in the present chapter was developed requires the annotation of specific items rather than a word-by-word annotation, and therefore requires manual annotation, described in the following section.

Applying Manual Annotation

The focus of the research project for which the methodology described in the present chapter was developed lies on non-standardized linguistic features, which are to be annotated manually. To do this, a custom tag scheme distinguishing five main

Table 5 Overview of tools for automatic annotation

Name	Annotation capabilities	License
CLAWS[a] (Garside 1987, 1996; Garside and Smith 1997; Leech et al. 1994)	Part-of-speech tagging	Academic/commercial
GATE[b] (Cunningham et al. 2011, 2013)	Part-of-speech-tagging, semantic annotation, named-entity recognition	Open source (GNU LPGL)
Python+NLTK[c] (Bird et al. 2009)	Part-of-speech tagging, syntactic parsing, named-entity recognition	Open source (Apache)
TreeTagger[d] (Schmid 1994, 1995)	Part-of-speech annotation, syntactic parsing	Non-commercial

[a] Available via http://ucrel.lancs.ac.uk/claws
[b] Available via https://gate.ac.uk
[c] Available via http://www.nltk.org
[d] Available via http://www.cis.uni-muenchen.de/~schmid/tools/TreeTagger

Table 6 Overview of custom annotation scheme

Category	Raw example	Annotated example
Code	They were kampung colors	They were `<code feature="switch" meaning= "village" language="Malay">kampung</code>` colors
Grammar	He want to sign on another fireman	He `<grammar feature="VP_person" observed= "BASE" standard="3SG">want</grammar>` to sign on another fireman
Lexical	You got handphone?	You got `<lexical feature="lexeme" standard= "mobile phone">handphone</lexical>`?
Phonology	In de street	In `<phonology feature="consonant_place" observed="d" standard="D">d</phonology>`e street
Spelling	But lissen	But `<spelling observed="lissen" standard= "listen">lissen</spelling>`

categories is applied to the corpus. The categories are defined below, while Table 6 illustrates each category with an example.

code   Code-switching or code-mixing to a language other than English.
grammar   Instances of non-standardized grammar.
lexical   Lexical innovations, or lexical items bearing different meanings than in standardized varieties.
phonology   Non-standardized spelling that affects pronunciation. Sounds are represented by SAMPA rather than IPA for easier data entry.
spelling   Non-standardized spelling that does not affect pronunciation, so-called *eye dialect*.

The non-standardized linguistic features are enclosed in a set of start-tag and end-tag corresponding to the appropriate category. In addition to said linguistic features, textual features are also annotated: the `<character>` tags previously inserted automatically are edited to contain additional information such as character identity, discourse type (direct, free indirect, free indirect), and medium (speech, writing, thought). The characteristics of a text's narrator or narrators are tagged as well, with a `<narrator>` tag that includes attributes such as identity, diegetic level (extradiegetic, intradiegetic), level of participation (heterodiegetic, homodiegetic), and person (1st, 3rd).[5] Finally, information relating to the overt marking of non-standardized features and commentary on language are marked with a `<meta>` tag.

These XML tags could be entered manually in a text editor. However, given the potential for typing errors,[6] a computer-assisted manual annotation process is

---

[5]Cf. Prince (2003), Rimmon-Kenan (1983) for definitions of these terms.

[6]One could unwittingly define multiple categories such as *phonology, phnology,* or *phonlogy* rather than a unique *phonology* category.

recommended rather than a purely manual equivalent. For this reason, a custom XML editor called *XmlCat* (Percillier 2015) (short for *XML Corpus Annotation Tool*) was designed for the purpose of the study. The software allows the user to insert pairs of start-tag and end-tag from a predetermined annotation scheme by selecting the stretch of text to be annotated, then selecting the appropriate tag and attributes by clicking through radio buttons. Although originally developed as an in-house tool, *XmlCat* and the current methodology can in principle be used in any project requiring manual annotation, given that the annotation is defined in a separate file. The data format of the tag set file is YAML (Evans 2009), a format simple enough to be easily read by people, yet consistent enough to be machine-readable. A simplified example of such an external tag set file is shown and commented in Appendix 3.

An example sentence from a Scottish text (Spence 2002, p. 1001) with basic annotation contrasted with its fully annotated equivalent is given in example (2). A sample text at various annotation stages is available on the companion website.

(2)   a.   `<p id='52'>`Robert nudged him. "`<character>`Wher's yer proddy god noo!`</character>`"`</p>`

       b.   `<p id='52'>`Robert nudged him. "`<character discourse= "direct" medium="speech" name="Robert"><spelling observed="wher" standard="where">`Wher`</spelling>`'s y`<phonology feature="vowel_place" observed="e" standard="u">`e`</phonology>`r `<lexical feature= "lexeme" standard="Protestant">`proddy`</lexical>` god n`<phonology feature="vowel_monophthongisation" observed="u" standard="aU">`oo`</phonology>`! `</character>`"`</p>`

Enabling Qualitative Analysis

As can be seen in example (2), a fully annotated corpus contains a wealth of information, but is difficult to read. In order to make the corpus readable while maintaining access to the annotation data contained in the tags, the display of a corpus can be modified using CSS (*Cascading Style Sheets*). CSS are generally used to define the layout of HTML websites, but also work with XML files.[7] When a link to a CSS file is specified in the XML file (as is done in the second line of the XML template shown in section "From Plain Text to XML"), the XML file can be viewed in a web browser in such a way that tags do not impede readability. By default, XML tags are hidden so that only the plain text is displayed. By specifying a style

---

[7]Another method for styling XML is XSL (*Extensible Stylesheet Language*), which is more powerful but also more complex. The recommendation by the *World Wide Web Consortium* (W3C) is "Use CSS when you can, use XSL when you must" (Bos 2015).

in a CSS file, this default behavior can be changed, e.g., stretches of text marked by a tag can be highlighted in color, or the name of a character can be displayed in the margin. A simplified example of such a CSS file is shown below, while an expanded example is available on the companion website.

```
header {border: 2px solid black; background-color: lightgrey;
    display: block; margin-left: 10%; margin-right: 10%;}

region,country,year,author,title {display: block;}

region:before{content: "Region: "}
country:before{content: "Country: "}
year:before {content: "Year: "}
author:before {content: "Author: "}
title:before {content: "Title: "}

p {display: block; margin-left: 10%;
    margin-right: 10%; line-height: 1.5;}

p:before {content: "P. " attr(id) " "; color: lightgrey;}

italic {font-style: italic;}

character {border: 2px solid red;}

character:before {position: absolute; left: 1%; width: 8%;
    border-style: solid; border-width: thin; font-size: 50%;
    content: attr(name) "\A(" attr(discourse) " "
            attr(medium) ")";
    text-align: center; white-space: pre-wrap;
    color: white; background: red;}

grammar {background: orange;}

grammar:hover:after {
    content: " feature: " attr(feature) ", observed:
    " attr(observed) ", standard: " attr(standard);
    color: white; background: black;}
```

The CSS file defines how tags should be displayed in a web browser. The format requires the name of the tag, followed by a set of curly brackets in which the display instructions are given. Individual display options have to be followed by a semicolon, even when only one such option is given.[8] For example, the first two lines provide instructions for the header to be surrounded by a black border that is solid and two pixels wide, to have a light grey background, to be displayed in block,[9] and to have margins on the left and right side that make up ten percent of the

---

[8]Only the semicolon is relevant, which means that users can specify all display options in one line for brevity, or give one option per line for greater clarity.

[9]A block display means that the element in question should not share horizontal space. In other words, preceding and following material will be on separate lines.

browser window width. The border and background color are to make the header visibly distinct from the main text. Multiple tags can share a set of instructions, as seen in the following line, where five tags are each to be displayed on separate lines. The following lines declare that an explanatory label should stand before individual items in the header. The display of paragraphs and italics is then defined, with paragraphs preceded by their running number in light grey.

The instructions concerning the tags <character> and <grammar> are the main point of interest, as they define how character passages and annotated features should be displayed. First, sequences of character speech are to be surrounded by a red frame. Following this, character labels are to be placed in the left-hand margin (which is the reason why a ten per cent margin was defined for the tags <header> and <p>). The character labels should be placed in the left margin, with smaller white text on a red background. The content of the labels is defined as the name of the character, and on a second line the attributes discourse and medium written in parentheses.[10] The following instructions highlight text tagged with the <grammar> tag.[11] Highlighting the tagged passages in color already provides helpful information without compromising readability, but the tag attributes can also be made accessible from within the browser view. The last set of instructions display the tag attributes after the tagged passage only when the mouse cursor is positioned over it, which is achieved with the :hover sequence. The attributes are to be displayed, separated by commas, in white text over a black background, each preceded by an explanatory label. Once the mouse cursor leaves the tagged area, the attributes are hidden again, leaving only the color highlighting.

The method of styling the display of XML files using CSS makes it possible to read an annotated corpus text, while seeing tagged areas as highlights, and having access to the tag contents "on demand" by dragging the mouse cursor over highlighted areas.

Quantitative Analysis

The practice of highlighting annotated text, as discussed in the previous section, can be of great help in any qualitative analysis. However, the full potential of annotation is achieved in a quantitative approach. The present section describes how an annotated corpus can be analyzed in *R* (R Core Team 2015), a programming language and software environment for statistics and graphics, in order to reveal empirical patterns that may have remained unnoticed in a qualitative analysis. *R* is

---

[10]The line break to place the two latter attributes on a separate line is marked by \A, which is a special sequence for line breaks in CSS.

[11]Only instructions for the *grammar* category are given in this example to avoid repetition, as the other tags require the exact same instructions, save for a different highlight color. An expanded version of the CSS file can be found on the companion website.

Table 7 Selection of statistical software

Title	License
R (R Core Team 2015)	Open source (GNU GPL)
SAS (SAS Institute 2013)	Commercial
SPSS (IBM 2015)	Commercial
Stata (StataCorp 2015)	Commercial
Python+SciPy[a] (Millman and Aivazis 2011; Oliphant 2007)	Open source (BSD-new)

[a] Available via http://www.scipy.org

an emerging standard for statistics and graphics in the field of linguistics, judging by the fact that a number of introductions to quantitative linguistics based on *R* have appeared in recent years (Baayen 2008; Gries 2009, 2013; Levshina 2015). However, other academic fields may use other tools for statistical analysis, some of which are listed in Table 7.

Preparing the Data

In order to analyze the corpus in *R*, it must first be converted in a format that *R* can easily work with, ideally CSV (*Comma-Separated Values*). The CSV format stores tabular data in plain text, so that such a conversion is recommended even if readers choose to work with a spreadsheet application rather than *R*. The aim is to have a CSV file in which each row corresponds to a non-standardized feature observed in the corpus, with columns specifying metadata about the text and attributes about the feature. The *Python* script used to perform this conversion is shown in Appendix 4. The script not only collects information contained in XML tags, but also performs word counts of narrators and individual characters, which is of crucial importance to the subsequent analysis.

Installing and Running **R**

R is available for download from the official website.[12] Optionally, readers can also install *RStudio*,[13] a software environment for *R* which groups all display windows as panes in a unified window, rather than individual windows in the standard *R* application.

The *R* interface consists of a console window and a script editor. Commands entered in the console are carried out as soon as the Enter key is pressed. In contrast, commands spanning multiple lines can be entered in the script editor. Code

---

[12] Available via https://www.r-project.org.

[13] Available via https://www.rstudio.com.

in the editor can be selected, and executed with the key combinations Control-R (Windows) or Command-Enter (Mac OS X). Code entered in the script editor can be saved as a file with the ending .R.

A Sample Quantitative Analysis

In the following sample quantitative analysis, the frequency of non-standardized linguistic features in literary works is investigated, contrasted by region. The code used for this analysis is shown and discussed below. It should be noted that unlike in *Python*, the code in *R* scripts can be run interactively line by line rather than all at once. Therefore, the *R* code can be executed bit by bit, and the content of every variable can be examined individually.

The first step in the *R* script is to import the CSV file previously created. The function read.csv() imports a CSV file as a data frame, in this case under the variable name features. The function contains two arguments, the first of which is the path to the file to be imported. An alternative, shown in the example below, is to use the file.choose() function, which opens a dialog window prompting the user to select the file. The second argument indicates that the semicolon character is to be used as a column separator. The following line creates a table, or matrix, by using the xtabs() function (short for *cross tabulation*). The first argument in the function is a formula specifying the names of the columns to be cross-tabulated, the second argument specifies the data frame from which these columns originate. The matrix is saved as the variable cXr (chosen as shorthand for *category × region*). Users can see the table by executing the variable as a command. The differences between feature categories across regions are tested statistically using Pearson's χ^2 test in the third line, which is achieved by executing the function chisq.test() on the matrix created in the preceding line. The differences are statistically significant ($\chi^2 = 3230.7$, $df = 8$, $p < 2.2 \times 10^{-16}$***).

```
features <- read.csv(file.choose(),sep=";")
cXr <- xtabs(~Category+Region,features)
chisq.test(cXr)
```

The raw frequencies used for the χ^2 test above should not be used for visual comparisons, as the possibility of varying sample sizes is not taken into account. To remedy this, a process called normalization [cf. (Gries 2010, pp. 270–271)] is described below, by which a common sample size is set, and the actual frequencies are transformed accordingly for purposes of comparison. In the present example, a common sample size of 10,000 words is used. To calculate normalized frequencies, the actual sample sizes for each region have to be obtained. To avoid repeating the same code block three times to obtain the sample size for each of the regions, the relevant code is defined once as a custom function called getRegionSize(). The function first isolates a subset of rows related to the region being treated from the original data frame. The square brackets serve to access a subset of the data frame. Given that a data frame is a two-dimensional object (rows and columns), two dimensions must be specified in the square brackets, separated by a comma. The first dimension of the subset selects only those rows whose value in the `Region` column is equal to the specified value. If, for example, "Europe" is supplied as a value, only the rows from European texts will be selected as part of the subset. The second dimension, referring to columns, is left blank, meaning that all columns of the selected rows are to be kept in the subset. The subset is enclosed by the `droplevels()` function to remove any unused categories from the subset. The next command in the function retrieves the word counts for every text in the subset. The function `tapply()` takes a vector of values given as the first argument, in this case the column containing the size of each text, and groups these values according to the categories in the vector specified as the second argument, in this case the titles of the texts. The third argument specifies a function to be applied to each group. As each entry in the `Size` column contains the word count for the entire text, only one entry per title is needed, and therefore any duplicates should be removed, which the `unique()` function achieves. The last command of the function sums the counts of all titles to obtain the word count for the region, which is the value to be returned by the function.

Now that the function is defined, it can be applied for the three regions under investigation in the corpus to obtain the sample size for each region. The normalized frequencies can now be calculated. A copy of the matrix containing the raw values is created under the name `cXr.norm`, to be edited without overwriting the original values. The columns of the copied matrix are changed one by one by dividing the values in each column by the sample size of the respective region, then multiplying the result by the normalization value. The resulting table contains normalized values, and can be visualized with the `barplot()` function (shown in the top-left pane of Fig. 1). The results suggest clear differences in terms of feature density, with European texts displaying the highest feature density by far.

```
getRegionSize <- function(region) {
  regionFeatures <- droplevels(
    features[features$Region==region,])
  regionWordCounts <- tapply(regionFeatures$Size,
                             regionFeatures$Title,unique)
  return(sum(regionWordCounts))
}
EURsize <- getRegionSize("Europe")
SEAsize <- getRegionSize("Southeast Asia")
WAFsize <- getRegionSize("West Africa")
cXr.norm <- cXr
normValue <- 10000
cXr.norm[,1] <- cXr.norm[,1]/EURsize * normValue
cXr.norm[,2] <- cXr.norm[,2]/SEAsize * normValue
cXr.norm[,3] <- cXr.norm[,3]/WAFsize * normValue
barplot(cXr.norm,legend=TRUE,
        main="Categories by region per 10,000 words")
```

A proportional comparison, for example in per cent, can be obtained with relative ease. The function `prop.table()` turns raw values of a table into proportional

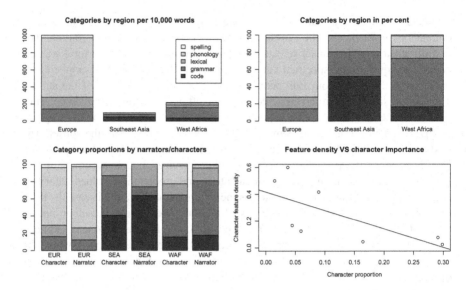

Fig. 1 Sample quantitative *R* plots

values. By default, values are changed so that the sum of the entire table equals one. The first argument is the table with the raw values. The second argument specifies whether the sum of one should apply to each row (1) or column (2) rather than the entire table. As columns correspond to regions, the latter option is chosen. The function calculates new values to achieve a sum of one per column. As per cent values are desired rather than "per one," the resulting table is multiplied by 100. The results, shown in the top-right pane of Fig. 1, clearly indicate that each region emphasizes a dominant feature category, which differs from region to region: phonology for European texts, code-switching/code-mixing for Southeast Asian texts, and grammar for West African texts.

```
cXr.perc <- prop.table(cXr,2) * 100
barplot(cXr.perc,main="Categories by region in per cent")
```

More fine-grained analyses are possible, for example, a contrast between feature proportions for characters and narrators. In order to produce such a comparison of narrators and characters, the information contained in the column `Character` is used, which provides the character name, or "NA" in case the feature is used by a narrator. As the current analysis does not distinguish individual characters, a broader division with only two levels, narrator and character, should be made. The code excerpt below does this by first creating a new empty column in the data frame, then by using a for-loop to process every row of the data frame. If the value in the `Character` column of the current row has the value "NA," then the value "Narrator" is written in the row's `CharacterStatus` column, otherwise the value "Character" is written. The values thus entered in the new column are cross-tabulated with the `Category` column for each region. The three individual tables are united to form one table, whose columns are then renamed. A conversion to percentage values is performed before plotting the results (as shown in the bottom-left pane of Fig. 1). The results show that narrators and characters use non-standardized linguistic features differently in Southeast Asian and West African texts, which suggests a certain reluctance to attribute non-standardized forms, accent features in particular, to narrators, which does not apply to European texts.

```
features$CharacterStatus <- ""
for (i in 1:nrow(features)){
    features$CharacterStatus[i] <- ifelse(
       is.na(features$Character[i]),"Narrator","Character")
}
EURnc <- xtabs(~Category+CharacterStatus,features,
              Region=="Europe")
SEAnc <- xtabs(~Category+CharacterStatus,features,
              Region=="Southeast Asia")
WAFnc <- xtabs(~Category+CharacterStatus,features,
              Region=="West Africa")
nc <- cbind(EURnc,SEAnc,WAFnc)
colnames(nc) <- c("EUR\nCharacter","EUR\nNarrator",
                 "SEA\nCharacter","SEA\nNarrator",
                 "WAF\nCharacter","WAF\nNarrator")
nc.perc <- prop.table(nc,2)*100
barplot(nc.perc,
        main="Category proportions by narrators/characters")
```

Analyses can also be performed at the level of individual texts. For example, a correlation between characters' importance and the density of their use of non-standardized linguistic features is investigated in the Scottish short story *The Orange and the Green* (Hanley 2002), as shown below. The first step in such an analysis is to isolate rows pertaining to the text from the original data frame. In this case, it is saved under the variable `toatg`, chosen as an abbreviation for the title of the text. The correlation test requires two vectors: one containing a relative measure of non-standardized linguistic features produced by each character, the other listing each character's relative importance in the text, measured as the number of words for each character divided by the total word count for characters. The number of features per character is obtained by counting the number of rows for each character, as each row stands for an observation of non-standardized linguistic feature in the text. The word count for each character is obtained using the `tapply()` function, in a similar manner to the estimation of regional word counts described earlier. The feature densities of each character are determined by dividing the vector containing the number of features per character by the vector containing the word count of each character. The relative character importance is obtained by dividing each element of the vector containing the character word counts by its sum, i.e., the total character word count. By using the `plot()` function, the correlation between the two measures can be visualized as a scatterplot. A regression line can be added to the graph by first calculating a linear model using the `lm()` function, which is then passed on to the `abline()` function, which uses the linear model to draw a regression line in the graph (cf. the bottom-right pane of Fig. 1). A correlation test, for example, Spearman's rank-sum correlation test, can be performed using the cor.test() function, which returns a statistically significant negative correlation ($r_s = -0.8809524$, $p = 0.007242**$). As such, the story's main characters present a low feature density in comparison to marginal characters. By using this pattern, marginal characters can quickly be given contours by their dense use of non-standardized features without taking additional space in the text.[14]

```
toatg <- droplevels(
    features[features$Title=="The Orange and the Green",])
characterFeatures <- xtabs(~Character,toatg)
characterSizes <- tapply(
    toatg$CharacterSize,toatg$Character,unique)
characterFeatureDensities <- characterFeatures/characterSizes
characterImportance <- characterSizes/sum(characterSizes)
plot(characterImportance,characterFeatureDensities,
    xlab="Character proportion",
    ylab="Character feature density",
    main="Feature density VS character importance")
abline(lm(characterFeatureDensities~characterImportance))
cor.test(characterImportance,characterFeatureDensities,
    method="spearman")
```

Conclusion

The methodology outlined in the present chapter describes the creation of a literary corpus, starting from a printed text to produce an annotated XML corpus, and showcases options for qualitative and quantitative analyses of the data. The individual steps of the process are summarized as a flowchart in Fig. 2.

The annotation used in the present chapter is geared towards a linguistic analysis of literary texts, more specifically the analysis of non-standardized linguistic features. However, the methodological principles put forward in the present chapter are not limited to linguistic analyses. For example, a quantitative literary analysis of texts may tag character passages, and optionally place individual chapters in tags, to objectively track which characters utter how many words in which part of the text, which can yield insights into character development and changes in character importance. Regarding the tagging of narrators, varying narratorial techniques throughout a text or an author's work can be investigated empirically. Given the flexibility of the XML format, researchers can add any number of new tags or attributes, e.g., a focalization attribute in a narrator tag, to annotate information

---

[14]A more thorough analysis of this correlation, found in Percillier and Paulin (2016), also includes characters that do not produce any non-standardized linguistic features. The results of both analyses are comparable as both point to a statistically significant negative correlation.

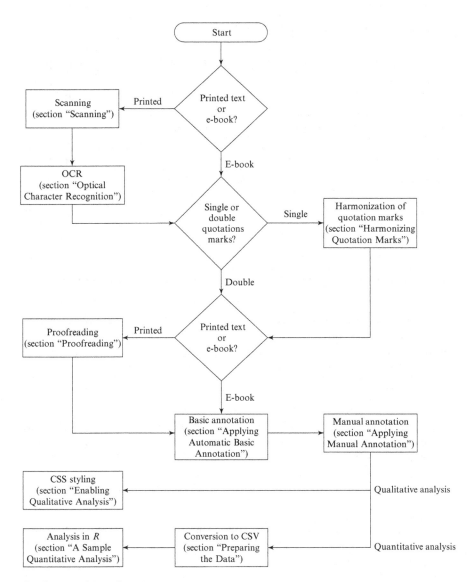

Fig. 2 Methodology flowchart

relevant to their research program. Beyond the fields of linguistics and literature, the methodology can be applied to any study requiring manual annotation so as to enable both qualitative and quantitative analyses.

Suggestions for Further Reading

The current chapter introduced a number of data formats and programming languages used in the research project for which the methodology was developed. Admittedly, following the code examples may be challenging for readers unfamiliar with programming in general. Moreover, the examples given may not necessarily be fit as user guides for readers who recognize the usefulness of the methods shown, but who have research projects of a different nature. To these readers, I can recommend some general introductions to *Python* (Shaw 2013; Sweigart 2015). Readers interested in *R* may consult general introductions (Kabacoff 2015; Teetor 2011), or introductions to *R* with an emphasis on linguistic analysis (Baayen 2008; Gries 2009, 2013; Levshina 2015), which may also be relevant to other fields in Digital Humanities.

Appendix 1: *Python* Script to Harmonize Quotations Marks

The first lines load necessary modules, i.e., components with additional features. Specifically, *codecs* adds the ability to read and write files in the Unicode format (cf. the recommendation in section "Optical Character Recognition"), and *re* enables the use of regular expressions.

```
import codecs
import re
```

The next step is to ask the user for the name of the file to be treated. The file name provided by the user is then used to open the file with this name. The file content is then read and saved as a variable called `text`.

```
iFileName = raw_input("Enter file name: ")
iFile = codecs.open(iFileName, encoding="utf-8",mode="r")
text = iFile.read()
```

The following two lines open an output file, whose name is the same as the input file save for the ending `-harmonized`. Note that the dot character in the `.txt` file ending has to be escaped with a backslash, as it would otherwise be treated as a wild card that stands for any character.

```
oFileName = re.sub("\.txt","-harmonized.txt",iFileName)
oFile = codecs.open(oFileName, encoding="utf-8",mode="w")
```

The harmonization of quotation is undertaken in two steps:

1. the replacement of closing single quotation marks by double quotation marks. In regular expressions, square brackets indicate a range of characters, so that the search term consists of one character from the set . , ; ! ? - followed by a single quotation mark character. Some of these punctuation marks are preceded by a backslash character because they are special characters, and therefore need to

be escaped. The range of punctuation characters enclosed in square brackets is surrounded by a set of round brackets. The reason for this is that we want to keep the punctuation mark when substituting the quotation mark character. The punctuation mark is solely used to detect the closing quotation mark and should not be deleted, which would happen without the round brackets. The second argument given to the function re.sub() is the replacement for the search term specified in the first argument. The \\1 sequence refers to the content of the round brackets in the first argument, which is then reproduced.

2. The opening quotation marks are handled in a similar fashion. The range [A-Z] refers to all uppercase letters from A to Z. The square brackets are preceded by _?, which means that the capital letter may or may not be preceded by an underscore, as one may have been placed as an italics marker in the proofreading process (cf. Table 4).

```
text = re.sub("([\.,;!\?\-])'","\\1"',text)
text = re.sub("'(_?[A-Z])","\\1',text)
```

The last three lines of the script write the modified text to the output file, then close the input and output files.

```
oFile.write(text)
iFile.close()
oFile.close()
```

Appendix 2: *Python* Script for Basic Automatic Annotation

After importing the required modules, as already discussed in the previous script, the script defines a custom function, which avoids repeating the block of code specified therein.[15] The instructions given in said block of code replace plain text markers with XML tags: underscores will be replaced with a set of <italic> tags, and double quotation marks will be marked with a set of <character> tags. As the start-tag and end-tag do not share the same format, simply replacing all underscores or double quotation marks with <italic> or <character> will not suffice. The strategy used instead is to number occurrences of underscore/double quotation marks, and replace odd instances with a start-tag, and even instances with an end-tag. To achieve this, a counter variable is defined, which will be used to keep track of the number of underscores or double quotations marks encountered.

```
import codecs
import re
def replaceMarker(marker,tag,text):
  counter = 0
  while re.search(marker,text):
```

---

[15]NB: The indentation shown is mandatory in *Python*, and is achieved by maintaining a consistent amount of spaces for each indentation level.

```
      counter += 1
      if counter % 2 == 1:
        text = re.sub(marker,"<"+tag+">",text,count=1)
      else:
        text = re.sub(marker,"</"+tag+">",text,count=1)
    return text
```

The next lines ask the user for an input file, which is then opened, and then proceeds to create an output file, in a similar fashion to the script in Appendix 1. In addition, two counter variables are created: one to determine the boundaries of the XML header, the other to keep a running count of paragraph numbers.

```
iFileName = raw_input("Enter file name: ")
iFile = codecs.open(iFileName,encoding="utf-8",mode="r")
oFileName = re.sub("\.xml","-basic.xml",iFileName)
oFile = codecs.open(oFileName,encoding="utf-8",mode="w")
headerStatus = 0
parCounter = 0
```

The lines of the input file are now read one by one in a for-loop. Lines occurring before the header, as well as the header itself, are to be copied to the output file without any modification. The headerStatus variable keeps track of the number of times a header tag has been encountered. The header ends once two such tags have occurred. Other lines to be copied without modification are the two <body> tags, as well as the </text> end-tag. All other lines are subject to basic automatic annotation before being written to the output file. First, the line is enclosed with a <p> tag (short for *paragraph*), which specifies the running paragraph number stored in the parCounter variable that has just been incremented. Subsequently, the custom function replaceMarker() defined above is used to replace plain text markers with XML tags, specifically underscores with <italic> tags, and double quotation marks with <character> tags. For the latter substitution, the quotation marks are reintroduced as they are part of the actual text. The modified line is then written to the output file. Once the for-loop has treated all lines of the input file, the input and output files are closed.

```
for line in iFile:
  if headerStatus < 2:
    oFile.write(line)
    if re.search("header>",line):
      headerStatus += 1
  else:
    if re.match("\n",line) == None:
      if re.search("<body>|</body>|</text>",line):
        oFile.write(line)
      else:
        parCounter += 1
        line = line.rstrip("\n")
        line = "<p id='"+str(parCounter)+"'>"+line+"</p>\n"
        line = replaceMarker("_","italic",line)
        line = replaceMarker('"',"character",line)
        line = re.sub("<character>",'"<character>',line)
```

```
        line = re.sub("</character>",'</character>"',line)
        oFile.write(line)
iFile.close()
oFile.close()
```

Appendix 3: Simplified Example of a Tag Set File in the YAML Format

The YAML file shown is divided into two parts, each beginning with - - -, and the sequence . . . acting as a separator. The first part defines the tag inventory and the possible attributes of each tag.[16] Hierarchy is marked by indentation.[17] Elements followed by a colon contain a list. Lists can be nested, as can be seen for the category *code*. Elements preceded by hyphens have no subordinate items. Tags are represented by elements at the top of the hierarchy. The elements at the bottom of the hierarchy are to be treated as tag attributes by *XmlCat*. Intermediate elements, such as mixing and switching in the *code* category, represent distinct features within their category and will be listed under a feature attribute by *XmlCat*. The second part of the YAML file specifies a color profile for the tags to be displayed. Highlighting tagged sequences makes it easier to read an annotated text. The practice is discussed in further detail in section "Enabling Qualitative Analysis."

```
    ---
    character:
        - discourse
        - medium
        - name
    narrator:
        - identity
        - level
        - participation
        - person
    code:
        mixing:
            - language
            - meaning
        switching:
            - language
            - meaning
    spelling:
        - observed
```

---

[16]The actual YAML file used for the project is over 200 lines long. The attributes for the categories *phonology*, *grammar*, and *lexical* have been left out in the present appendix due to their length, which would have made the example overly repetitive. Consult the companion website for a full example.

[17]Tab indents are not permitted. A consistent number of spaces, e.g., 4 spaces, should be used instead.

```
    - standard
...
---
header: gray
character: red
code: magenta
spelling: rosybrown
```

Appendix 4: *Python* Script to Convert XML Annotation to CSV

The first four lines import the required modules. The modules `codecs` and `re` are already known. The module `os`, specifically its subset `listdir`, allows to obtain a list of all files in a given folder. The module `bs4`, specifically its subset `BeautifulSoup`, makes it possible to parse XML data with relative ease.

Two custom functions that will be used on multiple occasions later on are then defined. The first function, `getCount()`, calculates the word counts of text marked by a specific tag. It will be used specifically to obtain word counts of individual characters. The purpose of the second function, `getAttribute()`, is to extract specific attributes from tags. In the first two lines of the function, the specific attribute is queried from the tag. Querying a non-existing attribute from a tag would produce a so-called key error, which would result in the program quitting immediately. To avoid this, the query is first tried, and an exception is defined, which states that the query should return "NA" in case the attribute cannot be found in the tag. Once the two custom functions have been defined, an output file is created and a header line with column names is written, with semicolons serving as column separators. The last character written in the CSV header line is a line break (\n), which corresponds to a new row in the tabular data.

```python
import codecs
import re
from os import listdir
from bs4 import BeautifulSoup
def getCount(tag,attribute,sample):
  tags = sample.find_all(tag)
  tagCount = {}
  for tag in tags:
    currentTagSize = len(tag.text.split())
    if tag[attribute] in tagCount.keys():
      tagCount[tag[attribute]] += currentTagSize
    else:
      tagCount[tag[attribute]] = currentTagSize
  return tagCount
def getAttribute(tag,attribute):
  try:
    value = tag[attribute]
  except KeyError:
```

```
        value = "NA"
    return value
outp = codecs.open("features.csv",encoding="utf-8",mode="w")
outp.write("Region;Country;Year;Author;Title;Size;")
outp.write("Paragraph;NarratorID;NarratorSize;")
outp.write("NarratorLevel;NarratorParticipation;")
outp.write("NarratorPerson;Character;CharacterSize;")
outp.write("Discourse;Medium;Category;Feature;Observed;")
outp.write("Standard;Language;Meaning\n")
```

A list of all files in the current directory is created, but only files with the ending
.xml are considered in the for-loop. Each XML file is treated in turn. It is first
parsed, and the metadata contained in the header is read and stored as variables. The
textual body is then isolated from the header, and the word count of the entire text is
accessed and stored. The function getCount(), defined earlier, is used to obtain
a word count for each individual character. An "NA" key with a matching value is
added to prevent key errors when a character word count is queried outside of a
character tag.

```
fileList = listdir(".")
for file in fileList:
    if re.search("\.xml$",file):
        xmlFile = codecs.open(file,encoding="utf-8",mode="r")
        parsedXml = BeautifulSoup(xmlFile,"xml")
        xmlFile.close()
        region = parsedXml.find("region").text
        country = parsedXml.find("country").text
        year = parsedXml.find("year").text
        author = parsedXml.find("author").text
        title = parsedXml.find("title").text
        body = parsedXml.find("body")
        textSize = len(body.text.split())
        charCount = getCount("character","name",parsedXml)
        charCount["NA"] = "NA"
```

A list of all feature tags in the corpus file is queried. Given that several tags fit into
this category, they are all queried at once using the pipe character, which stands for
"or." The query is placed in the re.compile() function as regular expressions
are not directly supported by the .find_all() method. The list of tags thus
obtained is then treated item by item in a for-loop. Before handling the tag attributes
themselves, data from superordinate tags are gathered, i.e., paragraph, narrator, and
character information. Every parent tag is checked, and if it belongs to the relevant
category, its contents are processed. Character attributes are assigned "NA" defaults
beforehand. These are to be replaced if a parent <character> is encountered,
i.e., if the feature tag occurs in character discourse as opposed to narrator discourse.
To obtain a word count for a <narrator> tag, it is not sufficient to count the plain
text enclosed. Rather, the word counts for character passages within the narrator
sequence should be excluded. For this reason, a character word count is calculated
for the current narrator passage, which is then subtracted from the total word count

of the narrator passage. Once the attributes of the parent tags have been processed, the attributes of the actual tag are accessed.

```
tagList = parsedXml.find_all(re.compile(
"code|grammar|lexical|phonology|spelling"))
for tag in tagList:
  charName,charDiscourse,charMedium = "NA","NA","NA"
  for parent in tag.parents:
    if parent.name == "p":
      para = getAttribute(parent,"id")
    elif parent.name == "narrator":
      narID = getAttribute(parent,"identity")
      narLevel = getAttribute(parent,"level")
      narPart = getAttribute(parent,"participation")
      narPerson = getAttribute(parent,"person")
      charsInNar = getCount("character","name",parent)
      charsInNar = sum(charsInNar.values())
      narCount = len(parent.text.split()) - charsInNar
    elif parent.name == "character":
      charName = getAttribute(parent,"name")
      charDiscourse = getAttribute(parent,"discourse")
      charMedium = getAttribute(parent,"medium")
  tagCategory = tag.name
  tagFeature = getAttribute(tag,"feature")
  tagObserved = getAttribute(tag,"observed")
  tagStandard = getAttribute(tag,"standard")
  tagLanguage = getAttribute(tag,"language")
  tagMeaning = getAttribute(tag,"meaning")
```

The remainder of the script mainly shows the writing of the collected data to the output file. In a similar vein to the header line, this process is shown in multiple lines rather than one very long line for reasons of clarity. As already mentioned, semicolons serve as columns separators and therefore occur between every data item. The last item is followed by a line break, which corresponds to a new row in the tabular data. Once the indented code block has been reiterated for every file, the program proceeds to the last line, which closes the output file, after which the program quits. The resulting output file is a CSV file listing every feature tag row by row, and can be opened in any spreadsheet application or imported into *R*.

```
  outp.write(region+";"+country+";"+year+";"+author+";")
  outp.write(title+";"+str(textSize)+";"+str(para)+";")
  outp.write(narID+";"+str(narCount)+";")
  outp.write(narLevel+";"+narPart+";"+narPerson+";")
  outp.write(charName+";"+str(charCount[charName])+";")
  outp.write(charDiscourse+";"+charMedium+";")
  outp.write(tagCategory+";"+tagFeature+";")
  outp.write(tagObserved+";"+tagStandard+";")
  outp.write(tagLanguage+";"+tagMeaning+"\n")
outp.close()
```

References

ABBYY, FineReader (2016). Available via http://www.abbyy.com/finereader. Cited 30 January 2016

C. Achebe, *A Man of the People* (Penguin, London, 1966)

Adobe, Acrobat (2016). Available via https://acrobat.adobe.com. Cited 30 January 2016

R.H. Baayen, *Analyzing Linguistic Data* (Cambridge University Press, Cambridge, 2008)

Bare Bones Software, TextWrangler. Available via http://www.barebones.com/products/textwrangler. Cited 19 March 2016

S. Behnel, lxml (2015). Available via http://lxml.de. Cited 26 January 2016

D. Biber, S. Conrad, R. Reppen, *Corpus Linguistics: Investigating Language Structure and Use* (Cambridge University Press, Cambridge, 1998)

S. Bird, E. Loper, E. Klein, *Natural Language Processing with Python* (O'Reilly Media Inc., Sebastopol, CA, 2009)

B. Bos, CSS & XSL (2015). Available via http://www.w3.org/Style/CSS-vs-XSL. Cited 1 April 2016

H. Cunningham, D. Maynard, K. Bontcheva, V. Tablan, N. Aswani, I. Roberts, G. Gorrell, A. Funk, A. Roberts, D. Damljanovic, T. Heitz, M.A. Greenwood, H. Saggion, J. Petrak, Y. Li, W. Peters, *Text Processing with GATE (Version 6)* (GATE, Sheffield, 2011)

H. Cunningham, V. Tablan, A. Roberts, K. Bontcheva, Getting more out of biomedical documents with GATE's full lifecycle open source text analytics. PLoS Comput. Biol. **9**(2) (2013). doi:10.1371/journal.pcbi.1002854

Distributed Proofreaders Foundation, DPCustomMono2 (2015). Available via http://www.pgdp.net/wiki/DPCustomMono2. Cited 16 January 2016

C.C. Evans, YAML (2009). Available via http://yaml.org. Cited 21 January 2016

R. Garside, The CLAWS word-tagging system, in *The Computational Analysis of English: A Corpus-based Approach*, ed. by R. Garside, G. Leech, G. Sampson (Longman, London, 1987), pp. 30–41

R. Garside, The robust tagging of unrestricted text: the BNC experience, in *Using Corpora for Language Research: Studies in the Honour of Geoffrey Leech*, ed. by J. Thomas, M. Short (Longman, London, 1996), pp. 167–180

R. Garside, N. Smith, A hybrid grammatical tagger: CLAWS 4, in *Corpus Annotation: Linguistic Information from Computer Text Corpora*, ed. by R. Garside, G. Leech, T. McEnery (Longman, London, 1997), pp. 102–121

S.Th. Gries, *Quantitative Corpus Linguistics with R: A Practical Introduction.* (Routledge, London, 2009)

S.Th. Gries, Useful statistics for corpus linguistics, in *A Mosaic of Corpus Linguistics: Selected Approaches*, ed. by A. Sánchez, M. Almela (Peter Lang, Frankfurt, 2010), pp. 269–291

S.Th. Gries, *Statistics for Linguistics with R: A Practical Introduction* (de Gruyter, Berlin, 2013)

E. Hamrick, D. Hamrick, VueScan (2016). Available via https://www.hamrick.com. Cited 30 January 2016

C. Hanley, The Orange and the Green, in *Scottish Literature in the Twentieth Century. An Anthology*, ed. by D. McCordick (Scottish Cultural Press, Dalkeith, 2002), pp. 765–767

D. Ho, Notepad++ (2016). Available via https://notepad-plus-plus.org. Cited 19 March 2016

IBM, SPSS (2015). Available via http://www.ibm.com/software/analytics/spss. Cited 21 March 2016

IRIS, Readiris (2015). Available via http://www.irislink.com/readiris. Cited 30 January 2016

R.I. Kabacoff, *R in Action: Data Analysis and Graphics with R* (Manning Publications, Greenwich, CT, 2015)

G. Leech, R. Garside, M. Bryant, CLAWS4: the tagging of the British National Corpus, in *Proceedings of the 15th International Conference on Computational Linguistics (COLING 94)*, Kyoto (1994), pp. 622–628

N. Levshina, *How to do Linguistics with R* (John Benjamins, Amsterdam, 2015). doi:10.1075/z.195

P. Maggi, P. Borelli, S. Frécinaux, J. van den Kieboom, J. Willcox, C. Celorio, F. Mena Quintero, gedit (2015). Available via https://wiki.gnome.org/Apps/Gedit. Cited 19 March 2016

Microsoft, OneNote (2016). Available via http://onenote.com. Cited 30 January 2016

K.J. Millman, M. Aivazis, Python for scientists and engineers. Comput. Sci. Eng. **13**, 9–12 (2011). doi:10.1109/MCSE.2011.36

T.E. Oliphant, Python for scientific computing. Comput. Sci. Eng. **9**, 10–20 (2007). doi:10.1109/MCSE.2007.58

C. Paulin, M. Percillier, Oral varieties of English in a literary corpus of West African and South East Asian prose (1954–2013): commitment to local identities and catering for foreign readers. *Etudes de stylistique anglaise* 59–79 (2015)

M. Percillier, XmlCat (2015). Available via http://lilpa.unistra.fr/fdt/ressources. Cited 29 March 2016

M. Percillier, C. Paulin, A corpus linguistic investigation of world Englishes in literature. *World Englishes* (2016). doi:10.1111/weng.12208

Project Gutenberg Literary Archive Foundation, Project Gutenberg (2015). Available via http://www.gutenberg.org/wiki/Main_Page. Cited 11 January 2016

G. Prince, *A Dictionary of Narratology* (University of Nebraska Press, Lincoln, 2003)

Python Software Foundation, Python. Available via https://www.python.org. Cited 15 January 2016

R Core Team, *R: A Language and Environment for Statistical Computing* (R Foundation for Statistical Computing, Vienna, 2015). Available via https://www.R-project.org. Cited 26 January 2016

L. Richardson, Beautiful Soup (2015). Available via http://www.crummy.com/software/BeautifulSoup. Cited 26 January 2016

S. Rimmon-Kenan, *Narrative Fiction: Contemporary Poetics* (Routledge, London, 1983)

SAS Institute, SAS (2013). Available via http://www.sas.com. Cited 21 March 2016

H. Schmid, Probabilistic part-of-speech tagging using decision trees, in *Proceedings of International Conference on New Methods in Language Processing*, Manchester (1994)

H. Schmid, Improvements in part-of-speech tagging with an application to German, in *Proceedings of the ACL SIGDAT-Workshop*, Dublin (1995)

Z.A. Shaw, Learn Python the Hard Way (2013). Available via http://learnpythonthehardway.org/book. Cited 1 April 2016

R. Smith, Tesseract (2015). Available via https://github.com/tesseract-ocr. Cited 30 January 2016

A. Spence, Its colours they are fine, in *Scottish Literature in the Twentieth Century. An Anthology*, ed. by D. McCordick (Scottish Cultural Press, Dalkeith, 2002), pp. 998–1005

StataCorp, Stata (2015). Available via http://www.stata.com. Cited 21 March 2016

A. Sweigart, Automate the boring stuff with Python (2015). Available via https://automatetheboringstuff.com. Cited 1 April 2016

P. Teetor, *R Cookbook* (O'Reilly Media, Sebastopol, CA, 2011)

Part III
Engaging Social Data

Content and Sentiment Analysis on Online Social Networks (OSNs)

Davide Di Fatta and Roberto Musotto

Abstract The growing importance of the internet and online social networks (OSNs) has opened new doors to the digital humanities. Researchers have started to explore approaches and strategies available through social media and particularly through OSNs, but this field is still little unexplored and it requires further study.

OSNs include social components, such as comment fields for users and evaluation form that are a great source of information about users' opinion, sentiment, and feelings. These data could be very attractive for the firm, therefore, how to exploit this information?

This theoretical study aims to shine a light over the application of content and sentiment analysis to the new field of OSNs, passing from opinion mining to integrated sentiment analysis (iSA). iSA is the contact point between sentiment analysis and opinion mining, held together in order to create a new method in order to capture not only the opinion, but also the polarity (positive or negative) of the sentiment.

Our conclusions rely on the following areas: the first is related to the importance of using content and sentiment analysis on the OSNs; the second conclusion is about the need to introduce appropriate new human resources able to manage social media marketing (SMM) instruments; the third is the ability to estimate the online activities performance through specific indicators; the last conclusion deals with the so-called social media return on investment, which is much debated in the literature and, therefore, represents a challenge for further study.

Introduction

Recently, scholars have increased attention on internet issues (Hanna et al. 2011; Kaplan and Haenlein 2011; Kietzmann et al. 2011; Leamer and Storper 2014).

D. Di Fatta, PhD (✉) • R. Musotto, PhD
University of Messina, Messina, Italy
e-mail: davide.difatta@unime.it; roberto.musotto@unime.it; robertomusotto@gmail.com

© Springer International Publishing AG 2017
S. Hai-Jew (ed.), *Data Analytics in Digital Humanities*, Multimedia Systems and Applications, DOI 10.1007/978-3-319-54499-1_5

The engagement between the humanities and social media could help the understanding of the digital humanities issue. Particularly, in recent years, researchers have focused on exploring the marketing approaches and strategies now available through social media (Ashley and Tuten 2015; Di Fatta et al. 2016) and the online social network (OSNs): many authors (Pak and Paroubek 2010; Kumar and Sebastian 2012; Takahashi et al. 2016) studied Twitter using sentiment and content analysis.

Social networks such as Twitter and Facebook have caused a revolution in our way of life: they are becoming an integral part of our life. From the economic point of view, OSNs are also a business opportunity. Most traditional online media include social components, such as comment fields for users and evaluation forms. Social network sites also provide rich sources of behavioral data. Profile and linkage data from ONSs can be gathered either through the use of automated collection techniques or through datasets provided directly from the social network owner (Ellison 2007). In other words, all these factors are a big source of data about users' feelings. How to exploit this communicational potential?

Our aim is to apply content analysis (Krippendorff 1980a), opinion mining, and sentiment analysis to OSNs in order to derive the economic implications helpful to the full understanding of the internet economy. All these methods can work together dealing with the computational treatment of opinion (i.e., sentiment) and subjectivity in text: this is the so-called iSA (Hopkins and King 2010), meaning integrated sentiment analysis, which will be explained later.

The work is structured as follows: firstly, we will propose the content analysis theoretical framework, dealing subsequently with the transition from opinion mining to the iSA. The next section is about application of content and sentiment analysis of the OSNs. Then we will discuss the problem of measuring online activities performance. Finally, a brief summary and conclusions will follow.

Content Analysis Theoretical Framework

"Content analysis involves replicable and valid methods for making inferences from observed communications to their context" (Krippendorff 1980a, p. 69). However, its definition has been various extensions for a large bundle of methods and approaches that study information from any kind of document. Rather than being a single method, Hsieh and Shannon (2002) show three distinct approaches to content analysis: conventional, directed, or summative. In the first (conventional content analysis), coding categories are derived directly from the text data. In the second (directed approach), analysis begin with a theory or relevant research findings as guidance for initial codes. The third (summative content analysis) is based on counting and comparisons, usually of keywords or content, followed by the interpretation of the underlying context.

Once the content analysis has been defined, what about the purpose? It aims to reach a broad and concise description of a document (Cavanagh, 1997) and it allows the researcher to better understand the data.

Content analysis requires valid methods. Any valid method requires internal and external validity. The first one consists of stable, reproducible, and accurate results. The second one is the ability to extent the results of a study, generalizing to other situations and data, such as other place, people, and time. External validity is the proper validity. It is the specific kind of information employed in the process of validation (Krippendorff 1980b).

According to this point of view, validity can be also product or process oriented. Product oriented validity (or pragmatical validity) focuses on the outcome and it evaluates the robustness of a method from the result obtained. Process oriented validity (or construct validity) is the degree to which a method is able to measure specific information.

Validity can be also correlational or predictive. The first is the degree to which findings obtained by one method correlate with findings obtained by another. The predictive validity is the degree to which predictions obtained by a method agree with directly observable facts. Correlational and predictive validity can also be distinguished by being direct or indirect. Direct methods of validation show the results of a content analysis for what they aim to describe. Indirect ones correlate the observable information with a not observable meaning or perception (Krippendorff 2004).

Before Krippendorf, other scholars were interested in content analysis. Indeed, another widely used definition of content analysis is that of Berelson (1952) who described it as a: "research technique for the objective, systematic and quantitative description of the manifest content of communication" (p. 18).

This definition has been confuted by Berger and Luckman (1966): they suggested that it is not possible to produce totally objective results, because the analysis will be always influenced by the interpreter of data. However, according to Sandelowski (1995), Berelson's argument has the great advantage of summing up every issue of content analysis: validity, manifest data, and accuracy. Nevertheless, Krippendorf's conceptualization is the most widely accepted in the literature.

However, some quantitative researchers are skeptical, because this method is not univocal and it is likely to remain a vague set of un-coded ideas (Rourke et al. 2001). Other authors consider content analysis a simple technique that does not reach a detailed statistical analysis (Hsieh and Shannon 2002).

The major problem of content analysis could be the absence of strict guidelines, but, on the other hand, this is also an advantage: it is a more flexible instrument that allows the identifying of critical processes inside documents (Lederman 1991). This in fact makes it a very versatile technique that can be adapted in various areas. The next sections will show in more detail how to analyze media messages using content analysis (Riff et al. 2014).

From Opinion Mining to Integrated Sentiment Analysis

The growing number of blogs and social networks has generated a large availability and popularity of opinion-rich resources. Therefore new opportunities and challenges arise by using information technologies to seek out and understand peoples' opinions and sentiments: some authors suggested Twitter as a corpus for opinion mining and sentiment analysis (Pak and Paroubek 2011). Recently Takahashi et al. (2016) used Twitter for the analysis of Coffee Service Quality and Customer Value and they found that opinions influence our behaviors, and perceptions of reality are filtered through sentiments, evaluations, and emotions.

Although sentiment analysis and opinion mining mostly refer to the same field, there are some differences between them: usually sentiment analysis refers more to the polarity (positive or negative) of a sentiment, while opinion mining relates to the motivations behind the sentiment (Dave et al. 2003; Pang and Lee 2008; Liu 2012).

Therefore, a better understanding of these concepts is required. More in depth, opinion mining is a discipline at the crossroads of information retrieval and computational linguistics, which concerns with the opinion expressed in a text (Esui and Sebastiani 2006). Opinion mining is used in a wide set of applications, ranging from tracking users' opinions about products or services, to customer relationship management.

Sentiment analysis is a method for evaluating the polarity of specific information in a document, i.e., through scoring or tagging (Nasukawa and Yi 2003). Scoring aligns a text along a systematic scale: thus, the scoring models are the best response to the need to create classifications, to profile and to predict behavior. The tagging technique evaluates sets of terms and categorized into macro semantic categories. In other words, a tag is a keyword (something like a label), which is associated with selected information.

Sentiment analysis is founded on four principles taken from Grimmer and Stewart (2013):

1. All quantitative models of language are wrong, but some are useful.
2. Quantitative methods augment humans, not replace them.
3. There is no globally best method for automated text analysis.
4. Validate, validate, validate (We must always validate the analysis).

Although they are different, opinion mining and sentiment analysis can work together in dealing with the computational treatment of opinion and subjectivity in text (Pang and Lee 2008). Hopkins and King (2010) proposed a new method to estimate the primary quantity of interest in many social science applications. Sentiment analysis and opinion mining are held together in order to create something new: this is the so-called integrated sentiment analysis (iSA), where individual and aggregate classifications of feelings and motivations are translated into statistics.

Integrated sentiment analysis gives approximately unbiased estimates of category proportions even when the optimal classifier performs poorly. The main advantage of iSA is flexibility: on the one hand, it gets on well with qualitative and quantitative methods (McDonald et al. 2007). On the other hand, it is possible to apply iSA in different fields: from the theoretical point of view, Lai and To (2015) proposed a grounded theory approach; from the practical point of view, Li and Wu (2010) applied iSA for online forums hotspot detection and forecast. Kuo et al. (2015) for users' social interaction patterns in micro-blogs. Menner et al. (2016) used iSA to identify relevant topics in tourism review. The common feature in all these studies is the iSA's versatility, which emerges as a flexible and multidisciplinary method.

Therefore, why do not apply these intuitions on the new social media and social network websites (i.e., Facebook and Twitter)? In the next section, we will show some insights about Content and Sentiment Analysis on OSNs.

Content and Sentiment Analysis to OSNs

The growing relevance of sentiment analysis coincides with the growth of social media and social networks (Liu and Zhang 2012). Online social networks (OSN) have attracted millions of users since their introduction, many of whom have integrated these sites into their daily practices. According to Faloutsos et al. (2010) OSNs have transformed the way users communicate. Therefore, in recent years, OSNs have also attracted the attention of academic researchers, intrigued by their affordances and reach. However, what are online social networks?

Although there are many differences, it is possible to outline some common characteristics among all the OSNs: (1) constructing a public or semi-public profile within a bounded system, (2) articulating a list of other users with whom they share a connection, and (3) viewing and traversing their list of connections and those made by others within the system (Boyd and Ellison 2007).

What makes social network sites unique is not that they allow individuals to meet strangers, but rather that they enable users to articulate and make visible their social networks.

Dealing with OSN, the reference point in the sector is Facebook, which was object of the first world-scale social network graph-distance computations (Ugander et al. 2011).

Before entering into results details, it might be useful to clarify the concept of network analysis: it was defined as a methodology for analysis of social and interpersonal relations by Burt (1984). Then, Wasserman and Faust (1994) theorized social network analysis (SNA) methods and applications.

For what concerns the purposes of this manuscript, the crucial point is to understand the concept of degrees of separation. Let us start from the analysis of an ordered theoretical network, meaning that each node of the network is connected to the next. Therefore, to move from point 1 to point 3, you must necessarily pass through point 2. In this case, there are two degrees of separation. Generally, we realize that there are many degrees of separation that combine elements are spatially distant.

Furthermore, for studying network connections, it is also useful to consider graph theory, which is a branch of mathematics. Graph theory studies the various ways in which certain points in the network are connected[1].

Coming back to Facebook, the results by Ugander et al. (2011) rely on three main observations: (a) this online social network is nearly fully connected, with 99.91% of individuals belonging to a single large connection. (b) The neighborhoods users graph[2] contains a dense structure. (c) There is a strong effect of age on friendship preferences, as well as a globally modular community structure driven by nationality, but there is not any strong gender effect. In other words, these findings means that Facebook is a compact network in which users are interconnected with each other in a dense way.

Other authors studied Facebook users (Backstrom et al. 2012) discovering that, at the time of research, there were 721 million users with 69 billion friendship links. They found an average distance of 4.74, corresponding to 3.74 intermediaries between the each node. These findings are also consistent with Barnett (2012), who found about four degrees of separation on Facebook.

Quite similar results arrived from studies carried out on Twitter (Cheng 2010). Analyzing more than 5.2 billion Twitter friendships and followers, it was discovered that Twitter is a social network site in which the average distance is 4.67, corresponding to 3.32 intermediaries between each node.

In other words, after visiting an average of 3.32 people within the friend network, Twitter users can expect to find one of their followers with a standard deviation of 1.25 (Cheng 2010).

These data serve to illustrate the relevance of the OSNs, but why they are so relevant for the firm?

There are at least two reasons: the first is that they are a virtual network that conveys the exchange of information between users. OSNs have a relevant role because they are an extraordinary source of data: many authors (Pak and Paroubek, 2010; Kumar and Sebastian 2012; Takahashi et al. 2016) suggested Twitter as a corpus for opinion mining and sentiment analysis. Similarly, Ortigosa et al. (2014) proposed the use of sentiment analysis on Facebook. They studied how adaptive e-learning systems support personalized learning, by considering the user's emotional state when recommending him/her the most suitable activities to be tackled at each time. On the other hand, the students' sentiments towards a course can serve as feedback for teachers, especially in the case of online learning, where face-to-face contact is less frequent (Ortigosa et al. 2014).

The second reason is that OSNs can provide an expression of sentiment. Therefore, sentiment analysis on the OSNs could be a very powerful tool. Indeed,

---

[1]From a graphical point of view, a graph consists of two sets, the so-called vertices and edges, and an incidence relation between them (Gross and Yellen 2005).

[2]The neighborhoods user graph is the graph with the set of all the vertices (i.e., users) adjacent to selected starting point. More generally, the ith neighborhood of v is the set of all vertices that lie at the distance i from v (Brouwer et al. 1989).

OSNs are not only sources of big data, but above all, they provide emotional reactions, generated by the various market players and social network users, which can be measurable.

How is it possible to be able to exploit this communicational potential? Yet, in the 2000s the first research path began (Goldenberg et al. 2001; Henning-Thurau et al. 2004) about the effect of word-of-mouth (WOM[3]) marketing on member growth within OSN.

For what concerns this study, the crucial point is the ability to analyze media messages, using quantitative content analysis. In this way, quantitative content analysis identifies the systematic assignment of communication content to categories according to some rules, and then the analysis of relationships involving those categories using certain statistical methods (Riff et al. 2014).

This definition lacks any specification of appropriate types of communication to be examined (e.g., newspaper, books, web sites, or blogs) or the types of content qualities explored: therefore why do not apply this method on the OSNs?

Through specific software systems, it is possible to classify documents, which deals with certain topics, in: instinctive-positive (e.g., love, fun, joy, excitement); rational-positive (e.g., gratitude, friendliness, satisfaction, surprise); instinctive-negative (e.g., fear, sadness, hate, anger, nervousness, aggression, pity, disgust); rational-negative (e.g., grief, shame, anxiety, disappointment, envy, humiliation, boredom, dissatisfaction).

Let us suppose that we have to study the sentiment for a given brand. We must consider the so-called instinctive sentiments, which identify the emotional reactions, without specific reasons (opposed to the rational sentiment, which will be discussed later).

Specifically the instinctive sentiments can be positive or negative: positive instinctive sentiments measure attachment to the brand; negative instinctive sentiments show a prejudice that takes the user walks away from the brand.

Conversely, the so-called rational sentiments identify a reasoned response. The positive ones are awards for the brand, while negative values are an expression of dissatisfaction or disapproval.

Crossing these variables, we developed a model where it is possible to identify six areas. At the extremes, we find the positive sentiment area, resulting from rational and instinctive (positive) sentiment; and the negative sentiment area, resulting from rational and instinctive (negative) sentiment. The other two areas can be divided into two other segments.

Users who express positive sentiment can be classified into an identification area (positive sentiment, without a clear motivation) and adhesion area (positive sentiment because of rational and precise evidence).

---

[3]For a definition of word-of-mouth communication (WOM) the main reference is Dichter (1966). The meaning involves the passing of information between a non-commercial communicator and a receiver concerning a brand, a product, or a service.

Table 1 Sentiment classification—authors' elaboration

Areas	Positive rational sentiment	Positive instinctive sentiment	Negative rational sentiment	Negative instinctive sentiment
Positive sentiment	x	X		
Negative sentiment			x	x
Identification		X		
Adhesion	x			
Disapproval			x	
Aversion				x

Users who express negative sentiment can be divided into a disapproval area (negative sentiment because of precise and rational elements) and aversion area (negative sentiment, without a clear motivation).

The above-defined six areas are summarized in Table 1.

This methodology could be very useful in order to capture customer preferences and feelings. Another advantage is that this model emphasizes not only quantitative aspects, but also qualitative approach to human behavior.

Online Activities Performance and Social Media Return on Investment

The previous section discussed the issue of determining the sentiment with a qualitative approach. However, the world of OSNs cannot give up a quantitative approach, especially with respect to results and performance. Therefore, a further question arises: how to measure the performance of online activities?

This is one of the most critical points of OSNs topic: on the one hand, it could be a limitation, on the other it can become a challenge for further research. The performance of online activities is mostly indirect and therefore it is difficult to quantify: increased online visibility, growing numbers of followers, greater appeal of the brand, product, or service (naming only a few examples).

This issue was raised by Hoffman and Fodor (2010), who wondered: is it possible to measure the social media Return On Investment (ROI)? Some authors have proposed a specific formulation of the ROI for online activities (Cosenza 2014). Other authors (Kumar and Mirchandani 2012; Kumar et al. 2013) studied how social media ROI affect general performance of the firm, focusing also on the indirect effects: the return on engagement (ROE), the return on participation (ROP), and the return on listening (ROL).

Instead, Blanchard (2009) suggested that it is impossible to quantify online activities performance, while acknowledging the existence of an indirect effect.

The debate is still open and there is no consensus in the literature (Fisher 2009). Our suggestion is that, regardless of the acronyms, it is necessary to implement a sort of measure of the performance for online activities. In other words, something must be measured. It is, indeed, possible to develop a check list of measurable attributes: web analytics (number of visitors, navigation time for each page, bounce rate), velocity (page load time, server timeout), attention (duration on site), participation (comments, trackbacks, citation), and social features (i.e., Facebook likes, Tweets, Pinterest Pins, etc.). They are proxy variables for measuring online performance.

With respect to social media activities, it is also possible to suggest some specific indicators. Murdough (2009) proposed a social media measurement process in five steps: concept, definition, design, deployment, and optimization. The first step (concept) relies on the conceptualization of the object of the analysis. The second step (definition) deals with the outline of the social media strategy, that is the way in which the defined goals are achieved; the third step is to develop social media tactics; the fourth step (deploy) implements and launches the program; the final step (optimization) synthesizes social performance drivers and identifies corrective actions and adjustment. Then, this kind of process is circular and virtuous: after the optimization phase, a new concept will arise and the process will re-restart.

As will be described in the conclusive section, there is a feel rouge that runs through this manuscript: the need to manage these new tools. In order to approach the OSNs, the presence within the company of specific professionals in the field is strictly required.

Conclusions

OSNs are becoming an integral part of our life: as discussed in the previous sections, most traditional online media include social components, such as comment fields for users and evaluation forms. Therefore, the growing of blogs and OSNs generated a large availability and popularity of opinion-rich resources. The explosive growth of sentiment analysis coincided with the proliferation of web related media. Firms have taken away the potential of this phenomenon, but still a long road must be traveled before coming to a full exploitation of these data. In light of this reasoning, managing OSNs is a key factor to understand the multiplicity of information surrounding us.

Concluding, our final suggestions rely on four areas. The first one is related to the importance of applying content and sentiment analysis on the OSNs in order to classify and to interpret the numerical data collected, for instance, on Facebook and Twitter. Calabrese et al. (2015) show that it is feasible to perform sentiment analysis on Facebook with high accuracy (83.27%): then it is possible to conclude that the results have a good reliability level.

The second conclusion deals with the need to introduce appropriate new human resources especially dedicated to organizing the activities on the web: indeed, according to Baye et al. (2016), new figures are emerging such as social media managers, web strategists, SEO (search engine optimization), or SEM (search engine marketing) consultants.

Social media marketing (SMM) considers all these aspects and takes advantage of social networking to help a company increase brand exposure and broaden customer reach. The SMM goal is usually to create content compelling enough that users will share it with their social networks. In other words, social media marketing is the professional use of social media in order to facilitate information or product/service exchanges between consumers and organizations (Tuten and Solomon 2014). The SMM, therefore, requires the use of qualified and specifically trained figures in order to handle social media in all its facets: the previous point is strictly related with this second suggestion. While recognizing the importance of OSNs, firms would risk nullifying their effort by entrusting the management of these aspects to people, who are inadequately qualified.

The third conclusion relies on the debate about how to estimate online activities performance. Planning marketing initiatives through social media clashes daily with the lack of universally accepted metrics. The debate still remains open (Fisher 2009). Our suggestion is that not only a performance measure is strictly necessary, but it also possible using the above-mentioned proxy variables. This is consistent with Murdough (2009) and Cosenza (2014).

Going to the fourth conclusion, as subspecies of the traditional ROI, we are going to propose some drivers useful for capturing online performance. These drivers are brand health and marketing optimization (measured by social signals such as the number of likes, tweets, and comments), revenue generator (conversions of visitors in buyers), operational efficiency (social networks are cost free), and customer experience (through rating and review systems). These metrics are not unanimously accepted in the literature; therefore, this point is also a challenge for further study.

Concluding, the common denominator to the above-mentioned conclusions is a necessary change of perspective towards OSNs. Managers and practitioners have to consider OSNs as sources of valuable information and, consequently, as a business opportunity.

References

B. Aljaber, N. Stokes, J. Bailey, J. Pei, Document clustering of scientific texts using citation contexts. Inf. Retr. **13**, 101–131 (2010)

N. Amblee, The impact of eWOM density on sales of travel insurance. Ann. Tour. Res. **56**(C), 137–140 (2016)

C. Ashley, T. Tuten, Creative strategies in social media marketing: an exploratory study of branded social content and consumer engagement. Psychol. Mark. **32**(1), 15–27 (2015)

L. Backstrom, P. Boldi, M. Rosa J. Ugander, S. Vigna, in *Four Degrees of Separation*. Proceedings of the 4th Annual ACM Web Science Conference, Web Science, 2012 (ACM, New York, 2012), pp. 33–42

E. Barnett, Facebook cuts six degrees of separation to four, Telegraph, 22 November, retrieved/May 2012, 2011

A. Barua, J. Pinnel, J. Shutter, A.B. Whinston, *Measuring the Internet Economy*, Center for Research in Electronic Commerce, (University of Texas, 1999)

M.R. Baye, B. De los Santos, M.R. Wildenbeest, Search engine optimization: what drives organic traffic to retail sites? J. Econ. Manage. Strategy **25**(1), 6–31 (2016)

C. Boyce, P. Neale, *Conducting In-Depth Interviews: A Guide for Designing and Conducting In-Depth Interviews for Evaluation Input* (Pathfinder International, Watertown, 2006), pp. 3–7

D.M. Boyd, N.B. Ellison, Social networks sites: definition, history, and scholarship. J Comp Mediated Commun **13**, 210–230 (2007)

L. Bjorneborn, P. Ingwerse, Toward a basic framework for webometrics. J. Am. Soc. Inf. Sci. Technol. **55**, 1216–1227 (2004)

A.E. Brouwer, A.M. Cohen, A. Neumaier, *Distance-Regular Graphs* (Springer-Verlag, New York, 1989)

D. Buhalis, E. Mamalakis, in *Social Media Return on Investment and Performance Evaluation in the Hotel Industry Context*. Information and Communication Technologies in Tourism 2015. (Springer International Publishing, 2015), pp. 241–253

P. Burnard, A method of analysing interview transcripts in qualitative research. Nurse Educ. Today **11**(6), 461–466 (1991)

R.S. Burt, Network items and the general social survey. Soc. Netw. **6**(4), 293–339 (1984)

B. Calabrese, M. Cannataro, N. Ielpo, in *Using Social Networks Data for Behavior and Sentiment Analysis*. Internet and Distributed Computing Systems (Springer International Publishing, 2015), pp. 285–293

K.R. Callahan, G.S. Stetz, L.M. Brooks, *Project Management Accounting, with Website: Budgeting, Tracking, and Reporting Costs and Profitability*, vol. 565 (Wiley, 2011)

M. Castells, Communication, power and counterpower in the network society. Int J Commun **1**, 238–266 (2007)

A. Ceron, L. Curini, S.M. Iacus, *Social Media e Sentiment Analysis: L'evoluzione dei fenomeni sociali attraverso la Rete*, vol. 9 (Springer Science & Business Media, 2014)

A. Cheng, *Six Degrees of Separation Twitter Style, Sysomos Inc* (University of Toronto, 2010)

R. Cohen, K. Erez, D. Ben-Avraham, S. Havlin, Resilience of the internet to random breakdowns. Phys. Rev. Lett. **85**, 4628 (2000)

D.J. Cooper, M. Rege, *Social Interaction Effects and Choice Under Uncertainty: An Experimental Study* (No. 2009/24) (University of Stavanger, 2008)

V. Cosenza, *Social media ROI: seconda edizione aggiornata* (Apogeo Editore, 2014)

I. Demirkan, D.L. Leeds, S. Demirkan, Exploring the role of network characteristics, knowledge quality and inertia on the evolution of scientific networks. J. Manag. **39**, 1462–1489 (2012)

D. Di Fatta, F. Caputo, F. Evangelista, G. Dominici, Small world theory and the World Wide Web: linking small world properties and website centrality. Int. J. Mark. Bus. Syst. **2**(2), 126–140 (2016)

E. Dichter, How word-of-mouth advertising works. Harv. Bus. Rev. **44**(6), 147–160 (1966)

P.S. Dodds, R. Muhamad, D.J. Watts, An experimental study of search in global social networks. Science **8**, 827–829 (2003)

G. Dominici, E-business model: a content based taxonomy of literature. Int J Manag Adm. Sci. **1**, 10–20 (2012)

P.T. Eugster, R. Guerraoui, A.M. Kermarrec, L. Massoulié, Epidemic information dissemination in distributed systems. Computer **37**(5), 60–67 (2004)

N.B. Ellison, Social network sites: definition, history, and scholarship. J. Comput. Mediated Commun. **13**(1), 210–230 (2007)

N.B. Ellison, C. Lampe, Social, capital, self-esteem and use of online social network sites: a longitudinal analysis. J. Appl. Dev. Psychol. **29**, 434–445 (2008)

A. Esuli, F. Sebastiani, in *Sentiwordnet: A publicly available lexical resource for opinion mining*. Proceedings of LREC vol. 6 (2006, May), pp. 417–422

M. Faloutsos, P. Faloutsos, C. Faloutsos, On power-law relationship of the internet topology. Comput. Commun. Rev. **29**, 251–262 (1999)

M. Faloutsos, T. Karagiannis, S.H. Moon, Online social networks. Netw. IEEE **24**(5), 4–5 (2010)

C. Fass, B. Turtle, M. Ginelli, *Six degrees of Kevin Bacon* (Plume Penguin Group, New York, 1996)

T. Fisher, ROI in social media: a look at the arguments. J. Datab. Mark. Cust. Strateg. Manag. **16**(3), 189–195 (2009)

L. Freeman, A set of measures of centrality based on betweeness. Sociometry **40**, 35–41 (1997)

J. Goldenberg, B. Libai, E. Muller, Tale of the network: a complex systems look at the underlying process of word-of-mouth. Mark. Lett. **12**, 211–223 (2001)

J.L. Gross, J. Yellen, *Graph theory and its applications* (CRC Press, Taylor & Francis Group, London, 2005)

T.W. Gruen, T. Osmonbekov, A.J. Czaplewski, eWOM: the impact of customer-to-customer online know-how exchange on customer value and loyalty. J. Bus. Res. **59**(4), 449–456 (2006)

R. Hanna, A. Rohm, V.L. Crittenden, We're all connected: the power of the social media ecosystem. Bus. Horiz. **54**(3), 265–273 (2011)

T. Henning-Thurau, K.P. Gwinner, G. Walsh, D.D. Gramler, Electronic word-of-mouth via consumer opinion platforms: what motivates consumers to articulate themselves on the internet? J. Interact. Mark. **18**, 38–52 (2004)

D.L. Hoffman, M. Fodor, Can you measure the ROI of your social media marketing. MIT Sloan Manage. Rev. **52**(1), 41–49 (2010)

S. Hollensen, *Marketing Management: A Relationship Approach* (Pearson Education, 2015)

D.J. Hopkins, G. King, A method of automated nonparametric content analysis for social science. Am. J. Polit. Sci. **54**(1), 229–247 (2010)

A.M. Kaplan, M. Haenlein, Two hearts in three-quarter time: how to waltz the social media/viral marketing dance. Bus. Horiz. **54**(3), 253–263 (2011)

J. Kietzmann, K. Hermkens, I. McCarthy, B. Silvestre, Social media? Get serious! Understanding the functional building blocks of social media. Bus. Horiz. **54**(3), 241–251 (2011)

J.H. Kietzmann, A. Canhoto, Bittersweet! Understanding and managing electronic word of mouth. J. Public Aff. **13**, 146–159 (2013)

J. Kleinfeld, *Six Degrees: Urban Myth?, Psychology Today*, vol.15 (Sussex Publishers LLC, 2002)

K. Krippendorff, *Content Analysis: An Introduction to Its Methodology* (Sage Publications, Beverly Hills, 1980a)

K. Krippendorff, in *Validity in Content Analysis*, ed. by E. Mochmann (Frankfurt, Germany, 1980b), pp. 69–112

K. Krippendorff, Reliability in content analysis. Hum. Commun. Res. **30**(3), 411–433 (2004)

R.A. Krueger, *Analyzing and Reporting Focus Group Results*, vol. 6 (Sage Publications, 1997)

V. Kulshreshtha, J. Boardman, D. Verma, Requirements dependencies: the emergence of a requirements network. Int. J. Comput. Appl. Technol. **45**(1), 42–56 (2012)

V. Kumar, V. Bhaskaran, R. Mirchandani, M. Shah, Practice prize winner-creating a measurable social media marketing strategy: increasing the value and ROI of intangibles and tangibles for hokey pokey. Mark. Sci. **32**(2), 194–212 (2013)

V. Kumar, R. Mirchandani, Increasing the ROI of social media marketing. MIT Sloan Manag. Rev. **54**(1), 55 (2012)

A. Kumar, T.M. Sebastian, Sentiment analysis on twitter. IJCSI Int. J. Comput. Sci. Issues **9**(4), 372–373 (2012)

Y.H. Kuo, M.H. Fu, W.H. Tsai, K.R. Lee, L.Y. Chen, Integrated microblog sentiment analysis from users' social interaction patterns and textual opinions. Appl. Intell. 1–15 (2015)

H. Kwak, C. Lee, H. Park, S. Moon, in *What is Twitter, a Social Network or a News Media?* Proceedings of the 19th International Conference on World Wide Web (ACM, New York, 2010, April), pp. 591–600

L.S. Lai, W.M. To, Content analysis of social media: a grounded theory approach. J. Electron. Commer. Res. **16**(2), 138 (2015)

E.E. Leamer, M. Storper, *The Economic Geography of the Internet Age* (Palgrave Macmillan UK, Springer, 2014) pp. 63–93

N. Li, D.D. Wu, Using text mining and sentiment analysis for online forums hotspot detection and forecast. Decis. Support. Syst. **48**(2), 354–368 (2010)

B. Liu, Sentiment analysis and opinion mining. Synth. Lect. Hum. Lang. Technol. **5**(1), 1–167 (2012)

B. Liu, L. Zhang, A survey of opinion mining and sentiment analysis. In *Mining Text Data* (Springer US, 2012), pp. 415–463

R. McDonald, K. Hannan, T. Neylon, M. Wells, J. Reynar, in *Structured Models for Fine-to-Coarse Sentiment Analysis*. Annual Meeting-Association for Computational Linguistics, vol. 45(1), p. 432 (2007, June)

R. Menner, W. Höpken, M. Fuchs, M. Lexhagen, in *Topic Detection: Identifying Relevant Topics in Tourism Reviews*. Information and Communication Technologies in Tourism 2016 (Springer International Publishing, 2016), pp. 411–423

C. Murdough, Social media measurement: It's not impossible. J. Interact. Advert. **10**(1), 94–99 (2009)

T. Nasukawa, J. Yi, in *Sentiment Analysis: Capturing Favorability Using Natural Language Processing*. Proceedings of the 2nd International Conference on Knowledge Capture (ACM, New York, 2003), pp. 70–77

G. Norris, J.D. Balls, K.M. Hartley, *E-business and ERP: Transforming the Enterprise* (Wiley, 2000)

A. Okafor, P. Pardalos, M. Ragle, in *Data Mining via Entropy and Graph Clustering*. Data Mining in Biomedicine (Springer US, 2007), pp. 117–131

T. Opsahl, F. Agneessens, J. Skoretz, Node centrality in weighted networks: generalizing degree and shortest paths. Soc. Netw. **32**, 245–251 (2010)

A. Ortigosa, J.M. Martín, R.M. Carro, Sentiment analysis in Facebook and its application to e-learning. Comput. Hum. Behav. **31**, 527–541 (2014)

B. Pang, L. Lee, Opinion mining and sentiment analysis. Found. Trends Inf. Retr. **2**(1–2), 1–135 (2008)

A. Pak, P. Paroubek, in *Text Representation Using Dependency Tree Subgraphs for Sentiment Analysis*. Database Systems for Advanced Applications. (Springer, Berlin Heidelberg, 2011), pp. 323–332

R.L. Paquin, J. Howard-Grenville, Blind dates and arranged marriages: longitudinal process of network orchestration. Organ. Stud. **34**, 1623–1653 (2013)

R. Ramanathan, L.S. Ganesh, Group preference aggregation methods employed in AHP: an evaluation and an intrinsic process for deriving members' weightages. Eur. J. Oper. Res. **79**(2), 249–265 (1994)

D. Riff, S. Lacy, F. Fico, *Analyzing Media Messages: Using Quantitative Content Analysis in Research* (Routledge, 2014)

L. Rourke, T. Anderson, D.R. Garrison, W. Archer, Methodological issues in the content analysis of computer conference transcripts. Int. J. Artif. Intell. Educ. (IJAIED) **12**, 8–22 (2001)

J. Shim, Social networking sites: a brief comparison of usage in the US and Korea. Decis. Line **39**(5), 16–18 (2008)

S. Takahashi, A. Sugiyama, Y. Kohda, in *A Method for Opinion Mining of Coffee Service Quality and Customer Value by Mining Twitter*. Knowledge, Information and Creativity Support Systems (Springer International Publishing, 2016), pp. 521–528

M. Trusov, R.E. Bucklin, K. Pauwels, Effects of word of mouth versus traditional marketing: findings from an internet social networking site. J. Mark. **73**, 90–102 (2009)

J. Ugander, B. Karrer, L. Backstrom, C. Marlow, *The Anatomy of the Facebook Social Graph* (Cornell University Library, Ithaca, 2011)

A. Van Looy, in *Search Engine Optimization*. Social Media Management (Springer International Publishing, 2016), pp. 113–132

S. Wasserman, K. Faust, *Social Network Analysis: Methods and Applications*, vol 8 (Cambridge University Press, Cambridge, 1994)

D.J. Watts, S.H. Strogatz, Collective dynamics of small-world networks. Nature **393**, 440–442 (1998)

M. Zirngibl, C.H. Joyner, L.W. Stulz, C. Dragone, H.M. Presby, I.P. Kaminow, LARNet, a local access router network. Photonics Technol. Lett. IEEE **7**(2), 215–217 (1995)

The Role of Data in the Evaluation of Networked Learning Effectiveness: An Auto-Ethnographic Evaluation of Four Experiential Learning Projects

Jonathan Bishop

Abstract Educator–learner interaction has been a key factor in the advantage traditional learning environments have had over electronic ones. This chapter explores four projects that have challenged this premise. The Young Enterprise Project showed that computers can play an important part of youth entrepreneurship, and subsequently the Emotivate Project showed how they can be an essential part of blending electronic learning with community activism and arts. The Digital Classroom of Tomorrow Project showed that it is possible to use eTwinning of the schools through networked learning. Finally, the Free Digital Project is discussed, which is an initiative that brought all the other projects together to show how through the Cloud young and disabled people can become Internet entrepreneurs.

Abbreviations

Blended Learning	Blended learning refers to the approach of merging offline and offline approaches to learning so as to combat the broadcasted approach to teaching
Classroom 2.0	Classroom 2.0 is an approach to networked learning that involves the partnering of learners from different schools or environments
Coasting School	A coasting school is one where the management is happy to have business as usual and where any ideas on how to improve that school might be rejected as to accept them would require accepting the school is coasting rather than improving
E-Learning	E-Learning refers to the use of digital technologies for learning and knowledge transformation

J. Bishop (✉)
Director of Centre for Research into Online Communities and E-Learning Systems (CROCELS)
e-mail: jbishop@crocels.com; bishop@crocels.ac.uk

© Springer International Publishing AG 2017   135
S. Hai-Jew (ed.), *Data Analytics in Digital Humanities*, Multimedia Systems
and Applications, DOI 10.1007/978-3-319-54499-1_6

Experiential Learning	Experiential learning refers to learning through doing learning activities rather than being expected to learn from listening to a teacher lecture in a broadcasted manner
Immediate Learning	Immediate learning is an approach to teaching and learning where the learning objectives of students are instantaneously paired with those of the educator, such as through guided inquiry or the flipped classroom
Networked Learning	Networked learning is a form of e-learning that involves using networked learning environments, such as multiple websites rather than one managed learning environment

Introduction

The term 'big data' has become a major buzzword for describing the harvesting and analysis of data from various sources for analysis in ways that were not intended (Bishop 2015; Brown et al. 2011; Labrinidis and Jagadish, 2012; Malgonde and Bhattacherjee, 2014; Woerner and Wixom, 2015). In educational environments data should be important for evaluating the effectiveness of learning and teaching. This is nowhere more important—and more possible—than in the case of networking learning, which is learning carried out online in networked learning environments. The use of website metrics in such situations is often overlooked but is nevertheless important in generating big data that can then be triangulated with observational data from video, such as in experiential or immediate learning contexts (Bishop and Goode 2014; Bishop, 2017).

Background

In looking at the role of big data in educational settings one must consider the different approaches to learning that data can be collected on and what the impacts of that data might be, such as whether educational establishments might not want to accept it when the data shows they are failing their students.

Approaches to Learning

Educator–learner interaction is an important part of any learning experience, regardless of whether the teachers and learners are communicating in-person or at a distance. Even where the computer is taking the place of a person, such as via CD-ROMs, Web-based learning or tablet apps, the engagement of a person with the system and trust in it is still important. The learning experience, whether or not enhanced by technology, is crucial to whether a teaching activity is successful or not.

Experiential Learning

Experiential learning is a process that is designed to link cognitive, social and emotional processes (Kolb, 1981). Every learner has different styles of learning and it is an important part of experiential learning to accommodate these (Eickmann et al. 2004). It is argued that conversation is an important part of constructing meaning from an experience (Baker et al. 2005). It follows therefore that communication between learner and educator needs to be a two-way process, where both are learning from one another.

Networked Learning

Networked learning is the concept that learning can occur collaboratively over the Internet, with educators and learners playing active roles not possible with traditional forms of computer-based learning (Goodyear et al. 2006). An example of networked learning that makes use of experiential learning is the eTwinning initiative. The eTwinning concept promotes the development of educators and learners through pairing their school with others at a distance (Vuorikari et al. 2011). It is based on the premise that collaboration between schools is and must be easy, democratic and the use of ICTs should be easily accessible by all (Scimeca et al. 2009). Examples include document sharing, and sharing of resources in general (Holmes and Sime 2012). With the focus of networked learning being on the social aspects of e-learning, it is easy to see how the approach can support cross-border activities that involve many different styles of teaching and learning (Hanraets et al. 2011).

Immediate Learning

Experiential learning and immediate learning often go hand in hand, as immediate learning allows learners to have concrete experiences in the moment, which are then reflected on Schuster et al. (2003). In terms e-learning, immediate learning has important implications for motivation, learning and course attrition (Hutchins and Hutchison 2008). Technologies like podcasting have made it easier for immediate learning to exist in a contemporary setting (Hendrickson et al. 2010).

Immediate learning often depends on verbal and non-verbal communication in classroom contexts (Turman 2008). E-Learning environments can therefore be seen as the perfect context for immediate learning, especially where it is possible for the user interface to be adapted based on the abilities and interests of the learners (Bishop 2012a, 2004). Some, however, argue that immediate learning can stifle creativity and reduce attention focus (DeHart 1975).

Blended Learning

Blended learning is a term typically used to describe the use of network learning technologies with traditional classroom approaches (Valiathan 2002). Blended learning can be the alternative to single instances of immediate learning, by having several stages where immediate learning is not just in the classroom, but can be on location at a specific point in the learning process. Blended learning is known to be able to allow for the facilitation of meaningful learning experiences not otherwise possible (Garrison and Kanuka 2004). This is possible because blended learning combines various forms of delivery, including teaching and learning styles (Heinze and Procter 2004).

Using Big Data to Evaluate the Effectiveness of Educational Projects

The evaluation of education projects is something that often results in politicians producing the so-called strategies that educational establishments do not follow as they do not take them seriously. Where opportunities exist for data analysis concerns of education establishment personnel is often about massaging it, such as taking out of the figures students with disabilities or those from minority backgrounds who the establishment are failing and want to avoid coming to terms with the fact that it is their management style that is failing and not the students that failed management style is holding back.

Investigation of the Projects

This section provides background information on three projects that made strong use of experiential learning, blended learning and networked learning. This includes the Young Enterprise Project, the Digital Classroom of Tomorrow Project and the Emotivate Project.

The Young Enterprise Project

The Young Enterprise Project, also known simply as the enterprise project, was an experiential learning initiative run at South Devon College between 1994 and 1996, which was available to students studying its GNVQ in Business Foundation course. South Devon College was one of the first colleges in the UK to have Internet access, which formed a core part of how students participated in the programme, including

Table 1 Objectives and outcomes of the Young Enterprise Project

Objective	Outcome
World of work	Provide young people with an exciting, imaginative and practical business experience
Personal skills	Enable young people to develop their personal skills
Life skills	Enable young people to develop knowledge and understanding of the processes of business and wealth creation

using it for market research. It is known that experiential learning in business studies can positively impact on a student's self-efficacy and self-confidence.

Table 1 shows the skills developed by the Young Enterprise Project (Ralph, 1996), which some of the participants used to gain certificates from the Associated Examining Board (i.e. AEB Basic Tests). The first stage of the enterprise project involved students market testing their ideas prior to being formally involved in the Young Enterprise programme. During this stage of the enterprise project they would come together as a group, decide what product they wanted to sell, and form a name and brand to sell the product. The important part of this enterprise project was that while technology was important, it was more important to develop ideas for making sales, pitching to customers and developing the product range in the first place. In one instance the project involved running a stall at the site of South Devon College and on another occasion attending a market. Software including Aldus PageMaker, Home Accounts 2, HyperPaint, among others were used to support the project's activities, being used as part of the project so much so they were not seen as out of the ordinary. The importance of developing the enterprise skills of students and the teaching and mentoring skills of education and business partners fed into the later projects discussed. The immediate learning in the project was perhaps more evident in the physical environment than through computer software, but it has direct relevance for online learning environments.

The Digital Classroom of Tomorrow Project

The Digital Classroom of Tomorrow (DCOT) Project in Wales started what became the Classroom 2.0 initiative (Bishop, 2007; Taddeo and Tirocchi, 2012). The aims of the Welsh DCOT Project were based on the Welsh Government's 2001 Learning Country initiative (Davidson, 2001). DCOT was adopted as Classi 2.0 in Italy, Escuela 2.0 in Spain and CAPITAL (Curriculum and Pedagogy in Technology Assisted Learning) in England (Bishop, 2007; Taddeo and Tirocchi, 2012). In Italy they were based on the Italian Ministry of Education's 2009 University and Research initiative (Cornali and Tirocchi, 2010). Both are set out in Table 2.

Immediate learning can be seen to be at the centre of the DCOT Project. Using advanced ICT techniques to tailor online learning environments to the students was an essential part of its scope. The importance of distance learning to the DCOT

Table 2 Comparing the objectives of classroom 2.0 in Wales and Italy

Factor	DCOT (Wales)	Classi 2.0 (Italy)
Persuasive	Encourage the development of bilingual educational and training materials relevant to Wales	To implement innovative teaching and learning methods
Adaptive	Develop flexible modes of provision tailored to the needs of the individual learner	Support the personalisation of the teaching process
Sociable	Strengthen distance learning and use ICT to move away from rigid timetables and classroom-based teaching	To re-organise school space and time management
Sustainable	Encourage the development of essential ICT skills throughout local communities	Develop close relationships with the local environment (other schools, companies, associations, parents and families, and so on)

Project allowed for self-directed immediate learning, as it is possible for education to be not based on set timetables, but accessed in an asynchronous fashion. The development of ICT skills in communities will increase the likelihood of informal immediate learning, such as in terms of accessing the Internet.

The Emotivate Project

The Emotivate Project is a community arts project where young people from a range of backgrounds and localities come together to improve their digital literacy, improve their understanding of the area and design murals reflecting the aspects of their community they think important to its past and what they'd like it to be like in the future. The project implemented many of the findings of the DCOT Project and Young Enterprise Project, and can be seen to embody immediate learning. For instance, the aim of the project was not just to transform the learning of the young people involved, but the teachers also. This could only be possible at the time through the experiential learning occurring in a physical setting where the social proof of the social change was immediately obvious. Equally, at the start of the project, the art teacher was sceptical that the social change would occur and then as part of the process saw that community regeneration through the arts was possible. Table 3 shows the objectives and outcomes of the project.

The Emotivate Project was the first to be grant-funded, requiring £15,261.59 start-up funding, which was made up of £2000 (13%) from local government, £8275 (54%) from grant-giving bodies, £786.79 (5%) from co-operatives and £4200 (28%) work in kind (Bishop, 2012b). This money went towards the paint and other materials the young people and artist needed, and was used in a way where the young people decided what the design was. There was no competition, such as who was the 'best' or anything like picking a 'winner'. The ethos of the project was that each participant could point at the mural and say 'I did that'. The credit was

Table 3 Objectives and outcomes of the Emotivate Project

Objective	Outcome
Visibility	Educating young people about the arts and make a visible contribution to the community by improving the local environment
Virtuality	Encouraging the use of electronic learning methods
Vitality	Improving cultural, economic and environmental development of the local communities
Viability	Increasing the social cohesion between the local communities
Environmentalism	Engaging with local community members and encourage participation in improving the local environment and the local community
Restitution	Engaging with socially excluded people within the community including young offenders and people on probation

therefore shared with no one taking more than the other, and importantly for no one part of the project to be singled out as belonging to one person or another.

Review and Consolidation of the Projects

The projects discussed above together provide many important insights into the design of experiential learning programmes, such as those which use blended learning and/or networked learning. It created a three-part instructional design model, namely 'Learn, Create, and Communicate.'

Aspect 1: The Learn Stage

The learn stage is an aspect of a learning activity where an educator imparts and develops knowledge. In the case of the Young Enterprise Project this involved a college lecturer and business mentor imparting knowledge and experience to participants. In the case of the DCOT Project this involved designing online instructional materials that put transferring information as the first stage. In the case of the Emotivate Project this involved the participants learning about the area's history and how to use digital technologies like Photoshop. This part of the learning process is probably least open to the experiential aspects of immediate education, but most suited to the asynchronous aspects of immediate education where distance learning provides for education to be conducted at a time of the learner's choosing.

Aspect 2: The Create Stage

The create stage is an aspect of a learning activity where learners are given the chance to put the knowledge they have gained into practice in order to develop through experiential learning. It is thus most suited to immediate learning, as workshops and fieldtrips are some of the best activities to enable this stage to happen. In the case of the Young Enterprise Project using software like HyperPaint and Aldus PageMaker allow for the design of marketing materials. It also involved deciding on a product range. In the case of the DCOT Project, examples of the create stage included online activities, such as registering for an employment website, providing instant access to current employment opportunities, providing immediate learning scenarios, that can be assessed for their relevance by participants. In the case of the Emotivate Project the create stage involved the creation of collages in Photoshop by drawing images from the Internet about the area's part and what they would like it to be like in the future, and the painting of those ideas onto boards that were then installed as a mural in the underpass. Applications used with a web browser, included Moodle and Google, and Photoshop was used alongside these.

Aspect 3: The Communicate Stage

The communicate stage is an aspect of a learning activity where the learners speak about their learning. In the case of the Young Enterprise Project this involved the participants making a speech at an end of year exhibition and speaking to others about the project at a stall. In the Digital Classroom of Tomorrow Project this has involved the use of weblogs as learning journals, the customisation of hand-outs and user data entry on sequential screens. In the Emotivate Project the communicate stage involved participants speaking to the media. The aspects of immediate learning that are suited to this stage are therefore, spontaneous opportunities for reflection.

Conclusions

There are a number of things to learn from the three projects referred to. This includes that technology works best when it is embedded into a programme of learning, rather than being seen as ancillary to it, as instant learning is more possible. Policies like 'bring your own device' could become essential to budgeting the cost of ICT into each lesson, especially at a point in time where there is pressure to slash public spending. This may improve instant learning through learners being more likely to engage in a state of flow, aiding experiential learning. The structured approach to designing instruction in the LCC model could be made available on all devices, such as using responsive programming. Figure 1 shows the revised Digital Classroom of Tomorrow Project conceptual framework, which takes account of the fact that a classroom should make use of a bring-your-own-device policy, even if the networked learning environment being used is controlled by an educator using their device.

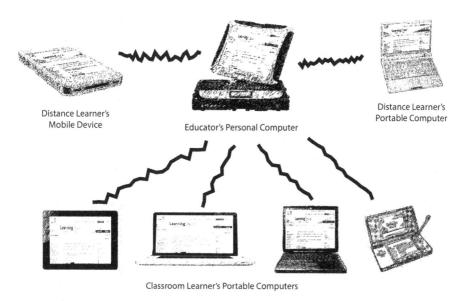

Fig. 1 The revised Digital Classroom of Tomorrow Project model

An Auto-Ethnographic Evaluation of the Three Experiential Learning Projects Into a Social Enterprise and a Coasting School

This section evaluates the success of three experiential learning projects and then applies them to two organisations to show instant learning can and/or should be implemented.

Methodology

The methodology behind the project is based on auto-ethnography. This is where the researcher is activity participating in a lead role in the setting being research and whom documents the project from the perspective they observe it through. Describing and defining auto-ethnography is a challenging task (Hayano, 1979). However, it has been argued that auto-ethnography is a more authentic approach because it relies on conveying the actual thoughts of the researcher rather than simply attempting to interpret the behaviours of others (Dyson, 2007). It is normal for auto-ethnographies to be written in the first-person rather than the third-person but the author, even as a Fellow of the Royal Anthropological Institute, prefers the third-person tense as it sounds more typical of academic texts where the aim is to be objective, even if it is impossible for humans to be objective because they are naturally subjective beings (Bochner, 2012).

Participants and Location

The participants and location of the project are the management, support staff and others relating to the organisations being studied.

Parc Lewis County Primary School

Parc Lewis County Primary School is a primary school based in South Wales. Its head teacher is Alun Roberts, the Chair of Governors is Geoff Herbert, a member of the support staff is Esther Thomas and the school's inspector is Merfyn Lloyd Jones. In the organisation, the researcher was a school governor, with responsibility for ICT and religious studies.

Crocels Community Media Group

The Crocels Community Media Group is the name given to a group of companies which cooperate to improve the West Wales and The Valleys region of Wales through multimedia education and community regeneration. The current and former directors include the researcher, Mark Beech, Tim Mazur and Gethin Rhys. The current contingent workers include Jason Barratt and Jeremy McDonagh.

Results

The results section sets out what was learned from the attempt to implement the lessons learned from the three projects into two organisations.

Parc Lewis County Primary School

Parc Lewis County Primary School is a school for children at primary school age, which is in Treforest, within the Pontypridd community. The make-up of the school includes students and travellers who are not in the area for long. This has caused the school challenges in terms of how it achieves adequate outcomes because of this. This section discussed the efforts by the researcher to implement Classroom 2.0 into the school during their role as school governor. In schools such as this, the individualistic approach can ensure that even with the steady flow of pupils through the school that each can be catered for and develop their own learning even if the classroom make-up changes.

Phase 1: Battling for Change (2008–2013)

During this stage the researcher had great difficulties in encouraging change to the school's IT policy. The head teacher presided over the greatest fall in performance seen at the school, with their key performance indicators set by governors not reflecting the fall in standards. The Chairman of the school, Geoff Herbert used all manner of methods to prevent the researcher from having influence on the school, including not passing his change of addresses on to the local authority. Geoff Herbert was then able to have the researcher excluded from the governing body, without giving him the chance to attend a meeting—through having the correspondence sent to his old address. On behalf of the Chairman, Esther Thomas defended Geoff Herbert not informing the council or school of the researcher's new address, saying: '*It is the responsibility of the school governor to formally notify the Clerk of the Governing Body of any changes to their personal details*'.

As can be seen in Fig. 2 below, the years at which the researcher was able to make interventions were the one in which the school had the highest performance. These were 2008 and 2012 to 2014. At the end of each intervention by the researcher the school's results were in the 80% are (81.8% in 2008 and 84.6% in 2012). When the researcher re-joined the school in 2012, the school's performance increases nearly 5% each year, before falling by over 10% in the year that he was no longer present (i.e. 2015).

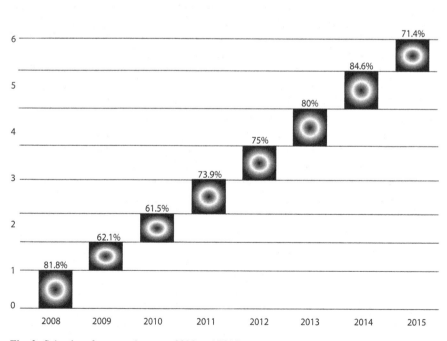

Fig. 2 School performance between 2008 and 2015

Table 4 Use of ICT resources

Local education authority	School inspector
There is a strong emphasis on meeting national priorities, particularly improving literacy, where the school's current self-evaluation has accurately identified that a significant minority of pupils have poorly developed reading skills.	Teachers' planning identifies appropriate opportunities for pupils to develop the key skills of numeracy, literacy and information and communication technology (ICT), but there are inconsistencies in some subjects when planning for these skills across the curriculum.
Robust systems have been introduced in this academic year to improve the school's focus on a skills-based curriculum, assessment for learning and improving literacy.	Most (pupils) say that they have enough books, equipment and computers to do their work.

During the year appointment of a new head teacher in 2011, the researcher was reappointed to the school governing body, and provided 'challenge' to the head teacher. In one instance the head teacher said to the researcher they were making changes. '*In school we have recently purchased 10 iPads for children's use initially in years 2 and 6, where our staff expertise in ICT is based*', he said. '*We are particularly interested in targeting boys writing through various apps that are available*', he continued. '*Our teachers have visited other schools that are successfully using them and we are aware that many schools are now 'dipping their toe' in this avenue (of adopting Classroom 2.0 principles)*'.

Table 4 presents the use of ICT resources from the point of view of the local education authority following the researcher disclosing his observations and that of the school inspector. As can be seen, whilst the LEA says that teachers are able to identify issues with pupils' learning, the school inspector, Merfyn Lloyd Jones, points out there is inconsistency across the curriculum. The school inspector also stated that the learners felt they had enough resources, but as Classroom 2.0 had not been introduced at this point, it is likely this was based on their acceptance of the status quo, rather than be said from the point of view what they could have.

Table 5 shows what the school inspector has said about differs from what the local education authority's own investigation showed. Under the current education arrangements in Wales, unlike many parts of England, local authorities still control many aspects of the education system. This creates a conflict of interest, as what the case at the school explored. For instance, the local education authority was so close to the head teacher and chair of governors that even though it was responsible for carrying out the investigation independent of the school, it still leaked information to the chair of governors, knowing that it would cause offense due to its 'derogatory' nature.

Phase 2: Winning the argument (2012–2013)

The school inspection by the statutory school inspectorate showed other key differences between what the local authority said in its investigation compared to

Table 5 Differentiation and behaviour management

Local education authority	School inspector
Throughout the school, pupils show a positive attitude and enjoyment of learning. They are helpful and co-operative and willing to talk about what they are doing in lessons.	The school has correctly identified those pupils who are more able and talented, but its provision does not always fully meet the needs of these pupils in order to challenge them appropriately.
All children spoke to agree that the school has effective ways of addressing issues such as bullying, and that their teachers help to ensure that all children behave well in class so that they can get on with their work.	Many say that the school deals with bullying well. Only a minority say that other children do not behave well so that they can get on with their work and do not behave well at playtime and lunchtime.

Table 6 Staff pupil development

Local authority	School inspector
'Nearly all children can describe how teachers use feedback and targets to help them to know how well they ate doing in class and what they need to do to improve, for example by referring to individual targets and feedback from teachers'.	*'However, on a few occasions where the teaching is less effective, teachers do not always provide suitable tasks for the range of abilities in a class and do not provide enough opportunities to enable pupils to write extensively across the curriculum'.*
'Continuing professional development (CPD) for all staff is now informed by more accurate self-evaluation and focussed on improving their ability to meet identified needs in the school'.	*'Clear, specific actions have been identified to improve the school environment and to develop skills-based learning. These are now being put into practice and are incorporated into the school's monitoring and evaluation cycle'.*

what was happening in practice. Table 6 shows this in the case of staff and pupil development. It can be seen that whilst the local authority investigation found that differentiation was the norm, the school inspector found it was lacking. The local authority said that staff development was a core part of the school's management, but the inspector said that it was only just being introduced.

The school had access to the Moodle e-learning system provided by the local university. However, the head teacher was focussed around his personal belief the use of this was limited because he thought the young people would not have access to technology at home. This was raised with the local authority, but again it turned out that what the local education authority found was different from that of the school inspector. Table 7 provides the comments on school performance. The researcher told the local education authority that the school was one of the worst performing, and the school inspector agreed. The researcher told the local education authority that the other governors were not playing an active role in ensuring the head teacher took tough decisions and the school inspector agreed that not enough challenge was being provided to the head teacher. The researcher told the local education authority that teachers were not willing to update their skills to help pupils and the school inspector agreed that the learning activities did not always meet the needs and abilities of learners. It was clear to both the researcher and the school

Table 7 School performance

ICT link governor (Researcher)	School inspector
'Parc Lewis is one of the worst performing schools in the county and needs to modernise'.	*'In comparison with schools with similar proportions of pupils entitled to free school meals, the school's performance at the expected outcome or better placed it in the bottom 25% in all learning areas'.*
'As a new headteacher you should be looking to reform the way the school works and not stick to old ways of doing things which clearly aren't working!' *'If you do not have what it takes to make tough decision why are you doing your job?'* *'The Governors at Parc Lewis Primary School playing no active Role'.*	*'The members of the governing body are very supportive of the school. They receive regular reports from the headteacher and are aware of the school's strengths and areas for improvement. They visit the school regularly and receive appropriate information about the school's performance. However, their role as critical friends is limited and they do not challenge the school enough about its performance'.*
'If teachers can't keep up with the times then they should be asked to leave!' *'If the teachers are not willing to learn new skills to do something about this then they should be sacked!'*	*'learning activities do not always meet the needs and abilities of all pupils well enough'.* *'Performance management procedures are in place for all members of staff'.*
'Alun (the head-teacher) says that our area isn't an affluent one, so people probably don't have these ICTs. If Alun went to near-by Pontypridd on market day, he would see that many of the things being sold are mobile phone accessories and most of the people buying them are on benefits!'	*'The school describes the overall socio-economic background of the area as economically and socially disadvantaged'.*

inspector that the head teacher focused on the fact the school was in a disadvantaged area, which the researcher saw as an excuse not to improve standards.

It was quite clear that after the school inspector reported that the researcher had won the argument, even if the local authority did not agree. At one meeting following the inspection the researcher proposed a cyber-bullying officer and the chair of governors said one should not be in place because he and other governors did 'not know enough about it'. And at the same meeting when the researcher made reference to the school system in England the local education authority's secretary said even though she was not entitled to speak, 'We are not in England'. The degree of conservatism in the school was perhaps behind its poor performance.

Phase 3: Outcomes of Interventions and Lack of Intervention (2013–2015)

Subsequent to that meeting, many of the policies suggested by the researcher were put into practice. This included a set of policies where the teachers would be subjected to disciplinary proceedings if they did not update their skills, and also

Table 8 Performance of Parc Lewis Primary School (2008–2015)

Group	2008	2009	2010	2011	2012	2013	2014	2015
School	81.8%	62.1%	61.5%	73.9%	75.0%	80.0%	84.6%	71.4%
Family	75.9%	78.9%	80.4%	77.1%	80.2%	83.4%	84.6%	87.5%
LEA	73.1%	74.1%	76.3%	77.1%	80.2%	83.4%	84.6%	85.8%
Wales	75.5%	77.0%	78.2%	80.0%	82.6%	84.3%	86.1%	87.7%

the school introduced more ICT into its set up. Table 8 sets out the performance of the school between 2008 and 2015. As can be seen from this table, when the researcher was present in 2008 and then 2012–2014 the school was performing better, perhaps because he was single handily providing challenge to the head teacher. The year following the researcher leaving the school, namely 2015, the school's performance had fallen again. This perhaps shows what can happen in schools where the management can escape scrutiny and carry on allowing the forces of conservatism to go unchallenged.

Crocels Community Media Group

The Crocels Community Media Group is the name given to a multimedia education and community regeneration partnership in the West Wales and the Valleys region of Wales. Its formation and transformation took place over 10 years, starting with the founding of the Centre for Research into Online Communities and E-Learning Systems in 2005 through to the incorporation of the partnership as a charitable incorporated organisation in 2015.

Phase 1: The Creation of the Digital Classroom of Tomorrow Project

The Digital Classroom of Tomorrow Project was founded in 2002 as an initiative to further the use of digital technologies in schools to provide an education to learners that is persuasive, adaptable, sociable and sustainable (Bishop, 2004). The DCOT Project grew out of an inspirational combination of the ACE initiative that used networking learning through web-cams (Reddy, 1997a, b) and the drive of the Welsh Government to transform Wales into 'The Learning Country' (Davidson, 2001). The DCOT Project caught on in England, Spain and Italy, transforming into the Classroom 2.0 initiative, which went in a slightly different direction to that envisaged by the DCOT Project.

Phase 2: The Incorporation of Glamorgan Blended Learning Ltd (GBL)

The creation of Glamorgan Blended Learning Ltd. (GBL) signalled the start of a project to bring together the communities in the East Glamorgan area, specifically the South Wales Central region. GBL could be seen to embody the enterprise project—the participants in the form of the company's directors (one having participated in the Young Enterprise Project) were developing enterprise skills that they have not previously gained. GBL was the first of several companies to be created, which was part of a vision to get dozens of students involved in work experience opportunities working through glocalisation, where they are both locally and globally minded. The skills of two of the directors (Jonathan Bishop was around Web development, so this formed an important part of the company's fund-raising offerings. Through the Emotivate Project, discussed above, GBL got together young people across several schools who would otherwise not meet. The idea being that due to the small world phenomenon, the same young people would bump into each other in the future and talk about their participation in the project, making the social change that much more meaningful.

Phase 3: The Incorporation of Jonathan Bishop Limited (JBL)

It became apparent that a significant amount of investment would be needed for Crocels to expand its product offerings to increase income for the community projects. On that basis, Jonathan Bishop Limited (JBL) was formed so that the risk could be shared between GBL and JBL where the director, Jonathan Bishop, would invest a lot of time into the project and with the financial support of GBL, he could then develop and market new products and processes that both he and the two companies would benefit from.

Part of this involved working with a team of programmers in India called iFlair. This was done collaboratively using tools like NetMeeting, Skype and email. Involving the programmers included paying amounts upfront as little as £90, but the value of these product development projects varied. The innovative products from JBL inspired the programmers. 'Because this is the real experience that we experienced while working with,' is what they said about one project. 'It does make it better the way you incorporate yourself within', they said about their buy-in to their vision.

Phase 4: The Creation of the Crocels Community Media Group

The creation of the Crocels Community Media Group (CMG) was an attempt to link and internationalise several companies. The increased collaboration between the companies occurred via the Cloud. In the first instance, it involved the renaming of Glamorgan Blended Learning Ltd. to Crocels CMG CYF, and this company became the lead company for the Group. The new mission of the Group was not easily

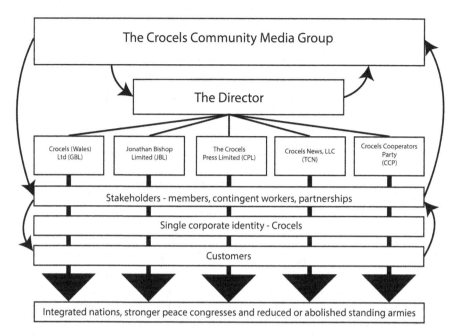

Fig. 3 Corporate structure of Crocels (2011–2014)

accessible to all, however. For instance, former director Tim Mazur said: '*I (he) was not aware 'world peace' featured in Crocels mission*'.

As can be seen from Fig. 3, the corporate structure of Crocels had expanded well beyond GBL at this stage.

Tim was a member of the company before the change, but Jason Barratt who joined the company after the change was more complimentary. '*Working for Crocels gives me everything I could want from working for the company*', he said. '*The work is relaxed, but always done in time, and aside from one person being late with time sheets, everything is satisfactory*'. Tim joined the company on a specific project—Assisting Human Interaction, or Vois—and his interest in the bigger picture therefore was not evident. '*Since my reduction in my hours worked for Crocels has very little effect on my life beyond my research interests into EI & ERD*', he said. '*My general experiences when discussing the VOIS system were demanding, interesting & frustrating*', he continued. '*However, the design of VOIS clearly lacks features and considerations needed to achieve what it set out to do*'. This shows the overall problem with learning organisations like CMG, where change is ongoing. With people joining at different times, and not always meeting face-to-face, the transitions can be difficult if people are not fully aware of them, or would rather things stay as they are.

Table 9 Aspects of the Free Digital Project

Aspect	Description and Examples
Freedom for digital teens from autocratic learning	The current education system is usually based on the 'sage on the stage model' where someone professing knowledge lectures to a class on what they should believe. The project gives young people the chance to developing themselves as individuals that work as part of a wider networked team.
Freedom for digital teens from autocratic leaders	The current employment system is not suited to the current generation of young people. The Free Digital Project gives them experience so they can go on to become self-employed and be their own boss.
Freedom for digital teens from abusive losers	The Free Digital Project gives young people an awareness of their abilities so that when they are criticised or bullied they know in themselves their true abilities.

Phase 5: The Realisation Through the Free Digital Project

The Free Digital Project was founded in 2012 as a way to take all the learning from the Emotivate Project and the Crocels companies to provide work opportunities to young people who have been let down by the system. Free Digital has derived its name from the beginning 'Freedom for Digital Teens from' then terms starting 'AA' followed by a word starting 'L' (Table 9).

The point of the Free Digital Project when it comes to the development of young people has been to help them develop a profitable business and by harnessing the Internet and the Cloud, it will mean that eventually state and grant funding will not be needed.

Phase 6: The Incorporation of the Crocels Community Media Group

The start of the incorporation of the Crocels Community Media Group singled what should be the final reform of the organisational structure. Whilst each company within CMG is independent and not a subsidiary of if, CMG will become the corporate director of all the companies within the Group. In terms of The Crocels Press Limited (CPL), it will have subsidiaries in the main territories covered by the Group's patents. At present this is Australia and the USA. Crocels News, Inc. currently covers the USA and a new company will be founded to cover Australia. As can be seen from Fig. 4, the new corporate structure of Crocels is not so based around a fixed number of companies. It is focussed on the tasks those companies perform, and the activities of the people operating within them. This should provide a greater inter-professional context to the company. For instance, it can be seen in the model that Crocels Press Limited is represented by the printer and the envelope and is responsible for the *'Production and Distribution'* side of CMG. In this lower part of the model would be all the contingent and other workers who cooperate to achieve the company's goals. So whilst the companies are present, they should

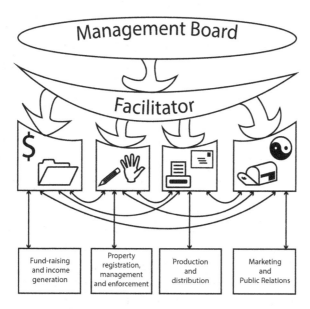

Fig. 4 Corporate structure of the Crocels Community Media Group (2014–2016)

ideally be invisible so that people see themselves working for Crocels and not the individual company with which they are associated.

An important aspect of the new corporate structure in Fig. 4 is the change in role for the director who has become a facilitator. This facilitator is still responsible for the day-to-day running of the company—as an office holder—but the group and its trustees are theoretically in control of the direction of the companies. A full working agreement between the companies is under way and will set out the divisions of labour between them and solidify the right for their members to veto a decision of the Group and/or the facilitator. It is likely that the corporate structure will change from that between 2014 and 2016 within 2017 as the outcomes of this study are implemented.

As can be seen from Fig. 5, there management structure of CMG now follows not a hierarchical one, but one based on the extent to which decisions are made by the facilitator and other C-Level executives (i.e. trustees). These executives can be seen to be the closest to the facilitator, sharing equal responsibility. It is the case that all the powers of the management board will be delegated to a committee of which the facilitator is the only member, making them the Chief Executive Officer of each company, but where there is a conflict of interest, such as where the facilitator is presented with a problem of which they have a direct interest, then the other C-Level executives must take the decision.

Next furthest from the facilitator are the technicians. These are people who have joined the Group, such as through the Free Digital Project, who need the most supervision from the facilitator or other C-Level executives. Furthest away are the

Fig. 5 The management
structure of the Crocels
Community Media Group
(2016)

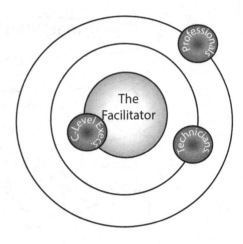

professionals, which are people who the facilitator has minimal control over, such as patent attorneys or accountants. The aim is that technicians will go on to become professionals through their professional development within Crocels.

Implications and Future Research Directions

This chapter has shown how there is the option of transforming educational institutions to be more business-minded and to focus on the individual development of their service users. There have been challenges in this regard with schools that are still tied to local education authorities, where these are managed by volunteers rather than experienced professionals. For instance, at Parc Lewis County Primary School in Wales, it took years of effort to convince the school to adopt ICT into part of the school's ethos. There is still an embedded 'forces of conservatism' in school governing bodies, which in the case of Parc Lewis led to the Chair of Governors arranging for the researcher's suspension when he voiced some home truths. Whilst this research has shown it is possible for young people, especially those with disabilities, to use the Tax Credits system in the UK to support themselves while they are developing their business, UK Government policy towards cutting these could mean the project would no longer be feasible outside of being a state-funded back to work scheme. Future research could therefore look at how the apprenticeship scheme run in the UK might be able to provide the skills development for Free Digital participants so that afterwards they can become self-employed afterwards. This would mean that the ethos of the Free Digital Project in terms of freeing digital teens from the constraints of the system could be embedded through work-based learning and realised afterwards.

Discussion

Educator–learner interaction has been a key factor in the advantage traditional learning environments have had over electronic ones. But this is only true if one considers that using technology in the teaching process makes the role of an in-person teacher redundant. This chapter explored four projects that have challenged this premise. The Young Enterprise Project showed that computers can play an important part of youth entrepreneurship, and subsequently the Emotivate Project showed how they can be an essential part of blending electronic learning with community activism and arts. The Digital Classroom of Tomorrow Project showed that it is possible to use eTwinning of the schools through networked learning. The findings from these projects were then applied through an auto-ethnography to two organisations—a social enterprise and a coasting school. Finally, the Free Digital Project was discussed, which is an initiative that brought all the other projects together to show how through the Cloud young and disabled people can become Internet entrepreneurs.

The study also looked at an investigation of a government maintained school between 2008 and 2015. It found that in the years that the researcher was present, providing challenge to the head teacher and the chair of governors, that the performance of the school was much greater. It found that the observations reported to the local education authority about the school, which were rubbished by them, were found to be supported by the school inspector. It can therefore be concluded that for schools to perform well there needs to be strong management, including through governors and similar taking the role of critical friends to ensure that the head teacher is focused on improving standards rather than relying on factors such as the local economy to justify an approach of 'business as usual'.

References

A.C. Baker, P.J. Jensen, D.A. Kolb, Conversation as experiential learning. Manag. Learn. **36**(4), 411–427 (2005)

J. Bishop, The potential of persuasive technology for educating heterogeneous user groups. Unpublished MSc, University of Glamorgan, Pontypridd GB, (2004)

J. Bishop, in *Evaluation-Centred Design of E-learning Communities: A Case Study and Review*. The 2nd International Conference on Internet Technologies and Applications (ITA'07), Wrexham, GB, 2007, pp. 1–9

J. Bishop, in *Didactic strategies and technologies for education: Incorporating advancements*, ed. by P. M. Pumilia-Gnarini, E. Favaron, E. Pacetti, J. Bishop, L. Guerra. Cooperative e-learning in the multilingual and multicultural school: The role of 'Classroom 2.0' for increasing participation in education (IGI Global, Hershey, PA, 2012a), pp. 137–150

J. Bishop, in *Didactic Strategies and Technologies for Education: Incorporating Advancements*, ed. by P. M. Pumilia-Gnarini, E. Favaron, E. Pacetti, J. Bishop, L. Guerra. Lessons from the Emotivate Project for Increasing Take-Up of Big Society and Responsible Capitalism Initiatives (IGI Global, Hershey, PA, 2012b), pp. 208–217

J. Bishop, in *Geo-Intelligence and Visualization Through Big Data Trends*. ed. by B. Bozkaya, V. Singh, Geo-demographic Big Data for Assessing Effectiveness of Crowd-Funded Software Projects: A Case Example of "QPress" (2015)

J. Bishop, in *Social Media Data Extraction and Content Analysis*, ed. by S. Hai-Jew. Devising Parametric User Models for Processing and Analysing Social Media Data to Influence User Behaviour: Using Quantitative and Qualitative Analysis of Social Media Data (IGI Global, Hershey, PA, 2017), pp. 1–41

J. Bishop, M.M.H. Goode, in *Gamification for Human Factors Integration: Social, Educational, and Psychological Issues*, ed. by J. Bishop. Towards a Subjectively Devised Parametric User Model for Analysing and Influencing Behaviour Online Using Gamification: A Review and Model (IGI Global, Hershey, PA, 2014), pp. 80–95

A.P. Bochner, On first-person narrative scholarship: Autoethnography as acts of meaning. Narrat. Inq. **22**(1), 155–164 (2012)

B. Brown, M. Chui, J. Manyika, Are you ready for the era of 'big data'. McKinsey Quart. **4**, 24–35 (2011)

F. Cornali, S. Tirocchi, in *Human Capital Formation and ICT: An Analysis of Education Policies*. International Conference on Teaching and Learning (IASK 2010), Siviglia, ES. pp. 201–214, 2010

J. Davidson, *The Learning Country: A Comprehensive Education and Lifelong Learning Programme to 2010 in Wales* No. (G/128/01–02) (The National Assembly for Wales, Cardiff, GB, 2001)

F.E. DeHart, Learning styles today: Implications for graduate library education, 1975

M. Dyson, My story in a profession of stories: auto ethnography–an empowering methodology for educators. Aust. J. Teach. Educ. **32**(1), n1 (2007)

P. Eickmann, A. Kolb, D. Kolb, Designing learning. Manag. Des., 241–247 (2004)

D.R. Garrison, H. Kanuka, Blended learning: uncovering its transformative potential in higher education. Internet High. Educ. **7**(2), 95–105 (2004)

P. Goodyear, M. de Laat, V. Lally, Using pattern languages to mediate theory-praxis conversations in design for networked learning. ALT-J Res. Learn. Technol. **14**(3), 211–223 (2006)

I. Hanraets, J. Hulsebosch, M. de Laat, Experiences of pioneers facilitating teacher networks for professional development. Educ. Media Int. **48**(2), 85–99 (2011)

D. Hayano, Auto-ethnography: paradigms, problems, and prospects. Hum. Organ. **38**(1), 99–104 (1979)

A. Heinze, C.T. Procter, Reflections on the use of blended learning. Paper presented at the *Education in a Changing Environment,* Manchester, GB, 2004

L. Hendrickson, R.H. Jokela, J. Gilman, S. Croymans, M. Marczak, V. Zuiker, et al., The viability of podcasts in extension education: Financial education for college students. J. Ext. **48**(4), 4FEA7 (2010)

B. Holmes, J. Sime, Online learning communities for teachers' continuous professional development: case study of an eTwinning learning event. Paper presented at the Proceedings of the 8th International Conference on Networked Learning, 2012

H.M. Hutchins, D. Hutchison, Cross-disciplinary contributions to e-learning design: a tripartite design model. J. Work. Learn. **20**(5), 364–380 (2008)

D.A. Kolb, Learning styles and disciplinary differences. The Modern American College, 232–255 (1981)

A. Labrinidis, H. Jagadish, Challenges and opportunities with big data. Proceedings of the VLDB Endowment **5**(12), 2032–2033 (2012)

O. Malgonde, A. Bhattacherjee, *Innovating using big data: A social capital perspective. Paper presented at the Twentieth Americas Conference on Information Systems* (Savannah, GA, 2014)

J.T. Ralph, *Annual report No. 1996* (Foster's Brewing Group Limited, Southbank, AU, 1996)

M. Reddy, *Using CU-seeme video conferening via the information superhighway to support distance learning of the ACE initiative at level 12 (Technical)* (University of Glamorgan, Treforest, GB, 1997a)

M. Reddy, in *The 2nd BP International Conference on Students as Tutors and Mentors*. Using the information superhighway to support the ACE initiative at level 12 (GB, London, 1997b)

D.T. Schuster, L.D. Grant, N. Moskowitz, Teaching Jewish adults. Ultimate Jewish Teacher's Handbook, 140–163 (2003)

S. Scimeca, P. Dumitru, M. Durando, A. Gilleran, A. Joyce, R. Vuorikari, European schoolnet: Enabling school networking. Eur. J. Educ. **44**(4), 475–492 (2009)

G. Taddeo, S. Tirocchi, in *Didactic strategies and technologies for education: Incorporating advancements*, ed. by P. M. Pumilia-Gnarini, E. Favaron, E. Pacetti, J. Bishop, L. Guerra. Learning in a "Classi 2.0" classroom: First results from an empirical research in the italian context (IGI Global, Hershey, PA, 2012), pp. 57–67

P.D. Turman, Coaches' immediacy behaviors as predictors of athletes' perceptions of satisfaction and team cohesion. West. J. Commun. **72**(2), 162–179 (2008)

P. Valiathan, Blended learning models. Learning Circuits, 2002

Vuorikari, R., Berlanga, A., Cachia, R., Cao, Y., Fetter, S., Gilleran, A., et al., in *ICT-Based School Collaboration, Teachers' Networks and their Opportunities for Teachers' Professional Development-A Case Study on eTwinning*. Advances in web-based learning-ICWL 2011 (Springer, 2011), pp. 112–121

S.L. Woerner, B.H. Wixom, Big data: extending the business strategy toolbox. J. Inf. Technol. **30**, 60–62 (2015)

Part IV
Applied Technologies for Data Analytics

Psychological Text Analysis in the Digital Humanities

Ryan L. Boyd

Abstract In the digital humanities, it has been particularly difficult to establish the psychological properties of a person or group of people in an objective, reliable manner. Traditionally, the attempt to understand an author's psychological makeup has been primarily (if not exclusively) accomplished through subjective interpretation, qualitative analysis, and speculation. In the world of empirical psychological research, however, the past two decades have witnessed an explosion of computerized language analysis techniques that objectively measure psychological features of the individual. Indeed, by using modern text analysis methods, it is now possible to quickly and accurately extract information about people—personalities, individual differences, social processes, and even their mental health—all through the words that people write and speak. This chapter serves as a primer for researchers interested in learning about how language can provide powerful insights into the minds of others via well-established and easy-to-use psychometric methods. First, this chapter provides a general background on language analysis in the field of psychology, followed by an introduction to modern methods and developments within the field of psychological text analysis. Finally, a solid foundation to psychological text analysis is provided in the form of an overview of research spanning hundreds of studies from labs all over the world.

Psychological Text Analysis in the Digital Humanities

The digital revolution has transformed the way that we interact with virtually everything. Televisions have built-in WIFI cards to stream media from sources all over the world. New refrigerator models can take pictures of their own contents with a digital camera and send them to your mobile phone. You can learn about world events, connect with your friends, and buy groceries with a few lazy swipes of the finger before you even get out of bed. For many of us, the technological shift has happened so quickly that we are still diligently attempting to understand just how

R.L. Boyd (✉)
Department of Psychology, The University of Texas at Austin, 108 E. Dean Keeton St., Stop A8000, Austin, TX 78712-1043, USA
e-mail: ryanboyd@utexas.edu

© Springer International Publishing AG 2017
S. Hai-Jew (ed.), *Data Analytics in Digital Humanities*, Multimedia Systems and Applications, DOI 10.1007/978-3-319-54499-1_7

drastically and diversely our world has changed in such a short amount of time. For many of the science fiction fans out there, these changes have not happened nearly fast enough ("Where *are* those hoverboards, anyway?").

One of the most obvious ways that advances in technology have impacted our daily lives is that we interact with information in completely new, unprecedented ways. This is particularly clear when considering how we both create and consume information. We are awash in human-created data 24/7, which can be seen as a great liberation of information or a scourge to quiet minds, depending on your point of view. People on both sides of the fence, however, generally agree that maximizing the benefit of our new abundance of information requires new ways of optimizing, managing, and processing data.

A New World of Research

Rather than create a great divide between fields of inquiry, the modern technological boom has instead helped to bring disparate areas of study closer together. The introduction of computational techniques has been particularly useful in the social sciences during this era of information. In the field of Psychology, we are primarily interested in the fundamentals of observable human thought, behaviors, and experience. Traditionally, psychology researchers have had to invite people into laboratory settings and prod them with stimuli and experimental conditions, hoping to coax real-world psychological processes out of them in a highly tedious, controlled manner. Alternatively, we could engage in painstaking field research by grabbing our pencils and paper, venturing outside, and carefully documenting what we could observe and survey from the population. These techniques are still incredibly useful for (and, in fact, central to) the careful, empirical study of psychological phenomena. However, with the proliferation of the internet and other digital technologies, we are finding not only new opportunities to study ourselves, but new methods to do so.

One of the most fascinating psychological methods to arise from the merging of disciplines has been the automated analysis of language. To many, this phrase may conjure thoughts of intricate, computer-generated linguistic diagrams or highly complex speech recognition programs. These are certainly triumphs of technology and deserve praise in their own right. Potentially even more fascinating to readers of this volume, however, are the scientific studies that have found that the common words a person writes, speaks, and types can be deeply revealing of their underlying psychology. Imagine a world where a few clicks on a computer can provide profound insights into whether a person is being authentic, how someone orients themselves socially, or even if a person is suicidal. You might be surprised to find that you are already living in this world. Decades of rigorous, empirical psychological research has found that there are profound links between the both content and style of a person's language and how they think, behave, and feel. The merging of psychology and computer science has been a driving force of such discoveries.

The goal of this chapter is to introduce to you three broad ideas from psychological research: (1) language analysis in the field of psychology, (2) two well-established techniques of automated psychological language analysis, and (3) an overview of psychological research that has successfully used automated text analysis. Some of the research that is introduced in this chapter has already been explored in the context of the Digital Humanities, however, the opportunities for future work are essentially limitless.

Importantly, the psychological analysis of text is conceptually quite different from those provided by techniques often referred to as "distant reading" (e.g., Moretti 2013; Ross 2014) and other natural language processing methodologies. The empirical methods and research discussed in this chapter are not necessarily about understanding texts themselves, modeling language structure, or capturing relationships between written works. Instead, these methods are emphatically *psychological* in their nature and applications. The analysis of language from this perspective allows us to understand the individual *behind* a given text—their motivations, preoccupations, emotional states, and other facets of their mental universe.

Language Analysis in Psychology

Language has been of long-standing intrigue in the field of Psychology. Dewey (1910) broadly philosophized about language as a vehicle for thought, and Freud (e.g., Freud 1891) theorized that people's words could provide insights into their emotions and hidden, deep-seated motives. While many of the specific theories from the psychodynamic movement have been modified or altogether abandoned, the overarching ideas about links between language and psychology took hold in empirical psychological research. In the middle of the twentieth century, researchers began codifying word clusters into "dictionaries" that could be used to assess people's needs for things like affiliation, achievement, and power (e.g., Lasswell et al. 1952). For example, people who used relatively high numbers of words like "win," "success," and "goal" were thought to be generally motivated by a striving for accomplishment. In fact, several lines of research often found such predictions to be true (e.g., McClelland et al. 1953).

The dictionary-based approach to measuring meaningful psychological processes continued to develop as mainframe computers were introduced in the 1960s. The focus of psychological text analysis swayed between studying culture and mass media versus individual motivations (e.g., Stone et al. 1966), but eventually returned to a more idiographic approach that focused on clinically relevant topics such as anxiety, schizophrenia, and coping in therapy (e.g., Martindale 1975; Mergenthaler 1996; Weintraub 1989).

A considerable drawback to most of the automated text analysis systems designed in the latter half of the twentieth century is that they were often wholly opaque. Many systems involved complicated rulesets that were difficult to interpret, idiosyncratic systems that prioritized certain words over others, or dictionaries that were rooted in highly specific theories of psychology that did not extend well outside of specific use-cases. A system of analyzing texts for a specific neo-Freudian process had little use when researching extraversion, for example, and an obtuse system that involved weighting various words made it difficult to evaluate the accuracy of a language-based measure for something like self-esteem from a psychological perspective. In effect, the ambitiousness of such systems proved to be a major hindrance and point of fault rather than providing accessible techniques that could be used to study human psychology broadly.

Linguistic Inquiry and Word Count

The impact of realizing that language can be quantified to reveal clues about a person's underlying psychology is difficult to overstate. The more that a person used words from certain, verified categories of language (such as words about anger or family), the more these concepts appeared to be a central dimension of that person's psychology.[1] However, in the late 1990s, psychologists were starting to discover that there was more to language than its content. Up to that point, virtually every text analysis technique in psychology focused on what we call *content words* (also referred to as "open class" words because they can take many different forms, such as "run," "running," and "runs"). Content words convey some kind of meaning (e.g., who, what, where, etc.) and constitute the majority of the words in a person's vocabulary. Consider the sentence:

Natalie drove to the store and bought some coffee.

The content words in this sentence give us the information of *who* (Natalie), *what* (drove, bought, coffee), and *where* (store). By looking only at the content words in the above sentence, we can get a fairly good sense of what is being said.

But what about the other words, like "to," "the," "and," and "some"? These have traditionally been treated as garbage words that convey no useful information—such words were thought to exist merely as an artifact of language that joins together the "important" words. If we look just at the grammatical words in the above sentence ("to the and some"), we get no clues as to what the sentence is about, what is being conveyed, etc.—virtually no useful information at all.

However, researchers such as George Miller (1995) were beginning to find that these small, meaningless words tend to be processed in different areas of the brain than content words and appear to serve other psychological purposes. This type

---

[1]Note that while it may seem trivial to create new categories of words to measure a psychological process, it can be an unspeakably difficult task in practice. Determining how specific words are often used out in the "real world," establishing whether certain words are related to psychologically meaningful processes, and creating dictionaries that possess adequate statistical properties is deceptively tricky. Many researchers have spent years working on word dictionaries that have ultimately proven to be meaningless.

of work hinted that there may be more to these *function words* (also called "closed class" words) than what we had initially thought. Indeed, researchers began noticing that the way that people used function words often signaled a person's psychological state as much as, and in some cases more than, their content words.

In essence, while we knew that *what* a person says can be important for inferring psychological patterns, we were beginning to learn that *how* a person says something can be just as telling. Additionally, because function words are generated in an essentially automatic manner by the brain in order to link meaningful words together, the way that function words are used is often unconscious. In other words, we seldom stop to think about which function words to use when speaking or writing—they are quietly generated from a very deep level of the mind.

At the same time as these realizations were being made, early versions of desktop applications were being developed to automatically analyze text in a more user-friendly manner. One of the first mainstream examples of these applications was named Linguistic Inquiry and Word Count (LIWC, pronounced the same as "Luke"; Pennebaker and Francis 1999). LIWC has gone through several iterations since its creation, with the latest version being LIWC2015 (Pennebaker et al. 2015). At its core, LIWC consists of two parts. The heart of the application is its dictionary that, in many ways, is similar to the dictionaries of older text analysis paradigms.

The LIWC dictionary contains word-to-category mappings for around 80 categories of words, including both common content words (e.g., words about family, emotions, biological processes) and function words (e.g., pronouns, conjunctions, articles, etc.). For example, the "cognitive processes" category contains words like "think," "understand," and "analyze," and the "articles" category contains the words "a," "an," and "the." Additionally, similar techniques have been used to translate various versions of the LIWC dictionary to multiple languages over the years, allowing researchers to conduct parallel work across different languages and cultures.[2]

The principal strength of the LIWC dictionary is bolstered by the fact that it was carefully developed using established, standard psychometric approaches such as validation on external psychological data, as well as techniques that ensure high internal reliability from a statistical perspective (see Pennebaker et al. 2015).

If the dictionary is the heart of LIWC, the program itself is the brain of the whole operation. The LIWC2015 software is, in a way, deceptively simple in how it works. The program operates by reading in batches of text files (e.g., plain text ".txt" files, MS Office ".docx" files, etc.), then counts the percentage of words that belong to each of the LIWC dictionary categories. For example, if 2 out of every 10 words in a text is a "social" word, and 1 out of every 10 words is a "cognitive process" word, the text will be scored as 20% social and 10% cognitive in nature.

---

[2]At the time of this writing, various translations of the LIWC dictionary exist in Spanish, Dutch, German, Italian, French, Korean, Chinese, Portuguese, and Turkish, among others. These translations are typically available from their respective translators rather than the LIWC creators, and most have accompanying peer-reviewed publications that evaluate the psychometric properties of the translated dictionaries.

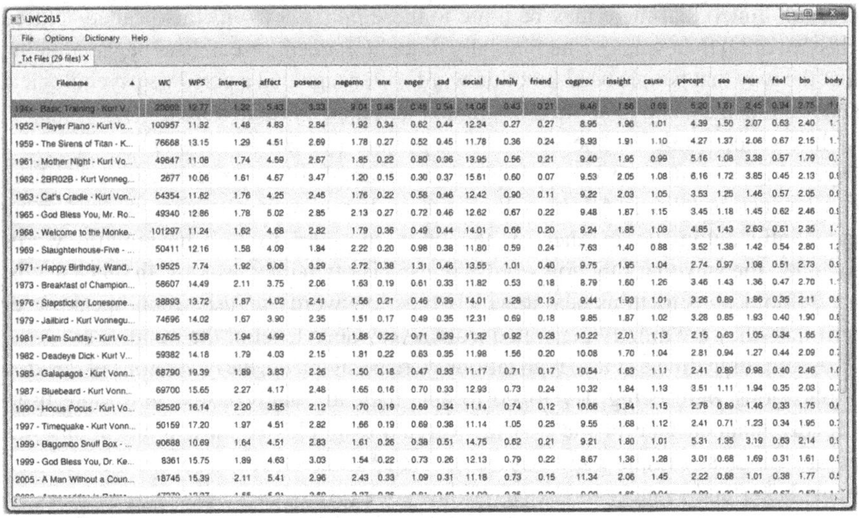

Fig. 1 Example of output provided by the LIWC2015 application. Output is provided in a table that shows filenames, summary measures (e.g., word count, average words per sentence), and percentage of words that belong to each category (e.g., percent of words reflecting anxiety, cognitive processing, tactile perception, etc.). LIWC output can be exported as one of many several standard file formats (CSV, Excel spreadsheets, etc.) for use in statistical packages such as R or SPSS

This task is done for each of the 80 categories in the LIWC dictionary (some other summary measures are calculated as well, such as word count, punctuation use, and so on), and output is produced in the form of a spreadsheet (see Fig. 1). Additionally, the LIWC2015 application is fairly open-ended—users can create and use their own custom dictionaries with the software to code for categories of words that are relevant to their own research interests.

The very basic "word counting" approach has been found to work extremely well across time and contexts for two primary reasons. First, as discussed earlier, we repeatedly find that when a person uses higher rates of certain topics/categories of language, they tend to show psychological patterns that correspond to their language. Second, the "word counting" approach of LIWC2015 takes advantage of the probabilistic properties of how people naturally use language—that is, people tend to use language in meaningful clusters. An angry person typically does not just use one or two anger words, they use constellations of words that express (or hint at) their anger. Someone who is actively working through a problem tends to use multiple cognitive words together as they talk or write relative to someone who is not working through a problem, and so on.

The word counting approach does occasionally miss or misclassify a word here and there, however, a well-made dictionary will correctly categorize words most of the time. If a person uses the word "sad" once, it is hard to determine with a computer program the precise meaning of the word in a single instance. Was the person being sarcastic? Were they relaying the fact that someone else looks sad? Were they talking about being *not* sad?[3] In extremely short texts (e.g., one or two sentences), these are very real concerns that should not be dismissed when using any form of automated text analysis. However, when aggregating across large amounts of text by the same person (hundreds, thousands, or tens of thousands of words), we almost always find that these issues are rendered moot, despite the occasionally misclassified word (see the section in Appendix "Preparing Texts for Analysis" for additional considerations on text preparation/word detection). Generally speaking, then, a word counting approach that ignores things like context and intended audience can still provide surprisingly clear insights into a person's psychology.

Meaning Extraction: A Complementary Approach

Over the years, an incredible amount of research from labs all over the world has demonstrated that each of the LIWC word categories exhibits distinct and often surprising relationships with specific social and psychological processes (for a fairly contemporary review, see Tausczik and Pennebaker 2010). Indeed, most of the research that is introduced later in this chapter relies directly on the LIWC dictionary for understanding how people think, feel, and behave. The LIWC dictionary does have one commonly cited drawback, however: it requires pre-defined sets of words to make psychological inferences. In the past decade, additional language analysis techniques have been created that are useful for inferring psychological processes in a more inductive, or "bottom-up," manner. In psychology, one of the most accessible techniques that have been created is called the Meaning Extraction Method (MEM; Chung and Pennebaker 2008).

The MEM is a way of automatically inferring what words are being used together, essentially resulting in a dictionary of word-to-category mappings from a collection of texts. In simple terms, this is achieved by finding words that naturally clump into "themes" using some basic statistical techniques. In practice, the MEM can be considered a series of steps that a researcher takes—this procedure begins with a collection of texts and results in psychologically meaningful word clusters:

1. Identify words in a corpus of texts that are relatively common.
2. Create a table that shows which texts use which common words.
3. Statistically identify words that tend to occur together throughout the corpus.

Conceptually, the MEM is fairly simple and straight-forward. However, in practice, there are several sub-steps that have to be completed in order to get from

---

[3]Interestingly, the negation of an emotion (e.g., "not sad") appears to be psychologically different from expressing the opposite of an emotion ("happy"). Research has found that people who think along a "sadness" dimension, even if they are repeatedly saying that they are "not sad" or talking about someone else's sadness, are psychologically different from those who are thinking along the lines of a different emotion altogether (Pennebaker et al. 1997).

the beginning of the process to the end. Recently, our lab has released free software called the Meaning Extraction Helper (MEH; Boyd 2016) that can automate the majority of the MEM process, making this approach readily accessible and easy to perform with minimal effort.

1. Identify words in a corpus of texts that are relatively common. Unlike a dictionary-based method that considers each document in isolation, the MEM considers a whole collection of texts at once. Like other topic modeling methods, the MEM works this way in order to determine how words are *typically* used within a given sample. As a first step, we need to identify those words that appear in enough different texts in order to understand not just idiosyncratic word use by one individual, but broader patterns across different people and texts. Moreover, when performing the MEM, we tend to care less about specific variations of words than the concepts reflected by each of the words—to account for this, we can do something called "lemmatization," which converts words to their most basic form (e.g., "drive," "driving," and "drove" are all converted to "drive"). Lemmatization is something that the MEH software is able to do this automatically for most English words (in addition to roughly a dozen other languages).

Once words are lemmatized, we create a list of all words and determine what percentage of texts use each word. Once all of this information has been collected, we decide which words we would like to omit based on what percentage of texts include each word, typically using a minimum of somewhere around 5%. This prevents any single text from unduly influencing our results: a single text may contain 500 instances of the word "enantiodromia,"[4] but this is hardly useful in understanding its broad psychological properties across different people. Lastly, we typically omit function words from our master list—because function words are so common, they tend to co-occur with *all* other words, making them difficult to statistically separate into meaningful themes (see Table 1 for an example of the frequency list generated by MEH).

2. Create a table that shows which texts use which common words. Once the commonly used words have been selected, we need to create a dataset with this information—this will allow us to extract common themes using some basic statistical procedures. The simplest way of doing this is to score each text using a "binary" method—that is, each text either does or does not use each word (see Table 2).

Before discussing the statistical particulars, take a close look at Table 2. By simply looking at the 1's in each row, one can get a decent sense of what each story is about. Story 1 clearly contains elements about school and social concepts, possibly a story about a school-related memory involving close relationships. Stories 3 and 5 appear to both have strong elements of time—an instinctive guess would suggest that the authors are focused on (or attentive to) time, order of events, or temporal sequences. The next step, listed below, is comprised of running a statistical

---

[4]To spare the curious reader from having to seek out a dictionary, "enantiodromia" refers to a tendency for something to convert into its opposite form.

Table 1 Example of a frequency list generated by MEH

Word	Raw Word Frequency Across All Texts	Percentage of Texts that Contain Word
the	600	100.00
a	542	98.12
life	320	67.89
school	187	53.45
time	133	35.33
people	98	21.66
year	91	8.99
day	82	6.72
family	72	5.51
friend	63	5.30
book	31	1.36
plant	15	1.21
enantiodromia	500	0.10

Note that uncommon words (even if used in high amounts by a single person) are excluded from subsequent steps. In this table words highlighted in black will be removed from subsequent steps because they are function words and, as the right-most column shows, will co-occur with virtually all other words in the sample (e.g., every single text includes the word "the," so it co-occurs with literally all other words). Words highlighted in gray will be excluded from subsequent steps because they appear in a small percentage of texts, even if they are highly common in terms of their raw frequency.

Table 2 An example of Step 2 in the Meaning Extraction Method: a binary table that reflects which texts used common words in a corpus

Text	Life	School	Time	People	Year	Day	Family	Friend
Story 1	1	1		1			1	1
Story 2					1	1		
Story 3			1		1	1		
Story 4		1		1				1
Story 5			1		1	1		1
...								

The left-most column shows which text is being considered, and each row highlights which words were present in each text. Note that for particularly long texts, other scoring methods may be preferable (e.g., percentage of text comprised of each word, known as a "verbose" score)

procedure that does a rather good job of extracting themes in a way that coincides with our intuitive judgments, albeit in a fairly broad manner.

3. Statistically identify words that tend to occur together. Conceptually, one can think of a Principal Components Analysis (PCA) as a method for finding groups of correlations—in essence, finding groups of words that tend to be used together. Fortunately, one does not have to be statistically savvy to run this analysis, as most statistical packages (such as SPSS and R) have ways to run a PCA rather easily. For our example above, a PCA would likely find that the words "time," "year," and "day" form a broader, meaningful theme about "time," and the concepts of "school," "people," and "friend" appear to be part of a broader social theme (see Table 3).

Table 3 Example results
from a Principal Components
Analysis performed in
Table 2

	Factor 1 ("time")	Factor 2 ("social")
Day	**0.67**	0.09
Year	**0.58**	0.02
Time	**0.42**	0.11
People	0.03	**0.88**
School	0.04	**0.75**
Friend	0.12	**0.70**
Life	0.16	0.00
Family	0.09	0.01

Technically, all words will have a 'loading' onto each of the themes extracted from a corpus of texts. Usually, a manually chosen cutoff is used (typically around 0.10 for very large samples and 0.25 for relatively small samples) to determine which words belong to which themes. In this table, shaded values indicate the theme onto which each word best loads using a conservative cutoff value. Words may also commonly load onto multiple themes.

What the PCA has done for us, then, is to identify 2 clusters of words that can be thought of as new categories of language to measure for psychological purposes. If we look back to Step 2, we find that these word clusters converge with our previous intuitions.

What Do We Do with these New Themes?

Ultimately, the steps that comprise the MEM are designed to help identify themes across our texts that can then be measured using the LIWC-style word counting approach. In some cases, identifying which common themes exist is telling in its own right—perhaps we are looking to discover common themes across international treaties to better understand the topics that they deal with, or what themes are most prevalent in famous jazz lyrics. However, as we have learned, these themes are often psychologically meaningful as well. By using a LIWC-style approach to quantifying each theme across texts, we can search for psychological patterns within or between individuals (e.g., did an author objectively fixate more on nature in earlier versus later works? How do time and culture influence the narrative of war?; see the section in Appendix "Working with the MEM and MEM Results" for additional notes on quantifying MEM themes in texts). In the coming sections, studies that have used the MEM to better understand psychological profiles of individuals across several types of research questions will be described.

The Statistical Analysis of LIWC and MEM Output

Once you have performed the above methods, you are left staring at spreadsheets full of rows of text names and hundreds of columns containing numeric representations of psychological dimensions. What does one *do* with all of those numbers? All of the methods described above are inherently quantitative in some form or another. While the quantified output of these procedures can still be used to facilitate qualitative psychological insights, they are particularly well-suited to statistical modeling and analyses. Given that each column of the LIWC and MEM datasets is numeric vectors, language-based psychological measures can fit into virtually any statistical algorithm that someone would use for any other quantified metric. How language-based measures of psychology are put to best use will vary widely depending on your research, goals, and interests. Like other types of measures and analyses, it is often important to understand the properties of your variables so that they may be optimally beneficial to your own work.

In terms of ensuring that your numerical data is of adequate quality, the primary statistical considerations in psychological text analyses typically revolve around the size of each text that you have processed—beyond this, most word counting methods are rather forgiving. Because most word counting methods deal with percentages, a minimum word count of 25 or 50 words per text is typically recommended.[5] For example, the sentence "That was a good doughnut" contains positive emotion words (good) and ingestion words (doughnut) both at the same rate: 1 out of 5, or 20%. This is an extremely high number for both categories: positive emotion words are typically in the 2–8% range, and ingestion words typically occur far less frequently (less than 1% of words in most cases). In larger bodies of text, the behaviors of language patterns tend to smooth out, resulting in more accurate and useful distributions of psychological categories. Omitting texts with too few words is equally important when running MEM analyses: if texts contain only 5 or 10 words on average, and half of these are function words, it becomes difficult to discover meaningful co-occurrence patterns unless you have an extremely large number of observations (e.g., a few hundred thousand texts).

Once language has been quantified and texts containing too few words have been dropped, an appropriate statistical model must be selected. The selection and execution of statistical models is usually informed by the nature of one's data and research design, and a full consideration of model selection is far beyond the scope of this chapter. However, it is important to note that the most actionable insights from psychological text analysis usually require transparent statistical models. In other words, if a statistical model is relatively easy to interpret (e.g., a simple Pearson correlation or a between-groups ANOVA), understanding the meaningful

---

[5]The general rule of thumb is that more data is almost *always* better. Data quantity is the foundation of both reliability and accuracy when quantifying psychological processes, which can be incredibly difficult to assess using *any* research method. The same holds true when using language to extract psychological information.

psychological patterns is far easier to come by than when using powerhouse algorithms that are largely impenetrable (e.g., a support vector machine with radial basis function kernels, deep-layer convolutional neural networks).

The use of powerful but opaque statistical techniques has rapidly become a serious problem for a number of studies that exist in the computational social sciences, particularly when using language to model human psychology. Many published studies are technically impressive from a Computer Science or Information Sciences perspective, but are ultimately useless to social scientists who seek to understand the nature of findings (e.g., "Did X *cause* Y?"; "How does X vary *as a function* of Y?"). In other words, being able to *predict* a phenomenon with a statistical model is conceptually quite different from being able to *understand* it and its implications. For example, virtually all of the research described in the next section has been made possible by the use of simple statistical models that are easily interpreted, resulting in valuable theoretical insights into the human mind.

The predict-versus-understand tradeoff is a major one that delineates most psychological text analysis techniques from those more frequently used in computational linguistics, the information sciences, and related fields. Ultimately, statistical decisions most often come down to properly understanding the intended goals of a research project and field-specific standards/traditions. A mismatch between the stated goals of a study and the domain expertise required to understand what types of decisions should be made during statistical analyses can too often result in dazzling statistical models that offer no insights beyond "X plus 50 other variables can predict Y".[6]

Psychological Research Using LIWC and MEM

In the past two decades, an incredible amount of research using both LIWC and MEM has been done that finds robust links between language use and psychological patterns—far too much to cover in a single chapter. What is presented below should not be taken as a comprehensive overview of this body of work. Instead, the goal of this section is to introduce you to some of the broader areas of psychological research that have been studied using automated language analysis, providing specific studies and experiments as examples of this work.

---

[6]These comments are in no way intended to disparage or discourage the use of heavy-hitting statistical algorithms and machine learning procedures. In fact, the author of this chapter uses these analytic techniques with absolute regularity in his own work, and he enjoys few things in life more than the intricacy of well-crafted, complex models (why yes, he *is* a huge hit at parties—how did you know?). However, the importance of considering tradeoffs between prediction power and being able to describe/understand one's model in practical terms cannot be overstated.

Language and Individual Differences

When we read a text, we are often trying to get a sense of who the author is as a person. How do they think? Are they young or old? What does their day-to-day life look like? Are they nice, independent, quick to anger, or deviously calculating? When asking these questions, we often have to rely upon our own subjective experiences and feelings to make evaluations of other people; this is especially true when all that we have to go on is a person's language. The central question, then, is "do different types of people talk in different ways?" Can we reliably infer characteristics of a person based solely on the words they use? As is discussed in this section, the answer turns out to be a resounding "yes."

These types of evaluations fall under the broader umbrella of *individual differences*, a large area of research that tries to understand the various ways in which people are psychologically different from one another, yet relatively consistent over time. Individual differences not only include personality evaluations like neuroticism and extraversion, but also include things such as gender, age, life experiences, and so on—things that differ between individuals but are not necessarily *caused by* internal psychology processes.

Language and Traditional Self-Report Personality Measures

In psychology, we generally refer to *personality* as collections of thoughts, behaviors, and emotions that are indicative of a person across time and situations. When we say that an individual is *neurotic*, for example, we really mean to say that they exhibit a cluster of specific, stable psychological patterns over time. A neurotic person tends to have difficulty regulating their emotions, they typically interpret ambiguous information as negative, and they consistently experience anxiety at above-average levels on a day-to-day basis. Personality descriptors like "neuroticism," then, do not refer to "real" things, but instead act as a sort of a shorthand term that we use to refer to these types of stable psychological patterns and clusters.

Early work on the consistency of language found that a person's language, like their personality, showed reliable patterns between multiple time points (Pennebaker and King 1999). Just as a person who is extroverted today is likely to be extroverted next week, next month, and next year, so too does a person's word use remain relatively constant over time. If someone uses high rates of conjunctions relative to other people today, they will most likely use high rates of conjunctions across different times and situations. This proved to be an invaluable finding for language research as it demonstrated that language use could be used to detect those stable psychological patterns that broadly characterize a person. In practice, what this means is that when we scientifically establish a link between a certain measure of language (e.g., use of negations such as "isn't" and "aren't") and personality (e.g., impulsivity), we can infer certain stable aspects of a person indirectly based exclusively on how they write or talk. That is to say, by measuring the rate at which someone uses negations, we can statistically estimate the degree to which they are also impulsive. Much recent research has found that it is possible to estimate a person's personality using LIWC- and MEM-based measures, albeit with some caveats.

An important point about studying personality is that psychologists typically assess an individual's personality using self-report questionnaires. In a standard social science research setting, self-report questionnaires can be an ideal personality assessment tool: they are easy to fill out, rather fast to complete, and require no fuss from the test-taker or the researcher.[7] Unfortunately, the self-report paradigm is of limited usefulness when conducting several other types of work. Until backwards time travel is invented (presumably this will come shortly after the aforementioned hoverboards), we cannot present questionnaires to historical figures such as Francis Beaumont or Franklin Pierce and politely ask them to "fill in the bubbles" at their convenience. Other sources of personality information can be problematic: observer reports of historical figures tend to be skewed, riddled with myth, and spotty, particularly as we look further back in history. Fortunately, the very foundations of personality (stable trends in thought, feeling, and behaviors) tend to be encoded in human language, allowing us to establish personality—language links and, subsequently, make scientifically grounded estimates of an individual's general psychological makeup.

When discussing personality, the most commonly used theoretical framework is known as the "Big 5" of personality (neuroticism, extroversion, openness to experience, conscientiousness, and agreeableness; see John et al. 2008). Most language research on personality that uses self-reports attempts to correlate language use with peoples' responses to Big 5 questionnaires, and the majority of these studies use the psychological measures generated by LIWC. Pennebaker and King (1999) initially found correlations between Big 5 personality measures and the language of students writing different types of stories and narratives. For example, people scoring high on self-reported neuroticism use fewer positive emotion words and high rates of negative emotion words, as we would expect, and participants who score higher on extroversion tend to use more social words. Since then, several other researchers have found that LIWC measures of language can be used to estimate someone's personality (Yarkoni 2010; Komisin and Guinn 2012), and some research has even been extended to automatically assessing the personality of fictional characters based on their language (e.g., Flekova and Gurevych 2015; Liberman 2015). Most research has found that LIWC-based approaches to estimating personality perform well above average, even when simple statistical models are used (e.g., Mairesse et al. 2007).

---

[7]Note, however, that self-report measures of personality are not without their own drawbacks and imperfections. In order to accurately answer a self-report question about yourself, you must have both accurate information about yourself in a given domain and a willingness/ability to make accurate self-reports. The literature on self-report biases and pitfalls is rather extensive but beyond the scope of this chapter.

Other research using the MEM has also found patterns of word use that can be used to understand personality as well. In a study that extracted themes from individual writing samples, Chung and Pennebaker (2008) found common social themes such as *sociability* (comprised of words like "independent," "fun," and "confident"), *maturity* ("mature," "successful," "caring"), and *psychological stability* ("satisfied," "healthy," "positive"). When quantifying these themes in peoples' writing, the researchers found that the degree to which each person invoked these themes was related to how they scored on self-reports of the Big 5. For example, people who used more words from the sociability theme tended to score higher on agreeableness, and people who wrote using words from the maturity theme tended to score higher on conscientiousness. This work revealed that even the common themes people talk about (and the way that people talk about them) can be telling of a person's personality, sometimes counterintuitively. Because the MEM extracts themes based on common content words, this approach can also be used to establish relevant lists of words to watch for when manually trying to infer personality based on an author's texts.

It is important to note that, while a considerable amount of research has been done attempting to link self-report questionnaires of personality to language use, this approach often results in weaker findings than studies that use other types of individual differences data. In the remaining portion of this section, the studies presented will generally focus on language use and its link to other forms of data, such as behavioral data (performance-based measures, such as test performance, and reports of specific actions in which people engage) and objective self-reports that are typically unbiased (e.g., age).

Language across the Lifespan

Pennebaker and Stone (2003) conducted two studies examining the effect of age on how people write. The researchers analyzed the writings of authors who wrote multiple works throughout their lifetime (e.g., Alcott, Austen, Shakespeare, Yeats) and found several consistent patterns. As authors aged, they tended to use more positive emotion words and future tense words. Aging was also found to be related to the use of fewer negative emotion words, past-tense verbs, and self-references. A second study of non-professional writing by psychology study participants found the same patterns, and these results converge with other research on age-related psychological changes (e.g., Watson 2000), as well as other studies of age-related shifts in language use (e.g., Schler et al. 2006).

Language and Core Values

Recently, Boyd et al. (2015) conducted a large-scale analysis of how a person's values are expressed in the language that they use. Using the MEM, they first asked participants to write about their core values (those principles that guide their lives, decisions, and behaviors), as well as their common behaviors. In their work, they found that they were able to extract word clusters that corresponded to distinct values, such as *religion, empathy,* and *personal growth.* Importantly, they found that the value-relevant themes that people used were strongly predictive of people's actual behaviors.

After establishing word-to-value mappings, the researchers conducted a large-scale analysis of Facebook users to explore the degree to which value-relevant language was present in unprompted writings by the general public. The results from their second study supported those of their first—greater use of value-related themes was broadly predictive of what types of behaviors people engaged in (and reported engaging in) online. People who invoked the *religion* core value theme were more likely to attend church, and individuals who used words from the *empathy* theme were more likely share messages in support of cancer awareness and friendship.

These types of language-based value—behavior links pave the way for assessing the values that a person holds central in their lives from their writings and verbal speech. Because the researchers established value-relevant themes using the MEM, these word lists can be applied to new domains in novel ways. The fact that a person's casual, innocuous words can be used to predict specific, concrete day-to-day behaviors may strike some readers as rather unnerving. Indeed, such findings highlight the power of psychological text analysis methods.

Language and Thinking Styles

In judgment and decision-making research, decades of work has found that different individuals tend to solve problems and make decisions in two broad ways: (1) slowly and deliberately, or (2) quickly and intuitively (see Kahneman 2011; also sometimes referred to as "rational" vs. "experiential" decision-making, respectively). These "decision-making styles" tend to be fairly static over time; someone who is an "intuitive" decision-maker today will tend to make decisions in the same way across time and contexts (Fetterman and Robinson 2013). Rational decision-makers tend to be highly analytic, do well in school, and can sometimes be perceived as socially cold or distant (a relatively common television/movie cliché that, as it turns out, has some basis in reality). On the other hand, experiential decision-makers tend to rely more on their emotions, social events, and narratives to make decisions, and are typically perceived as being more socially open and warm than rational decision-makers.

By analyzing function words with LIWC, Pennebaker et al. (2014) were able to develop a language-based measure of thinking styles named the Categorical-Dynamic Index (CDI) that corresponds to how people make decisions and mentally engage with the world. At the high end of the CDI are people who primarily use high rates of articles and prepositions while, conversely, people on the other end of the CDI tend to use lots of pronouns, negations, adverbs, and other types of function words. Using the CDI, Pennebaker et al. (2014) were able to predict measures pertaining to college performance, such as student GPA and pre-college SAT scores, as a function of students' admission essays. Using the same measure, Jordan and Pennebaker (2016) found striking differences between the 2016 Democratic and Republican US presidential candidates during debates, with Democratic candidates generally scoring on the "rational" side of the CDI and Republican candidates scoring on the "experiential" side.

Authorship Attribution Using Psychological Analyses

The LIWC application and dictionary are used regularly to help understand authors precisely because of the stable nature of language use by individuals. By building on the findings showing that a person's linguistic patterns are markers of their underlying psychology, and that both exhibit relatively static trends over time, it is theoretically possible to aggregate several language-based measures of a person's psychology into a "psychological fingerprint" that is unique to them. For example, Petrie et al. (2008) used LIWC measures of the Beatles' lyrics to identify the unique psychology of each Beatles member, and also found which songwriter's style was predominant in Beatles songs that were written collaboratively.[8]

What do we do when the authorship of a work is unknown or disputed? Over the years, several methods of automated stylometry have been developed to try to establish authorship using word distributions (e.g., Juola 2006; Koppel et al. 2008). Many of these methods are rather effective, however, they can conceptually oversimplify the individual by reducing them to single words rather than human beings with complex mental lives. By combining several of the measures outlined in this chapter (e.g., LIWC-based measures of personality, the CDI, MEM-derived themes), Boyd and Pennebaker (2015) were able to statistically establish the likelihood that Shakespeare authored the long-disputed play *Double Falsehood.*

In their study, Boyd and Pennebaker (2015) found that three possible authors— William Shakespeare, John Fletcher, and Lewis Theobald—all had highly distinct psychological patterns of language use across their respective solo works. In fact, each author's psychological fingerprint was so unique that all three authors could be reliably distinguished with near-100% accuracy using exclusively language-based psychological measures. After establishing each author's unique psychological attributes, the researchers were able to automatically extract a new psychological composite from the play *Double Falsehood,* then statistically compare the disputed play to each author's unique psychological fingerprint. Their findings overwhelm-

---

[8]Another interesting analysis of the Beatles using LIWC was performed by Kasser (2013), who explored the interpretation of the song *Lucy in the Sky with Diamonds* from a psychological perspective. While the song is often cited as being overtly about drug use, Kasser (2013) found that the psychological fingerprint of the song was generally quite similar to other lyrics authored by John Lennon. Kasser did find linguistic markers consistent with drug experience descriptions, however, *Lucy in the Sky with Diamonds* also scored relatively high on language measures that pertain to distancing oneself from painful experiences, such as a lack of emotional content and very few markers of "here and now" thinking (sometimes called "psychological distancing").

ingly supported the notion that Shakespeare was the primary author of the original play, with modest contributions from John Fletcher and likely later editing on the part of Lewis Theobald. Additionally, because the language-based measures were principally revealing of the authors' respective personalities, the researchers were able to compare the psychological fingerprints to historical accounts of each author. Boyd and Pennebaker's (2015) analysis largely converged with historical and observer reports, such as Fletcher having been a highly social individual and Theobald having been highly intelligent but cold and confrontational.

Language and Mental Health

Given that much of the early psychological interest in language dealt with disorders and mental health issues, it is perhaps not surprising that much of the modern work using automated text analysis also began in this area. By analyzing the language of an individual, it is possible to uncover areas that are particularly problematic in their lives. Depression, emotional upheavals, and childhood traumas can leave lasting marks on the ways in which a person communicates that are nearly impossible to detect with the naked eye. However, by using automated text analysis, the subtle differences in function word use and thematic relationships can be quite striking and powerfully telling of a person's current and past emotional difficulties.

Depression and Suicide

One of the best-explored areas of mental health and language includes research on depression and suicide. For example, Stirman and Pennebaker (2001) analyzed 300 poems by 18 poets (9 of whom committed suicide) with LIWC in order to test for language patterns indicative of risk for depression/suicide. The researchers found that the poets who committed suicide used language patterns consistent with a social withdrawal, such as increased first person singular pronouns (I, me, my) and decreased first person plural pronouns (we, us, our). These patterns were particularly pronounced when poems were written close to the time of an author's suicide. The findings of this study revealed that those poets who committed suicide increasingly suffered from an inability to extract themselves from their own mental worlds, instead exhibiting an elevated focus on the self and decreased attention to their social environments.

Other studies have found the same language patterns leading up to an author's suicide. An analysis of Marilyn Monroe's personal writings published in *Fragments* found similar first person pronoun patterns leading up to her death (Fernández-Cabana et al. 2013). Additionally, various cognitive and emotional patterns indicative of suicide and depression, such as decreases in cognitive complexity, were found in *Fragments*. While such patterns of language use are not *proof* of suicide, they strongly suggest suicidal perturbations in Monroe's psychological functioning.

Similar language patterns of self-focus and social isolation were found in the written works of Henry Hellyer, a ninetieth century surveyor and explorer whose death was ruled a suicide (Baddeley et al. 2011).

The work on links between language and depression/suicide has been extended to other areas as well. Such work includes research on comparisons between individuals who committed suicide versus spree killings (Egnoto and Griffin 2016), women suffering from post-partum depression (De Choudhury et al. 2013), and even depression support forums (Ramirez-Esparza et al. 2008).

The Impact of Traumatic Events on Psychology and Language Use

A sizeable portion of psychological text analysis research has examined the links between language and how people process and come to understand traumatic events. Indeed, the original version of LIWC was initially created as a way to automatically analyze narratives written by people coping with trauma in their own lives (known as "expressive writing"; see Pennebaker and Evans 2014).

In a study of psychological changes in response to traumatic events, Gortner and Pennebaker (2003) conducted an archival study of newspaper articles surrounding the 1999 Aggie Bonfire collapse, an event that caused the death of 12 people at Texas A&M University. Using a LIWC analysis of local newspaper articles spanning a timeline of 1 month before to approximately a year after the event, several psychological patterns mined from the articles' language followed a "social stages of coping" model that appeared to capture broader psychological trends in the community. For example, social words and cognitive words showed an immediate increase after the incident, suggesting a general increase in the need for social and mental engagement with the world. Additionally, the linguistic shifts seen in the newspaper articles were predictive of rates of illness in the affected community, acutely reflecting the effects of stress on individual physical health (Sapolsky 1994). Cohn et al. (2004) conducted a study of online journals kept by individuals living in the USA by analyzing entries in the 2 months prior September 11, 2001 and the 2 months following; they found strikingly similar results regarding pre- and post-trauma language patterns.[9]

Recently, psychological research on language and coping has begun to adopt more of the "bottom-up" language analysis techniques such as the MEM. Stanton et al. (2015) conducted an analysis of texts written by women who were survivors of childhood sexual abuse (CSA) using the MEM. In their analysis, word patterns and themes were identified that differentiated these individuals from women who had experienced no sexual abuse (NSA) during their childhood. Stanton et al. found that women who had experienced some form of sexual abuse during childhood showed

---

[9]Interestingly, this study and others suggest that higher use of both positive and negative emotion words may generally reflect greater immersion a given writing topic (e.g., Holmes et al. 2007; Tausczik and Pennebaker 2010).

different thematic patterns when talking about sex than those women who had not. For example, women who were CSA survivors tended to use less language related to virginity and relationships and more language related to physical attraction than their NSA counterparts; these results converge with other psychology research on the relationship between a history of sexual abuse, physical attraction, and sexual risk-taking behaviors (e.g., Senn et al. 2006).

In a follow-up study, Pulverman et al. (2016) found that as CSA women underwent cognitive therapy for their experiences of abuse, their conceptualization of sex (measured via their language) came to resemble those of women who had never experienced sexual abuse. Similar studies of alcohol abuse (Lowe et al. 2013) and inpatient psychotherapy aftercare (Wolf et al. 2010) have found that the themes invoked by individuals around certain topics allow us to both understand the common ways that people think about their situations, but also help to infer whether someone has experienced certain types of upheavals in their life.

Language and Social Processes

It may be something of an understatement, but language is, at its core, inherently social. Up to this point, the research highlighted in this chapter shows an unspoken awareness of the social nature of language, yet seldom touches upon this fact directly. Nevertheless, the past few years have seen a growth in the automated psychological analysis of social interactions as a way to extract and better understand social processes. Multiple empirical studies by Molly Ireland and colleagues have found that people not only coordinate *what* they talk about as conversations unfold (i.e., content words), but *how* they talk as well (function word use).[10]

Ireland et al. (2011) explored the degree to which two peoples' function words synchronize in the context of romantic relationships. In a study of introductory conversations in speed daters, the researchers found that those couples who engaged in higher *language style matching* (LSM) showed increased mutual attraction to each other, suggesting that they were keenly focused on each other to the point where they even began to speak similarly. The researchers' second study looked at instant messages between partners in romantic relationships, finding that couples with higher LSM tended to exhibit greater relationship stability. In fact, Ireland et al. (2011) found that by calculating LSM in these brief conversations between romantic partners, they were able to statistically predict relationship longevity more accurately than the people who were actually *in* the relationships.

In another study, Ireland and Pennebaker (2010) conducted LSM analyses of three pairs of famous writers across their relationships by analyzing function

---

[10]The degree to which people synchronize their function words is often not directly perceptible, however, higher language style matching among individuals can foster perceptions of social connectedness and support (Rains 2015).

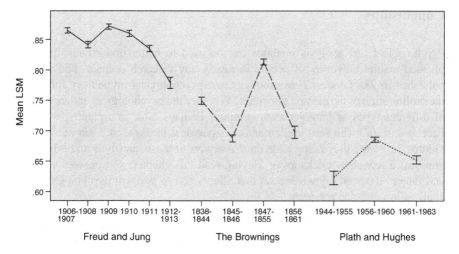

Fig. 2 Language style matching across time for famous writers and their relationships with close others (reprinted from Ireland and Pennebaker 2010; originally published by the American Psychological Association)

word synchrony in poetry and personal letters using LIWC. In their analysis, the researchers found that function word synchrony in the personal correspondence between Sigmund Freud and Carl Jung, one of Freud's students, mirrored their relationship trajectory. Freud and Jung had a notoriously contentious relationship as Jung gradually began to break away from the teachings of Freud, eventually accusing Freud of arrogance and stubbornness. LSM successfully captured the evolving (and later deteriorating) stages of the pair's relationship over a 7-year period (see Fig. 2).

Elizabeth Barrett Browning and Robert Browning's relationship is also quite infamous for its ups and downs. Points of interpersonal synchrony and asynchrony are revealed in the couple's poetry, with function word use being most similar during times of harmony in their marriage. Similarly, the works of Sylvia Plath and Ted Hughes, two influential poets who were married in 1956, exhibited LSM peaks during times of harmony and a gradual decline up to the time of Plath's suicide.

While still a relatively new measure, LSM has begun to see use in various forms of psychological research that reveal much about the importance of synchrony in understanding human interactions. Borelli et al. (2016) have found that higher LSM is found in strong mother–child attachments, with securely attached children exhibiting higher function word similarity to their mothers. Other research finds that crime suspects are more likely to confess to a crime when their language style coordinates with that of their interrogator (Richardson et al. 2014), and LSM during US presidential debates is even related to public perceptions of US presidential candidates (Romero et al. 2015).

Conclusions

Psychological text analysis methods can be used to better understand the complicated mental universes of people in nearly any research domain. Did articles published in *The London Times* show greater psychological immediacy following the proliferation of the electric telegraph? What are the psychological underpinnings of different types of humor across cultures? Perhaps most importantly, was that Facebook friend who sent you an amorous personal message at 3 am *really* "just kidding," or were they being authentic? Answers to these questions and others are now just a few short clicks away. Having read this chapter, you possess a robust and rather advanced knowledge set that allows you to perform psychological text analysis in your own research.

Generally speaking, perhaps the strongest advantages of psychological text analysis techniques include their wide availability, their extensive validation, and their ease to use. If desired, you can begin using these techniques within minutes of finishing this chapter. Texts that have been closely poured over for decades, and even centuries, have hidden psychological information embedded within them that is waiting to be revealed, and you could very well be the first person to make previously unimagined discoveries.

Each of the methods introduced in this chapter has its own strengths: LIWC is extremely easy to use "out of the box," whereas MEM (and the MEH software) allows for more fine-tuned analyses of text collections, albeit with a bit more effort/analysis required. Both types of methods, and particularly LIWC, have seen extensive use in psychological research and have been adopted by other fields as well, including computer/information sciences, sociology, business, and medicine, to name a few. Such methods are adaptable to virtually any field of interest that involves humans, and new discoveries are being made almost every day.

As technology pulls disparate fields closer together, unprecedented insights will result from combining techniques and information hailing from different disciplines. New techniques like automated psychological text analysis will not wholly replace subjective readings of texts but, rather, these two approaches will strengthen and complement each other. Various methods, including historical reports, psychological text analysis, subjective interpretation, and automated methods of understanding within- and between-text relationships, can all inform one another to create benefits that no single method in isolation could ever hope to achieve. As new techniques emerge, they too will be integrated into systems of understanding the human condition that are currently difficult to imagine. The prospects for newer, faster, and more accurate understandings of human experience are expanding every day. It is a very exciting time for innovation.

Acknowledgments Preparation of this chapter was aided by grants from the National Institute of Health (5R01GM112697-02), John Templeton Foundation (#48503), and the National Science Foundation (IIS-1344257). The views, opinions, and findings contained in this chapter are those of the author and should not be construed as position, policy, or decision of the aforementioned agencies, unless so designated by other documents. The author would like to thank Elisavet

Makridis, Natalie M. Peluso, James W. Pennebaker, and the anonymous reviewers for their helpful feedback on earlier versions of this chapter.

Appendix

When preparing and processing texts using psychological text analysis, there are some widely accepted (but often unspoken) guidelines that are quite commonplace. These guidelines serve to ensure accurate insights both while processing texts and in subsequent statistical analyses. This appendix can be thought of as a basic "need to know" reference and primer for technical considerations when performing psychological text analysis. Feel free to treat this appendix as a "cheat sheet" for the methods covered in this chapter—one that should help to give you a head start in the world of research with language.

Preparing Texts for Analysis

One of the most common questions that people ask during their first romp into the world of psychological text analysis is this: "How should I prepare my texts?" Ultimately, there is no answer to this question that will apply in all cases, as guidelines will vary as a function of text source, research questions, and goals. However, there are some basic considerations that apply to virtually all cases. As a general rule when it comes to the *psychological* analysis of text, "good enough" really is "good enough" for most purposes. One could literally spend years preparing a collection of text files so that they are 100% perfect for analysis, however, the conceptual (and, more importantly, statistical) gains from doing so are often nil.

Spelling and Spelling Variations

It is tempting to worry about correcting texts so that all words that could potentially be captured by a dictionary are successfully recognized. Note, however, that word distributions follow what is known as a Zipf distribution (see Piantadosi 2014), wherein a relatively small number of words constitute the majority of words actually seen in texts, verbalizations, and so on. Translated into practical terms, what this means is that unless a very common word is misspelled with high frequency, it is unlikely to have a measurable impact on LIWC-based and MEM-based measures of psychological processes. For example, if a single text has the misspelling "teh" two times, yet contains 750 uses of other articles in the whole text, the measured percentage of articles in a text will differ from the actual occurrence of articles by such a small amount as to be negligible.

Texts with several high-frequency misspellings, however, may benefit from correction. Multiple software programs exist that allow users to automatically batch-correct text files to avoid the tedious job of manual spelling correction (e.g., GNU Aspell; http://aspell.net). While most of these applications are useful only for the technically savvy, other options exist that allow users to find specific misspellings and replace them with corrections, such as Find and Replace (FAR; http://findandreplace.sourceforge.net). Relatedly, regional spelling variants may benefit from standardization, depending on the nature of one's research question. For example, given that the MEM looks for co-occurrences of words, we might expect the words "bloody," "neighbor," and "color" to co-occur more often than "bloody," "neighbor," and "color." Unless we are interested in identifying culture-specific word co-occurrences, we would want to standardize regional variants to have parallel spellings across all texts, ensuring more accurate psychological insights.

Finally, certain special circumstances arise when analyzing transcribed verbal exchanges, particularly when using software such as LIWC. Several categories of "utterances" (such as nonfluency words like "uh" and "um," and filler words like "like" and "y'know") are psychologically meaningful (Laserna et al. 2014), but are often transcribed idiosyncratically according to certain traditions. The word "like" is particularly problematic given its various meanings as a result of homography (e.g., expressing evaluation—"I like him"—or filling spaces—"I, like, love sandwiches"). Primarily in the case of verbal transcriptions, many utterances must be converted to software-specific tokens that are recognized explicitly as filler words to improve text analysis accuracy (LIWC, for example, uses "rrlike" for filler word recognition).

Working with the MEM and MEM Results

When performing any type of topic modeling procedure, including the MEM, several decisions must be made by the researcher performing the analysis. These typically include answering questions such as "What is the correct number of themes to extract?" and "How do I know what label to give each of these themes?" Topic modeling results are occasionally dismissed as purely subjective, however, this is seldom the case. Indeed, while some steps occasionally require some (arguably) arbitrary decisions, such decisions are typically made by relying on domain expertise. The author's recommendation is that, when in doubt, the best course of action is to consult with experts familiar with the type of research being conducted.

How to Extract/Understand Themes Using MEM

While the heart of the MEM is a statistical procedure known as a Principal Components Analysis (PCA), most of the typical guidelines that are recommended for a PCA do not extend to the modeling of language patterns. Instead, it may be more useful to think of the MEM as co-opting a statistical procedure to reach an end-goal, rather than the PCA being the goal itself.

When extracting themes using a PCA, a researcher must specify a k parameter, with k being the number of themes for which a PCA must solve. What is the ideal k parameter? In other words, how many themes should be extracted? Is it 10? 15? 50? This is a contentious issue in virtually every field that uses some form of topic modeling. The best answer at this time comes in the form of another question: "What makes sense given your research question?"

When attempting to perform a psychological analysis of text, domain expertise on psychological constructs is immensely helpful. The primary recommendation for determining the optimal k parameter is to test multiple k's, settling on the k parameter that appears to best represent the problem space. The ideal k parameter is also directly influenced by the amount of data that you are processing. If you have an extremely large number of wordy texts, you will be able to extract many, many more themes than if you are analyzing 100 posts made to Twitter.

Even with extremely large datasets, however, the smallest number of themes that can be coherently extracted is typically the most optimal, particularly in cases of psychological research. Whereas it is not uncommon to see sophisticated studies that extract hundreds (or even thousands) of topics from a corpus, 95% of these topics will end up being an uninterpretable and highly inter-correlated grab-bag of words that does not represent anything in particular. Extracting large numbers of topics may still be highly useful in predictive modeling, however, this practice is often problematic from a social sciences/digital humanities perspective and also leads to serious concerns about the replicability of one's findings.

Finally, when it comes to labeling themes that have been extracted using MEM or other topic models, there are no hard and fast rules. Labels assigned to word clusters should primarily be treated as a shorthand for referring to word clusters and should not treated as objective operationalizations during research in most cases. For example, one researcher may see the words "happy," "cry," and "shout" cluster together in a MEM analysis and label this as a broad "emotion" theme. Another researcher may see the same word clusters and see a "joyous" theme, believing that the words "cry" and "shout" are being used in a positive manner in conjunction with happiness. Most of the time, the labels are fairly simply to agree upon (e.g., a word cluster comprised of "college," "study," "test," and "class" is unlikely to be anything other than a broader "school" theme). However, when in doubt, one of the best ways to understand or interpret a questionable theme is to look for texts that score high for that theme, then read them closely to see how the theme-related words are used.

How to Score Texts for MEM Themes

We will typically want to score each text in our corpus for each theme that has been extracted. Once themes have been extracted using the MEM, there are two primary ways to make this information useful for subsequent statistical modeling. In the first method, "factor scores" can be calculated using a statistical approach, such as regression scoring. In this approach, each word is weighted for its "representativeness" of a given theme—these weights correspond to the "factor loadings" of each word to each theme. For example, if a theme is extracted pertaining to animals, the word "cat" may have a factor loading of 0.5, the word "bird" has a loading of 0.25, and so on. These scores can be used in a multiple linear regression model:

$$y = (ax) + (bz) + \ldots \text{ etc., or}$$
$$\text{Animal Theme} = (0.5*\text{cat}) + (0.25*\text{bird}) \ldots \text{ etc.}$$

This procedure is used to score a text for the "animal" theme, and so on for all other themes extracted during the MEM. Some statistical software, such as IBM's SPSS, have options that allow users to perform this scoring method automatically.

If using the regression approach to scoring texts for MEM themes, it is extremely important to note that the MEM typically requires that one performs their PCA with something called a VARIMAX rotation. Without going too far into the details, an orthogonal axis rotation such as VARIMAX ensures that all themes are mathematically 100% independent of each other. In practical terms, this means that regression scores for themes will be perfectly uncorrelated, which is often not an accurate reflection of psychological processes. This method is occasionally used in the literature but is not recommended for most purposes unless you have a well-articulated reason for doing so.

The second method for scoring MEM themes in texts is conceptually much simpler and strongly recommended. Essentially, this alternative method uses the MEM as a means of theme discovery or, in other words, simply determining what common themes exist in a corpus, as well as which words are indicative of which themes. Following this, a return to the word counting approach used by LIWC is used to score texts for each theme. For example, imagine that your use of the MEM uncovers two broad themes in your texts: a color theme (including the words "red," "blue," "green," and "brown") and a clothing theme (including the words "dress," "shirt," "shorts," and "jeans"). The next step is to create a custom dictionary that places the "color" and "clothing" words into separate categories. You would then rescan your texts with software like LIWC to calculate the percentage of words pertaining to color and clothing, respectively. Unlike with the regression method of scoring texts (which would force a perfect zero correlation between the two themes), one would likely find that use of color words and clothing words shows modest bivariate correlation, which makes sense from both and intuitive and psychological perspective.

References

J.L. Baddeley, G.R. Daniel, J.W. Pennebaker, How Henry Hellyer's use of language foretold his suicide. Crisis **32**(5), 288–292 (2011)

Borelli, J. L., Ramsook, K. A., Smiley, P., Kyle Bond, D., West, J. L., K.H. Buttitta, Language matching among mother-child dyads: associations with child attachment and emotion reactivity. Soc. Dev. (2016). doi:10.1111/sode.12200

R.L. Boyd, MEH: Meaning Extraction Helper (Version 1.4.13) [Software]. Available from http:// meh.ryanb.cc (2016)

R.L. Boyd, J.W. Pennebaker, Did Shakespeare write double falsehood? Identifying individuals by creating psychological signatures with text analysis. Psychol. Sci. **26**(5), 570–582 (2015)

R.L. Boyd, S.R. Wilson, J.W. Pennebaker, M. Kosinski, D.J. Stillwell, R. Mihalcea, Values in words: using language to evaluate and understand personal values, in Proceedings of the Ninth International AAAI Conference on Web and Social Media (2015), pp. 31–40

C.K. Chung, J.W. Pennebaker, Revealing dimensions of thinking in open-ended self-descriptions: an automated meaning extraction method for natural language. J. Res. Pers. **42**(1), 96–132 (2008)

M.A. Cohn, M.R. Mehl, J.W. Pennebaker, Linguistic markers of psychological change surrounding September 11, 2001. Psychol. Sci. **15**(10), 687–693 (2004)

M. De Choudhury, M. Gamon, S. Counts, E. Horvitz, Predicting depression via social media, in Annual Proceedings of the 2013 AAAI Conference on Web and Social Media (ICWSM) (2013)

J. Dewey, *How we think* (D.C. Heath, Boston, 1910)

M.J. Egnoto, D.J. Griffin, Analyzing language in suicide notes and legacy tokens: investigating clues to harm of self and harm to others in writing. Crisis **37**(2), 140–147 (2016)

M. Fernández-Cabana, A. García-Caballero, M.T. Alves-Pérez, M.J. García-García, R. Mateos, Suicidal traits in Marilyn Monroe's fragments. Crisis **34**(2), 124–130 (2013)

A.K. Fetterman, M.D. Robinson, Do you use your head or follow your heart? Self-location predicts personality, emotion, decision making, and performance. J. Pers. Soc. Psychol. **105**, 316–334 (2013)

L. Flekova, I. Gurevych, Personality profiling of fictional characters using sense-level links between lexical resources, in Proceedings of the 2015 Conference on Empirical Methods in Natural Language Processing (EMNLP) (2015)

S. Freud, *On Aphasia* (International Universities Press, London, 1891)

E. Gortner, J.W. Pennebaker, The archival anatomy of a disaster: media coverage and community-wide health effects of the Texas A&M bonfire tragedy. J. Soc. Clin. Psychol. **22**(5), 580–603 (2003)

D. Holmes, G.W. Alpers, T. Ismailji, C. Classen, T. Wales, V. Cheasty, A. Miller, C. Koopman, Cognitive and emotional processing in narratives of women abused by intimate partners. Violence Against Women **13**(11), 1192–1205 (2007)

M.E. Ireland, J.W. Pennebaker, Language style matching in writing: synchrony in essays, correspondence, and poetry. J. Pers. Soc. Psychol. **99**(3), 549–571 (2010)

M.E. Ireland, R.B. Slatcher, P.W. Eastwick, L.E. Scissors, E.J. Finkel, J.W. Pennebaker, Language style matching predicts relationship initiation and stability. Psychol. Sci. **22**(1), 39–44 (2011)

O.P. John, L.P. Naumann, C.J. Soto, in *Handbook of Personality: Theory and Research*, ed. by O. P. John, R. W. Robins, L. A. Pervin. Paradigm shift to the integrative big-five trait taxonomy: history, measurement, and conceptual issues (Guilford Press, New York, 2008), pp. 114–158

K. Jordan, J.W. Pennebaker, How the candidates are thinking: analytic versus narrative thinking styles. Retrieved January 21, 2016, from https://wordwatchers.wordpress.com/2016/01/21/how-the-candidates-are-thinking-analytic-versus-narrative-thinking-styles/ (2016)

P. Juola, Authorship attribution. Found. Trends Inf. Retr. **1**(3), 233 (2006)

D. Kahneman, *Thinking, Fast and Slow* (Farrar, Straus and Giroux, New York, 2011)

T. Kasser, *Lucy in the Mind of Lennon* (Oxford University Press, New York, 2013)

M. Komisin, C. Guinn, Identifying personality types using document classification methods, in Proceedings of the Twenty-Fifth International Florida Artificial Intelligence Research Society Conference (2012)

M. Koppel, J. Schler, S. Argamon, Computational methods in authorship attribution. J. Am. Soc. Inf. Sci. Technol. **60**(1), 9–26 (2008)

C.M. Laserna, Y. Seih, J.W. Pennebaker, J. Lang. Soc. Psychol. **33**(3), 328–338 (2014)

H.D. Lasswell, D. Lerner, I. De Sola Pool, *The Comparative Study of Symbols: An Introduction* (Stanford University Press, Stanford, 1952)

M. Liberman, Linguistic dominance in house of cards. Retrieved March 12, 2015, from http://languagelog.ldc.upenn.edu/nll/?p=18147 (2015)

R.D. Lowe, D. Heim, C.K. Chung, J.C. Duffy, J.B. Davies, J.W. Pennebaker, In verbis, vinum? Relating themes in an open-ended writing task to alcohol behaviors. Appetite **68**, 8–13 (2013)

F. Mairesse, M.A. Walker, M.R. Mehl, R.K. Moore, Using linguistic cues for the automatic recognition of personality and conversation in text. J. Artif. Intell. Res. **30**(1), 457–500 (2007)

C. Martindale, The grammar of altered states of consciousness: a semiotic reinterpretation of aspects of psychoanalytic theory. Psychoanal. Contemp. Thought **4**, 331–354 (1975)

D.C. McClelland, J.W. Atkinson, R.A. Clark, E.L. Lowell, *The Achievement Motive* (Irvington, Oxford, 1953)

E. Mergenthaler, Emotion-abstraction patterns in verbatim protocols: a new way of describing psychotherapeutic processes. J. Consult. Clin. Psychol. **64**(6), 1306–1315 (1996)

G.A. Miller, *The Science of Words* (Scientific American Library, New York, 1995)

F. Moretti, *Distant Reading* (Verso, London, 2013)

J.W. Pennebaker, J.F. Evans, *Expressive Writing: Words that Heal* (Idyll Arbor, Enumclaw, 2014)

J.W. Pennebaker, M.E. Francis, *Linguistic Inquiry and Word Count (LIWC): A Computer-Based Text Analysis Program* (Erlbaum, Mahwah, NJ, 1999)

J.W. Pennebaker, L.A. King, Linguistic styles: language use as an individual difference. J. Pers. Soc. Psychol. **77**(6), 1296–1312 (1999)

J.W. Pennebaker, L.D. Stone, Words of wisdom: Language use over the life span. Pers. Processes Individ. Differ. **85**(2), 291–301 (2003)

J.W. Pennebaker, T.J. Mayne, M.E. Francis, Linguistic predictors of adaptive bereavement. J. Pers. Soc. Psychol. **72**, 863–871 (1997)

J.W. Pennebaker, C.K. Chung, J. Frazee, G.M. Lavergne, D.I. Beaver, When small words foretell academic success: the case of college admissions essays. PLoS One **9**(12), e115844 (2014)

J.W. Pennebaker, R.L. Boyd, K. Jordan, K. Blackburn, *The Development and Psychometric Properties of LIWC2015* (University of Texas, Austin, TX, 2015a)

J.W. Pennebaker, R.J. Booth, R.L. Boyd, M.E. Francis, *Linguistic Inquiry and Word Count: LIWC2015* (Pennebaker Conglomerates, Austin, TX, 2015b)

K.J. Petrie, J.W. Pennebaker, B. Sivertsen, Things we said today: a linguistic analysis of the Beatles. Psychol. Aesthet. Creat. Arts **2**(4), 197–202 (2008)

S.T. Piantadosi, Zipf's word frequency law in natural language: a critical review and future directions. Psychon. Bull. Rev. **21**(5), 1112–1130 (2014)

C.S. Pulverman, R.L. Boyd, A.M. Stanton, C.M. Meston, Changes in the sexual self-schema of women with a history of childhood sexual abuse following expressive writing treatment. Psychol. Trauma. **9**(2), 181–188 (2016). doi:10.1037/tra0000163

S.A. Rains, Language style matching as a predictor of perceived social support in computer-mediated interaction among individuals coping with illness. Commun. Res. **43**(5), 694–712 (2015)

N. Ramirez-Esparza, C.K. Chung, E. Kacewicz, J.W. Pennebaker, The psychology of word use in depression forums in English and in Spanish: texting two text analytic approaches, in Annual Proceedings of the 2008 AAAI Conference on Web and Social Media (ICWSM) (2008)

B.H. Richardson, P.J. Taylor, B. Snook, S.M. Conchi, C. Bennell, Language style matching and police interrogation outcomes. Law Hum. Behav. **38**(4), 357–366 (2014)

D.M. Romero, R.I. Swaab, B. Uzzi, A.D. Galinsky, Mimicry is presidential: Linguistic style matching in presidential debates and improved polling numbers. Personal. Soc. Psychol. Bull. **41**(10), 1311–1319 (2015)

S. Ross, In praise of overstating the case: a review of Franco Moretti, distant reading. Dig. Humanit. Q. **8**(1), 1 (2014)

R.M. Sapolsky, *Why Zebras Don't Get Ulcers: A Guide To Stress, Stress Related Diseases, and Coping* (W.H. Freeman, New York, 1994)

J. Schler, M. Koppel, S. Argamon, J.W. Pennebaker, Effects of age and gender on blogging, in Proceedings of the 2005 AAAI Spring Symposium: Computational Approaches to Analyzing Weblogs (2006)

T.E. Senn, M.P. Carey, P.A. Vanable, Childhood sexual abuse and sexual risk behavior among men and women attending a sexually transmitted disease clinic. J. Consult. Clin. Psychol. **74**(4), 720–731 (2006)

A.M. Stanton, R.L. Boyd, C.S. Pulverman, C.M. Meston, Determining women's sexual self-schemas through advanced computerized text analysis. Child Abuse Negl. **46**, 78–88 (2015)

S.W. Stirman, J.W. Pennebaker, Word use in the poetry of suicidal and nonsuicidal poets. Psychosom. Med. **63**, 517–522 (2001)

P.J. Stone, D.C. Dunphy, M.S. Smith, D.M. Ogilvie, *The General Inquirer: A Computer Approach to Content Analysis* (MIT, Cambridge, 1966)

Y.R. Tausczik, J.W. Pennebaker, The psychological meaning of words: LIWC and computerized text analysis methods. J. Lang. Soc. Psychol. **29**(1), 24–54 (2010)

D. Watson, *Mood and Temperament* (Guilford Press, New York, 2000)

W. Weintraub, *Verbal Behavior in Everyday Life* (Springer, New York, 1989)

M. Wolf, C.K. Chung, H. Kordy, Inpatient treatment to online aftercare: e-mailing themes as a function of therapeutic outcomes. Psychother. Res. **20**(1), 71–85 (2010)

T. Yarkoni, Personality in 100,000 words: a large-scale analysis of personality and word use among bloggers. J. Res. Pers. **44**(3), 363–373 (2010)

Parsing Related Tags Networks from Flickr® to Explore Crowd-Sourced Keyword Associations

Shalin Hai-Jew

Abstract With the broad popularization of content-sharing social media platforms, researchers have developed methods to extract information from social related metadata. One approach is to extract related tags networks from freeform "folk" tags (keywords) used to describe imagery from Flickr®. These tag networks, graphed at 1, 1.5, and 2 degrees, show co-occurrence of related tags (above a certain threshold) to a target seeding tag. This work describes how these networks may be acquired and different ways that the extracted data may be used analytically in a digital humanities context.

Introduction

In the digital humanities, there is a range of tools and methods that enable researchers to tap into social media data for insight, whether it is to understand trends, capture individual voices, listen in on group discussions, explore online communities, and study user-generated multimedia. Some social media information is content data or the information that is shared; other type of common social information is from trace data, the recording of various types of interactions (such as replies, likes, forwarding, follows and unfollows, and so on); and finally, there's metadata, labeling data about data (such as "folk" tags, descriptions, and so on).

Social tagging involves interactive distributed cognition, with large groups of users co-tagging their own shared contents (and sometimes that of others), based on shared understandings. For people to engage with others, their tags have to make sense to others—and so are informative as social cues. Proper tagging is a sign of topic-based savvy and belongingness in the social media platform and/or groups within that platform.

For massive Web-scale collections of multimedia, such as imagery and video, one less direct way for researchers to engage that information is through the study

S. Hai-Jew (✉)
Kansas State University, Manhattan, KS 66506, USA
e-mail: shalin@k-state.edu

© Springer International Publishing AG 2017
S. Hai-Jew (ed.), *Data Analytics in Digital Humanities*, Multimedia Systems and Applications, DOI 10.1007/978-3-319-54499-1_8

of related tags networks. (Those who want to engage the direct contents are limited by human slowness against "big data" and/or the costs and complexity of engaging machine vision and "big data" analytics on noisy data-rich contents.)

A related tag network, at core, shows a target seeding tag and its ties to other tags with which it co-occurs in the description of particular user-generated contents. In other words, when a user shares an image or a video, he or she will apply keywords to describe that object. In the labeling, multiple tags are usually applied, and some will co-occur more frequently because of their applicability to the content and the mental associations of the sharer of the image. For example, a hiker shares a photo of a cactus that has been partially burned during a controlled burn of the prairie (to protect plant diversity). The hiker uploads the image to an image-based content-sharing site with the tags "cactus," "Konza_prairie," "#Konza," and "controlled_burn." She adds some personal tags, such as "day_hike," "6_miles," "92_degrees." Later, after some research to figure out what sort of cactus it was, she updates the tags describing the image as well. When she runs a related tags network with "konza" as the seeding tag for a 1.5 degree network, she finds a network with 17 vertices and 146 unique edges. The reciprocated vertex pair ratio is fairly high at 0.280702, and the reciprocated edge ratio is 0.438356. The maximum geodesic distance (graph diameter) is two, which is to be expected with related tags networks at 1.5 degrees. The graph density is high at 0.536764. The other related tags are not what she shared though but are more generic: tallgrass, prairie, tree, nature, grass, landscape, path, summer, Kansas, flinthills, hills, Nikon, sunset, Manhattan, and sky. Two groups or clusters are identified with the Clauset–Newman–Moore clustering algorithm. In Fig. 1, the group on the left seems to be focused around place and the Konza's relationship to other named locations; the one on the right seems more generic and related to natural landscapes.

The related tags network consists of a core target tag and co-occurring tags which occur above a certain threshold, for networks at one-degree, 1.5 degrees, two degrees, and so on. The higher the degree of connectivity, the more diffuse the apparent connections between the tags, and the more noise is mixed in with the signal. For this particular work, related tags networks from Flickr® will be explored at 1, 1.5, and 2 degrees: at 1 degree, the focal tag has direct ties to the include tags (based on a certain threshold established in the software tool); at 1.5 degrees, the network shows not only direct tag ties but also the transitivity between the alters in the tag neighborhood (the likelihood that tags with direct ties to the target tag also co-occur with other similar tags); at two degrees, the graph network captures all the prior and the respective tag neighborhoods of the alters. ("Alters" are also known as "first neighbors" or those with direct ties to the focal node or "seeding tag" in this case. "Second neighbors" are nodes without direct connection to the focal node but are connected to each other through the same intermediary.) It helps to note that while the graphs are directed ones (in which the edges or links have arrows showing directionality), the association is usually only one direction, from the target tag to the other tags. Just because a certain tag co-occurs with the target tag does not mean that the converse is also true. In general, the directionality of tag linkage is not reciprocated; in other words, the top co-occurring tags for the seeding

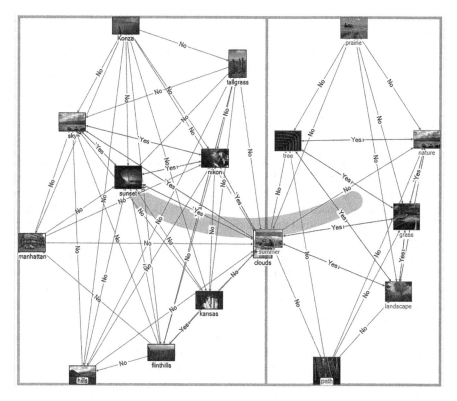

Fig. 1 "konza" related tags network on Flickr® (1.5 deg.)

tag do not often also have the original seeding tag as a high-level co-occurring tag (at the established threshold level to be selected as a co-occurring tag). The dyadic tag connection is often only one-directional in a structural sense. Tags that tend to co-occur commonly may have bidirectional reciprocal relationships (more on this follows later).

Essentially, the study of related tags networks is one narrow method that enables the exploration of relatedness between a focal "folk" tag and other tags with which it often co-occurs. This analysis enables the identification of the keywords which the broader public uses in relation to a particular tag, so this is a way to tap the collective subconscious or unconscious in understanding tag context. This can be a rich endeavor when certain semantic words are used as tags, such as particular social media-originated phrases, #hashtag tags, region names, proper nouns, context-dependent words, related sets of words, and others. (The Flickr® API does not enable the uses of certain function words like articles, prepositions, coordinate conjunctions, and such, for populating a related tags network, and a perusal of some of the images in the Flickr® collection show that many terms of semantic ones, including nouns and adjectives.) Tag terms may be further ambiguated (with richer senses of polysemy) in some senses and further disambiguated (with clarification and delimitations of its uses) in others. In other words, while the method itself may seem somewhat straightforward, it stands to add value as a data point, in a way that is complementary to the research context.

On Flickr®

Flickr® was created in 2004 by Ludicorp and purchased by Yahoo in 2005. As of June 2015, this platform boasted 122 million users in 63 countries, with a reported million photos shared daily on the service; further, there were over two million groups on Flickr® based around shared user interests (Smith 2016). While this started out as a platform for image sharing, it has since broadened out to host short videos as well.

Flickr® has a generous policy of sharing its contents and has created various application programming interfaces (APIs) for developers to create applications to access their contents and information. For users to access their data, they have to apply with a verifiable email in order to acquire a "key" and "secret" from the Flickr® App Garden (https://www.flickr.com/services/). Using the key, a researcher may access "raw" related tags network data (https://www.flickr.com/services/api/flickr.tags.getRelated.html). (In NodeXL, users may fire up the import feature to access Flickr® related tags network data and access the App Garden application from within the tool.)

There are built-in summary statistics about tags on the Flickr® site itself, to encourage user exploration. The "Trending Tags–Now" feature showcases popular tags in descending order. At the time of this capture, the tags were pretty general. They read, in descending order: buildings, winter, españa, mar, stone, America, and truck. The "Trending Tags—This Week" feature included the following: macromondays, flag, anythinggoes, holiday, and serene. A third feature was "Tags—All Time Most Popular." This list included the following, in descending order: sunset, beach, water, sky, flower, red, blue, nature, night, tree, white, green flowers, portrait, art, snow, light, dog, sun, clouds, cat, winter, park, street, landscape, summer, trees, sea, city, yellow, Christmas, lake, family, bridge, people, bird, river, pink, house, car, food, bw, old, macro, new, music, orange, garden, me, and baby. The trending tags page is available at https://www.flickr.com/photos/tags. The first two categories tend to be quite dynamic. As such, this page works like a summary dashboard. The information is helpful for an overview, but these may not directly answer the questions of researchers.

With the rollout of auto-tagging in 2015, Flickr®'s site offered a popup message to describe the "TagsBETA": "Tags are keywords that make photos easier to find in Flickr® search. The ones you add will show up in dark gray. Flickr®'s friendly robots will try to help out by adding some for you; these will appear with just a gray outline." The added tags may describe type ("portrait"), subject or contents ("people," "food," "plant," "vehicle," "architecture"), space ("outdoor," "indoor," "landscape," "cloud," "skyline," "seaside," "shore"), photographic features ("depth of field," "black background," "bright"), time of day ("dusk," "sunrise," "sunset"), mood ("serene"), and other features. Some images only have human tagging. Some images human-tagged as "sunrise" are contradicted by the auto-tagged "sunset" and "dusk." From a human point-of-view, it is unclear what the rules are for what is tagged and how, although inferences may be made. The auto-added tags may be removed by the users who shared the original photo or image. Also, users of the site may opt-out of the auto-tagging feature (Perez 2015). Beyond auto-tagging, there have been various ideas for tag refinement to try to improve the quality of human-assigned tags which are assigned on-the-fly and in-the-moment in an unstructured and emergent way, without a priori semantics. In order to compare related tags networks across different content-sharing platforms, it will be important to define how tagging is operationalized (by end user license agreement and policies and policy enforcement, by technological practices, by deployed robots, and other factors) within the socio-technical systems. The various social media services have differing standards for inclusiveness of their social tagging features and none with full inclusiveness based on the Inclusive Universal Access paradigm (Derntl et al. 2011).

Even more elusive is what the insider rules are for how Flickr® controls for tagging contents. Most social media content providers have clauses against certain types of information sharing—to prevent illegal, offensive, hateful, private, and other contents. Video sharing services, for example, will block copyrighted video, audio, and still imagery, from shared videos; they will enable blocks of content sharing based on laws in certain countries, so as to prevent offense and to prevent legal challenges. In the same way that search providers head off potential offense by preventing certain autocompletion terms to be found in searches, social media service providers also control for potential offense by blocking certain tag results. The idea is to keep customers and to avoid bad press while maintaining a sense of authenticity and credibility with users. As yet, there have not been apparent efforts to harmonize user-applied tags to the image. Unless a social media corporation encourages its staff to publish information broadly about what goes into their algorithms and processes for returning certain results, it will be hard to definitively define the rules from the outside except by using many queries and then applying inferences. External to the organization, a number of research works have explored Flickr® and its contents in rich ways (Spyrou and Mylonas 2016).

While this work only addresses extracting related tags networks from Flickr®, such networks can be extracted from any system that enables tagging and which enables data extraction through application programming interfaces or scraping or other methods. To understand the types of tags extracted, it is important to understand the demographics and geographies of the participants using the particular social media platform, the cultural influences, the language influences, and similar factors. It is also important to understand the platform and its underlying affordances for users. For example, are those tagging shared contents only those users who personally uploaded the contents, or can their social networks on the social sharing platform also tag? Or can anyone who is interested tag, with or without an account on the platform? How common is it to have batch uploads of images with batch tagging? Is there an auto-tagging feature, and how does it function? How are tags used by the users of the content-sharing social media platform, and how does usage affect the types of tags used?

NodeXL

The software used to extract the Flickr® related tags networks is NodeXL Basic (Network Overview, Discovery, and Exploration for Excel), a free add-on to Microsoft Excel. This free tool is downloadable from the CodePlex platform (https://www.codeplex.com/). The tool that enables extraction of Flickr® data from the Yahoo Flickr® application programming interface (API) is a third-party-created add-on to NodeXL. Using an add-on to Excel precludes the need for programming skills or command line interactivity or knowledge of how to handle JSON or XML. Also, the extracted data may be processed within NodeXL with various clustering algorithms and motif algorithms. The three clustering algorithms—Clauset–Newman–Moore, Wakita–Tsurumi, and Girvan–Newman— offer fairly wide-ranging group counts and varying informative value of the data. The motifs extractions show connections between smaller groups of nodes (dyadically, triadically, and so on), but motifs are useful in more complex networks and with higher degrees of connectivity and so are not as relevant here. There are ways to extract the most giant component in the network, and that is also almost redundant given that a related tag network at one degree is one giant component at one degree is one giant component only (generally speaking), but this may be a little more useful at 1.5 and 2 degrees.

The resulting related networks may be visualized as various types of node-link diagrams based on various layout algorithms. In NodeXL, the various types of layout algorithms include the following: Fruchterman–Reingold (force-based layout algorithm), Harel–Koren Fast multiscale, circle (ring lattice), spiral, horizontal sine wave, vertical sine wave, grid, polar, polar absolute, Sugiyama, random, and others. While Excel is not a typical go-to for professional data scientists, it provides a rich range of functions for data analytics and data visualizations for digital humanities researchers. (All the graphs used in this work were with NodeXL 1.0.1.336.) However, any intermediating software tool may have built-in limits in terms of the amount of data that is extracted. Too much data will overwhelm the tool's ability to show coherent graphs in two-dimensional space, so artificial ceilings are emplaced which limit the amount of information captured. Social media platform application programming interfaces (APIs) that enable data access are also often rate-limited in order to enable access for a broad range of users. While specifics may be elusive, any extracted data has to be understood as a sampling, and likely very non-random sampling at that.

Other methods of data extraction, data processing, and data visualization may produce larger graphs with more underlying data. Other methods may enable the changing up of parameters for inclusion of a tag in a related tags network. However, whatever information is available will depend on the limits of the Flickr® API as well. For example, the thumbnail images that illustrate particular tags are static (non-changing), and how they were selected to represent a particular tag is unclear. For example, were they selected by a person, a team, at random by computer, or some other way (at Flickr®)? Also, using NodeXL to create related tags networks is somewhat "non-consumptive." In other words, the underlying source data is only partially accessible. The tags not included are not captured. The long tail or tags are not captured. The only visual samples available are those thumbnail images linked to a particular tag by Flickr®, but the underlying image set is not fully capturable, and what may be captured is a very small percentage of the theoretically available imagery. A related tags network captured in the way described here is only a summary of the information with only a smattering of the underlying data. This offers a light drive-by observation of related tags networks based on freeware and open-source tools. (Employing other methods with a developer or with robots that can engage the Flickr® API for more information will most certainly mean more complex related tags networks and richer analytics. These approaches will also require comfort with database and data queries and data visualization packages.)

This analysis of related tags enables inferentially exploring other types of questions and answers beyond crowd-sourced tagging associations. Such networks may be suggestive of research leads and other tags to explore to study a particular phenomenon. The co-occurrence of tags used for particular image objects show undefined associations, and it is left to the researcher to explore what the related tags networks mean. A related tags network may provide insights about the following: the image holdings of one content-sharing platform over another, the differing tagging habits of different people groups around certain tags, the differing tagging habits of communities in different geographies or cultures, and so on. If the content-sharing platforms are truly global, then it may be possible to use related tags networks to understanding something of global collective thinking of particular issues, based on implicit links of co-occurring tags used on the shared imagery.

In the digital humanities, related tags networks may serve as anything from a "conversation starter" or "word art" or the "telling detail" to deeper analysis. The study of social tagging goes well beyond related tags networks, with studies of "tag streams, tagging models, tag semantics, generating recommendations using tags, visualizations of tags, applications of tags, integration of different tagging systems and problems associated with tagging usage" (Aggarwal 2011, p. 13), and other approaches. Folksonomies relate to tag sets that show how online crowds classify information in an unstructured way (without a controlled vocabulary or a formal taxonomy), whether on social tagging systems (applied to Web and Internet data) or in-system content-sharing sites. Folksonomies are created as multimodal networks, consisting of tripartite networks of (1) users (actors), (2) contents (images, videos), and (3) freeform open-ended tags (labeling metadata). By comparison, related tags networks are single-mode networks with the nodes consisting of tags alone.

There are limitations to the approach described in this introductory chapter. As mentioned earlier, the tag sampling is limited, so the set of co-occurring user-generated tags related to a seeding tag is not the full set (no N = all) but only a sampling with co-occurrences which reach a particular threshold. Ideally, it would help to have a full set, so a wider range of data may be explored. (For example, it would help to explore the long tail of tags—to look at those which are used rarely in relation with a seed tag but which may still offer research insights.) There is not external validation or invalidation of the tag findings. Ideally, it would be important to cross-check the data using other software tools and other methods. As-yet, there have not been baseline studies that show what related tags networks look like typically in terms of terms used (Are there more nouns than other parts-of-speech? Are there certain preferred types of adjectives? Are there certain preferred types of emotion words? Are certain seeding tags more insightful for use in related tags networks—like those with richer connotative meanings than denotative meanings?)

Finally, there is not much in the way of other research studies on related tags networks and how to informatize such data extractions. Should researchers select a seeding tag and hypothesize what they might find in terms of related tags and base research on those hypotheses vs. what they actually find? Should researchers extract related tags networks and make inferences about the millions of image holdings related to that network? Should researchers use related tags networks to identify large-scale trends and collective associations? Should researchers try to start tagging movements to change the collective associations of one tag with another?

In the same way that surrounding text to multimedia may be used to understand the contents of multimedia, tags may be mined ("tag mining") for informational value (Zha et al. 2012, p. 361). Related tags networks offer a way in to understanding a small part of the massive collections of shared imagery and videos on social media platforms. While these networks are built on labeling metadata, particularly noisy, unstructured, and informal keyword labeling, these structures provide insights about implicit links between the tags, and by extension, collective mental associations. Such associations are often latent to the individual user and are only revealed through computational processes that enable their visibility.

Review of The Literature

Based on the Konza tagging example above, several findings from tagging research emerge. When people tag the image contents they share on social media, they tend to think semantically and so choose words that carry meaning. They do not often use function words or syntax words. Also, people tend to think egoistically, based on their own local experiences; they use colloquial words which are comfortable to them even if the words are uncommon and informal. People are situated socially within particular social groups, and content-sharing sites are socio-technical spaces. People's selection of tag terms is influenced by their peer groups. People go online to connect socially, with many posing to their imagined audiences of social peers, many of whom are in physically closer proximity. Researchers have found that when people shared photos close in to their familiar spaces, they tagged more about "time, space, and motion" and did not provide more informational words as would someone unfamiliar with the area (such as a tourist) tends to; also, those familiar to a place tend to share more emotional or affect words about that place than informational ones because of the personal ties (Ahmed and Guha 2012, pp.1–2).

People think in terms of narratives and sequences, based on their own experiences. "Folk" or amateur tagging tends to mix differing levels of granularity. The freeform tags may refer to insider understandings among friends and family, in the sense that shared imagery may be narrowcast to a small audience. For outsiders, people's tags may be unclear or incoherent or inaccessible. Sometimes, users tag image-by-image, and other times, they tag *en masse* by applying the same tags to a bulk upload of related images. Also, people tend to share in a way that is informative of their native language(s) and culture(s), which may inform what is relevant. A related tags network is one form of the so-called emergent self-organization. At the individual levels, users do their own thing, but in their local choices, at the macro levels, a pattern starts to form that describes group behavior. Collectively, though, at a high level, tags that co-occur at a sufficient threshold to be linked dyadically to the seeding tag tend to be more generic and less individualistically ego-based. They tend to be unigrams or one-grams instead of phrases. Individual patterns of tagging do not necessarily repeat at the macro level. Also, tags seem to be related linguistically to other tags, with little in the way of multilingual tags in a particular related tags network. When seeded with a word in a particular language, many of the other co-occurring tags are also in that original tag's language. On Flickr®, singular and plural forms of a tag are treated as separate tags.

Various studies on tagging have explored why people tag, initially to enable future retrieval of the shared contents and also to make their contents available to a broader audience. The colloquial features of tagging make images more human-browsable; for example, colloquial labeling of regions is more effective for human search than more formalist labeling (Thomee and Rae 2012). Researchers have found that there are within-gender preferences for tagging (Popescu and Grefenstette 2010), with males preferring how males tag, and females preferring how females tag. Some researchers suggest that tagging is analogous to laying down pheromone trails to serve as wayfinders (from source to source) to lead others to discover their digital resources with tags acting as "a medium for social collaboration, navigation and browsing" and further that there is "an overall stable equilibrium . . . among tag patterns due to the social nature of the tagging process" (Kannampallil and Fu 2009, p. 165). While related tags networks show tags that occur at fairly high frequency, there is value in social media tags in the long tail. As one research team has observed, even one co-occurrence of a tag with another dyadically may be insightful, as is identifying the tags that constitute the long tail of a target tag (Kordumova et al. 2016). The rarity of tags on the long tail frequency distribution often means that such tags are "overlooked" (Kordumova et al. 2016, p. 51).

Exploring "Usual" and "Unusual" Related Tags Networks on Flickr®

This section contains a walk-through of six related tags networks, three using "usual" as a seeding tag, and three using "unusual" as a seeding tag, to see how this all works. These two seeding tags were selected because they are relativistic terms. What is unusual for one may be wholly usual for the other. The related tags networks may unearth some surprises.

To extract a related tags network from Flickr® using NodeXL (Network Overview, Discovery, and Exploration for Excel), a user has to ensure that the third-party data importer for Flickr® has been downloaded and installed. Also, he or she should have acquired a key from Flickr® in order to access the data. The general sequence of extracting a related tags network using NodeXL goes like this:

1. Open NodeXL. Ensure that the third-party social media data extraction for the Flickr® platform is downloaded and enabled.
2. In the ribbon, go to the NodeXL tab. In the Data area, select Import. In the dropdown menu, select "From Flickr® Related Tags Network."
3. Type in the desired tag as the seeding term.
4. Place the API key.
5. Select whether the network should be at 1, 1.5, or 2 degrees.
6. Select whether or not to capture sample image files.
7. Click OK.
8. Once the data is collected, go to the Analysis area of the NodeXL tab on the ribbon. Capture the Graph Metrics. These include number of vertices, number of unique edges, self-loops, reciprocated vertices, reciprocated edges, connected components, the maximum geodesic distance (graph diameter), average geodesic distance, graph density, and other measures (including modularity).
9. Go to the Groups in the Analysis area of the NodeXL tab on the ribbon, and choose the clustering method desired.
10. In the graph pane, create the respective data visualizations.
11. If labeling is desired for the graph, go to the Autofill Columns feature in the Visual Properties area of the NodeXL tab of the ribbon.
12. Likewise, if there is a desire to include the captured images related to the tags in the network graph, there are several adjustments that need to be made in multiple locations to enable this.

All the underlying related data is available in the worksheets labeled Edges, Vertices, Groups, Group Vertices, Overall Metrics, and so on. It is valuable to explore the underlying data. The vertices may be exported, for example, into a linguistic analysis tool, in order to map linguistic patterns in the data.

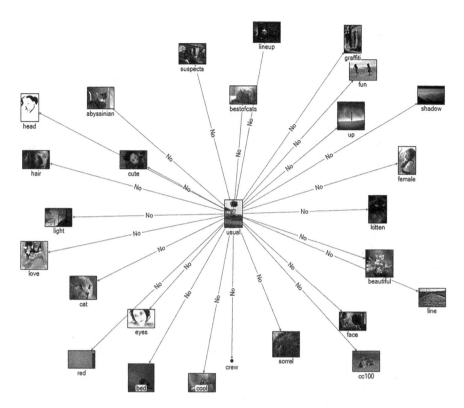

Fig. 2 "Usual" related tags network on Flickr® (1 deg.), with dyadic vertex relationships identified

Seeding Tag: "Usual"

For the related tags network seeded with "usual" as the tag for a one-degree network (direct ties between first neighbors and the target tag), there were 27 vertices and 26 unique edges. The maximum geodesic distance of this network was two. The graph density was 0.037. In terms of non-reciprocated tags, a majority of the edges were non-reciprocated (meaning that the other tags, when they were placed at the center of their own respective related tags networks, did not include the "usual" tag as one of the more common co-occurring ones) (Fig. 2).

The related tags network around the "usual" seeding tag at 1.5 degrees resulted in a network with 27 vertices and 183 unique edges (Fig. 3). The reciprocated vertex pair ratio was 0.196078, and the reciprocated edge ratio was 0.327868. The maximum vertices in a connected component were 27, and the maximum edges in a connected component were 183. The maximum graph diameter (or maximum geodesic distance) was two, with an average geodesic distance of 1.5. The graph density was 0.260684. Four clusters (subgroups) were identified from this graph using the Clauset–Newman–Moore clustering algorithm (a community

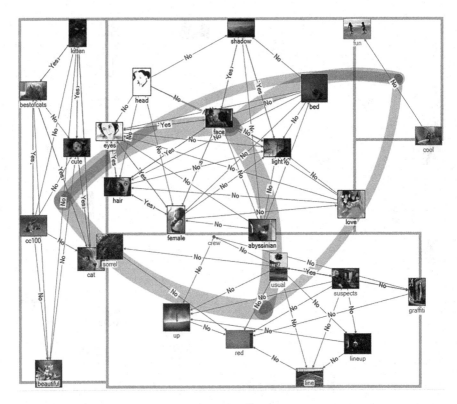

Fig. 3 "Usual" related tags network from Flickr® (1.5 deg.), with labeled edges showing (non)reciprocation

analysis algorithm). This may be seen in a layout using packed rectangles. In this figure, the edges show some reciprocal tag ties: light-shadow, face-shadow, face-eyes, cute-kitten, female-hair, and hair-eyes, which suggest deeper bidirectional tag associations.

A two-degree related tags extraction of the "usual" tag on Flickr® resulted in a graph with 453 vertices and 1376 edges. The reciprocated vertex pair ratio was 0.022288, and the reciprocated edge ratio was 0.043604. The maximum geodesic distance or graph diameter was four, and the average geodesic distance was 3.2. The graph density was 0.00672, so there was not a lot of density. In other words, when people conceptualize "usual," there were a wide range of tags used without a lot of connectivity (cohesiveness of conceptualization?) between them. Using the Clauset–Newman–Moore clustering algorithm, seven groups or clusters were identified (Fig. 4). When the same data (at 2 deg.) was run for motifs, 52 motifs were identified, which suggests complex small-scale interrelationships among the diverse tags.

The next section contains related tags networks seeded with the "unusual" tag.

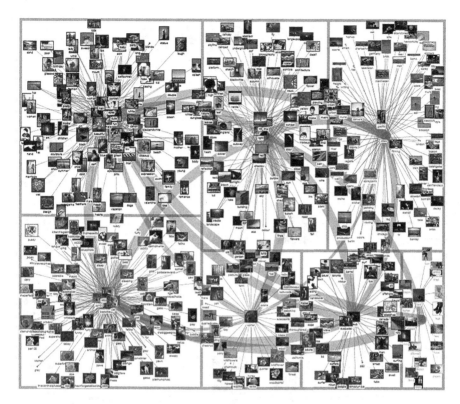

Fig. 4 "Usual" related tags network from Flickr® (2 deg.), with treemap layout for groups

Seeding Tag: "Unusual"

For the "unusual" related tags network at 1 deg., the graph itself contained 55 vertices with 54 unique edges. There was only one connected component, and the maximum geodesic distance (graph diameter) was two. The graph density was 0.01818, which identifies the actual presence of links divided by the possible number of links, suggests disparate non-connectivity among the extracted tags. With terms that are relativistic like "usual" and "unusual," one might expect less cohesion because there may be less collective agreement of what the tag may mean. The extracted tags identify various nouns: wildlife, plant, art, architecture, sky, nature, water, clouds, tree, and other tags. There are colloquial partial synonyms to "unusual" like the following: weird, surreal, strange, unique, and odd. Various descriptive color-based adjectives are included (Figs. 5 and 6).

At 1.5 degrees, the "unusual" related tags network on Flickr® resulted in 55 vertices (as of the one-degree network) but 1181 unique edges. The reciprocated vertex pair ratio was 0.28649, and the reciprocated edge ratio was 0.445385. The maximum geodesic distance (graph diameter) was two, and the graph density was

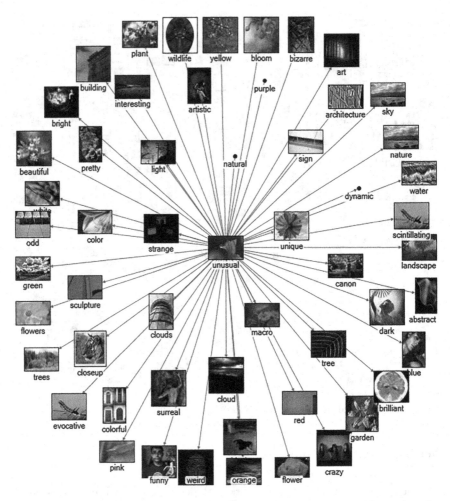

Fig. 5 "Unusual" related tags network on Flickr® (1 deg.), Clauset–Newman–Moore clustering algorithm, laid out with Harel–Koren fast multiscale layout

0.397643. Using the Clauset–Newman–Moore cluster algorithm, two clusters were identified. Clusters, by definition, have some deeper ties based on link density than other parts of the network; how the groupings are labeled (the explanation for the clustering) have to be done by the researcher. In Fig. 7, the top cluster shows links to particular human-made phenomena like "architecture" and "building" and "sculpture," and synonymous adjectives but also objects that may be described as "unusual"; the bottom cluster is full of adjectives and nouns related to nature. In both groups, the inclusion of images linked to the respective tags provides deeper understanding of the clusters.

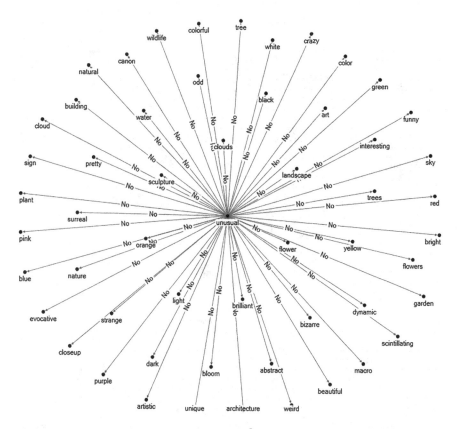

Fig. 6 "Unusual" related tags network from Flickr® (1 deg.), with labeled vertices indicating (non)reciprocation

In Fig. 8, the same data as Fig. 7 is reprocessed using the Wakita–Tsurumi clustering algorithm, which found three groups or clusters. The top group provides nature-based contextual descriptors. The one on the bottom left refers to structure, art, and signage. The one at the bottom right focuses around clouds and landscapes. The groupings do not necessarily lend themselves to easy distinctions or separations.

In Fig. 9, the 1.5 degree "unusual" related tags network was reprocessed using the Girvan–Newman clustering algorithm. This resulted in 11 extracted groups, with some of the groups consisting of one tag only. In the figure, the main connected component in the large group seems to tell a more complex story of what "unusual" means than the smaller groups at the bottom (which may serve as a kind of "long tail" frequency distribution within the related tags network).

It is important to note that users of NodeXL may apply a wide range of adjustments to the graph visualizations. They may describe how the groupings are portrayed (treemap diagram, packed rectangles, or force-directed group layout), the nature of the borders between groups, and the presence/absence of connectors

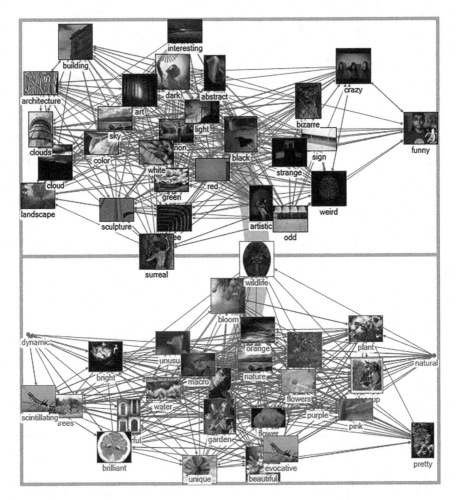

Fig. 7 "Unusual" related tags network from Flickr® (1.5 deg.), Clauset–Newman–Moore clustering algorithm

between groups. In the Autofill Columns, users may decide how the vertices and edges are depicted visually and labeled. In the graph pane, other features of the graph may be explored. Within that the Dynamic Filters may be used to select out data in a non-destructive way in order to explore the related tags network in more depth. In Fig. 10, reciprocation labels have been applied to the edges of a 1.5-degree related tags network in two clusters (without the thumbnail images included).

At two degrees, the "unusual" related tags network on Flickr® resulted in a graph with 455 vertices and 2670 edges. The reciprocated vertex pair ratio was 0.109265, and the reciprocated edge ratio was 0.197003. The maximum geodesic distance (graph diameter) was four, with the average geodesic distance at 2.89. The graph

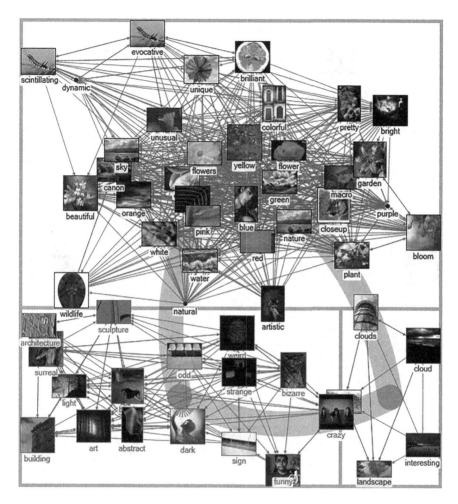

Fig. 8 "Unusual" related tags network from Flickr® (1.5 deg.), Wakita–Tsurumi clustering algorithm

density was 0.012925. Using the Clauset–Newman–Moore clustering algorithm, five groups were identified; the Wakita–Tsurumi clustering algorithm, 7 groups; and the Girvan–Newman clustering algorithm, 122 groups. Analyzing the terms and images related to each grouping gives a sense of how the clusters are organized. For example, some are based around "unusual" images from certain locations, like London, or there may be a topical organizing concept, like wildlife. The graphs are more effective when engaged with interactively, such as by zooming in and out. Fig. 11 shows how the one underlying dataset may vary greatly in terms of clustering based on the clustering algorithms applied.

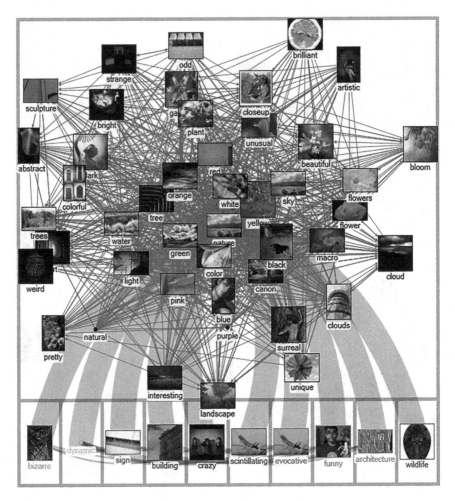

Fig. 9 "Unusual" related tags network from Flickr® (1.5 deg.) with Girvan–Newman clustering algorithm

In none of the three clustering algorithms do users have to pre-define how many clusters are required (unlike for k-means cluster algorithm). There is, however, a need to analyze the outcomes to see which clustering algorithm is more informative for the underlying related tags contents and the tag subgroups. In the research literature, the Clauset–Newman–Moore measures groupness or modularity in a network based on a "Q measure." The authors write, "If the fraction of within-community edges is no different from what we would expect for the randomized network, then this quantity will be zero. Nonzero values represent deviations from randomness, and in practice it is found that a value above about 0.3 is a good indicator of significant community structure in a network" (Clauset et al. 2004, p. 2).

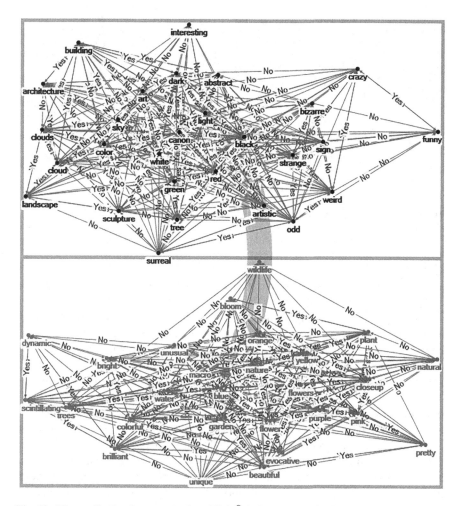

Fig. 10 "Unusual" related tags network on Flickr® (1.5 deg.) with dyadic ties noted

The Clauset–Newman–Moore clustering algorithm is a bottom-up "agglomerative clustering" method to extract subgroups from a network by merging pairs of nodes into clusters. Here, the algorithm is used to calculate the distances between the most similar members for each pair of clusters and will merge the clusters with the least distance (Clauset et al. 2004, p. 2). Other researchers suggest that the CNM community detection algorithm is computationally expensive and does not scale well beyond half a million nodes (Wakita and Tsurumi 2007a, p. 1275). To address this, the Wakita–Tsurumi team built on the CNM algorithm by adding heuristics that "merge community structures in a balanced manner" to "improve community structure analysis" at larger scale (Wakita and Tsurumi 2007a, p. 1275). This team introduced the idea of "modularity" in a network's community structure

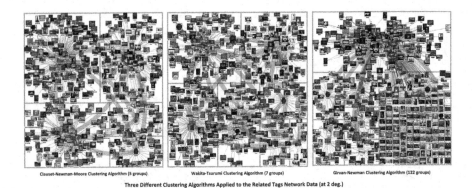

Clauset-Newman-Moore Clustering Algorithm (5 groups) Wakita-Tsurumi Clustering Algorithm (7 groups) Girvan-Newman Clustering Algorithm (122 groups)

Three Different Clustering Algorithms Applied to the Related Tags Network Data (at 2 deg.)

Fig. 11 Three different clustering algorithms applied to the related tags network data (at 2 deg.) in a triptych

as "a quantitative measure of the quality of clusterings (i.e., a graph partitioned into a set of subgraphs)" against which other clusterings of the same network may be compared (Wakita and Tsurumi 2007b, p. 2).

The Girvan–Newman Algorithm begins with the entirety of the network and all extant links among the nodes, and it detects communities by gradually removing edges from the original network. The authors write, "The connected components of the remaining network are the communities. Instead of trying to construct a measure that tells us which edges are the most central to communities, the Girvan–Newman Algorithm focuses on edges that are most likely 'between' communities" (Girvan–Newman Algorithm 2015, p. 1). The nodes that have high betweenness are bridging nodes that are highly centralized and connect various communities in a network. Node betweenness is based on "the number of shortest paths between pairs of nodes that run through it"; those that are most central will be the ones used to move information and goods in a network (Girvan–Newman Algorithm 2015, p. 1). The Girvan–Newman Algorithm also explores "edge betweenness," defined as "the number of shortest paths between pairs of nodes that run along it. If there is more than one shortest path between a pair of nodes, each path is assigned equal weight such that the total weight of all of the paths is equal to unity. If a network contains communities or groups that are only loosely connected by a few inter-group edges, then all shortest paths between different communities must go along one of these few edges. Thus, the edges connecting communities will have high edge betweenness (at least one of them). By removing these edges, the groups are separated from one another and so the underlying community structure of the network is revealed" (Girvan–Newman Algorithm 2015, p. 1). The Girvan–Newman Algorithm is considered a top-down type of processing that begins with the entire network first, and the network breaks into different communities with the successive removal of the links until what is left is a hierarchical dendrogram, with the leaves as individual nodes (Girvan–Newman Algorithm 2015).

Actual Image Sets from Seeding Tags

A perusal of the "usual" image set (1103 items) shows artworks, landscapes, people in costumes and dress-up, screen grabs from videos, aircraft, a baby leaning forward in his/her high chair to stuff a giant uncooked turkey which is larger than him/her, a pair of feet in slippers, a new haircut from various angles, body art, a pet dog, politician images, and others. A perusal of the "unusual" image set (791 thumbnail images) shows cloud formations, second Life virtual world art, a man holding his face in his hands like a removable mask while his own facial area is blurred, various body art tattoos, a poolside seal lying on a lounge chair next to a guy—with both sleeping, crystal formations, posed stuffed animals, a couple kissing, wildlife, a birthday cake, flowers, plants, shadows and light, a child with a snake around her neck, and artworks. Some of the images are created ones, with clever image editing, and others are "found" from-the-world. It would seem, without forcing the assertion, that one person's "unusual" might be another person's "usual."

In terms of comparisons with the actual scraped image set based on the seeding tag, it was not possible to get any sort of a real match. At the level of abstraction of a related tags network, that seemed to be done at a level of abstraction that was not directly reflected at the level of the actual shared imagery for either the "usual" or "unusual" image collections (Fig. 12).

Discussion

Content-sharing social media platforms are high dimensional spaces with complex messaging in imagery, audio, and video. Related tags networks, which are built from arbitrary "folk" tags applied to such contents, may be helpful in formulating some early understanding of the contents and the crowd-sourced mental associations linked to the contents.

This chapter introduced the creation of related tags networks from Flickr® using NodeXL and an integrated third-party data exporter to access the Flickr® API for related tags networks. This work showed how related tags may be explored at 1, 1.5, and 2 degrees. Also, it showed how linked thumbnail images to the respective tags may be viewed for a light image sense of the term. Also, this showed how subgroups may be extracted from the various networks using three different algorithms, and how meanings may be extracted from the respective clusterings. Finally, a scrape of the images based on the target seeding tags were done with some observations of the image sets.

Related tags networks tend to reach a certain equilibrium and may remain stable for months and even years (based on data extractions by this author). This stability may be due in part to the social influences of co-taggers; co-taggers share knowledge based on how they tag, and they enhance the specificity and richness of tagging

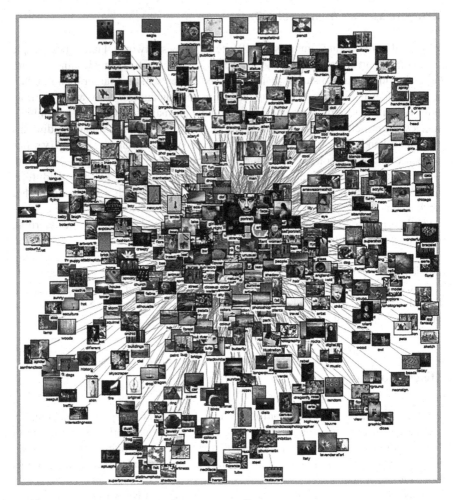

Fig. 12 "Unusual" related tags network from Flickr® (2 deg.), as a connected component

sets based on mutual influence through distributed cognition (Ley and Seitlinger 2015). The shared labors of users on content-sharing sites contribute to crowd-sourced semantic stabilization of tags around particular topics. The equilibrium of related tags networks may also come from the difficulty of achieving the threshold of co-occurrence given the massness of the social imagery and the applied tags. Lesser-occurring tags—which are the majority—will exist in the long tail of the frequency distribution curve and not even register as one of the top few that co-occur with a target seeding tag-based graph/subgraph. These networks may reveal tag associations that may suggest something of the underlying image sets. While the seeding text co-occurs with the first neighbors and second neighbors in the related tags network, the reciprocation levels between nodes are not high; the first and second neighbors may not relate back to the seeding tag if those tags were used as the focal or seeding tag of their own related tags networks. While the relationships between tags are implicit in related tags networks and may change over time, there are ways to extract more explicit relationships between terms—such as by running the tags through linguistic analysis for more formal parts of speech analysis.

Future Research Directions

The application of related tags networks to research in the digital humanities is promising as a way to understand complex phenomena. As such, there is plenty of space for researchers to build their own "use cases" based on this approach. It would be helpful to have baseline understandings of related tags networks and how they form and evolve over time. It would help to know if related tags networks have a generic form and if different types (based on seeding tags) show different characteristics. For example, are related tags networks different based on tags which are concrete vs. abstract, single-meaninged vs. polysemic, commonly used vs. uncommonly used, ambiguated vs. disambiguated, social-media-originated vs. traditional dictionary denotated (semantically), material-based vs. ephemera-based, or other sorts of comparatives? Do tag–tag relations emulate other relations in formal word relationships? Other contexts?

It would be helpful to not only explore popular co-occurring tags in a related tags network but also understand unrelated tags networks (such as those with total mutual exclusion or which are never used in combination); it would be interesting to understand the "long tail" distribution of tags used only once or twice with a target focal tag and what insights may be available from such long tails.

Conclusion

With the change in Yahoo's fortunes and the rise of Google Photos, Flickr® itself may be "flickr'd out" (Murabayashi 2016). Further, the age of human manual and batch-tagging may be coming to an end. "Folk" tagging of mostly amateur-created contents has long been seen as noisy and error-ridden, informed by users' own mixed motives, both private and public. For many contexts, such as geo-tagging, the preference has long been for going with locational data from apps and equipment, which communicate exact degree coordinates and sea levels. With the major advancements in machine vision and image object recognition, images shared on the Web will all likely be auto-tagged. The value in human "folk" tagging may be in their sharing of private narratives by providing information that would not otherwise be machine-observable or known from the image itself.

Computational tagging and tag mining will likely affect researchers who engage with Web-scale social imagery and related tags. The manual content analysis of

S. Hai-Jew

imagery has never been really scalable, except in the rare crowd-sourced project. Related tags networks are capturable because of computational affordances, but even before their full value as research tools has been exploited, even more complex tag networks are enabled—with creative mixes of users, the shared contents, shared commenting, and tagging, or mixes of these elements to address more complex research questions.

References

C.C. Aggarwal, in *C.C. Aggarwal's Social Network Data Analytics*. An introduction to social network data analytics. Ch. 1 (Springer, New York, 2011), pp. 1–15

S.I. Ahmed, S. Guha, Distance matters: an exploratory analysis of the linguistic features of Flickr photo tag metadata in relation to impression management, in The Proceedings of DBSocial '12, Scottsdale, Arizona, 2012, pp. 1–6

A. Clauset, M.E.J. Newman, C. Moore, Finding community structure in very large networks. Phys. Rev. **E70**(6), 066111 (2004)

M. Derntl, T. Hampel, R. Motschnig-Pitrik, T. Pitner, Inclusive social tagging and its support in web 2.0 services. Comput. Hum. Behav. **27**(2011), 1460–1466 (2011)

Girvan–Newman Algorithm, (2015) Wikipedia. Retrieved June 5, 2016, from https://en.wikipedia.org/wiki/Girvan%E2%80%93Newman_algorithm

T.G. Kannampallil, W.-T. Fu, in *Augmented Cognition. HCII 2009. LNAI 5638*, ed. by D. D. Schmorow et al.. Trail patterns in social tagging systems: role of tags as digital pheromones (Springer-Verlag, Berlin, 2009), pp. 165–174

S. Kordumova, J. van Gemert, C.G.M. Snoek, in *MultiMedia Modeling*, Lecture Notes in Computer Science, ed. by Q. Tian et al.. Exploring the long tail of social media tags, vol 9516 (Springer, Cham, 2016), pp. 51–62

T. Ley, P. Seitlinger, Dynamics of human categorization in a collaborative tagging system: how social processes of semantic stabilization shape individual sensemaking. Comput. Hum. Behav. **51**(2015), 140–151 (2015)

A. Murabayashi, Flickr'd out: the rise and fall of a photo sharing service. PetaPixel. Retrieved June 5, 2016, from http://petapixel.com/2016/03/22/flickrd-rise-demise-photo-sharing-service/ , 2016, Mar. 22

S. Perez, After backlash over upgrade, Flickr considers letting users opt-out of auto-tagging. Tech Crunch. Retrieved June 9, 2016, from http://techcrunch.com/2015/05/12/after-backlash-over-upgrade-flickr-considers-letting-users-opt-out-of-auto-tagging/, 2015, May 12

A. Popescu, G. Grefenstette, Image tagging and search—a gender oriented study, in The Proceedings of WSM '10. Oct. 25, 2010, Firenze, Italy, pp. 9–14

C. Smith, By the numbers: 14 interesting Flickr stats. DMR. Retrieved June 5, 2016, from http://expandedramblings.com/index.php/flickr-stats/, 2016, May 6

E. Spyrou, P. Mylonas, A survey on Flickr multimedia research challenges. Eng. Appl. Artif. Intell. **51**, 71–91 (2016)

B. Thomee, A. Rae, in *The Proceedings of MM '12, Oct. 29–Nov. 2*. Exploring and browsing photos through characteristic geographic tag regions (Association of Computing Machinery, Nara, Japan, 2012), pp. 1273–1274

K. Wakita, T. Tsurumi, Finding community structure in mega-scale social networks (extended abstract), in The Proceedings of WWW 2007, May 8–12, 2007a, Banff, Alberta, Canada, pp. 1275–1276

K. Wakita, T. Tsurumi, Finding community structure in mega-scale social networks, Preprint arXiv:cs/0702048, pp. 1–9 (2007b).

Z.-J. Zha, M. Wang, S. Jialie, T.-S. Chua, in *C.C. Aggarwal & C.X. Zhai's Mining Text Data*. Text mining in multimedia (Springer, New York, 2012), pp. 361–384

Part V
Sense-Making in the World

A Case Study of Crowdsourcing Imagery Coding in Natural Disasters

Cobi Smith

Abstract Crowdsourcing and open licensing allow more people to participate in research and humanitarian activities. Open data, such as geographic information shared through OpenStreetMap and image datasets from disasters, can be useful for disaster response and recovery work. This chapter shares a real-world case study of humanitarian-driven imagery analysis, using open-source crowdsourcing technology. Shared philosophies in open technologies and digital humanities, including remixing and the wisdom of the crowd, are reflected in this case study.

Introduction

Digital humanities research is characterized by values of transparency and collaboration through online networks (Spiro 2012, p. 17). This means that digital humanities can contribute to fields of work beyond academia, such as in humanitarian disaster responses. Visual media data shared during disasters are a source of information for humanitarian responses and research. They can also be a source of information for digital humanities researchers. This data can inform acute emergency responses as well as longer term research to prevent and mitigate future disasters. Given the time dependencies and short funding cycles of disaster response work, the digital humanities can support humanitarian activities through longer term research and analysis that may have academic and humanitarian outcomes. This chapter shares a real-world case study of humanitarian-driven imagery analysis using open-source crowdsourcing technology. Potential links to digital humanities are emphasized, with the hope that in future, data analyses and academic work in digital humanities may be able to support humanitarian goals.

Cobi Smith is a PhD candidate at Australian National University. She took leave from her PhD in Australia to work in Geneva as a consultant for the United Nations. She worked on the GeoTag-X project within the United Nations Institute for Training and Research Operational Statellite Application Programme (UNITAT-UNOSAT). This research was part of the Citizen Cyberlab project, funded through EU FP7.

C. Smith (✉)
Australian National University, Canberra, ACT, Australia
e-mail: cobi.smith@anu.edu.au

© Springer International Publishing AG 2017
S. Hai-Jew (ed.), *Data Analytics in Digital Humanities*, Multimedia Systems and Applications, DOI 10.1007/978-3-319-54499-1_9

GeoTag-X was developed at the United Nations Institute for Training and Research (UNITAR) Operational Satellite Applications Programme (UNOSAT) in Geneva and built using the Pybossa open-source crowdsourcing platform. It was funded through the European Commission 7th Framework Programme for Research and Technological Development as part of Citizen Cyberlab. The broader Citizen Cyberlab research project aimed to research and evaluate online collaborative environments and software tools for creative learning. Most other applications were focused on citizen science; GeoTag-X was unique in its humanitarian disaster response focus.

GeoTag-X aims were aligned with best practices in humanitarian knowledge management (King 2005; Cervigni and Smith 2014):

- identify media relevant to a disaster or emergency that are not already being categorized and geotagged;
- analyze content to generate associated metadata for sharing, pooling, comparison, verification and mapping;
- establish a community of practice involving individuals in multiple organizations to develop tacit knowledge associated with explicit knowledge generated through the project and with the knowledge of other organizations;
- focus on geotagging, to facilitate visualization and accessible representations of complex data and information;
- prototype humanitarian application of an open-source crowdsourcing platform and use prototype data and information to answer questions and respond to identified information needs;
- recognize the value of tacit knowledge gained from field experience, collaboration, and learned expertise;
- research if and how such knowledge can be passed on to new digital volunteers;
- promote the use of GIS technologies and internet technologies, including PyBossa for open-source crowdsourcing and GitHub for virtual collaboration and version control.

These aims yielded data designed for use in humanitarian disaster response contexts. The project's open philosophy meant that outcomes could also contribute to digital humanities projects, given open licensing supports uses unanticipated by original users.

Aims of the project were drawn from the Information Systems for Crisis Response and Management (ISCRAM) community (Van De Walle and Turoff 2006), through which related technologies have been documented. Existing research anticipated system development needs, for example, challenges in data storage and integrating new social media sources (Schram and Anderson 2012). Complementary systems existed to support disaster responses, for example, an Australian system developed in collaboration with official crisis coordination teams. This system was motivated by a 2009 Australian Royal Commission on bushfires, which heard evidence that official services lacked information reported in near-real-time on social media (Yin et al. 2012, p. 54). Another system used mobile phone calling data to inform emergency responses (Madey et al. 2006). GeoTag-X differed from existing systems in focusing on crowdsourced imagery coding and analysis, as well as having an explicitly open ethos, of relevance for digital humanities research.

ISCRAM research can be described as crisis informatics, which has been defined as the study of social, technical, and informational concerns in emergency response. This includes interactions and concerns of formal responders as well as affected citizens (Palen et al. 2010a; Starbird et al. 2012; Cervigni and Smith 2014, p. 8). Discussion about the value of volunteer participation in disaster responses reflects collaborative and crowdsourced values of digital humanities, as well as debates about how to value expert knowledge (Spiro 2012, p. 20).

> By viewing the citizenry as a powerful, self-organizing, and collectively intelligent force, ICT has the potential to play a remarkable and transformational role in the way society responds to mass emergencies and disaster. Furthermore, this view of a civil society that can be augmented by ICT is based on social and behavioral knowledge about how people truly respond in disaster, rather than on simplified and mythical portrayals of people unable to help themselves. Research has shown that disaster victims themselves are the true first responders, frequently acting on the basis of knowledge not available to officials (Palen et al. 2010b, pp. 1–2).

Debates about the merits of expert and public contributions are shared across digital humanities and humanitarian disaster response work.

Crowdsourcing is a form of volunteer participation. The speed and willingness that digital volunteers have shown in collecting and compiling information in disaster responses has already influenced the United Nations Office for the Coordination of Humanitarian Affairs (UNOCHA). Digital volunteers have helped to collect information for relevant datasets much more rapidly than officials could alone, with huge potential impacts on officials' responsibilities in information management (UNOCHA 2011). Crowdsourcing can involve people feeling a need to help (Lowe and Fothergill 2003) who might not have opportunities to help in other ways.

However, crowdsourcing remains controversial. Research has questioned the ethics of crowdsourcing from the perspective of employees' rights (Felstiner 2011), which is mitigated in humanitarian disaster response circumstances in which people volunteer regardless of crowdsourcing (Finkelstein and Brannick 2007). Crowdsourcing challenges the privileged role of individual experts (Spielman 2014). Research has indicated that unpaid crowds can produce results of high quality regardless of the type of task (Borromeo et al. 2016). A systematic review of crowdsourcing in health and medicine found that it can improve the quality of a research project, as well as increase speed and reduce cost—however, also called for standardized guidelines on crowdsourcing metrics and reporting methods for clarity and comparability (Ranard et al. 2014). This call is consistent with principles of open research, to which discussion of the GeoTag-X method is intended to contribute.

Method

The name GeoTag-X expressed key components of the system:

1. *Geo*: all media should be georeferenced as accurately as possible;

2. *Tag*: all media should have metadata relevant to the humanitarian and disaster response community, compatible with existing disaster response methodologies;
3. *X*: the system should be adaptable for diverse disaster situations anywhere in the world.

An early iteration of the platform in 2011 was called CyberMappr (Bromley 2012), which engaged volunteers in finding and georeferencing online photographs depicting damage resulting from conflict.

Source code for the GeoTag-X project, which was adapted from the open-source Pybossa code, is available at github.com/geotagx. This includes code for the overall website as well as specific projects, modules, and tasks. A project is typically a disaster event, such as the 2014 Ebola outbreak in West Africa or flooding of the Yamuna river in India in 2013. Modules are analyses of imagery that forms a dataset associated with a project. For example, the Ebola outbreak project included a module about analyzing images for responders' use of personal protective equipment. Another Ebola module was about geotagging the images. The Yamuna project included modules about analyzing flood waters and pollution, as well as separate modules analyzing impacts on people and animals. Tasks were individual analyses of images within modules. Task design reflected that of the underlying Pybossa code.

GeoTag-X was designed so that new modules with different questions could be flexibly developed depending on human input in response to environmental conditions, typically a new disaster event. This meant the system had potential to reflect a diverse range of values and cultural perspectives. Rather than claiming to be a neutral, anonymized data analysis platform, GeoTag-X transparently communicated humanitarian values and objectives through descriptive text. Participants could consider for themselves the questions used in the system and could contact developers to suggest new modules or projects asking different questions. This is why GeoTag-X was framed as a citizen science project with learning objectives as part of Citizen Cyberlab, as well as a technology platform for disaster response.

In GeoTag-X system design, data was collected in association with a particular project and analyzed through modules associated with a project. A project was typically a disaster event, for example, the 2013 Yamuna monsoonal floods, while a module was a type of analysis, for example, geotagging or recording whether photos feature shelter. Modules built using HTML and Javascript were a series of analysis steps; the same code for modules could be applied in different projects. For example, the same code for geotagging photos in a project about a flood in India could be used for a project about landslides in Peru. Volunteers could codesign a module with a particular dataset in mind; media with which they frame their understanding of potential questions for analysis and develop shared understanding. Once a module was published within a project category, volunteers could add more media to the initial dataset. The open nature of the module code as well as resulting data means that digital humanities researchers could explore values and assumptions embedded in the system, as well as resulting datasets.

A taxonomy of information management in disaster response (King 2005; Tatham and Spens 2011) was adapted for the GeoTag-X project in a project report (Cervigni and Smith 2014).

Data

A collection of related facts usually organized in a format such as a table or database and gathered for a particular purpose. In this sense, GeoTag-X produced image analyses as data tables associated with specific modules.

Information

Data that has been interpreted, verbalized, translated, or transformed to reveal the underlying meaning or context. In this sense, the images shown on the GeoTag-X platform represented raw data, while volunteers' image analyses created information that was saved as data tables.

Knowledge

Internalization of information, data, and experience. In this sense GeoTag-X was a learning and training project building on data analyses. Knowledge can be further sub-divided into two categories.

1. Tacit Knowledge
   Personal knowledge resident within the mind, behavior, and perceptions of individual members of the organization. Transforming the tacit knowledge of core project participants into explicit knowledge for sharing happened through project documentation.
2. Explicit Knowledge
   Formal, recorded, or systematic knowledge that can easily be accessed trans-mitted or stored in computer files or hard copy. Explicit knowledge was what GeoTag-X aimed to generate for humanitarian disaster responses.

Research about citizen science and crowdsourcing indicates that volunteers should be able to usefully contribute limited time to a project, supported by results of usability studies (Jennet and Cox 2014) which found that the GeoTag-X website, modules, and tutorials needed to be as simple as possible to avoid people becoming frustrated and discontinuing analysis.

Steps within prototype learning modules were able to be categorized as one of the three types: polar analyses, geotagging analyses, or multiple-choice analyses. However in all cases, even polar analyses, participants were given the option of choosing a "don't know" option. The importance of actively labelling uncertainty was noted in a review of the accuracy of OpenStreetMap digital volunteers' assessments of damage (Westrope et al. 2014). Types of analysis questions are explained from a technical perspective, followed by explanation of how each of the modules was developed from a participatory perspective.

Binary or Polar Analyses

Binary or polar analyses focused on yes or no, absent or present analyses. Volunteers were asked to consider a pair of alternatives and select which one to associate with the media being analyzed. However, all questions included a "don't know" option, so participants could respond if they were not comfortable with the binary options. Below is an example of how a binary question was coded in Javascript in the system[1]:

```
{

"question":"Can you see any water in the photo?",

"key":"water",

"type":"binary",

"branch":{

"no":"end"

}
```

The Javascript code above instructed the system to move on to another question if the participant answered no. If they answered yes, they were asked further questions about the water. If they responded saying they didn't know, they were thanked for their time and given a new analysis task. Every module began with the polar analysis step of determining whether media is spam or not, so polar analyses were the base step for all modules.

Geotagging Analyses

Another standard type of analysis is geotagging media on a map. Given the name and focus of GeoTag-X, geotagging analyses were core to the project. Below is an example of the typical code for geotagging tasks:

---

[1]Example from the project.json file available at: https://github.com/geotagx/geotagx-project-yamuna-floodwaters-2013/.

```
{

"question":"Can you geo-localize the photo?",

"key":"latlancoords",

"type":"geotagging"
}
```

Geotagging relied on OpenStreetMap instances embedded in the module. Users viewed an image on the right of the screen, then on the left of the screen either zoomed into a map area where they thought the image was located, or searched for a specific place name, which the map then displayed.

Multiple-Choice Analyses

Some modules contained multiple-choice steps asking volunteers to identify, for example, specific crops, animals, water, or landscape features. An example of code for a single-answer multiple-choice question comes from a module analyzing agricultural crops in Somalia during drought.[2]

There were two types of multiple-choice analyses: single-answer and multiple-answer. These two sub-categories of multiple choice are different both from technical and theoretical perspectives. These two types of multiple-choice categories lead to different answers in surveys and so cannot be assumed to be interchangeable in interpreting results.

Technically, single-answer analyses resulted in a single value associated with a media URL, while multiple-answer resulted in several new associated values. Single-answer values are studied in behavioral psychology and decision science because it means volunteers must make a forced choice, even if that choice is "don't know." Research suggests forced-choice analyses encourage deeper processing of response options (Smyth et al. 2006). This is not practical, however, in situations where multiple choices are relevant data. Furthermore, displaying several valid values together as options may support learning in the form of pattern recognition, valuable if learning is an intended outcome.

For data verification, the PyBossa platform had a default value of 30 individual user analyses, given this value is commonly used for statistical analysis. It is this repeat analysis that makes PyBossa a crowdsourcing platform. Users (anonymous and authenticated) only participated once per analysis. After completing an analysis the system invited them to complete a different one. Developers could prioritize how

---

[2]Example from the project.json file available at: https://github.com/geotagx/geotagx-project-somalia-crop-identification/.

```
{
"question":"Can you see the method of cultivation?",
"key":"agCultivation",
"type":"checklist",
"parameters":{
"options":[
{
"label":"Manual cultivation",
"value":"Manual"
},
{
"label":"With animals",
"value":"Animals"
},
{
"label":"By machine",
"value":"Machine"
}
]
}
```

the system would serve users new analyses. For example, a particular emergency response task could be prioritized to be presented to the next 30 users, quickly yielding a crowdsourced dataset. This might have potential ethical implications during simultaneous disasters and limited volunteer resources. So developers could alternatively prioritize a random task to be assigned to the next 30 users.

Results

Given that development of GeoTag-X was a research project, results were not only outputs as datasets but also development of the project modules themselves. Thus the development of question module types described in the method above were a project outcome. The outputs of modules were also results, as were their development. How modules were structured reflected technological limitations of the Pybossa open-source code, as well as what kind of questions for analysis were valued.

Results were exportable as raw data in JSON or CSV format. A sample output of data from a single task in a module displayed in the format below, with identifying numbers replaced with x.

{
"info": {
"isRelevant": "Yes",
"latlancoords": "2.626953125, 41.7138671875",
"img":   "http://www.railnews.co.in/wp-content/uploads/2013/06/6171_3530_
yamu.jpg",
"task_id": 582
},
"user_id": xxxxx,
"task_id": 582,
"created": "2014-05-02T14:01:03.821552",
"finish_time": "2014-05-02T14:01:03.821572",
"calibration": null,
"app_id": 27,
"user_ip": xxxxx,
"timeout": null,
"id": 441
},

This example data output from a geotagging task is reproduced from Cervigni and Smith (2014, p. 31), in JSON format.

Analysis of data from the authenticated users (Cervigni and Smith 2014, p. 35) showed that GeoTag-X reflected the norm of online communities in which a minority of participants engage heavily while the majority engage little (Wilkinson 2008). This was evidenced in the bounce rate showing that more than a third of users of the website simply visited the front page without contributing any analyses. Analysis in 2014 also showed that two-thirds of users were contributing anonymously while one-third were authenticated users (Cervigni and Smith 2014, p. 35).

Discussion

The *Digital Humanities Manifesto* (Schnapp and Presner 2009) promoted remixing, openness, and the wisdom of the crowd (Spiro 2012, p. 22). The values of openness and crowdsourcing were reflected in the GeoTag-X project, nonetheless the idea of remixing was of concern to some in the disaster response community. Given that disaster response imagery can include sensitive data, there are risks that such data might be used inappropriately if analyses were invited from volunteers rather than experts. This risk was mitigated by the GeoTag-X system not storing imagery data or support uploading functions. Rather, the platform was designed to collate and analyze images already available via citizen or professional journalism online. This meant the GeoTag-X project itself was an example of remixing. GeoTag-X involved volunteers collating imagery about a particular disaster spread across the internet and collating it in a dataset for use in disaster response contexts. This was remixing news and social media content into a dataset for explicitly humanitarian aims.

The ethics of exposing volunteers to disaster response imagery was discussed in a 2014 workshop at the University of Vienna during a Science in Society Catalyst (SiS Catalyst) conference on science communication and social inclusion (Smith 2014). A primary discussion in this workshop was whether a "walled garden" or closed platform should be developed, allowing staged levels of participation, in contrast to the entirely open platform in which users were randomly assigned tasks. A "walled garden" would support, for example, restricting potentially gory disaster modules to people of a certain age. Debates about how open or closed projects should be also occur in digital humanities beyond this disaster response technology case study (Berry 2011, p. 11).

There was no consensus but rather active debate among the group of conference participants about whether a walled garden should replace the open platform. The current open platform stores media URLs from a range of online news sources that young people can access without restriction. The main argument against moving youth participation to a closed platform was that young people see these news stories and may face disasters in real life, so censoring this does not support their learning. Development of technologies like GeoTag-X could teach participants to view such media from a humanitarian perspective, rather than as a passive media consumer, which may have psychological and social benefits.

There was discussion about the potential for GeoTag-X to support learning about potential careers in humanitarian fields and how to respond to potentially distressing situations as a proactive and effective first responder. At the same conference Dawson (2012, 2014) experimented with GeoTag-X and shared perspectives about engaging with migrant communities to geotag content from their home countries. Considering impacts on volunteer users of the platform reflected the humanitarian context of the project.

The implications of different analysis types used in the project have been discussed. An untested type of analysis is one in which volunteers freely tag images with metadata of their choice. Researchers have suggested that allowing volunteers to freely tag images with metadata of their choice may be as productive for generating useful information as developing prescribed modules. Stewart Buckfield, a creator of Flickr, one of the photo services used in GeoTag-X, discussed classification schemes:

> I think the lack of hierarchy, synonym control, and semantic precision are precisely why it works. Free typing loose associations is just a lot easier than making a decision about the degree of match to a predefined category (especially hierarchical ones). It's like 90% of the value of a proper taxonomy but 10 times simpler (Bishr and Kuhn 2007, p. 18).

Future research could explore information and learning outcomes comparing step-by-step analytical approaches used in GeoTag-X modules with free tagging of the same media. A hypothesis could be that modular analyses support greater learning, through volunteers questioning the reasons and values behind the programming of module steps. The challenges and extra effort involved in decision making about predefined categories may be associated with more learning, in contrast with free tagging that may generate useful information, but without learning outcomes for those volunteering to crowdsource.

Imagery analysis differs from text analysis given linguistic barriers are removed. While text can be understood only by those people or machines literate in the given language, images can be interpreted by people from diverse cultural and linguistic backgrounds. Images do not need to be translated for different societies, though different people may consider different parts of an image significant. This diversity, while more challenging to manage within an information technology system, can also be a strength. The algorithms and machine interpretations built into any system design reflect certain values. Research has indicated that volunteer-based crowdsourced sentiment analysis is more accurate than an automatic sentiment analysis algorithm (Borromeo and Toyama 2015). Machine learning classifiers still need training for different events as well as validation (Starbird et al. 2012; Cobb et al. 2014), so expectations of greater responsiveness or accuracy from machines alone may be unrealistic.

Designing a system for sharing information between organizations during complex and time-dependent disaster situations is challenging (Comfort et al. 2004; Kapucu 2006; Ren et al. 2008). Poor information sharing and coordination during disaster responses negatively impact collective decision-making and resulting outcomes, including resource allocation, delayed evacuations, and casualties (Bharosa et al. 2010). Crowdsourced media analyses will not solve these broader challenges. New challenges may be introduced; for example, researchers have called for more critical analysis of content emerging from social media in disaster situations given fake images may be shared (Gupta et al. 2013). Disaster responses remain challenging scenarios given timeframes, however, crowdsourcing may alleviate some challenges in information sharing. Digital humanities research typically has longer time frames and less political pressure than disaster response work, so digital humanities researchers have opportunities to contribute to humanitarian work through engagement with open technology projects.

Conclusion

Digital humanities suggest not only the promise of collective intelligence but also collective intellect (Berry 2011, p. 2011). Values in the digital humanities include transparency and collaboration through online networks (Spiro 2012, p. 17). These values are compatible with explicitly humanitarian values, particularly given the emergence of open technology platforms driven by humanitarian organizations such as the UN. Open-source crowdsourcing platform Geotag-X engaged volunteers in analyzing media about disasters, to contribute information and knowledge to disaster response agencies. Given the acute nature of disaster responses, digital humanities researchers may have more capacity to contribute to long-term projects for developing collective intellect than disaster response workers. Considering not only the datasets resulting from projects but also the questions embedded in the structures of crowdsourcing technologies could be a meaningful contribution of digital humanities researchers to humanitarian projects.

References

D.M. Berry, The computational turn: thinking about the digital humanities. Cult. Mach. **12**, 2 (2011)

N. Bharosa, J. Lee, M. Janssen, Challenges and obstacles in sharing and coordinating information during multi-agency disaster response: propositions from field exercises. Inf. Syst. Front. **12**(1), 49–65 (2010)

M. Bishr, W. Kuhn, *Geospatial Information Bottom-Up: A Matter of Trust and Semantics* (The European Information Society, Springer, Berlin, 2007), pp. 365–387

R.M. Borromeo, M. Toyama, Automatic vs. crowdsourced sentiment analysis, in Proceedings of the 19th International Database Engineering and Applications Symposium, July 2015, ACM, pp. 90–95

R.M. Borromeo, T. Laurent, M. Toyama, The influence of crowd type and task complexity on crowdsourced work quality, in Proceedings of the 20th International Database Engineering and Applications Symposium, July, 2016, ACM, pp. 70–76

L. Bromley, UNOSAT, open data, and the crowd. Proceedings of the Environmental Systems Research Institute (ESRI). 4 April 2012. Accessed online 21/10/2016 at: https://s3.amazonaws.com/webapps.esri.com/esri-proceedings/unic12/papers/unosat_open_data_and_the_crowd.pdf

E. Cervigni, C. Smith, Learning modules on media interpretation and disaster response data generation. Report. Deliverable 4.4 in EU Citizen Cyberlab: Technology Enhanced Creative Learning in the field of Citizen Cyberscience: http://cordis.europa.eu/project/rcn/106216_en.html (2014)

C. Cobb, T. McCarthy, A. Perkins, A. Bharadwaj, J. Comis, B. Do, K. Starbird, Designing for the deluge: understanding and supporting the distributed, collaborative work of crisis volunteers, in Proceedings of the 17th ACM Conference on Computer Supported Cooperative Work and Social Computing, February, 2014, ACM, pp. 888–899

L.K. Comfort, K. Ko, A. Zagorecki, Coordination in rapidly evolving disaster response systems the role of information. Am. Behav. Sci. **48**(3), 295–313 (2004)

E. Dawson, Non-participation in public engagement with science: a study of four socioeconomically disadvantaged, minority ethnic groups, Doctoral dissertation, King's College London, 2012

E. Dawson, Reframing social exclusion from science communication: moving away from 'barriers' towards a more complex perspective. JCOM **13**(02), C02 (2014)

A. Felstiner, Working the crowd: employment and labor law in the crowdsourcing industry. Berkeley J. Emp. Lab. L. **32**, 143–569 (2011)

M.A. Finkelstein, M.T. Brannick, Applying theories of institutional helping to informal volunteering: motives, role identity, and prosocial personality. Soc. Behav. Personal. Int. J. **35**(1), 101–114 (2007)

A. Gupta, H. Lamba, P. Kumaraguru, A. Joshi, Faking Sandy: characterizing and identifying fake images on Twitter during Hurricane Sandy, in Proceedings of the 22nd International Conference on World Wide Web Companion, May 2013, International World Wide Web Conferences Steering Committee, pp. 729–736

C. Jennet, A.L. Cox, Report. Deliverable 6.1 evaluating the design of citizen Cyberlab pilot projects and platforms in EU Citizen Cyberlab: technology enhanced creative learning in the field of citizen cyberscience: http://cordis.europa.eu/project/rcn/106216_en.html (2014)

N. Kapucu, Interagency communication networks during emergencies: boundary spanners in multiagency coordination. Am. Rev. Public Admin. **36**(2), 207–225 (2006)

D. King, Humanitarian knowledge management, in Proceedings of the Second International ISCRAM Conference, Brussels, Belgium, 2005, vol. 1, pp. 1–6

S. Lowe, A. Fothergill, in *Beyond September 11th: An Account of Post-Disaster Research*, ed. by M. F. Myers. A need to help: emergent volunteer behavior after September 11th (Natural Hazards Research and Applications Information Center, University of Colorado, Boulder, CO, 2003), pp. 293–314

G.R. Madey, G. Szabo, A.L. Barabási, in *Computational Science–ICCS 2006*. WIPER: the integrated wireless phone based emergency response system (Springer, Berlin, 2006), pp. 417–424

L. Palen, K.M. Anderson, G. Mark, J. Martin, D. Sicker, M. Palmer, D. Grunwald, A vision for technology-mediated support for public participation & assistance in mass emergencies and disasters, in Proceedings of the 2010 ACM-BCS Visions of Computer Science Conference, April 2010a, British Computer Society, p. 8

L. Palen, S. Vieweg, K.M. Anderson, Supporting "everyday analysts" in safety-and time-critical situations. Inf. Soc. **27**(1), 52–62 (2010b)

B.L. Ranard, Y.P. Ha, Z.F. Meisel, D.A. Asch, S.S. Hill, L.B. Becker, A.K. Seymour, R.M. Merchant, Crowdsourcing—harnessing the masses to advance health and medicine, a systematic review. J. Gen. Intern. Med. **29**(1), 187–203 (2014)

Y. Ren, S. Kiesler, S.R. Fussell, Multiple group coordination in complex and dynamic task environments: Interruptions, coping mechansism, and technology recommendations. J. Manag. Inf. Syst. **25**(1), 105–130 (2008)

J. Schnapp, P. Presner, Digital Humanities Manifesto 2.0, accessed 14 October 2010 http://www.humanitiesblast.com/manifesto/Manifesto_V2.pdf (2009)

A. Schram, K.M. Anderson, MySQL to NoSQL: data modeling challenges in supporting scalability, in Proceedings of the 3rd Annual Conference on Systems, Programming, and Applications: Software for Humanity, October 2012, ACM, pp. 191–202

C. Smith, GeoTag-X. Page 4–5 in SiS Catalyst Newsletter. October. Accessed online 5 December 2016 at: http://archive.siscatalyst.eu/sites/default/files/Newsletteroctober2014.pdf (2014)

J.D. Smyth, D.A. Dillman, L.M. Christian, M.J. Stern, Comparing check-all and forced-choice question formats in web surveys. Public Opin. Q. **70**(1), 66–77 (2006)

S.E. Spielman, Spatial collective intelligence? Credibility, accuracy, and volunteered geographic information. Cartogr. Geogr. Inf. Sci. **41**(2), 115–124 (2014)

L. Spiro, in *Debates in The Digital Humanities*. "This is why we fight": defining the values of the digital humanities, vol 16 (Oxford University Press, Oxford, 2012)

K. Starbird, G. Muzny, L. Palen, Learning from the crowd: collaborative filtering techniques for identifying on-the-ground twitterers during mass disruptions, in *Proceedings of 9th International Conference on Information Systems for Crisis Response and Management,* ISCRAM, Vancouver, Canada, 22–25 April 2012

P. Tatham, K. Spens, Towards a humanitarian logistics knowledge management system. Disaster Prev Manag **20**(1), 6–26 (2011)

UNOCHA, OCHA Lessons Learned [Publicly Editable]–Collaboration with VTCs in Libya and Japan. Accessed online 26/08/2014 at: https://docs.google.com/document/d/1wut8oDRo9BYSlc0hQ34Ng8qQ-pLVGlRO95WOvR3MN78/edit?hl=en_US (2011)

B. Van De Walle, M. Turoff, ISCRAM: growing a global R&D community on information systems for crisis response and management. Int. J. Emerg. Manag. **3**(4), 364–369 (2006)

C. Westrope, R. Banick, M. Levine, Groundtruthing OpenStreetMap building damage assessment. Procedia Eng. **78**, 29–39 (2014)

D.M. Wilkinson, Strong regularities in online peer production, in Proceedings of the 9th ACM Conference on Electronic Commerce, July 2008, ACM, pp. 302–309

J. Yin, A. Lampert, M. Cameron, B. Robinson, R. Power, Using social media to enhance emergency situation awareness. IEEE Intell. Syst. 27(6), 52–59 (2012)

YouTube Comments as Metalanguage Data on Non-standardized Languages: The Case of Trinidadian Creole English in Soca Music

Glenda Alicia Leung

Abstract This chapter takes an innovative look at YouTube comments as a source of language attitudinal data, otherwise known as metalanguage. Social media sites are linguistically emancipatory spaces where users of non-standardized/non-codified languages are free to communicate, interact, and collaborate as they see fit, free from prescriptivism and censure. Within the framework of indexicality, specific units of language (e.g., vocalic/consonantal sounds or words) may become associated with multiple social correlates such as gender, socio-economic class, and education. At higher levels of indexicality or indexical orders, the same unit of language may index particular stances in specific contexts. In this analysis, YouTube comments on soca music—a genre of party music popularized during Trinidadian carnival and performed in non-standardized Trinidadian Creole English—are treated as metalanguage data. A model of indexical orders associated with a particular Trinidadian Creole English vowel is proposed, based on YouTube metalanguage and data from other established empirical studies. The analysis highlights how this particular Trinidadian Creole English vowel indexes oppositional stances against respectability in a carnival context. Overall, the chapter positions computer-mediated communication via social media as a powerful means through which users of non-standardized/non-codified languages can display and exert their social and linguistic agency.

Introduction

In this small data project, I use data from social media (Web 2.0) to gain insight into the non-standard language variety Trinidadian Creole English (TCE)—which is spoken in Trinidad, a former British colony and Caribbean island in the West Indies. This case study relies on YouTube comments as a source of folk metalanguage data to explore social meanings attached to the particularly salient phonetic vowel variant/ ɒ/ in Trinidadian Creole English when enacted in the performance of soca

G.A. Leung (✉)
Independent Researcher, Manhattan, Kansas, USA
e-mail: glendaleung13@gmail.com

© Springer International Publishing AG 2017
S. Hai-Jew (ed.), *Data Analytics in Digital Humanities*, Multimedia Systems and Applications, DOI 10.1007/978-3-319-54499-1_10

music—the party and carnival music of Trinidad. In these songs, the TCE vowel /ɒ/ occurs in the hook, "that part of a song's musical and lyrical material through which the song remains in popular memory and is instantly recognizable in popular consciousness" (Shepherd and Horn 2003). Because of the saliency of the language variant in the hook, rich folk metalanguage is found in YouTube comments. The hook also has the call-response function (Smitherman 1977) of inviting the listener to identify ideologically with a certain type of vagabondage that is licensed during carnival, and to embody a response through louche, improvisational dance. I hypothesize that the use of this vowel indexes jocularity and defiance and ruptures the bounds of respectability. Additionally, this preliminary inquiry highlights the richness of YouTube comments as a complementary data set and its utility in hypothesis generation, especially when investigating non-standard or non-codified languages.

Computer-Mediated Communication

The examination of language in digital communication started in the early 1990s, giving rise to a research area known as Computer-Mediated Communication (CMC). CMC research has made significant incursions into linguistic areas such as discourse analysis, pragmatics, and sociolinguistics. (See Androutsopoulos (2006) for coverage on the various waves of CMC research.) Given the prominence of digital humanities, CMC researchers have recognized the importance of carving out their space into this evolving field. (See Georgakopoulou and Spilioti (2016) and Squires (2016) for recent collections on CMC.) As regards CMC inquiry into creole languages, notable research has been done on codeswitching in Jamaican Creole and English (Hinrichs 2006), orthography in Jamaican Creole, Bahamian English, and Mauritian Creole (Moll 2015; Oenbring 2013; Rajah-Carrim 2009), and lexicon in Nigerian Pidgin (Heyd 2014).

Early CMC research examined data from synchronous (e.g., e-chat and instant messenger) and asynchronous communication (e.g., mailing lists and discussion boards). However, the advent of the participatory web (Web 2.0) opened up access to rich, socially situated discourse from sites such as Facebook, Twitter, and YouTube (Schneider 2016). Interestingly, Androutsopoulos (2013) frames the discourse structure of YouTube as a "vernacular spectacle" where a YouTube video is like a "game," whereas the webpage houses video and its comments are comparable to a "spectacle" (Androutsopoulos and Tereick 2016, p. 356). YouTube research typically belongs to one of two lines of inquiry: (a) discourse structuring and sequencing of comments or (b) attitudes towards the video itself and participation in the evolving discourse (Androutsopoulos and Tereick 2016). This study is concerned with the latter thread since YouTube comments are taken as attitudinal data (metalanguage) in response to language data, in this case lyrics sung in Trinidadian Creole English.

Carnival Culture

Before delving into the intricacies of the data, let us examine the language complex in Trinidad. In many post-colonial, West Indian territories, the language of the former colonizer (a highly codified, standard language) coexists with a local vernacular (typically a creole language that may or may not be codified). Diglossia, where one variety is used in specific contexts or circumstances rather than another, results in the functional compartmentalization of language usage (Ferguson 1959). For example, the standard or high variety (H) is often the language of government, education, and broadcast news, whereas the creole or low variety (L) may be used in conversations with familiars or in folk performance (Wardhaugh and Fuller 2015).

In Trinidad, this diglossic situation is evident in the musical soundscape. Soca, a musical genre indigenous to Trinidad, is exclusively written, sung, and performed in the local vernacular: Trinidadian Creole English. While soca music may be generated all year round, soca's peak playtime is during the carnival season, which is the period leading up to lent. The onset of the carnival season starts right after Christmas on Boxing Day and culminates on Carnival Monday and Carnival Tuesday (known as Fat Tuesday in New Orleans). Trinidadian carnival is predominantly an outdoor affair. Festivities are characterized by outdoor fetes, soca and calypso singing competitions, steel drum competitions in the open space of the Queen's Park Savannah, and various costume parades where masqueraders "go on de road," parading through the streets.

Notable pre-lenten carnivals in the Old World are the carnival of Venice and Cologne carnival, held, respectively, in Italy and Germany. Famous carnivals in the New World include Mardi Gras in New Orleans, Brazilian Carnival, and Trinidadian Carnival. Pre-lenten New World carnivals find their origination in colonialism. The carnivals of New Orleans, Brazil, and Trinidad are syncretic, cultural by-products of the Catholic plantocracy and the African chattel slave population.

Carnival practices and the carnivalesque have long been associated with subversion and inversion (Bakhtin 1968). Within Bakhtin's analysis of medieval carnivals, there is the reversal of governing structures and hierarchies, manifest in the inversion of the authority of Church and State. However, in the analysis of contemporary New World carnivals, the added dimension of intensification is explored, most notably in Scheper-Hughes' (1992) anthropological work on carnival in Brazil. For Scheper-Hughes carnival is a ritual of reversal as much as it is a ritual of intensification, meaning that carnival has the capacity to "emphasize ordinary and everyday social realities" (p. 482).

Scholars with an interest in West Indian carnivals treat and theorize it as a "dialect of inside and outside and of private and public." This "dualistic value system" (Burton 1997, p. 162) reveals a tension between respectability and reputation that underpins West Indian values and life (Abrahams 1983; Burton 1997; Riggio 1998; Wilson 1973). The overarching tension between respectability and reputation has been delineated through a number of binary oppositions, shown in Table 1.

Table 1 A delineation of the respectability-reputation duality in West Indian life (Abrahams 1983; Burton 1997; Riggio 1998; Wilson 1973)

Respectability	Reputation
Christmas	Carnival
Home	Street
Private	Public
Order, Discipline	Chaos, Bacchanal
Decorum, Being behaved	Rudeness
Work, Job	Play, Liming
Self-restraint	Self-dissipation, Display
Quiet, Harmony	Noise to annoy
Standard English	Creole
Writing	Speech
Clock time	Trini-time

What I am concerned with here is the ideological opposition and resistance to respectability that dominates carnival. I hypothesize that this stance is indexed through specific linguistic resources within soca music. To contextualize this hermeneutic process of how I used small data to generate this hypothesis, an explanation of the various analytic frames that sociolinguists use to investigate language variation is warranted here.

Indexicality

In sociolinguistics, language variation may be investigated with respect to social correlates such as gender, socio-economic class, age, ethnicity, or geographical region. At a more nuanced, interpretive level, how speakers construct social meaning vis-à-vis language variation may also be examined, particularly in highly contextualized scenarios where language variants are employed to perform stylistic work (Coupland 2007). Social meaning is the ideological stance conveyed and interpreted in the deployment of a particular linguistic form.

Indexicality is when an *index* or linguistic sign assumes nuanced meanings from "the context of an utterance, with the context understood very broadly, including aspects of the speaker, hearer, and speaking situation" (Jaffe 2009, p. 177). Coulon (1995) defines indexicality as "all the contextual determinations that are implicitly attached to a word" (p. 17). Simply put, a word contains linguistic as well as indexical information within it. While a word can carry indexical information (e.g., Kiesling 2004; Wong 2005), so too can smaller units of language such as a phoneme (e.g., Johnstone and Kiesling 2008), which represents the single, "smallest contrastive unit in the sound system of a language" (SIL 2004). Indexicality is an approach which interrogates relationships between linguistic variation and multiple layers of social meaning, by appealing to *orders of indexicality* (Silverstein 2003). For instance, mapping linguistic variation to social categories (e.g., geographical region, ethnicity, etc.) is an example of first-order indexicality, whereas more nuanced associations of a linguistic variant to local or context-specific ideologies are

Table 2 Summary of data sets by Song and YouTube metadata

Song	YouTube metadata
Wotless (Kes the Band 2011)	Canchozi 743 comments 1,900,147 views Uploaded Dec 6 2010
Hard Wuk (Montano 2011)	JulianpromosTV 85 comments 227,940 views Uploaded Jan 8 2011
Tusty (Blaxx 2009)	Back on de scene 168,907 views 87 comments Uploaded Jan 16 2009
	Ayinde Olatunji 208,985 views 135 comments Uploaded Feb 19 2009

considered second- or third-order indexicality, and so forth. What follows here is my proposed indexical orders for the vowel variant in question, which I have generated using two types of data: (a) sociolinguistic studies on vowel variation in Trinidadian English (Leung 2013; Wilson 2014; Winford 1978) to derive first- and second-order indexicals and (b) YouTube commentary data to generate my hypothesis on higher order indexicals.

The linguistic detail I examine occurs in words such as *work, dirty, worth,* and *thirsty.* These words are said to belong to the NURSE lexical set (Wells 1982) because they share the same vowel pronunciation in a particular variety of English (e.g., *nurse* and *work* in several varieties of English: Standard American English [nɚs], [wɚk]; British Received Pronunciation [nɜːs], [wɜːk]; Trinidadian Standard English (TSE) [nɜːs], [wɜːk]; Trinidad Creole English /nɒs/, /wɒk/). Our sociolinguistic understanding of Trinidadian English vowel variation comes from three key empirical studies (Leung 2013; Winford 1978; Wilson 2014).

In a nutshell, here is what we know about the NURSE lexical set in Trinidadian English (i.e., in the standard and creole varieties). From Winford's (1978) first rigorous Labovian sociolinguistic inquiry into the vowel system, we know that TSE NURSE /ɜː/ is a prestige norm and TCE NURSE /ɒ/ is a vernacular variant. This is consistent with contemporary attitudes towards these two variants (Leung 2013).[1] Winford (1978) also found that TSE NURSE /ɜː/ was associated with urban speakers, whereas TCE NURSE /ɒ/ was used more frequently with rural speakers. In Leung's (2013) more recent sociophonetic analysis, both urban and rural speakers preferred to use the /ɜː/ variant in interview settings and in elicitation

---

[1]It should be noted that Winford (1978) analyzed speech data collected in the 1970s so attitudes and usage will likely have shifted over the last four decades for some variants.

Fig. 1 First- and
second-order indexicals for
TSE NURSE /ɜː/ and TCE
NURSE /ɒ/ (Leung 2013;
Winford 1978)

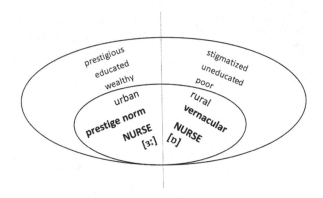

tasks (with the exception of a few rural residents), a finding that is somewhat different to Winford's (1978). Leung (2013) also conducted a verbal guise task to investigate language attitudes towards vowel variants. TSE NURSE /ɜː/ was positively evaluated; survey respondents judged the speaker using this variant as educated, intelligent, competent, successful, and wealthy. In contrast, TCE NURSE /ɒ/ was evaluated very poorly (and rated lowest across all the creole vowel variants surveyed), revealing TCE NURSE /ɒ/ is a highly stigmatized pronunciation in Trinidadian English and is less likely to be used in formal contexts. In Wilson's (2014) innovative study on language ideology in Trinidad, she investigated attitudes towards Trinidadian varieties in context of choral singing where British English pronunciations are a favored target. In her analysis, she describes TSE NURSE /ɜː/ as a low order indexical, meaning that in the context of choral singing there was little metalinguistic awareness around its usage (e.g., it was not problematic for singers to produce or there were no strong attitudes, either favorable or prejudicial towards it). Wilson does not report on TCE NURSE /ɒ/ probably because since prestige varieties such as Trinidadian Standard English and British English are targets for choral singers, they would avoid a phonetic variant such as TCE NURSE /ɒ/ that is so prominently marked as a vernacular feature and stigmatized (cf. Leung 2013). On the basis of the three aforementioned studies, I visualize the indexicals associated with TSE NURSE /ɜː/ and TCE NURSE /ɒ/ in Fig. 1, presenting them as binaries relative to each language variety.

In the innermost oval are the core associations with each variety, which refer to two dimensions: norms of usage, followed by geographical associations. The second oval highlights more nuanced indexical meanings connected to the dimensions of social status. Here we see how linguistic variables become imbued with social meaning—whether that social meaning is reflective of social factors, stereotypes, or social identities.

Another layer to consider is how the soundscape of carnival intersects with social constructs:

> Soundscapes are the totality of all sounds within a location with an emphasis in the relationship between individual's or society's perception of, understanding of and the interaction with the sonic environment. (Payne, Davies, and Adams 2009)

The relevance of Trinidad carnival in the construction of individual and national identity cannot be understated; Trinidad carnival has been described as "the true sinew" and "basic value system ... that directly or indirectly sustains or holds the society together" (Coomansingh 2011, p. 120). Furthermore, carnival potentially impacts the psyche as evidenced in cultural behaviors such as carnival mentality. Maharajh and Kalpoo (2012) note a duality in carnival mentality. During the carnival, season, the carnival mentality manifests as a rupture to decorum or an inversion to respectability as "it is a 'time to free up', 'time to break away and get on bad' or take part in every carnival activity or event, and indulging in alcohol, immoral, vulgar, and promiscuous activities without thinking of the consequences." In contrast, outside the carnival season, carnival mentality has the element of intensification as it references a "non-stop party mentality" where every opportunity is an excuse "to lime or party" (Maharajh and Kalpoo 2012, p. 140). Elsewhere, carnival mentality has been defined as "An attitude towards work which makes a person very energetic about carnival costumes and fetes, and very lazy the rest of the year about anything else" (Winer 2009, p. 173). What interests me here is the intersection and coalescence of language, social meaning, national identity, and performativity.

Data

The data used to generate higher level indexicals come from YouTube comments for three soca songs. These data were accessed in December 2014 for the following songs: "Wotless" *worthless* /'wɒt,lɛs/ by Kes the Band (2011), "Hard Wuk" *hard work* /haːd wʊk/ by Machel Montano (2011), and "Tusty" *thirsty* /'tɒs,ti/ by Blaxx (2009). However, I have elected to report primarily on the data for "Wotless," performed by Kes the Band (CanchozI 2010), since analysis of the YouTube data from "Tusty" by Blaxx and "Hard Wuk" by Machel Montano yields similar descriptions. See Appendices B and C for YouTube data samples from "Tusty" (Back on de Scene 2009; Olatunji 2009) and "Hard Wuk" (JulianspromosTV 2011).

The linguistic variants being investigated are words belonging to the NURSE lexical set, where the TCE NURSE /ɒ/ variant occurs both in the title and in the hook of the song. It is also important to note the creole orthography in the title of the songs; because TCE NURSE /ɒ/ is highly salient, it prompts a non-standard spelling to index or reference the creole. YouTube comments about either TSE or TCE are treated as folk metalanguage. Folk metalanguage, or conscious, overt commentary about language by non-linguists (Niedzielski and Preston 2000), is one resource which lends insight into ideologies associated with additive or higher orders of indexicality (i.e., second-, third-, etc.).

Method

The analysis of the YouTube comments was conducted in two stages. First, any metalanguage regarding the meaning of the creole word in question (e.g., *wotless, tusty,* or *wuk*) was described using emergent codes that were developed during the analysis (Strauss and Corbin 1998). Next, themes were identified in any other metalanguage that was noted (i.e., metalanguage that did not address the meaning of the creole word). Lyrics were also examined and described using the binaries of respectability and reputation presented in Table 1 as a priori codes.

Analysis

Here I report on the overall patterns that emerged from the YouTube comments. Generally speaking, the metalanguage observed in the soca YouTube comments concerned: (a) questions and/or explanations about the semantics (e.g., meaning or definition) of a creole word, primarily located in the title of the song or hook; (b) questions and/or explanations surrounding the etymology of a creole word; and (c) engaged responses in which commenters identified on an affective level with the behavior expressed in the song title. Whenever a YouTube user posed a question about the meaning of a creole word, various types of responses were observed in the data. YouTubers employed a combination of strategies to define the creole term. Some users simply offered explanations *[general explanation/definition]*. Others defined the creole word in context *[contextualized explanation/definition]*. Others referenced or filtered the meaning of the creole word through the standard (e.g., *tutsy* means *thirsty*; *wuk* is how we say *work* in Trinidad) *[referenced explanation/definition]*. Through close interpretative reading of the YouTube comments, two sets of dualities were evident: (a) linguistic duality between standard-creole and (b) behavioral duality between respectability-reputation, both of which I will illustrate below in the analysis of "Wotless," performed by Kes.

Wotless

According to Lise Winer (2009), author of *Dictionary of the English/Creole of Trinidad and Tobago*, the adjective *wutless* (also *worthless*) is defined as "unreliable; dishonest; bad; RUDE; Sometimes said affectionately, e.g. of a loveable rogue" (p. 974). The noun *wutlessness* (also *worthlessness)* means "Rudeness; vulgarity; rubbish" (p. 975). In the context of carnival, the act of being wotless describes a specific kind of vagabondage.

In Kes' soca song *Wotless*, the first verse starts with Kes confessing that he is dancing (known as *wining* in the Caribbean; also synonymous with *getting on*) and enjoying it. Then he goes on to say if he wins a million dollars in the annual Soca Monarch competition, he will be the "talk of the town." He also boasts about revelling without a care:

	Verse 1
Ln 1	And ah feel like I just win a million dollars.
	Everybody watching meh,
	Wearing a million colors.
	You wanna talk, talk 'bout this.
Ln 5	Cuz when ah wine you go talk 'bout dat.
	When ah getting on you go talk 'bout dis.
	Call yuh friends and den talk 'bout dat.
	Down south dey go talk' 'bout dis.
	Uptown dey done talk 'bout dat.

This type of carefree, self-display, and being the center of attention is how Kes envisions getting reputation. Additionally, Kes welcomes positioning himself in public (e.g., down south and uptown, lines 8 and 9) for others to talk about his less than respectable behavior. In the chorus that follows, it is clear that reputation comes at the expense of respectability of which Kes is aware:

	Chorus
Ln 1	I don't care what you say
	Cuz right now I just wotless.
	And I don't really care less.
	Meh girlfriend she go get vex.
Ln 5	Meh family go send text.
	But I don't care I wotless.
	They say I moving breathless.
	But I don't really care less.
	This year I moving fearless.

In the chorus, Kes claims ownership of his behavior, declaring he is wotless, which is his license to display himself and engage in rudeness. His declaration of not "caring less" in lines 3 and 8 is an antithetical response to discipline and respectability. Lines 4 and 5 capture an ultimate defiance: not caring what family and loved ones think of his behavior during this carnival season.

In the YouTube comments, *claudiabigail23* asks, "What does wotless mean?" User *happystar1000* gives this comprehensive explanation:

[W]otless is trini dialect and slang for saying "worthless" *[referenced]* and has many meanings in this respect, as was rightly said like giving trouble. [O]ften when children misbehave, parents would say. "yuh too damn wotless" meaning ur good for nothing but giving trouble *[general]*. It [i]s a similar meaning in this song, him having a good time dancing with other women would be seen as him being wotless or "worthless" by his girlfriend and her family *[contextualized]*.

Here *happystar1000* defines *wotless* by referencing it through TSE *worthless*, while acknowledging that *wotless* is a TCE word. Furthermore, *happystar1000* gives the general definition for the term, but also what *wotless* would mean in the song, and by extension in a carnival context. Other users give similar explanations—some more evaluative than others:

- *Jabari200666666@FirstGeneration2011* Multiple uses and meanings generally it means carefree, lighthearted or most cases lackadaisical *[general]*.
- *yizzlemanizzle@Jabari200666666* Wotless is the word Worthless *[referenced]*. You're right about the connotation though, it's been bastardized over the years to mean slack, lascivious, or lecherous *[general]*.
- *Christopher7708@ahoradamelomio* It means "worthless" *[referenced]* which is used to describe having no shame *[general]*... getting on bad (in a good way ... party atmosphere) *[contextualized]*. A word meaning to not care profoundly about anything, and just having a hell of a time not caring what anyone says or thinks of you *[contextualized]*.
- *Kirwina@claudiabigail23* In trini slang, it means someone who is no good or giving trouble *[general]* but in terms of the song, it may mean someone who is having a wonderful time or grinding alot in a party *[contextualized]*. You would really understand the unique Trinidad and Tobago culture to really comprehend.

Many users identified with being wotless, expressing this in different ways. For some users, the affective identification was captured in a simple reiteration of the word *wotless* or of the hook (e.g., *MrsMusic84* Rite Nw I Jus WOTLE-SS!!! :D). Other users identified explicitly with being wotless and described its psychosomatic effects and how this "wotlesssness" might manifest itself. YouTuber *HOTTGAL1989* comments, "i cah stop whinin fuh dis song omg... & dah beat BEEESSSSSSSSSS :)))))... AH WOTLESS," while user *wesley hamilton* describes a deeper tension between self-restraint and self-dissipation: "I shouldn't listen to this song, but oh gosh, it biting meh, look how meh head moving.....oh gosh, I fraid to be wotless... my gosh, it biting meh... "

The act of being wotless was also marked as happening in public spaces and in the street parades for carnival. Acts of wotlessness were envisioned on Caribbean soil as well as in North America metropoles where diasporic carnival celebrations have taken root (e.g., Caribana in Toronto, Labor Day Carnival in Brooklyn, and Miami Broward Carnival hosted around Columbus Day). This is best illustrated in *Jolene Smith*'s comment in which she describes an urgency to display herself dancing in the Baltimore/DC carnival:

Yuh really just have tuh wine reaaaal wotless when yuh hear this song, man i had to break out on stage in DC when this played. I just keep listening to it over and over cah stop dance man!!! Just have to drop hard, trini style.

Wotless behavior was also described as a trait that marked Trinidadian identity. YouTuber *buttercup535* declares, "all yuh trinis we wotless and we careless to[o] so true." Evenly more interestingly, the questioning of Trinidadian authenticity was particularly noted in YouTubers' responses to dislikes. YouTuber *Daniel Mitchell* expresses his disgust at the dislikes: "The 6 people that dislike this video definately not wotless....dey full ah shit and probably go be in dey bed monday and tuesday." Going out on the street on Carnival Monday and Tuesday is the quintessential display of Trinidadianness. Here *Daniel Mitchell* condemns those for not liking the song. By saying that they are "not wotless," he implies that they are proper, respectable folk who would probably avoid carnival altogether by being "in dey bed monday and tuesday." Another interesting dislike comment came from *relhardwine1* who surmises that the people who did not like the song could not have been Trinidadians: "the 22 dat dislike this song is probably bajans...hahhahaha." Although wotlessness might index Trinidadian identity, YouTubers of West Indian heritage or extraction also identified with wotless behavior. YouTube *kingala*, who we can assume has barbadian roots, writes, "uptown dey gon talk bout dis!!! ah doan care ah wotless!! *insert bajan wukup*"[2] YouTubers representing St. Vincent, Antigua, the Cayman Islands, Guyana, and other West Indian territories also claimed to be wotless.

To summarize, the YouTube comments from Kes' "Wotless" highlighted: affective identification with vagabondage; indexing of Trinidadian and West Indian authenticity and identity; and license for public dissipation. Using these findings, I hypothesize higher order indexicals, which will be discussed in the following section.

Discussion

Recall that diglossia, the functional compartmentalization of language usage, is commonplace in the West Indies, because in many territories a standard language coexists with a creole language. The tension between these two varieties is captured, conceptualized, and explained via Allsopp's (2003) hierarchy of formalness. In the *Dictionary of Caribbean English*, lexicographer Richard Allsopp establishes a four-level hierarchy of formalness in his codification of Caribbean English: formal, informal, anti-formal, and erroneous. Here, formal refers to language that is "accepted as educated...[where] no personal familiarity is shown when such [language] is used" (p. lvi). Informal is "accepted as familiar...[and is] usually well-structured, casual, relaxed speech, but sometimes characterized by...features of decreolization." Note well that "neither inter-personal tenseness nor intimacy is

---

[2] *Wukking up*—a term used most notably in Barbados, Guyana, and the US Virgin Island—is defined as "to dance suggestively or erotically, with vigorous gyrations of the waist and hips" (Allsopp 2003, p. 613). *Wukking up* is synonymous with *wining* (Springer 2008).

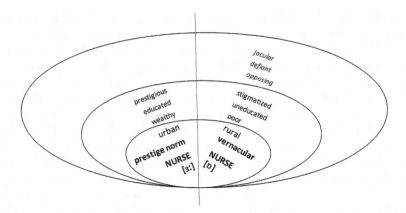

Fig. 2 Lower- and higher-order indexicals for TSE NURSE /ɜ:/ and TCE NURSE /ɒ/

shown when such items are used" (Allsopp 2003 p. lvi). The level of Allsopp's hierarchy of formalness that is most relevant to this case study is anti-formal, which he defines as "Deliberately rejecting Formalness; consciously familiar and intimate; part of a wide range from close and friendly through jocular to coarse and vulgar; any Creolized or Creole form or structure surviving or conveniently borrowed to suit context or situation" (p. lvii). Allsopp goes on to say that "when such items are used an *absence or a wilful closing of social distance* [emphasis added] is signalled" (Allsopp 2003, p. lvii). Allsopp's hierarchy acknowledges the overall oppositional stance that creole structures have the potential to index.

Partially inspired by Allsopp, I motivate and propose the following higher indexicals, represented in the outermost oval of Fig. 2. As explained above, the indexical orders in the inner and middle ovals were substantiated, drawing upon empirical studies (Leung 2013; Wilson 2014; Winford 1978). What is known from Trinidadian English sociolinguistic scholarship is the NURSE lexical is highly sensitive to the indexing social information and meaning, most prominently the norms of usage and geographic distribution, followed by characteristics of social status, more so than other lexical sets. (See Leung (2013) on her coverage of other lexical sets, e.g., STRUT, LOT, and BATH.) Eckert (2008) notes it is possible that "variables that historically come to distinguish geographical dialects can take on interactional meanings based on local ideology" (p. 462). It is precisely these nuanced interactional meanings in context of local carnival ideology that I wish to account for in hypothesizing higher order indexicals.

West Indian life is characterized by tensions between respectability and reputation. This is also true in Trinidadian society. These tensions come most prominently to the fore during the Trinidadian carnival season where inversion and intensification are permissible. Through a close reading of the data on *wotless*, *wuk*, and *tusty*, overtones of jocularity, defiance, and opposition to respectability imbue these terms in context of carnival. Furthermore, these terms take on new interpretations which are called to be enacted in dance. Thus, jocularity, defiance, and opposition are not purely mental or emotional stances; these stances are physically portrayed through improvised/spontaneous dance connected to carnival.

Whether it is the word itself or the vowel (phonetic variant TCE NURSE /ɒ/) that has indexical power is not entirely clear from these data. It may be argued that each individual word (i.e., *wotless*, *tusty*, and *wuk*) has higher order indexical meaning in context of carnival. This explanation is valid. However, because these words all belong to the NURSE lexical set, then it begs the question whether the vowel is the variable that is doing the indexical work. I take the latter position because of the overall sensitivity of the TCE NURSE /ɒ/ variant. To make a case for the markedness of TCE NURSE /ɒ/ variant in Trinidadian English, I rely on previous empirical work (as explained above) as well as on *linguistic intuition* or introspective judgments about language. While there is controversy surrounding the relevance and reliability of linguistic intuition (cf. Devitt 2014; Maynes 2012; Wasow and Arnold 2005), I take the position that examining linguistic intuition is a starting point for observation of linguistic phenomena. Here, I do not subscribe to using linguistic intuition in lieu of linguistic evidence or data. Rather, linguistic intuition can play a role in hypothesis/theory construction and ultimately hypothesis/theory testing for which I strongly advocate.

In each set below, there are three sentences of equivalent meaning in TSE, TCE, and TCE with the most conservative creole pronunciation of NURSE /ɒ/, respectively. What is of interest is if there is any semantic difference between sentences (b) and (c).

(1) a. The house burnt [bɜːnt] down. (TSE)
   b. The house burn [bɜːn] down. (TCE)
   c. The house burn [bɒn] down. (TCE—conservative pronunciation)
(2) a. He cursed [kɜːst] at the man. (TSE)
   b. He curse [kɜːs] at the man. (TCE)
   c. He curse [kɒs] at the man. (TCE—conservative pronunciation)
(3) a. The house is dirty [dɜːti]. (TSE)
   b. The house dirty [dɜːti]. (TCE)
   c. The house dirty [dɒti]. (TCE—conservative pronunciation)
(4) a. The child is thirsty [θɜːsti]. (TSE)
   b. The child thirsty [tɜːsti]. (TCE)
   c. The child thirsty [tɒsti]. (TCE—conservative pronunciation)

The difference between TCE sentences (b) and (c) in the above sets is one of degrees; sentence (c)—rendered with the most conservative creole pronunciation /ɒ/—differs by degree of extremity, intensity, or urgency. For example, sentence 1(c) gives the impression that the house was completely destroyed. Sentence 2(c) implies that the man who was cursed was the recipient of some extremely harsh words. Sentence 3(c) suggests that the house was exceedingly unclean or untidy. Lastly, sentence 4(c) indicates that the child was extremely thirsty. Since TCE NURSE /ɒ/ has the potential to connote extremity, intensity, or urgency, then it is not implausible that indexicality in the soca data is operating at a phonetic rather than a lexical level.

This line of reasoning relies on the triangulation of various information types: extant empirical studies, close readings of YouTube metalanguage, and linguistic intuition. Overall, because TCE NURSE /ɒ/ is marked as a highly creole feature, it can be harnessed for stylistic and stance work.

Conclusion

Considering folk metalanguage is particularly useful in investigating non-standard, oftentimes stigmatized, language varieties such as creoles. Non-elicited folk meta-language is challenging to source, especially if the language variety does not have a standardized orthography. However, growing accessibility to the participatory Web (Web 2.0) has resulted in social media technologies being instrumental in generating communities. The broad-based participation that social media facilitates makes posting or publishing on the internet a social act, giving speakers of non-standardized languages social and linguistic agency as shown in this study. This study also highlighted how social media can provide rich, complementary data for linguistic analysis. From my perspective as a sociolinguist—who examines language operating in social, societal, and cultural contexts—what makes the participatory web groundbreaking is the proliferation of digital data, their accessibility, and ways in which today's technology shapes our communication, language, and discourse. In short, today's technology and digital world have opened up new spaces for digital experiences and digital culture to flourish.

Thematized YouTube Comments (CanchozI 2010) for "Wotless" by Kes the Band (2011)

General identification

- *KC Smoke* wooooooooooooooooooooooooooooooe wotless dis song bigg love it bad bad
- *sweetbabypuppy* right i just wotlessssssssssssssssssssssssssssss . . . i dnt care what u say . . . mad man!!!!!!!

Affective self-identification

- *Msscpb@uncensoredreality* Same dam thing i sayin! Music jus get inna me head, creep unda me skin and me jus feel real wotless!
- *wesley hamilton* I shouldn't listen to this song, but oh gosh, it biting meh, look how meh head moving . . . oh gosh, I fraid to be wotless . . . my gosh, it biting meh . . .
- *fuckumlivinglife* right now ii juss wotlessssssssssssss buss a winee;
- *HOTTGAL1989* i cah stop whinin fuh dis song omg.......& dah beat BEEESSSSSSSSS:)))))...AH WOTLESS;
- Ursulav83 WOTLESS!!!!!!!!!!! WOOOOOOOO DANCING LOL.

Behavior in a place

- *cooyahfab* Me wotless in the club . . .
- *MultiJ0rdan* big tune boiiii WE WOTLESS for J'ouvert 2011!!
- *calypsoking23* ohh goshhhhh, rite now i juss wotless!!!!! ready for de parkway already
- *Jolene Smith* Yuh really just have tuh wine reaaaal wotless when yuh hear this song, man i had to break out on stage in DC when this played. I just keep listening to it over and over cah stop dance man!!! Just have to drop hard, trini style

Behavior and Trinidadian identity

- *nichelle hector* WE TRINI PEOPLE REL WOTLESS . . . AN WE DOH REALLY CARELESS YUH DONE KNOW!
- *buttercup535* all yuh trinis we wotless and we careless to so true
- *Stanley Grant* Ah wotless Trini to the bone,wait yall check out a new artist by the name of Dyce Man tune name Thicky Thicky it mad summer anthem yes we wotless
- *trini1405* Gosh I cah decide between this and Benjai's Trini tune for groovy!! Both ah dem sweeeet. Iza Trini who make good company and ah wotlesss!

Behavior and national/regional identity

- *galfriend3* Vincy, Vincy, VINCY MAAAS!! WE WOTLESS!!
- *tyrone neale* Antigua wotless
- *Beverley Yearwood* Bajan and wotless wwooiii
- *Ashley Joseph* I WOTLESS! I love being Carbbean!!
- *Myson* Labor Day In Brooklyn Wotless!!
- *liltrina4* Miami Carnival I will wotless!!!
- *modelo81292* I was wotless today in brooklyn the parade was madd and when they play this tune I was goin madd!
- *Sajeev Swarupan* im wotless. TORONTO BIG UP!
- *LANI11433* I'm jamming to my cousin song WOTLESS! I'm gonna be WOT-LESS for da next few days till LABOR DAY!
- *VINCYJEWEL* BOY OH BOY I WAS JUS WOTLESSSSSSSSSSS FOR CARIBANA LUV KES STR8888888 RIGHT NOW I JUS WOTLESSSSSSSS DIS CHUNE CANT DONE
- *Gabrielle Gabby* I am a happy to be a trini and half Jamacian we run tingz cuzz RIGHT NOW WE JUST WOTLESSSS!!!!!!!!!!!!!!!!
- *Cherry* Yadunno <<guyanese straiight wotlesss!!!!
- *kingala* uptown dey gon talk bout dis!!! ah doan care ah wotless!! *insert bajan wukup*
- *sexilika1* Iza vincy and ah wotlessssssssssssssssssssssss, and i doh really careless
- *roni mitchell* I luvv dis song to de fullest mann! Me need to go backk home to Trinida and be WOTLESS! !
- *Tata Bus* KES The Band in Cayman Islands right now!!!! Right now ah just WOTLESS!

- *Ambryana Campbell* Right Now I Just Wotless And I Dont Really Careless... Mi Rep JA Buhh Dhiss Is The SHit

Responses to dislikes

- *Kirtzjacob* only one person dis like dis? wam yuh wotless awa?
- *LinnDonn Adams* who eva dislike dis is a raw ass... i go wotless fa weekz till i bak to normal [Whoever disliked this is a raw ass. I'll be wotless for weeks until I'm back to normal]
- *Ragga Muffin* i think d 1 person who click "dislike" clicked the wrong one
- *riazman* It have chree wotless people bout here.sen puncheon!
- *Daniel Mitchell* The 6 people that dislike this video definately not wotless... dey full ah shit and probably go be in dey bed monday and tuesday
- *mervstar* Ack, I hit dislike by mistake... oh gosh nuh, I wotless.
- *MsLionheart29* 11 people wotless but pretending
- *gizzerts* 11 people are not wotless at the moment
- *spicey ryan* 11 people are acting. Like they r NOT wotless
- *divababii1227* the 12 people that dislike this song is deff not Wotless and Dumb like how can you dislike this songg this songg is thee best and pluss why would you look up a songg and dislikee itt #verydumb
- *SempaiAlex* Unlike those 13 people who are VERY wotless right now, I have a sense of taste. Kes is besssssssst!
- *squeaknique1* 13 people had wotless partners this carnival...
- *VTEC_LOL* 13 people are not Trinidadians...
- *SuperAshleyrawr* 14 chupid ...i izza trini && ah wotless... i doh biz wa pplz say... woi woi trini tuh d bone yo:)
- *relhardwine1* the 22 dat dislike this song is probably bajans... hahhahaha
- *JUSTIIN JACKSON* For the 22 dat dislike dis sng.u hear wah di man say.kall he name lml

Definitions, Selected Lyrics, and Selected YouTube Comments (Back on de Scene 2009; Olatunji 2009) for "Tusty" by Blaxx (2009)

According to the Urban Dictionary, user *sub27* defines *tusty* as "slang for 'thirsty' with specific reference to interaction with the opposite sex; *see soca song 'Tusty' by Blaxx (2009)*" (Urban Dictionary 2009). It should be noted that a definition for this term does not appear in either Winer's (2009) or Allsopp's (2003) dictionaries

Selected lyrics for "Tusty" by Blaxx (2009)
Sample definitions of *tusty* from YouTube comments (Olatunji 2009)

- *Huging* banging song! So what exactly is a "TUSTY"???
- *cluckyclucky @ Huging* Tusty is just the way we say "thirsty" *[referenced]*

Chorus
Ah tusty (repeated) . . .
Ah tusty for wine, mama
Ah tusty to grind, mama
Ah tusty for wave, mama
Ah tusty is ah pain, mama
Show me what you got.
Give me dat (repeated)
Verse 2
Doh feel no way if ah put a bump on you
Ah tus- tusty, ah tus- tusty.
Say pardon me if I take a jump with you
Ah tus- tusty, ah tus- tusty.
I grabbing anything I see
Right now I tusty tusty
Ah doh care who talking 'bout me
Right now I tusty tusty
Bridge
Country people getting a beer
Social people get out of here
Put dem big ting up in de air
Right now I declare that we get on bad, bad, bad
Bad, bad, bad (repeated)
Get bad, bad, bad (repeated)

- *Dswanky @Huging* tusty isnt something....its when u want someting very bad . . . so wen u see a girl that u want badly . . . we would say, ur tusty!! *[general]*
- *Huging* I see, I see:) Up here we call that 'horny'
- *Reddiamonds87 @ Huging* cluckyclucky is right.he saying he thirsty meaning he want 2 really have fun and dance with the woman *[contextualized]*

Sample definitions of *tusty* from YouTube comments (Back on de Scene 2009)

- *Akeliahsmusic89 @ tambienme4* its just broken english for thirsty . . . in this tune blaxx is sayn hes cravin a gud wuk up or dance from a girl *[contextualized]*
- *IVEMER 5* Ain't dat kool or wat? We west Indians have a unique language: D
- *SWANKS17@tambienme4* it means thirsty...WE TRINIS JUS SAT TUSTY . . . thas how we speak:) *[referenced]*

Definitions, Selected Lyrics, and Selected YouTube Comments (JulianspromosTV 2011) for "Hard Wuk" by Machel Montano (2011)

One of the meanings of the verb *wuk* is to "give strenuous sexual exercise" (Winer 2009, p. 971). Winer does not provide and definition of *wuk* connected to dancing. Wuking and winning are synonymous. The verb *wine* (also wind) means "while dancing, to gyrate the pelvis in a sexual manner" (Dalzell and Victor 2015, p. 842).

Selected lyrics for "Hard Wuk" by Machel Montano (2011)

Chorus	
What dey want? Wuk! Hard wuk.	
When we wining. Wuk! Hard wuk.	
When we jamming. Wuk! Hard wuk.	
When we grinding. Wuk! Hard wuk.	
	Verse 1
Ln1	She want me to take de time when ah wine
	But ah only sharing hard wuk.
	When she get de wuk, she change she mind
	And decide she want the hard wuk
Ln 5	It does worry me when I cannot give it
	Cuz I'm a man with plenty stamina
	So this year any gyal out dere
	Who want to come and get a taste of meh wuk
	When I behind de truck on de road.
Ln 10	Better tick tock. It like a time bomb and make that mini bumper explode.
	Anything you want me do, I want to do it for you
	Once it have to do with the wining
	Once it have to do with the sharing
Ln 15	I does more give more than I take
	Make no mistake, I'm a hard worker, hard worker, hard worker

Sample definitions of *wuk* from YouTubers (JulianspromosTV 2011)

- *RRmanutd98* Wtf does wuk mean??!!
- *niquentae @ RRmanutd98* work *[referenced]*
- *JazzyBae97 @RRmanutd98* it means to dance. lik "wuk up on a girl" *[contextualized]*
- *DigitalIslandboy* Wuk was "Work" with a Caribbean accent *[referenced]*... As in to "workup" (wukkup) your waistline. *[contextualized]*

References

R.D. Abrahams, *The Man-of-Words in the West Indies: Performance and the Emergence of Creole Culture* (Johns Hopkins University Press, Baltimore, 1983)

R. Allsopp, *Dictionary of Caribbean English Usage* (University of West Indies Press, Kingston, 2003)

J. Androutsopoulos, in *Discourse 2.0: Language and new media*, ed. by D. Tannen, A. M. Trester. Participatory culture and metalinguistic discourse: Performing and negotiating German dialects on YouTube (Georgetown University Press, Washington, DC, 2013), pp. 47–71

J. Androutsopoulos, Introduction: sociolinguistics and computer-mediated communication. J. Sociolinguist. **10**(4), 419–438 (2006)

J. Androutsopoulos, J. Tereick, in *The Routledge handbook of language and digital communication*, ed. by A. Georgakopoulou, T. Spilioti. YouTube: language and discourse practices in participatory culture (Routledge, New York, 2016), pp. 354–370

Back on de Scene, Tusty – Blaxx (Trini soca 2009) [Video file] (2009), Retrieved from https://www.youtube.com/watch?v=9Qau6VxRoFU.

M. Bakhtin, *Rabelais and His World* (MIT Press, Cambridge, MA, 1968)

Blaxx, *Tusty*, in *Soca gold 2009 [CD]* (VP Records, Jamaica, NY, 2009)

R.D. Burton, *Afro-Creole: Power, Opposition, and Play in the Caribbean* (Cornell University Press, Ithaca, 1997)

CanchozI, Kes the Band – Wotless (soca 2011) [Video file] (2010), Retrieved from https://www.youtube.com/watch?v=n0DvbOk8rs4.

J. Coomansingh, in *Island Tourism: Towards a Sustainable Perspective*, ed. by J. Carlsen, R. Butler. Social sustainability of tourism in a culture of sensuality, sexual freedom and violence: Trinidad and Tobago (CAB International, Wallingford, 2011), pp. 118–128

A. Coulon, *Ethnomethodology* (Sage, Thousand Oaks, 1995)

N. Coupland, *Style: Language Variation and Identity* (CUP, Cambridge, 2007)

T. Dalzell, T. Victor, *The Concise New Partridge Dictionary of Slang and Unconventional English* (Routledge, New York, 2015)

M. Devitt, Linguistic intuitions and cognitive penetrability. Balt. Int. Yearb. Cogn. Logic Commun. **9**(1), 4 (2014)

P. Eckert, Variation and the indexical field. J. Socioling. **12**(4), 453–476 (2008)

C.A. Ferguson, Diglossia. Word **15**(2), 325–340 (1959)

A. Georgakopoulou, T. Spilioti (eds.), *The Routledge Handbook of Language and Digital Communication* (Routledge, New York, 2016)

T. Heyd, Doing race and ethnicity in a digital community: Lexical labels and narratives of belonging in a Nigerian web forum. Discourse Context Media **4**, 38–47 (2014)

L. Hinrichs, *Codeswitching on the Web: English and Jamaican Creole in e-mail Communication* (John Benjamins Publishing, Amsterdam, 2006)

A. Jaffe, *Stance: Sociolinguistic perspectives* (OUP, New York, 2009)

B. Johnstone, S.F. Kiesling, Indexicality and experience: Exploring the meanings of/aw−monophthongization in Pittsburgh. J. Socioling. **12**(1), 5–33 (2008)

JulianspromosTV. Machel Montano: Hard wuk 2011 Trinidad Carnival (produced by Mr. Roots) [Video file] (2011), Retrieved from https://www.youtube.com/watch?v=vcAO5iMDT6g.

Kes the Band, *Wotless*, in *Wotless: The carnival album [CD]* (Kes the Band, Trinidad, 2011)

S.F. Kiesling, Dude. Am Speech **79**(3), 281–305 (2004)

G. Leung, A synchronic sociophonetic study of monophthongs in Trinidadian English (Doctoral dissertation), (2013), Retrieved from https://freidok.uni-freiburg.de/data/9015.

H.D. Maharajh, A. Kalpoo, in *Perspectives in Caribbean Psychology*, ed. by F.W. Hickling, B.K. Matthies, K. Morgan, R.C. Gibson. Culture and behaviour: Recognition of cultural behaviours in Trinidad and Tobago (Kingston, Caribbean Institute of Mental Health and Substance Abuse, 2012), pp. 131–160

J. Maynes, Linguistic intuition and calibration. Linguist. Philos. **35**(5), 443–460 (2012)

A. Moll, *Jamaican Creole goes web: Sociolinguistic styling and authenticity in a digital 'Yaad'* (John Benjamins Publishing, Amsterdam, 2015)

M. Montano, *Hard wuk,* in *The return [CD]* (Ruf Rex Records/Xtatik Ltd., Trinidad, 2011)

N. Niedzielski, D. Preston, *Folk linguistics* (Mouton de Gruyter, Berlin, 2000)

S. R. Payne, W. J. Davies, M. D. Adams, Research into the practical policy applications of soundscapes concepts and techniques in urban areas. DEFRA report NANR200, June 2009

R. Oenbring, Bey or bouy: Orthographic patterns in Bahamian Creole English on the web. Engl. World-Wide **34**(3), 341–364 (2013)

Olatunji, A. (2009, February 19). *Blaxx-Tusty (offical soca music video 2009) [Video file].* Retrieved from https://www.youtube.com/watch?v=JvsZT2wo4PU

A. Rajah-Carrim, Use and standardisation of Mauritian Creole in electronically mediated communication. J. Comput. Mediat. Commun. **14**(3), 484–508 (2009)

M.C. Riggio, Resistance and identity: carnival in Trinidad and Tobago. Drama Rev. **42**(3), 7–23 (1998)

N. Scheper-Hughes, *Death without weeping: Everyday violence in Brazil* (University of California Press, Berkeley, 1992)

E. Schneider, World Englishes on Youtube: treasure trove or nightmare? in *World Englishes: New Theoretical and Methodological Considerations,* ed. by E. Seoane, C. Suárez-Gómez (Benjamins, Amsterdam, 2016), p. 253–282

J. Shepherd, D. Horn (eds.), *Continuum encyclopedia of popular music of the world: Performance and Production,* vol 2 (Continuum, New York, NY, 2003)

M. Silverstein, Indexical order and the dialectics of sociolinguistic life. Lang. Commun. **23**(3), 193–229 (2003)

SIL International, What is a phoneme? (2004), Retrieved December 10, 2016, from http://www-01.sil.org/linguistics/glossaryoflinguisticterms/whatisaphoneme.htm

G. Smitherman, *Talkin and testifyin: The language of Black America* (Wayne State University Press, Detroit, MI, 1977)

J.T. Springer, "Roll it gal": Alison Hinds, female empowerment, and calypso. Meridians **8**(1), 93–129 (2008)

L. Squires (ed.), *English in Computer-mediated Communication: Variation, Representation, and Change* (De Gruyter Mouton, Berlin, 2016)

A. Strauss, J. Corbin, *Basics of Qualitative Research: Techniques and Procedures for Developing Grounded Theory* (Sage Publications, Inc., Thousand Oaks, CA, 1998)

Urban Dictionary, Tusty [Online dictionary] (2009), Retrieved from http://www.urbandictionary.com/define.php?term=tusty&defid=3757629.

R. Wardhaugh, J. Fuller, *An Introduction to Sociolinguistics* (John Wiley & Sons, Malden, 2015)

T. Wasow, J. Arnold, Intuitions in linguistic argumentation. Lingua **115**(11), 1481–1496 (2005)

J.C. Wells, *Accents of English 3: Beyond the British Isles* (CUP, Cambridge, 1982)

G. Wilson, *The Sociolinguistics of Singing: Dialect and Style in Classical Choral Singing in Trinidad* (Verlag-Haus Monsenstein und Vannerdat, Monsenstein, 2014)

P.J. Wilson, *Crab Antics: the Social Anthropology of English-Speaking Negro Societies of the Caribbean* (Yale University Press, New Haven, 1973)

L. Winer, *Dictionary of the English/Creole of Trinidad & Tobago: On Historical Principles* (McGill-Queen's Press, 2009)

D. Winford, Phonological hypercorrection in the process of decreolization: the case of Trinidadian English. J. Linguist. **14**(2), 277–291 (1978)

A.D. Wong, The reappropriation of tongzhi. Lang. Soc. **34**(05), 763–793 (2005)

Creating Inheritable Digital Codebooks for Qualitative Research Data Analysis

Shalin Hai-Jew

Abstract In qualitative, mixed methods, and multi-methodology research, a codebook captures how research data may be analyzed for insight. Codebooks serve multiple purposes: they enable researchers to explore data; identify patterns; advance their research, and develop insights. Codebooks, also referred to as code lists, may be created using emergent methods (based on researcher interaction with the target data), a priori methods (based on theories, frameworks, models, and other extant sources), and combined approaches (informed by a priori sources and insights from the coding). With the affordances of Computer Assisted Qualitative Data AnalysiS (CAQDAS) tools, contemporary codebooks may originate in more ways than manual coding. NVivo 11 Plus enables the development of semi- and fully autocoded codebooks based on three main methods: sentiment autocoding (unsupervised), automated theme extraction (unsupervised), and coding by existing pattern (supervised). The use of technologies fundamentally influences the evolution of codebooks and the applied coding to the research data. This work introduces some of these interaction effects between a researcher and a CAQDAS technology in the development of a codebook from initial conceptualization through the evolution and finalization of a digital codebook for qualitative research. Further, this work suggests that contemporary digital codebooks may be designed to be inheritable or transferable, which is an assumption more common in fields using mostly quantitative research approaches. If there are more common distribution channels for qualitative, mixed methods, and multi-methodology research codebooks, research may be advanced in many areas.

Introduction

A codebook in qualitative, mixed methods, and multi-methodology research essentially describes how research data is analyzed for meaning and insight. Most such codebooks are unique to the project and the data; in other words, by general practice,

S. Hai-Jew (✉)
Kansas State University, Manhattan, KS 66506, USA
e-mail: shalin@k-state.edu; haijes@gmail.com

© Springer International Publishing AG 2017
S. Hai-Jew (ed.), *Data Analytics in Digital Humanities*, Multimedia Systems and Applications, DOI 10.1007/978-3-319-54499-1_11

the coding structures are not usually inherited from other researchers or research projects. The codebooks are not usually pre-created in other research contexts, but they may be informed by particular selected theories, models, frameworks, or other concept-based sources (in a priori or pre-existing method coding). Some projects involve "emergent coding," in which a coding structure is grounded in fresh readings of the data, with the data informing the development of the codebook, and the emerging codebook informing the analysis of the data.

While codebooks stand to inform their respective research domains and other arenas of study, qualitative methods codebooks are often a hidden aspect of modern research, with many published works using these to scaffold the data analysis but with codebooks considered something privy and even embargoed, like researcher notes and journals, which are critical as working papers but are not thought to be of archival value unless the researcher reaches a certain level of prominence. Much time, effort, and expertise go into the development of codebooks, yet the culmination of these efforts are often unshared and lost to history. In some cases, when codebooks are shared, they are mentioned in passing in the methods sections of publications, or snippets may be shared in the body of a paper or in the appendices; in some rare occasions, codebooks may be included in their entirety in the appendices. In even rarer cases, a few codebooks have been shared as stand-alone publications, some with front matter, research source citations, and desired bibliographic information. In this digital age, most of what is shared is preserved for the future, but there are not dedicated efforts at codebook preservation per se.

The shared qualitative codebooks tend to be team-built objects related to evolving datasets; as such, these are generally co-evolved over time, and new variables are added by consensus [sometimes overseen by the originator(s) of the codebook or committees/organizations] as a field advances. (The few that the author has seen have been from political science, and the codebooks and datasets tend to be more aligned with quantitative research practices than qualitative ones.)

And yet, codebooks used in qualitative research stand to offer rich insights, particularly in research contexts with low "N's" and the need to approach research precision in multiple ways, sometimes without statistical significance or with different types of statistical significance for non-parametric data (such as chi-square measures of non-parametric cross tabulation tables). Certainly, qualitative researchers and theorists have created a wide range of methods for supporting research rigor over the many prior decades. Shared codebooks may offer clarity as to how data was approached and conclusions were reached in research. Ideally, they could offer the following:

- Tactics and strategies for research designs, data collection, data analysis, code-book creation (and collaborative codebook co-creation), and other research work related insights;
- A meta-level and condensed perspective of the data analytics, with insights about the research hypotheses and data discoveries in a research context and domain;
- Efficient and effective methods for codebook creation and evolution;

  - Discernments about how research insights relate to the applied research methods and the raw primary data (with exemplars coded to each part of a codebook, and also exemplars for what was not coded to particular codes; coding frequency distributions across the codebooks, and other aspects of coding and the underlying source data);
- Applied methods for coding new data in different research contexts;
- Entrée into understanding a particular domain or field or professional practice;
- Understanding of respective researchers' coding "fists" (by reverse engineering their codebooks to their unique insights, their "hidden hand" in the analytical work, and their research gaze);
- Understandings of ways to reapply these researcher coding "fists" to different data through computational means
  - This concept of a "fist" comes from the unique ways that Morse code operators handled their telegraph keys, communicating through dots and dashes. A "good fist" involves communicating the messages clearly and efficiently, and a "poor fist" involves being unclear and inefficient. In coding, a person's "fist" encapsulates what that researcher sees that others do not. Coding is an extension of the researcher's personality, intellect, skill, and professional insight;
- Ways to understand codebook inspiration, creation, and evolution through process mining (of event logs, research journals, and the codebooks)
  - Are there phases that codebooks go through? What important steps occur when?
  - Are there requisite steps that have to occur for a successful codebook? Are these steps required to be in a particular order or not, and why or why not?
  - Are there ways to enhance the process of creating effective codebooks through process mining, in what van der Aalst (2011) calls "enhancement process mining" (p. 45)?

Rethinking the sharing of qualitative codebooks has come about in part because of the current state of the world. There is negligible cost to digital memory. Most information may be digitized. Prior stored information on media may be transcoded into a fairly easy-to-handle digital format, no matter what the original type of data storage was, even cassette tapes, eight-track tapes, and vinyl (although the transcoder consoles are more and more difficult to acquire commercially). The popularization of Computer Assisted Qualitative Data AnalysiS (CAQDAS) tools has made it easier for researchers to create codebooks and apply them to various types of data.

For many researchers using empirical data from the world for their studies, there is a sentimental tie to embodied data analytics approaches. There is the charm of using markers, butcher paper, tape, and sticky notes. There is charm to having notepads and pencil and ink pens. Many will say that having physical objects to engage with in a physical space can be freeing and relaxing for the difficult cognitive and thinking work. Such stances are valid based on research into the role of proprioception in learning. One light rebuttal is that digital means can emulate physical thinking processes. There are advances in widely available technologies that enable the digital re-creation of some of these spaces, with touch screens, stylus and tablet devices, digital audio recording devices, and others. A researcher and a research team have to accept technologies to some degree for this approach to work. To avoid CAQDAS technology, though, is to leave a lot of information unexploited and latent.

This approach is not about forgoing effective methods for researchers, who may feel that technologies are making incursions into human research. Technologies are augmentations to human capabilities, and many technological affordances are informed by human interests and are designed to serve people. Many computational models are compared against expert insights when measuring the efficacy of these programs. Interestingly, qualitative research is about learning in depth from small samples, but even here, there are computational means to extract insights from even one exemplar, by extracting relevant features and applying logic methodically and rigorously (Winston 2010). For many, computational supports for qualitative research findings may bolster human researcher insights. "But for" the use of the technology, some codes would not be extracted and observed because they would not be observable to the unaided human eye.

Historically, codebooks in qualitative research have not been broadly shared as any sort of stand-alone resource. Rather, if they are mentioned at all, they are occasionally included in the Methods sections of a publication or placed in the Appendices. These are almost never released with datasets, which are considered proprietary and at-risk of data leakage and participant re-identification. Historically, most codebooks are applied to the unique research context, and only those which are applied to continuing data collection are released broadly (to modify the dataset and promote deeper researcher understandings of the data).

This paper describes some light research in qualitative codebooks or "CAQDAS code lists" and some of the affordances of NVivo 11 Plus for the creation of transferable codebooks.

Review of the Literature

At the simplest level, a codebook consists of a listing of codes and then descriptive information about what fits within each code category and what does not. Codebooks may be built off of pre-defined categories, based on theories, models, constructs, frameworks, and other elements from a research domain; these are known as a priori codebooks, and these are usually created prior to the actual usage against a set of data or text corpus. Emergent codebooks, by contrast, are those that are created from a researcher's read-through of the collected data; emergent codebooks do not have any prior structure but are an extraction from the raw data. And then there are codebooks that have some initial early structure but which evolve based on researcher observations of the raw data. As a qualitative research tool, codebooks generally are used to make summary and analytical sense of the underlying raw data. Codebooks in qualitative research tend to be one-offs, except in a situation where the researcher continues along the same line of research over multiple years and multiple projects. Generally, these tend to be essentialist and condensed, inspired by expertise and prior work but also partially derived from analyses of the raw data.

A codebook "is an abstract of a collection of data items that have been assembled for studying some topic of interest" (Bettinger 2012, Slide 3). The prior phrasing suggests more of an emergent focus for this conceptualization of a codebook. Of interest is how this author describes characteristics of the code and their respective representations, with codebooks include both continuous and categorical variables. For the first, Bettinger suggests that basic descriptive statistics be included: "mean, standard deviation, range, mode, median" and visualizations including "box-and-whisker plots, contour plots, heat maps, and 3D surface diagrams." For the latter, he suggests "frequency histograms, mosaic plots, bubble plots" to represent the categorical variables (Bettinger 2012, Slide 3). Like models, codebooks should be parsimonious, with selected variables. Not everything deserves to be observed and listed in a codebook.

In the research literature, codebooks may be used to set a level of rigor in understanding particular in-world phenomena and events (Sullivan and Koch 2008). They may be deeply integrated into the research design and take years to build and evolve, some involving researchers from multiple countries (Treiman 1998).

In terms of formats, some new codebooks are seeded with the so-called start lists, which enable researchers to begin their coding work and evolve a codebook from there. Others pre-define the entire codebook (or code list) with a mix of a priori details. Some codebooks come in tabular form (like a data table), and these are referred to as tabular codebooks. There are some codebooks that take on more complex forms, such as some emulating the periodic table (as an organizing construct and visualization) (McGrew 2014). Researchers often set rules for the coding, such as whether information coded to one "node" may also be coded to others. In many contexts, there are multiple cycles of coding and subcoding and refinement of the codebook (Miles et al. 2014). The structure of codebooks into layers suggests both an awareness of the unit of measure (granularity, level of abstraction) and of hierarchical and network relationships in terms of data.

While a very basic codebook involves merely codes ("nodes") and rules for coding to that node, more detailed codebooks may include the following:

- *"Short description* – the name of the code itself
- *Detailed description* – a 1–3 sentence description of the coded datum's qualities or properties
- *Inclusion criteria* – conditions of the datum or phenomenon that merit the code
- *Exclusion criteria* – exceptions or particular instances of the datum or phenomenon that do not merit the code
- *Typical exemplars* – a few examples of data that best represent the code

- *Atypical exemplars* – extreme or special examples of data that still represent the code
- *"Close, but no"* – data examples that could mistakenly be assigned this particular code" (Saldaña 2013, p. 25).

In addition, it may be helpful to have even more information, particularly about contexts from which the codebook is being released. This is especially so for stand-alone contexts of codebooks, which will not be held in place in a particular research sequence and context.

- A disambiguated codebook name (with an apt acronym),
- A history of the codebook development (and main decision junctures),

  - The sequence of the codebook creation, data processing sequences (the codes extracted from data are sensitive to sequential and methodological processing), and related macros,

- How intermediate or advanced the codebook is in the particular area of research (is the codebook just an initial draft or something that has been used for decades and has settled into a stable state or something else?),
- Descriptions of applicable research and/or data analytics contexts (as conceptualized by the developers of the codebook),
- How the codes were created, particularly those extracted from theories, models, frameworks, and other extant approaches and then from the data analytics (as relevant), given the universe of possibilities and the high dimensionality of data in qualitative research,
- Any pilot testing of the codebook (methods, insights, and changes to the codebook),
- References to any related datasets, whether publicly available or not,
- Known limitations to the use of the codebook tool,
- A bibliographic listing of sources which informed the creation of the codebook,
- Applied data pre-processing or data cleaning,
- Sample coded data,
- An authors' listing (and direct contact information and terms of invited contact),
- Sample citation for the usage of the codebook,
- Linked prior published research (using the codebook),
- Suggested methods for building onto the codebook,
- Creative Commons licensure for intellectual property releases, and other relevant information.

Meta-analytic applications of codebooks As noted earlier, codebooks created for qualitative, mixed methods, and multi-methodology research could be applied for various meta-aims: (1) coder exploration, (2) data exploration and pattern identification, (3) research advancement, and (4) domain and non-domain insight creation. Meta aims are additional ambitions overlaid to the original usage of the codebook. What do these four applied categories mean? Table 1: "Four Objectives for Qualitative Research Codebook Analysis" summarizes some practical applications.

Table 1 Four objectives for qualitative research codebook analysis

Digital codebook creation process. The creation of a digital codebook is thought to fit into a qualitative, mixed method, or multi-method research sequence, which goes something like this:

conceptualization of the research < – > review of the literature < – > research design < – > research design approval < – > data collection < – > data pre-processing and cleaning < – > digital codebook development (informed by the prior elements and the following elements) < – > data analysis (including data queries) < – > machine coding over the raw data < – > coding queries based on coding in the project (such as matrix coding queries, and others) < – > data visualizations < – > write-up < – > research publication/presentation <-> codebook preparation for sharing < – > codebook distribution <-> codebook archival < – > codebook supports –>.

Each of the steps in the process includes complexities which have not been addressed here. The process here is generally linear but includes recursive elements, therefore, the two-ended processes arrow heads. It helps to note that a digital codebook is informed by both upstream and downstream processes, and there is a degree of recursion in the steps, in this conceptualization. Also, this process suggests that the researcher and research team go through disciplined thinking and work in order to emerge with research insights. The value in creating a codebook is in the process, which opens up discoveries to the researcher, and not necessarily in the finalized product alone.

Early observations of codebook structures: The structure of codebook depends on a number of factors:

• Underlying applied concepts (whether from theories, models, frameworks, or other sources),

• Research domain,

• Researcher conceptual models, expertise, and education (whether consciously, subconsciously, or unconsciously applied),

• Research question(s) and hypothesis(ses), including related sub-questions and sub-hypotheses,

• Captured source data,

• Serendipity, and other factors.

The above factors will have interaction effects. For example, if an a priori coding structure is applied, but there is no observation of a particular concept or phenomena, that coding node will be left empty except for its name and description. An empty node in the software tool will mean that if "coding by existing pattern" is applied as a supervised machine learning tool, that node will not have any exemplars to lead, and nothing will be machine coded to that particular node. (With supervised machine learning in NVivo 11 Plus, no new nodes will be created based on a run over the data, but the machine will emulate the human coder based on exemplars coded to the respective nodes.) This node without examples coded to it will receive less attention than other nodes populated with text-based examples. If a concept lies outside a research domain, it may be difficult to find references to it in amounts that are meaningful. The research question(s) or hypothesis(ses) will affect the contents of the codebook because these define certain observable phenomena of interest as expressed in the data. Serendipity (beneficial coincidences and chance) likely will play a role, too, as it does in most contexts. Each of these elements will influence the final codebook to varying degrees. Said another way, no two codebooks will be exactly alike because most if not all the input factors will vary.

(continued)

Table 1 continued

Making a codebook ready for public stand-alone release and inheritance. A codebook, then, is designed for a local applied purpose of coding captured data, but it may also be used for meta-purposes and fresh insights. It may be applied to other research contexts. It has an inherent informational value. The prior realities beg the question of what additional work may need to prepare a codebook for stand-alone release. Researchers who inherit a codebook will not necessarily have direct background with that particular type of research or the research data. They will need sufficient contextual information to properly understand the codebook and the related coded data and how to apply it.

For researchers who are thinking about sharing their codebooks broadly, this question of how to make their stand-alone codebook more usable may arise earlier rather than after the research and data coding has been completed. Given the cognitive load of managing complex research, it may be better to keep the transferability of a codebook a somewhat separate process either at the end of the main research and coding work (1), or as dedicated periods of time throughout the research work (2), as may be seen in Fig. 1. In this latter case, some additional steps have been added to the prior sequence:

---

conceptualization of the research(*and what a codebook may look like; initial notetaking for a conceptualized codebook*) < – >

---

review of the literature(*with theoretical and practical inputs into a codebook; initial drafting of a digital codebook*) < – >

---

research design(*with anticipated coding defined*) < – >

---

research design approval < – >

---

data collection(*with an eye for collecting sufficient data to inform the potential categories of a codebook*) <–>

---

data pre-processing and cleaning < – >

---

digital codebook development (informed by the prior elements and the following elements) (*codebook building; documentation of the codebook development from various data streams, including the research journal; citation of formal published sources and gray literature used for the development of the coding structure; memo-ing at the level of each node for documentation; automated event logging*) < – >

---

data analysis (including data queries) (*documentation of the macros and sequences for the codebook documentation; selection of exemplars for each node category*) < – > machine coding over the raw data (*documentation of macros and sequences for the codebook documentation*) < – >

---

coding queries based on coding in the project (such as matrix coding queries, and others) (*documentation of macros and sequences for the codebook documentation*) < – >

---

data visualizations (*consideration for inclusion of some data visualizations into the codebook*) <– >

---

pilot testing of the codebook for transferability (*design of the pilot testing methods; documentation of the pilot testing of the codebook*)* < – >

---

revision of the codebook post pilot testing (*responses to the findings of the codebook pilot testing; documentation of the revisions*)* < – >

---

write-up (*analysis of the influence of the qualitative codebook to the research findings; limited inclusion of the codebook in a formal publication and / or presentation; write-up of the full stand-alone codebook with support information*) < – >

---

research publication / presentation (*rollout of the stand-alone codebook as well*) < - >

---

codebook preparation for sharing (*codebook finalization*) < - >

---

codebook distribution < - > (*formatting to align with the digital and / or analog platform*)

---

codebook archival < - >

---

codebook supports -> (*evolving design of strategy and tactics for codebook supports; creation of digital or other objects*)

The asterisk refers to two added steps in the semi-linear occasionally recursive sequence

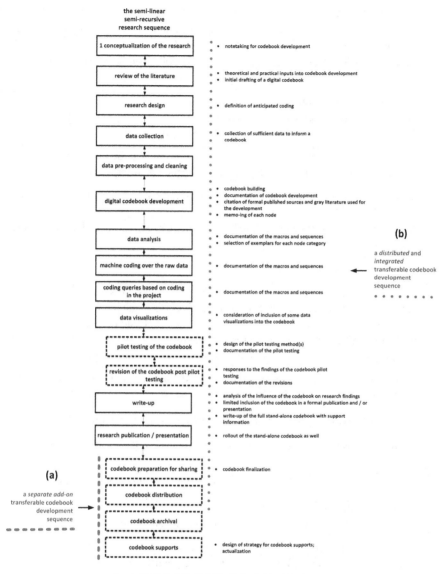

Transferable / Inheritable Digital Qualitative Codebook Development:
(a) Separate Add-on Process or (b) Distributed and Integrated Development Process

Fig. 1 Transferable/inheritable digital qualitative codebook development: (**a**) separate add-on process or (**b**) distributed and integrated development process

Coder exploration:
- What is the researcher (or research team) "hand" that may be seen in the development and evolution of the particular codebook?
- What are the built-in subjectivities and biases observable in the research data coding?

Data exploration and pattern identification:
- What data and information are in the dataset?
- What is seen and not seen in the raw data? The processed information?

  – In terms of what is not seen, why isn't a particular code category filled with raw source information? How may that absence be interpreted?

- What external (non-included) information may be analyzed with the particular codebook for research value?
- What apparent patterns exist in the data? (whether "inherent" or based on a pre-determined model)

  – What do these patterns suggest?

- Based on grouping variables (of case nodes—or interview subjects, focus group subjects, survey interviewees), are certain patterns seeable? If so, what would these patterns suggest? (Grouping variables include basic demographic features and other attribute data about the respective subjects.)
- In terms of machine coding, what are observed sentiment patterns?

  – Why might such sentiment patterns exist, and what do they mean in the context?

- In terms of machine coding, what are theme and subtheme patterns?

  – How do these extracted themes and subthemes compare across similar text sets?

- What are some unexploited ways to explore the data through the codebook?

Research advancement:
- What research discoveries were made in the data analytics?

  – What are some inferences from these findings?
  – In terms of deductive logic, what are some potential insights?
  – What are various interpretation methods? Are there unexplored interpretations?

- Are there other contexts in which this codebook may be used for research insights?
- What are some new methodologies of data analytics based on what may be observed in the codebook?

  – How transferable are these new research methodologies?
  – How transferable are the new codebook design strategies and tactics?

- What research questions have not been addressed?
- What are some important potential future research directions?

Domain and non-domain insight creation:
- What does the codebook suggest about how researchers in a particular domain conduct research? Collect information? Value information and insights? Practice particular professional ethics, especially around data?
- What are some possible domain-based and non-domain-based insights from the coded research and data analytics?
- What are some observed data insights not found in the codebook (and left uncoded)? What do the gaps suggest?

Some additional points for the development of a transferable/inheritable digital qualitative codebook include the following considerations:

- *Modularizing the digital codebook*: Is it possible to modularize the codebook for easier transferability? By having multiple sections that focus on particular aspects of the topic, sections may be more heritable than the entirety.
- *Necessary sequencing*: Does the codebook assume particular steps to the research sequence, such as for data cleaning or for analysis/re-analysis or for machine learning sequences? Are these sequences absolutely required or just preferred? Are there value-added sequences that may benefit the research and data analytics work?
- *Standards setting*: Do the creators of a codebook assume that there has to be a certain level of data capture before data saturation is attained? Before some level of validity or invalidity is reached? Are there assumed data ranges?
- *Versioning the codebook for various levels of tech access*: Is it a good idea to use proprietary software, or is it better to have an open-source version, too (but without built-in analytics functionality)? Is it a good idea to version a codebook, so it may be used by researchers with differing levels of technology access? If there are different versions, are there different names for the respective versions?
- *Versioning protocols*: If other researchers want to build off a released codebook, what are the terms by which this may be done? Are there versioning protocols (v. 1.0.1)? At what point does a codebook become one that is renamed wholly? What happens to prior codebook developer rights as a codebook evolves?
- *Virtual communities*: In some cases, if a tool becomes highly popular and if there are interested parties, virtual communities of users will arise around the usage of particular tools. They will share data and methods. They will often help co-evolve a tool. This may occur around highly useful codebooks. Such communities do need some support to maintain the social health and constructiveness of these groups. What sort of effort should go into these?

Setting parameters for the application of the digital codebook   Based on usage and new insights, any used codebook will be changed and refined over time. Changes to the affordances of the CAQDAS tool will also affect any codebooks built using that technology. How a codebook is applied in the tech tool—such as settings for the aggressiveness of the coding, settings for the levels of language similarity applied, such as the granularity of the coding (applied to sentences, paragraphs, or cells, for example, in NVivo 11 Plus), will affect the efficacy of the codebook.

What Makes for Effective and Transferable Digital Codebooks for Qualitative, Mixed Methods, and Multi-Methods Research?

Some CAQDAS software tools enable supports for virtually every phase of the research work. For NVivo 11 Plus, this software may be used for the following (and likely more than is listed here):

Data collection
- Literature review (published data)

  - Inclusion of metadata from third-party bibliographic tools for resources from commercial subscription and open-source databases, repositories, and referatories

- Online survey data download
- Social media data download (such as through the NCapture web browser add-on)
- Inclusion of digitized gray literature
- Inclusion of embed text to public videos on YouTube
- Inclusion of multimedia data
- Inclusion of multilingual data (anything that can be represented using the UTF-8 character set of Unicode).

Multimedia data curation
- Ability to ingest a wide range of multimedia and text-based files (unstructured data) and datasets (structured data)

  - Function like a heterogeneous database (with easy application of metadata and the easy findability of multimedia contents)

- File management: file (re)naming, file movement, file inclusion, file deletion, folder structures, and others
- File export (in usable formats)
- Autocoding of interview, focus group, survey, and other such data *by style or structure* for ease of ingestion and the ability to create grouping variables (based on linked classification sheets).

Data annotation
- Manual adding of transcripts to video and audio files
- File-level memo-ing
- Automatic capture of metadata (such as coder, day of annotation, and other information)

- Event logging (at the project level)
- The ability to maintain a catch-all folder of discarded insights, sources, and coding (for later re-review and possible re-consideration, and ultimately for non-destructive/non-lossy coding).

Research documentation
- Maintenance of research journal
- Memo-ing (at the source level)
- Event logging.

Team coding
- Ability to ingest and synthesize others' projects to enable team coding (even with a non-server version of the software), within the 10 GB project size limit
- Real-time team coding with server version of the software.

Computer-assisted and fully automated data analytics
- Structured queries of the text in the project (such as word frequency count, text search, coding queries, matrix queries, coding comparisons, and other advanced queries)
- Capture of macros (or query sequences) for re-querying new data
- Sentiment analysis (unsupervised machine learning based on a built-in and un-editable sentiment dictionary)
- Theme and subtheme extraction (unsupervised machine learning)
- Coding by existing pattern (machine emulation of a human coding "fist").

Data visualizations
- Ability to output a variety of data visualizations based on data ingestions (such as from social media platforms), data queries, and machine learning

  – Examples include bar charts, 2D and 3D cluster diagrams, dendrograms (both vertical and horizontal), circle (ring lattice graphs) diagrams, tree maps (with and without color overlays), word clouds, word tree maps, sunburst hierarchy charts, geolocationally pinned maps, sociograms, and others

- Ability to create 2D visual models (node-link diagrams) either manually or in an automated way or in a combination of manual-automated drawing
- Ability to use interactive functionality in the data visualizations to access underlying data.

Codebook editing
- The ability to build nodes in outlines and layers (parent, child, grandchild, and other node layers)
- The ability to code/uncode data to and from nodes
- The ability to meld similar nodes; the ability to split dissimilar nodes
- The ability to create, delete, and revise nodes.

Reportage and report export

- Ability to create and export a codebook with selected elements (usually in an alphabetized listing of nodes and their definitions, but may be editable outside of the software)
- Ability to export a text event log linked to a project
- Ability to export memos
- Ability to export data tables, and others.

Codebooks that are created using CAQDAS software are of a type that would not have been possible before without the current computational capabilities. Modern codebooks may be informed by much bigger and multi-modal data than before. They may be informed by rich annotations and notetaking. They may be fairly easily co-created with researchers. They may be informed by data visualizations. They may be informed by autocoding or the use of various types of data mining and machine learning. CAQDAS tools enable analysis of the amounts of code coded to each node, to give a sense of frequency of coding based on the identified concepts and phenomena. A researcher's computer-mediated interactions with data affect what is knowable and what is ultimately created. If a technology is sufficiently well defined to be research method "agnostic" and is sufficiently flexible to include a broad range of approaches and uses, it may be deployed for effective research data analytics applications and codebook creation. (A codebook is a necessary byproduct of data analytics in qualitative, mixed methods, and multi-methodology approaches.)

Multiple projects per research project. During the span of work for research, it is possible (and even advisable) to use multiple projects for the research particularly in different phases. For example, it may help to have one project for the review of the literature, another for the analysis of interview or focus group or survey data, another for fieldwork videos and notes and imagery, another for related social media channel, and so on. Likewise, for any qualitative, mixed method, and multi-methodology project, it is possible to have several codebooks over the lifespan of a project, and these may be stand-alone and not truly able to be integrated. For example, the coding used in the review of the literature may be used to create a codebook to apply to the raw primary-sourced data, but not every element of the initial codebook from the review will be applicable to the next stage; further, as the raw data is coded, there may be new nodes and insights that are a function of the new collected data with features not found in the precursor literature review.

Coding for codebook transferability The affordances, of course, go beyond the listings above. If codebooks are designed or retrofitted for transferability, these may be broadly distributed for usage by others. There are implications to the sharing of codebooks with other researchers and the broader public. In digital format, codebooks

- May be directly linked to the underlying data (and archived with the underlying data);
- May be much more than text, with integrations of visuals and other informative content;

- May be easily transferred to other researchers (assuming fairly wide usage of and familiarity with the CAQDAS software).

The ability to include important exemplars in each node is an important capability, given the polysemic nature of language and the inherent ambiguity in terms of its usage. The multimedia capabilities for a richer codebook than text is another important digital capability. The ability to share codebooks through databases, repositories, referatories, and registries is yet another new capability, which may change research practices broadly. (It may not be a good idea to have publications dedicate space to codebook publishing as that will mean more competition for already limited reputable publishing spaces for academic research dissemination.) Qualitative codebooks may not only be one-offs but may be abstracted, portioned out, augmented, and otherwise applied to other research contexts.

Providing a venue for the publishing and dissemination of codebooks may benefit the codebook developers as well, by enabling them to identify other researchers with shared interests and providing a distribution channel for extending their scholarship to new audiences. Having a sense of audience may help researchers be more self-aware of their research work. Having an audience may motivate codebook developers to better explain and document the development of their codebook as well, moving it from the realm of a private research aid to a publishable and polished work. Shared codebooks do not have to be in a finalized state but may be provisional and early draft versions—sufficient for a research endeavor but not in finalized format. In cases where others use a dedicated codebook in their own research work, the codebook itself may have a more extended shelf life (through a wider range of applied usage and application); in contexts where it is revised or augmented with other code lists, the codebook may be strengthened for broader data coverage. Also, codebooks which are instantiated into macros may serve as automated programs to be run on new data, with expert human insights encoded into the program and illuminated by the sample code (again, in reference to NVivo 11 Plus's "coding by existing pattern").

This is not to say that codebooks are not related to the contexts from which they emerge. Even codebooks which are released as stand-alone objects will have a history, ties to its developers, ties to particular research designs and methods, and ties to research conclusions. An assumption is that when decontextualized codebooks are released, their histories will still follow them. A necessary condition for a successful stand-alone codebook though is that it can transfer effectively to other research and data analytic contexts.

Ability to enable consistency of understanding or practice in a field in terms of some approaches to particular types of data analytics.

How to Check the Quality of a Codebook for Possible Heritance?

The selection of another researcher's codebook is not one that is entered into lightly. A codebook is an important part of research design, and its structure will affect what insights are surfaced. One key requirement is that the codebook has to fit the research interests of the researcher or research team. It has to have sufficient comprehensiveness to address the issues of concern but also not be too unwieldy to use; it has to be somewhat parsimonious. If there is excessive data residua that is not addressed, then it is possible for the researchers to create their own module or other parts to address what is missing in the original codebook? Or is this extraneous work a disincentive to use the particular codebook? The codebook has to be sufficiently developed and original to be useful; otherwise, other researchers may develop their own (at a cost of time, effort, and money). Also, a codebook has to enable new insights that were not discovered earlier in part because repeats of former findings will often not result in publications or presentations. Some codebooks may involve cost to use. Even if there is not a financial cost though, there may be a reputational one because a researcher or research team needs to credit the original developer(s) of the codebook.

Another way to understand the value of a codebook may be by their meta-analytic value. As cited in Table 1: "Four Objectives for Qualitative Research Codebook Analysis," there are at least four general insights from codebooks, related to coder exploration, data exploration and pattern identification, research advancement, and domain and non-domain insight creation.

In addition, there are some other more general features of a codebook quality to consider for heritance. These are described in five broad areas: (1) codebook validity, (2) credibility of the coder-codebook developer, (3) practical usability, (4) technical alignment with CAQDAS technologies, and (5) support for heritance.

1. Codebook Validity

   - *Alignment to underlying concepts*: If the codebook is designed around particular identified theories, models, frameworks, and so on, are well aligned are the codes to the underlying concepts? Are there important variables or parts missing? Are aspects of the underlying theories . . . misconstrued?
   - *Internal and external (in)validation*: Does the codebook have a record of effective usage? What is its track record of (in)validation?

2. Credibility of Coder-Codebook Developer

   - *Coder-codebook developer "hand"*: Is the coding "fist" sufficiently transferable and flexible or too specific to the original researcher?

     - Does the codebook creator allow room for others to use the codebook without interference? Without political cruft? Are the stated and unstated terms of use sufficient for the inheriting researcher?
     - Does/do the original creator(s) of the codebook have a positive earned reputation in the field?

3. Practical Usability

- *Practical address of research challenges and applied problem-solving*: Does the codebook solve the stated research challenges it was designed to solve? The applied problem-solving?
- *Applicability to other domain data*: Does the codebook "overfit" to the researcher's original context, or is it sufficiently general to apply to other domain data (without leaving too much uncoded residua)? (An overfit codebook is suitable to analyze only the particular questions and specific data that the researcher has captured in a particular research context. It does not have code that can apply to other research situations.)
- *Novel approaches*: Are there compelling and novel theories, approaches, or insights related to a codebook and its usage? Does the inheriting researcher want to build on that novelty with a fresh approach?
- *Sufficient scope and ambition*: Is the scope or ambition of the codebook sufficient for the research?
- *Suitability to engage a range of data types*: Is the codebook applicable to a wide range of data types? Data sources?

  - Are there accommodations for coding multimedia? Textual data? Other high dimensionality data types?

- *Details on data pre-processing/data cleaning*: Does the codebook include information on data pre-processing?
- *Sufficient documentation and detail*: Are all aspects of the codebook's development sufficiently described? Is its provenance clear?

4. Technical Alignment with CAQDAS Technologies

- *Alignment to CAQDAS tools*: Is the digital codebook well aligned to the underlying CAQDAS or other software tool and its functionalities?

  - Does the digital codebook function as advertised?
  - Is it clear how much the inheriting researcher is supposed to do and how much he or she hands over to the computer for processing?
  - If the codebook functions within custom software program, how well does it function? Is the software program well designed? Is it secure and trustworthy?

5. Support for Heritage

- *Codebook "how-to"*: Is the codebook sufficiently detailed for application by other researchers?

  - Are the codes named clearly and with parallel construction?
  - Do all the nodes have sufficient descriptors for inclusion?
  - Are there logical described standards for how raw source contents should be coded?

- Can the source contents be coded to multiple nodes simultaneously? What is the logic behind the advisement?
- Are there exemplars for each of the codes? Is the level of abstraction /unit of analysis clear?
- Is the codebook correctly revised and edited?

- *Legality to use*: Is the codebook released for public use without obvious potential legal challenges?
- *Support for usage*: How much developer support is there for codebook use? Is there a community of users? Is the original codebook developer or codebook development team available to support the usage of the tool?

Delimitations The above concepts may be difficult to wield, particularly for new researchers. This work has not provided examples of codebook "overfit" or "novelty" or "validation." To do so would require codebook samples that are publicly available and easy-to-access and cite. Examples would also be somewhat limiting to the generality of the ideas and potentially hinder transfer. What these respective aspects of codebook quality mean will differ based on the research contexts.

Discussion

The concept of shared codebooks is common in a number of fields with common quantitative research practices. In a qualitative, mixed methods, and multi-methodology approach, the assumptions themselves would differ. One major difference is in the concept of reproducibility of research, which is not at all an assumption in qualitative approaches. The researcher subjectivity is an important part of qualitative understandings, but this is seen as both a strength and a weakness—the strength being the power of researcher insights and the weakness being that subjectivities may mean blind spots. CAQDAS tools have some adoption among qualitative researchers, and their use for creating codebooks is widely known and accepted. The concept of shared digital codebooks for qualitative, mixed methods, and multi-methods research, though, is not so common. The contention is that there can be wider benefits to focus on codebook development not only for the local research but also to a wider context. Computational means can be highly beneficial to a transferable codebook particularly if researchers have access to the same tools and can engage autocoding, data querying, and data visualization capabilities within the software tools.

This approach is not without risks. It will be important to be vigilant about unintended and possibly negative effects to shared digital codebooks. In some contexts, there may be "first mover" advantage in the sense that an early shared codebook may be adopted broadly and close out other contender codebooks. For example, if certain codebooks are adopted and become dominant, these may mean much less attention to fresh and original codebooks applied to unique research contexts. Shared codebooks may mean fewer innovations and less variety in the particular domain field. Also, anything released to the public may be mis-used with some researchers taking undue credit or third-party publishers usurping copyrighted works to drive traffic to disreputable sites.

Also, per institutional review board (IRB) oversight, the data collected in human subjects research has to be carefully protected against a wide range of potential misuses. It is important to de-identify the data and to prevent re-identification. As such, codebooks may be a source of unintended data leakage, and as such, those who would release these publicly should scrub the data and metadata of all related files.

Future Research Directions

At heart, this work proposes a rethinking of qualitative, mixed methods, and multi-methods codebooks (created with CAQDAS tools) as objects that may be inherited for use by researchers in a domain and also for researchers who are interested in pursuing meta-analytics of the codebooks themselves and what they may suggest about coding, coders, and research domains. This work suggests fresh value propositions to datafy and informatize codebooks.

This propositional work suggests a number of potential future research directions. If there are some who agree to share their inheritable digital codebooks, they may wish to write up how they generated these and enhanced the heritability through design and technological means. If this sharing becomes more common practice, there may be works describing helpful principles, practices, and technologies that optimize transferability.

If codebooks become common fare for sharing, it will be possible to categorize codebooks in various ways. The typologies would require categories and descriptions of those respective categories. These typologies may help in codebook distribution by increasing findability.

As researchers inherit codebooks, they may describe the process: how they selected particular codebooks, how they made adjustments in order to adapt the respective codebooks, how they created added modules, and what they learned about codebook inheritance from the experience. There may be professional etiquette issues for how to inherit codebooks effectively. If codebooks are inherited and fundamentally updated or changed, how do they evolve, and on what variables and dimensions? It may be that there are recognizable patterns for how codebooks evolve over time. If they do advance by punctuated equilibrium, what could contribute to these forward motions and advancements: new data, new research methods, new theories, adoptions by major funders, adoptions by leading researchers?

Codebooks may be used to apply to past research and historical data. In those cases, what are some fresh insights (made possible with more contemporary coding methods)? Likewise, it may help to conceptualize codebooks as applying to the future and to future-collected data. Of note would be NVivo 11 Plus's "autocoding by existing pattern," which enables supervised machine learning of textual data based on the code structure and example code by an individual researcher or research team. Are there special considerations when trying to design a codebook with future applicability (in an anticipatory way)?

How do research groups or teams inherit qualitative codebooks? Teams usually train on how to effectively co-code, and is this different when the coding comes from inherited codebooks? Is interrater reliability harder or easier to achieve?

Another approach to future research involves technological affordances. Some CAQDAS tools may be found to be more effective than others for heritability and transferability of digital codebooks. There may be uniquely coded codebooks that are shared, say, through GitHub. Also, there may be different platforms for digital codebook distribution with various types of affordances and constraints.

If digital codebooks are distributed through electronic means, capturing metrics about codebook popularity and usage will be likely par-for-the-course. If the codebooks are sufficiently documented, it will be possible to examine which features of a codebook are associated with its popularity or lack-of-popularity. Another way to come at this would be to analyze the references to particular inherited codebooks in the published academic research literature, for yet another data point.

Finally, future research in this area may include optimal ways to present and distribute codebooks for usage among researchers.

Conclusion

Broadly sharing digital codebooks from qualitative, mixed methods, and multi-method approaches may be highly disruptive to the *status quo*. What is traditionally mysterious and hidden could well become part of common research understandings and interchanges.

This early work suggests that the sharing of codebooks will enable researchers to informatize what is already created as a "byproduct" of their work by forefronting these tools as valuable and publishable and distributable—as it is in other non-qualitative research approaches. This work summarized the application of NVivo 11 Plus capabilities to the development and design of codebooks, generally, and has argued for the broader sharing of digital codebooks in the humanities and more broadly, to advance data exploration, enhance pattern identification, support research, and expand data-based insights. If there are more common and democratic distribution channels for digital codebooks, and more common practices of research codebook and data sharing, deeper advances may be made in various domains.

Acknowledgment I am deeply grateful to the anonymous reviewers who provided feedback on this work. It is hard to gain perspective when one is so deeply focused on a work. Thanks!

References

R. Bettinger, SAS rule-based codebook generation for exploratory data analysis. Modern analytics (2012), Retrieved on 29 Jun 2016, from http://www.slideshare.net/RossBettinger/sas-rule-based-codebook-generation-for-exploratory-data-analysis-wuss-2012.

K. McGrew, The CHC periodic table of cognitive elements: 'What are you made of?' Now available on a t-shirt. IQ's Corner, (2014), Retrieved 17 Jul 2016, from http://www.iqscorner.com/2014/06/the-chc-periodic-table-oc-cognitive.html.

M.B. Miles, A.M. Huberman, J. Saldaña, *Qualitative Data Analysis: A Methods Sourcebook*, 3rd edn. (2014)

J. Saldaña, *The Coding Manual for Qualitative Researchers*, 2nd edn. (SAGE Publications, Los Angeles, 2013), pp. 24–25

P.L. Sullivan & M.T. Koch, Military Intervention by Powerful States (MIPS) Codebook (2008), vol. 2, pp. 1–36, Retrieved 28 Jun 2016, from https://www.researchgate.net/publication/228601442_Military_Intervention_by_Powerful_States_MIPS_Codebook.

D.J. Treiman, Life histories and social change in contemporary China provisional codebook (1998), Retrieved 28 Jun 2016, from http://data-archive.library.ucla.edu/lhsccs/ccb_1.pdf.

W. Van der Aalst, Process mining: Making knowledge discovery process centric. ACM SIGKDD Explor. Newsl. **13**(2), 45–49 (2011)

C. Weston, T. Gandell, J. Beauchamp, L. McAlpine, C. Wiseman, C. Beauchamp, Analyzing interview data: The development and evolution of a coding system. Qual. Sociol. **24**(3), 381–400 (2001)

P.H Winston, Lecture 15: learning: near misses, felicity conditions. Artificial intelligence series. Massachusetts Institute of Technology. MIT OpenCourseWare YouTube Channel (2010), Retrieved 17 Jul 2016, from https://www.youtube.com/watch?v=sh3EPjhhd40.

Part VI
Support for Digital Humanities Work

Is It Worth It? The Library and Information Science Degree in the Digital Humanities

Hannah Lee

Abstract The last several years have seen a marked upturn in society's use of electronic information as the internet has greatly altered the very nature of information access. Although academics and professionals in the library and information sciences (LIS) seek ways of improving the connection between individuals and information, public perceptions often question the importance of LIS-based work in a world where everything is so freely and readily available online.

Therefore, the question becomes how relevant is the library and information science degree today in the world of electronic information? Using the theoretical framework of system theory and cybersemiotics, this chapter seeks to investigate the importance of LIS in the growing discipline of the digital humanities (DH). More specifically by focusing on data analytics, this chapter will demonstrate the practicality of LIS in an online environment and its necessity in giving information structure and meaning.

Introduction

The internet brought with it the ability for everyday people to find information on their own with near instantaneous results. Whereas the information-seeking society before the internet required a better understanding of where and how to find information, searching for information now is as simple as typing in a few keywords in a search engine. "Just Google it" has become the standard phrase when referencing the search for information with the expectation that anything and everything is available online. The complex algorithms that make up the everyday mechanisms of online interaction makes the internet seem quite intuitive and easy.

In reality, the internet is anything but simple. The kind of information-seeking society that has developed gives the illusion that average internet users are expert searchers. If someone cannot find their answers within the first page of a search result, then common attitude of internet users is that the information

H. Lee (✉)
Human and Organizational Development and Change Fielding Graduate University,
Santa Barbara, CA, USA
e-mail: 00HannahLee@gmail.com

© Springer International Publishing AG 2017
S. Hai-Jew (ed.), *Data Analytics in Digital Humanities*, Multimedia Systems
and Applications, DOI 10.1007/978-3-319-54499-1_12

is notavailable at all. Because of modern society's understanding of information through the internet, the library and information sciences (LIS) is often seen by the public as obsolete or utterly useless in an era of digital information.

Even though LIS professionals have been applying traditional library practices online (Lynch 2003; Hong et al. 2002) and the ability to use a library's resources online becoming the norm rather than a novel exception (Tenopir 2003), the process of translating traditional practices to the internet has been slow. However, it is often the case that many within the digital landscape are not aware that the LIS degree exists, much less the need for it as the internet and as information systems continue to grow. Furthermore, despite its wide application in a variety of professional fields, the assumption by the public is for LIS degree holders to work exclusively in libraries as librarians. Much of what the public perceives as LIS work reflects an outdated understanding of the degree or ignorance of the infrastructure needed for today's internet society.

Thus, the purpose of this chapter is to answer the question, "how relevant is the library and information science degree in today's electronic information world." The first step is to briefly explain some of the misconceptions of library and information sciences. Then, this chapter argues for a theoretical framework of system theory and cybersemiotics that gives a perspective of interconnectedness between field (LIS) and discipline (DH) in the USA. By focusing specifically on the challenge of data analytics in an online information environment, this chapter seeks recognition that the LIS degree contributes towards the information structures that make up the foundation of modern, online information society.

Misconceptions about Library and Information Sciences

In general, perceptions of the library and information sciences field are often at odds with public perception. As a result, misconceptions of the field severely devalue the work of LIS academics and professional. However, as society becomes information enriched, the work of those in the LIS field becomes all the more important. The following is a brief introduction to some of the public misconceptions of LIS.

First, there is strong evidence that the LIS degree is a severely undervalued degree. Quite frequently, and annoyingly so for those within LIS degree-based professions, the master's degree in library and information sciences is described as the following: "The low pay rank and estimated growth rank make library and information science the worst master's degree for jobs right now" (Dill 2015; Smith 2012). The poor use data analytics of popular news sites notwithstanding, it is disheartening when the value of an entire degree reduces down to a single profession (librarians) with the focus being purely on pay and ignoring other factors like job satisfaction. One recent survey of those with a Masters in Library and Information Sciences (also known as MLIS, MLS, or MILS) found that even though approximately 94% of respondents found intrinsic value in their degree, the same survey concluded that there was an increase in overall negative comments regarding the MLIS degree from 3 years prior in 2008 (Teglovic et al. 2012). Therefore, it is not only the public who question the value of an LIS degree but those holding the degree as well.

In studies investigating those who do choose careers in LIS, the key fallacy that endures over the history of LIS professionals is (1) lack of awareness of the LIS profession and (2) misunderstandings of the LIS professionals' roles (Moniarou-Papaconstantinou et al. 2015; Newbutt 2008). Without simple awareness of an entire professional and academic field, of course it is difficult to formulate opinions other than ones presented through common media stereotypes like the "shusher" or the "sexy librarian" (Vassilakaki and Moniarou-Papaconstantinou 2014).

These kinds of perceptions point towards a larger problem of not knowing exactly LIS work involves. In an internet-dependent information society like the USA, the common attitude is that "everything is available online" (Dougherty 2010; Herring 2014). However, everything is not available online. Even though the internet and search engines are able to bring answer to easy question (NPR 2014), the internet is not the Holy Grail of information.

And, despite its name, the library and information sciences is more than librarians working in libraries. There are numerous subfields/specialties found in the LIS field (Hjorland 2002) but the image of librarians is intrinsically linked to the degree. It is difficult for many to see beyond the seemingly hushed and dusty aisles of book stacks where the only forms of life are dust motes or college students making out. These stereotypes greatly misrepresent what it is that the LIS field actually does that is detrimental in an information era that is heavily dependent on the internet.

In other words, there is a great deal more LIS professionals, institutions, and work has to offer to current information society than what the public believes is available. This section is but a brief introduction to the some of the common stereotypes the LIS field and the LIS community face. In order to dispel this misconception, the remainder of this chapter will work towards understanding the role of LIS in today's information-rich online environment.

Theoretical Frameworks of Interconnectedness

Two theories provide the basic framework for this chapter: system theory and cybersemiotics. System theory (or general system theory), introduced by Ludwig von Bertalanffy in the 1940s, examines the entirety of a system and its place in an environment. This broad, general theoretical framework seeks inclusivity that is important when addressing the wide range and reach of LIS and the humanities. Cybersemiotics, developed more recently by Søren Brier, observes the intersection of information, cognition, and communication by integrating systems theory and cybernetics. This particular theory provides a framework that seeks better understanding of the digital aspect of DH and the use of the internet in fostering human understanding.

The following sections explore specific aspects of system theory and cybersemiotics in order to add to a broad discussion of LIS and data analytics in DH by demonstrating how connected (and interconnected) information is in internet society.

Thinking in Systems

Systems theory is composed of two basic concepts: systems and wholeness. Together, these concepts produce a theory with characteristics that emphasize wider, meta-level views rather than individual part.

First, the term "system" refers not to technological systems (e.g., computers), systems of control (e.g., classification schemes), or even abstract, grouped ideas (e.g., "Fight the corrupt system"). Rather, system in this chapter means a "set of elements or parts that is coherently organized and interconnected in a pattern or structure that produces a characteristic set of behaviors" (Meadows 2008). In other words, systems are groups of things that behave as one. If any given piece does not behave with or moves against the rest of the system, then it is either (1) not part of the system or (2) an indicator that there is something wrong within a system. As this chapter progresses, any differences between understanding system as a theory and other kinds of systems (especially the kinds of technological or control systems listed above) will be made apparent.

Second, system theory in general advocates the perspective of viewing the entirety of a given system rather than its parts; the wholeness of a system instead of in minutiae. The benefits from having a theory advocating wholeness are that it is easier to see how an issue (like information) affects the system at large and easier to see the connection to and from other systems. Alternatively, discarding a wider system view and instead focusing on the individual details result in professional specialization or academic silos. Although there are benefits to being an expert rather than a generalist (Berlin 2013), what is lost is when focusing on the components rather than whole of the system is the perspective of how systems connect with other systems existing within an environment.

The environment is one critical component when discussing system theory. The term "environment" can mean anything that is not the system itself. This definition does not mean that the scientific of environment is completely ignored. In fact, von Bertalanffy was a biologist who developed system theory from his observation of nature and his objections to the prevalent scientific theories of closed systems during his time (von Bertalanffy 1968). An environment constitutes anything that is not of the system itself. Therefore, environment encompasses that which is out of the system including that natural world (i.e., The Environment), society, physical space, and culture. There are also certainly environments that exist within a system/organization and the differences between the two concepts will be made apparent if necessary.

While the way systems theory is explained above makes system theory seem like the theory of everything, it is not without its flaws. One of its major drawbacks is that it is holistic by nature and because of its broader perspective; there are complexities that can easily be overlooked or exaggerated. It is more of a way of thinking than a hard theory with empirical processes. Also, the attempt to define or formalize system theory will paradoxically "limit its generating power" (Mesarovic 1964). Perhaps more so that other fields of research that creates its own, unique vocabulary, systems theory also suffers from having a shared terminology with a non-specific, generalized concept of systems and theories. Unlike medicine where specific terms refer to a limited number of concepts, systems theory language reflects its inclusive nature.

There are many other intricacies and issues surrounding systems theory but that is beyond the scope of this chapter. Understanding that systems are interconnected groups within an environment valuing the whole rather than the sum of its parts is the necessary requirements for this discussion.

Cybersemiotics: Towards a Theory of Everything

Although von Bertalanffy's system theory developed his background in the hard sciences, its organic qualities or "cloudy metaphysics" is a criticism of some scholars (Brier 2008, 39). In order to address the limitations of system theory and similar theories around the theme of communication, cognition, and information, Brier developed cybersemiotics as a way of unifying these separate theories.

Cybersemiotics offers a way of combining theories of information, computing, semiotics, communication, and meaning into a single theory (Brier 2013). Specifically, Brier approaches cybersemiotics in a two-pronged approach. On one hand, he builds upon the theoretical frameworks of system theory and cybernetics. On the other, he relies upon the semiotic work of Charles Sanders Peirce.

First, cybernetics closely relates to systems theory in that they developed approximately the same time to explain systems but the theories take on different perspectives. System theory focuses on the structure of systems while cybernetics focuses on exploring system functions (Heylighen et al. 1999). Alternatively, another way of viewing the cybernetics-system theory relationship is that system theory focuses on the broader relationship between systems and systems within an environment, resulting in a broader, myopic view of systems. In contrast, cybernetics is the mechanics of systems including feedback loops, controls, and communication capabilities that looks inward towards systems themselves as self-reflective examination of its functions (Glanville 2014). Therefore, system theory is an inter-system perspective while cybernetics is an intra-system perspective.

While it is important to have an understanding of system theory and cybernetics for the connection and working of systems, semiotics is necessary for providing and understanding to how individuals process information. To briefly explain semiotics, it is the study of signs and symbols as well as their use or interpretation. Peirce theorized that the process of producing meaning of signs involved three categories: Firstness, Secondness, and Thirdness. Without delving into the philosophical and technical details of this particular theory, briefly, these categories are, respectively, described as the following. Firstness is a sign's quality that is "accessed through feeling," meaning that it is the initial, responsive reaction without any thought (Southern Semiotic Review 2013). Secondness is the reaction to a sign and how individuals experience signs. Thirdness is the laws or other constraints (e.g., laws of physics) that limit individuals' ability to understand a sign (Southern Semiotic Review 2013). For Peirce, this process reflects an interconnectedness of signs; every sign is represented by this trio of categories and signs are not limited by the form (Treaude 2011).

In turn, this triad of sign (i.e., information) processing allows Brier to have framework for how internet users can understand information through individuals' initial reaction to a sign, individuals' experience of a sign, and the laws governing a sign. Because systems theory and cybernetics do not adequately explain the role of cognition in its theory, (Peirce) semiotics bridges the gap between the system and understanding. The broad applicability of Peirce's semiotics also lends to Brier's efforts in cybersemiotics in proposing a unified theory of information science.

Therefore, Brier combines the complementing qualities of universality and interconnectedness found in system theory, cybernetics, and semiotics for a unified theory of information. The theories are universal because of the broad perspective of inter-systems relationships (system theory), intra-systems relationships (cybernetics), and individual-information relationships (semiotics) promoted inclusivity. The argument for interconnectedness is based on the premise that the theories cannot stand independent of or by itself: systems theory connects systems and the environment; cybernetics connects systems and its inner mechanics; while semiotic connects individuals and information.

Although Brier does examine other theories involving information and cognition, he found theories contradicting one another when attempting to explain cognition and information (Brier 2008). System theory provides the general view of interconnected relationships of systems and environments, cybernetics provide the machine-mind process of information, and semiotics provide the framework of understanding sign (i.e., information) cognition. Combined, cybersemiotics is a theory that brings together how individuals understanding information in an electronic information age.

Theory Applied to Discussion

The two theories presented here, system theory and cybersemiotics, provide unique perspectives when discussing LIS and DH. Through wider lenses, these theories allow a basic framework for understanding how to connect information environments to the LIS system.

Applying Theory to LIS

More than just the work of librarians within libraries, the LIS degree runs the gamut of issues and concerns about information. It can, for example, cover philosophical meta-questions of information (Furner 2010) to the mechanics of what is the difference between data, information, and knowledge (Borgman 2015). The scholars and practitioners utilizing an LIS degree usually work under narrow subfields that directly apply to their work: archivists handle subject-specific collections; scholars hone in on one, narrow area of study; and user experience researchers work with specific audiences. To reflect this state of specialization, much of the scholarly literature reflects the understanding of individual areas of the library and information sciences.

The issue at hand is not the lack of scholarly literature or active practice in the individual LIS professions. Rather, the issue here is that there is a lack of discussion of the library and information sciences as a whole. As explained earlier, the ability to see systems as a whole and its relation to other systems within an environment creates a better understanding of the state of a system. The LIS degree is in desperate need of this wider lens because its very nature creates silos of specialization (Marty and Twidale 2011; Chisita and Abdullahi 2012; Oliver 2010) as it encourages specializations (Cox and Rasmussen 1997). While it is useful to have experts when expertise is required, it is easy to lose sight of the larger picture of LIS in society when having such a myopic focus.

The broader, system-level discussions currently found in the literature cover the debate on governing LIS theories or debates on the nature information itself (Brier 2008; Hjørland 2000; Bates 1999) or even the very nature of LIS (Furner 2015). However, the focus of these debates looks inward in the attempt to further define the LIS field for the LIS community.

In order to demonstrate the importance of LIS to those outside of the field/community, a macro-level lens of LIS as a transdisciplinary metadiscipline is necessary. This is achieved by examining LIS as a system (i.e., as a system according to system theory) to investigate the components that make it a system.

Attempting to categorize LIS into a single field is quite difficult. Information is prevalent in all facets of life with libraries and books dedicated to every single topic imaginable. Much like systems theory, the attempt to clearly define the boundaries of LIS creates a paradox; the attempt to delineate its characteristics in precise applications limit what is part of the LIS system. Conversely, the attempt at pigeonholing LIS as a subcategory of another field based on select properties limits the capabilities of LIS (Konrad 2007). Instead, having a better grasp of LIS involves breaking down shared points of commonality.

One LIS scholar approaches LIS as an intellectual domain around the documents produced through human activity (Bates 1999). With a systems theory perspective in mind, Bates' investigation into the need for better articulation of theories and research in LIS reveal three reoccurring components of LIS: information; individuals (or groups); and connections between the two (Bates 1999). Some people dedicate their entire lives into the investigation of information including its definition, its preservation, and the policies surrounding it. Others have focused on the people using information, whether it is in the form of library users or internet users. The remainder of the LIS population is concerned with ways of connecting information and individuals along with the machines and software aiding them. Consider how most academics dedicate years to studying a single aspect of the field then it becomes apparent how fragmented and non-systems thinking the LIS degree can become.

Even though much of the literature, academics, and professional concentrations focus on a component of LIS, these components behave in conjunction with each other to form an LIS system. Understanding LIS as a system then allows for a discussion on how it works within the social, cultural, and technical environment of information.

Applying Theory to Data, Information, and Knowledge on the Internet

The previous section discussed the components that make up an LIS system: information (and data), individuals (or groups), and connections between the two. This section applies theory to data, information, and knowledge within the digital landscape of the internet.

The two methods of approaching data, information, and knowledge here are through the concept of the environment in system theory and cybersemiotics. Before beginning this discussion, it is important to know the difference between data, information, and knowledge. Of over 130 definitions of data, information, and knowledge that varies because of theoretical framework or fields of research (Zins 2007), the definition used here is limited within the context of how these terms are applied in digital humanities and/or understood through the theoretical framework of cybersemiotics (Brier 2008). As such, data as defined by this paper is considered facts without context; data is/are strings of symbols (numbers, letters, and other signs) that represent this world. Information is data with context; it is data that has been interpreted and analyzed. Knowledge is the cognitive understanding of information by individuals. These definitions are important because from its name, the focus of data analytics appears to be data. However, the purpose of data analytics is to "derive insight" by creating information from data in order to add to human knowledge (Ridge and Rogers 2015). For the sake of brevity, data, information, and knowledge will be collectively referred as "information" unless otherwise stated.

A system theory approach to information here is an environmental approach. In other words, the cultural, societal, and technological environment of data, information, and knowledge currently are different from other non-internet or non-digital time periods.

The internet changed the information environment as it allowed for increased connectedness and accessibility of information between individuals far beyond any real-world limitations like distance or country borders. As internet users find more interesting and innovative ways to use the internet as a communication tool, the data/information/knowledge environment has also changed (Newhagen and Rafaeli 1996; Papacharissi and Rubin 2000). The amount of information processed daily is incredible; no longer is society measuring the internet in kilobytes and megabytes but in petabytes and exabytes. One estimate puts annual global IP traffic to surpass 1 zettabyte by the end of 2016 (Cisco 2015)—1 zettabyte is equal to 1 trillion gigabytes. Entire libraries can now fit their digital information onto devices smaller than a fingernail. Technology is getting smaller and faster with new advancements. Even though there are many issues to resolve, the internet and the accompanying technologies have become integral parts of daily life.

To complement this growth, recent years have seen an increasingly semantic and interconnected internet. A semantic web is a concept that allows cross-platform data sharing (Berners-Lee et al. 2001). Rather than replicating the same information over and over and over again for different platforms, a semantic web takes those different platforms and links towards the same data. As a result, there is less duplication of effort as the initial input (i.e., the data) is the same and the only thing that changes is the output (i.e., the platforms). This kind of internet creates the opportunity to connect information in a dynamic manner that was not possible before. That is not to say that these kinds of processes were not *at all* possible—it just takes a lot more effort and duplication of data in order to achieve the same effect. However, what this increasingly semantic web represents is the kind of interconnectedness found in system theory not possible in pre-internet society.

The cybersemiotics of information is the difference of pre-internet society and current internet society's understandings of searching for information. Imagine the internet as an ant farm with its users as ants. In the early years of the internet (i.e., dial-up), users have puttered around by digging through heaps of informational dirt until they found the right information pocket. This method of internet navigation was quite easy when there were a limited number of sites and literally everything could be cataloged by Yahoo like numbers in a phone book.

Internet users quickly grew out of the ant farm. Now, internet ants can navigate through entire worlds of information with very little guidance. The most popular form of traversing the information environment is through keyword searching. This type of information-seeking behavior helped foster an information society so used to getting their answers within the first page of Google that good enough has become enough. When satisficing (the acceptance of what is available versus the best option) becomes the norm of current information and internet society, it is easy to see how complacent internet society has become in understanding the support that information needs in order for its users to make sense of it (Prabha et al. 2007).

Therefore, not only has the method in which access information has changed due to the popularization of internet information society, the ubiquity of the internet has made information universal to anyone with internet access. Certainly there are those without the ability to participate within this digital landscape; a recent

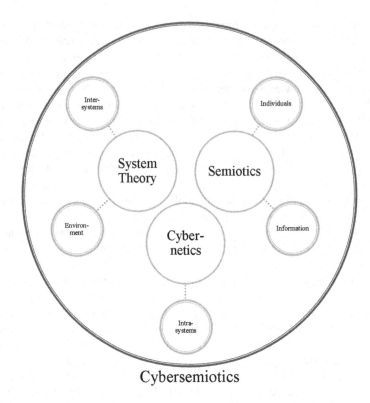

Fig. 1 Breakdown of the components of Cybersemiotics including system theory, cybernetics, semiotics, and their individual components

2015 study found approximately 80% of adult Americans without internet access at home whether in the form of broadband or through smartphones (Horrigan and Duggan 2015). There are many aspects to take into consideration when citing these numbers; social, economic, and political environments are just some of the factors influencing internet systems. However, the general trends of these report numbers reveal a growing trend of internet users moving towards a digitally literate society.

Summary

Altogether, internet society shifted its use of data/information/knowledge according to the cybersemiotic relationship between systems and cognition. The ways in which information is sought by internet users expects immediacy in an information deluge (Borgman 2015). Within this deluge, the increasingly semantic web represents an interconnected digital information era that can lead to a truly global information network. System theory and cybersemiotics are theoretical frameworks that provide the foundation for understanding precisely the shift in LIS and data/information/knowledge in today's internet society. It is the connection made between users and systems in information environments (as well as the attempt to better those connections) that is the heart of the discussion here. Even though the work of LIS community members focus on one narrow aspect of an LIS system, the behavior the system as a whole operate within an information environment to create connections between individuals and information.

In Context: LIS and Data Analytics in DH

While the previous section connected theory with analogies to current literature and practices, the following section will focus on applying theory within the practical context of data analytics in the digital humanities. There are many challenges that LIS face within the context of data analytics including the nature of data itself, connecting users to data, and data governance for future use. The following section addresses these challenges as well as how the library and information sciences meet those challenges.

Data Analytics in the Digital Humanities

One of the clearest definitions for modern DH is that it is the "digital humanities is the use of digital media and technology to advance the full range of thought and practice in the humanities" (Cohen 2011). The early days of DH saw the "digital" in "digital humanities" play an important but ultimately supporting role to the humanities. Now, the internet has created the opportunity for the "digital" in DH to become better integrated into the humanities. No longer are digital humanists limited by the technology; instead, they are finding new ways of using them. Digital society has even gone so far as to see examples of the humanities moving entirely onto a digital landscape and new forms developing regularly.

For the digital humanities, the movement towards internet interconnectedness means the ability to increase *what* can be investigated and *how*. The issues and research arising in DH tackle the traditional humanities and apply it towards new perspectives made possible by the internet.

Data analytics is "any activity that involves applying an analytical process to data to derive insight from the data" (Ridge and Rogers 2015, 4). This is a broad definition that reflects data analytics' multi-faceted approach to techniques, applications, domains, and purpose. As such, the multi-faceted approach of data analytics well suites the equally multi-faceted approaching of the digital humanities in its various theories, frameworks, fields, etc. Additionally, the application of the data analytics to DH addresses the longstanding criticism of the wont for the humanities and humanities research to be qualitative in nature (Brier 2008).

There are many more discussions possible from investigating only the relation-ship between DH and data analytics but that is beyond the scope of this chapter. In order to demonstrate the importance of LIS as it applies to data analytics in the digital humanities, this section breaks down challenges in the life cycle of data analytics as used by digital humanities from the perspective of LIS. In such a life cycle, the first step is the preparation of data long before its use. Next is the focus on use; this is the process that involves connecting users with data. Finally, the last part of this life cycles looks towards the future and the future use of data generated.

Challenge of Data

To reiterate, data refers to facts without context (Zins 2007). However, "without context" does not mean that data are a series of numbers or combinations of ones and zeroes. Instead, data are facts that lack subjective or objective interpretation (the inclusion of interpretation would transform data into information). What this means is that even though data are one of the rawest forms of facts, it still needs descriptions, labels, and other forms of metadata in order to differentiate between X and X.

Yet, one of the major challenges with being able to use data is that data often lacks description (i.e., metadata). In turn, this makes individuals' discovery of data difficult from the beginning. Part of this challenge involves making data searchable through metadata is from the sheer amount of digital data. The size of digital traffic is now measured in exabytes and as such, there is an incredible backlog of data that need descriptions from data created now (Hey and Trefethen 2003). In addition to metadata for digitally born data, there is an even bigger backlog for the digitized data. Although concrete numbers are sparse and very much dependent on the institution, digitization, and the associated metadata needed to make data discoverable is costly and time-consuming (Lee 2001).

Another challenge with metadata is interoperability. That is to say, the standards governing metadata of a data object can change. Within libraries, classification systems like the Dewey Decimal System (DDS) or Library of Congress (LoC) Classification are metadata standards in the USA while some international metadata standards include Dublin Core or digital object identifies (DOI). However, these standards can change (and have changed) in order to reflect changing society and technologies: LoC recently changed the subject heading "Illegal Aliens" (Dechman 2016) while debates on international standards still endure (Baell 2006; Guenther and McCallum 2003).

Additionally, digital data has a very limited lifespan. In comparison to written texts that could last for centuries given optimal circumstances, digital data depends upon the technology available at the time. This means that when data are created (whether digitally born or digitally transferred), its longevity depends on the then-current technology that may or may not be tested. When a product claims that it will keep data stored on a DVD for 100 up to one hundred years (University Products, Inc 2010), there is no way of guaranteeing such a claim. Moreover, the software and hardware that determines how data are read quickly change, affecting interoperability. On average, technologies quickly become obsolete in 5–10 years (Bellinger et al. 2002) as software and hardware evolve for the next generation. One of the few ways to overcome this challenge is through emulators that simulate outdated software and hardware or through digital migration. However, both of these options pose issues: emulators will not always guarantee usable, readable data; while data can be lost in migration (Bellinger et al. 2002).

To illustrate the challenges of data, one team of researchers dramatized their ordeal in obtaining a data set from another researcher who was funded by the National Science Foundation (NYU Health Sciences Library 2012). In addition to only having one copy of the data on a USB drive using outdated, proprietary software to read the data, the original researchers used vague data fields like "Sam1" and "Sam2" without any indication on how to interpret the fields (NYU Health Sciences Library 2012). This one example demonstrates how issues like metadata (bad labeling) and storage/preservation data (one copy on a USB drive) are challenges for LIS.

Listed here are only a few of the many more challenges of data. As internet/information society generates and utilizes data, the challenges researchers will face will grow upon existing issues not discussed here (like issues of data privacy, data quality, or data mining) while also finding new challenges.

Challenge of Connections

The next part in the challenges of data analytics is in connecting users with data. Connecting users to data means not only having a place for data to exist, it means that users need to know how access the data in order to use data that may or may not be within their realm of expertise. The barriers that prevent researchers from accessing information are the focus of this section.

Data repositories are, as the name suggests, digital spaces allowing researchers to store their data. Some of the literature calls for better degrees of interoperability between repositories (Park 2009), while other literature focus on data repositories and its use is one method of data curation and sharing (McLure et al. 2014). However, data repositories as they are currently used have not encountered many issues yet but should be kept in mind for future discussions on the challenge of data analytical research in DH.

Instead the kind of data storage discussed here is in terms of databases. While open source databases exist with the operating principles of shared scholarly knowledge, most scholarly knowledge is hidden behind paywalls that require costly subscriptions (Montgomery and King 2002; Franklin 2005). When data and information is only accessible with expensive per-article costs or even more expensive yearly subscription costs, of course this issue is a challenge for data analytical research. Unless a scholar is part of a major research university, then it becomes difficult to access the fundamental resources of academia. In turn, the cost of databases and its publishers lead to issues of price gouging and authors taking on the brunt of publishing their own work become issues of scholarly communication and general affordability of knowledge (Van Noorden 2013).

But given the assumption that the accessibility of data is not an issue, the next challenge is on what to do with that data. Having access to data does not mean that a researcher automatically knows how to handle it. Unlike other fields of research that has had decades to centuries of history, the digital humanities as it is known and used now has not reached its full potential since it is still an expanding field (Liu 2012). As such, the tools for analyzing data are still being developed and, as discussed earlier, under the threat of becoming obsolete within a few years as new technologies develop. Software like IBM's Many Eyes or the University College, London's Pie-Slice (Dombrowski 2014; Machlis 2015) are a couple of examples that have been developed as data visualization software but now defunct. Additionally, popular tools like Google Analytics that track data of websites can only collect data once it has been implemented; the attempt for data collection before implementation is lost.

Therefore, many of challenges surrounding connecting with data here investigate not only the cost of accessing data itself but, once accessed, the tools used to analyze data in a field that is still developing the software.

Challenge of the Future

Some of the challenges the future of data analytics in the digital humanities hold includes many of the challenges already discussed; access, storage, and other challenges related to technology that will continue to be issues in the future. However, one of the key challenges of the future is changing the way that researchers manage their data in the present for use in the future.

Again, finding studies or hard data on the digital humanities itself (rather than research under the DH banner) is difficult since it is still a growing field. A small study on the effectiveness of data management of faculty members in higher education found that several surprising results: nearly half of respondent reported they have and will continue store/share data in data repositories (56.8%); the remaining sample will not store and/or not store data (43.2%); but as many of 80% of were unaware of institutions repositories (Diekama et al. 2014). Additionally, only a small number of respondents had institutions with current or planned data management plans (17 or 8.5%)—this included contractual obligations of funding agencies (Diekama et al. 2014). What these numbers mean to this discussion on data analytics in the digital humanities is the need for better understanding of the tools and resources that is available by its users. In turn, creating a better understanding means the researchers and other individuals working within the digital humanities and using data analytics tools need instruction.

On one hand, the ability to analyze data in the digital humanities in the digital setting of the internet is still quite a relatively recent development, and many of the challenges of data analytics are largely theoretical. On the other hand, one of the areas that can contribute to future challenges in the data analytics of digital humanities can be found in those who contribute data for future use like scholars and faculty of higher education.

Overcoming Challenges

To sum, the challenges of data analytics in the digital humanities is one of the basic challenges LIS face: the information, connecting users to information, and the users themselves.

One of the easiest ways of imagining this issue is when a customer coming into a bookstore and asking for a book with a blue cover. Without knowing anything else about the book like the author, publisher, plot, or title, finding the book a customer has in mind is going to be nearly impossible. The same is true with finding digital information. LIS professionals (primarily those in the archives and library fields) ascribe descriptions to digital objects. To achieve this, there are entire subfields of LIS addressing description: metadata, cataloging, archival descriptions, etc., are limited by subject area (e.g., government data versus medical data) and area of concentration (e.g., Library of Congress classification, encoded archival description (EAD), etc.).

Providing useful, rich descriptions is one of the major steps in making data accessible. So, if a graduate student wants to find the latest government data on the Indian Ocean and its link in the global economy of South and East Asia (N.A. 2016), having descriptive data makes the process so much easier than a random set of numbers. It is through the work of LIS professional who give data descriptions and the academics who work alongside them who determine standards. However, LIS needed to develop data practices slowly in order to consider its use in the long term rather than temporarily (Borgman 2015). If the LIS community immediately adopts that latest practice as soon as it develops, then it falls into the trap of becoming obsolete within a few years.

LIS also provides structure to the internet as it gives rules for data that categorizes like properties together. There are rules that LIS academics and professionals developed in order to ensure that X is different from X by assigning metadata or classification scheme. These methods of categorization have many different types of standards in order to ensure the right metadata is attributed to a field or object; titles have designated spots/tags and images are labeled as such. Therefore, an elementary school student constructing a report on Abraham Lincoln needs little more than some images and a basic biography on the 16th US president. This can easily be achieved with a quick search on Google with an even quicker click to the "Images" link for images.

Although this is a very simple example to the kind of complex structure that LIS provides, it demonstrates the kind of work utilized by individuals to better connect with data/information. As the digital humanities continue to develop, these kinds of infrastructure become all the more critical. Given the sheer amount of data and information that is available, the ability to extract meaningful (and useful) data and information is a matter of navigating uncharted lands with or without a guide. Already LIS is present in many forms as scholarly databases demonstrate. While databases like Web of Science or JSTOR require a small measure of skill, navigating through these electronic places becomes easier when LIS infrastructures allow users to refine by source types, dates, or subject manner. Anyone who attempts to navigate Google Scholar knows how limiting keyword searching can be or how unhelpful it is to have only two sorting options (i.e., sort by relevance and sort by date).

However, as explained earlier, databases are expensive. Despite its cost, libraries (academic libraries in particular) and archives take on the cost of subscriptions to these expensive databases that can cost tens of thousands of dollars for a single database (Montgomery and King 2002). But even beyond libraries and archives, information architects investigating user experience design or human–computer interaction (HCI) seek to better connect users to information within the information environment of websites or software (Rosenfeld and Morville 2002). These professionals research the best ways of presenting information through a variety of qualitative and quantitative research methods for an informationally connected society.

LIS also play a pivotal role in providing support to those who seek out data analytical software. Once again, studies investigating data analytical software instruction in the library and information sciences are sparse but most academic libraries have research guides (e.g., LibGuides) that introduce scholars on the tools and resources available in a given field. Depending on the institution, librarians may also include instruction on how to use data software which includes analysis and visualization.

Furthermore, LIS professionals and academics are educating individuals in order to have them become participants within the internet, not simply users. Just like the example of the researcher inappropriately labeling his data as "Sam1" and "Sam2," LIS people working under the title of data management librarians or project managers are demonstrating the need for the information rules (NYU Health Sciences Library 2012). Digital humanists need not only consider the information they are using, they must also take into consideration that information they are generating. Many LIS people are already working towards making sure that the information that is available makes sense by assigning information rules and making sure that it is digitally available. However, there is a huge information backlog problem; some have entire careers in cataloging and digitizing past records.

In order to ensure that future information seekers are able to find information digitally, there is a growing sector within LIS dedicated towards making sure that researchers consider their research for future use. The digital humanities is an area where such a harmonious working environment can exist. Since digital humanists need information, create meaning through research, and make available their work, LIS can provide the structure and the environment for meaning that is needed for all these stages.

By giving rules to information, LIS individuals create meaning for individuals. As a result, the connection between the two grows stronger. In short, LIS provides

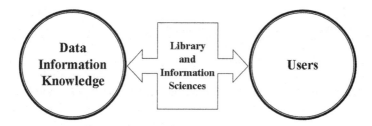

Fig. 2 Library and information sciences as intermediary between data/information/knowledge and users

the digital data infrastructure that helps make much of data analytical research possible.

It is through the desire to create better connections between individuals and information that is the heart of the discussion here. The digital humanities is the proving grounds where LIS work can truly shine. A small (but time-consuming) part of this is the ability to have information digitally available along with the accompanying politics and policies. The other, larger part is to make the available information make sense. Keyword searching is wholly inadequate to the kind of dynamic work being done in DH now. Some DH projects include three-dimensional mapping of ancient civilizations, reverse engineering historical buildings, and the translational networks of literature (University of California, Los Angeles N.D.). All these projects could eventually be done through the use of keyword searching or other simple information searching functions. However, the structure and connection that LIS provides makes these projects not only easy to create but also easier to use and reuse. With DH and data analytics, so much information policies, procedures, and ethics must be taken into consideration when researching. LIS degree holders become the first line of defense who guides information users towards information structures that accounts for efficiency as well as ethics.

In short, LIS provides better connections between information and its users in order to create better interconnectedness between subjects in the digital humanities. Taking on the view of LIS as a structural environment that DH as the systems that operate within it, it becomes quite apparent just how interconnected everything is. Failing to acknowledge and advocate for better ways of connecting, online society falls to the trap of being internet ants stuck in the ant farm, blinding digging through a seemingly endless source of informational dirt until society hopefully (maybe) find the connections it is looking for (Fig. 2).

Conclusion

To paraphrase one political commentator, infrastructure is not sexy (J. Oliver 2015). However, not only does information need infrastructure, it is required. The internet provides a virtual landscape for today's information environment to grow exponentially beyond anything previously imagined. In a digital era where Google is thought to provide all the answers, the internet brought with it many misconceptions of the role of the library and information sciences.

In fact, LIS has not been sidelined by Google but made all the more important. Because there is now so much information available in the digital landscape that information infrastructure provided by LIS is incredibly important. Using the theoretical framework of system theory and cybersemiotics that provide ways of viewing the LIS system within an information environment, this chapter has demonstrated the importance of having a broad view of interconnected systems and environments.

The question posed here brings together the relevancy of LIS in a world of electronic information within the context of data analytics in the digital humanities. This chapter argues that the components working together to create the behavior of the LIS system mirrors the very challenges of data analytics in DH: the information; connecting users to information; and the users themselves. The challenges posed by information itself questions are issues of description, interoperability between technical systems, and its permanence. Not only are the databases that hold most academic data held behind expensive paywalls, the ability to use data through software is precarious. Data analytical tools as they are used by the digital humanities are continually developing and constantly in danger of becoming obsolete. Finally, although it is difficult to anticipate challenges of the future, how digital humanists and other researchers handle information now affects future practices.

In order to meet the challenges of data analytics in DH, LIS is a system that attempts to resolve challenges of issues involved with information, its users, and connecting the two in an overloaded information environment. Even when public perceptions question its relevancy as outdated ideas of libraries dominate its image and many are simply not aware of it as a field, LIS provides for the digital humanities and data analytics the infrastructure necessary in today's information society.

References

J. Baell, Dublin core: An obituary. Library Hi Tech News **21**(8), 40–41 (2006)

M.J. Bates, The invisible substrate of information science. J. Am. Soc. Inf. Sci. **50**(12), 1043–1050 (1999)

M. Bellinger et al, The state of digital preservation: An international perspective. *Council on Library and Information Resources.* (Documentation Abstraccts, Inc., Washington DC, 2002). pp. 1–95.

I. Berlin, *The Hedgehog and the Fox: An Essay on Tolstoy's View of History* (Princeton University Press, Princeton, 2013)

T. Berners-Lee, J. Hendler, O. Lassila, *The Semantic Web* (Scientific American, 2001), **284**(5): 28–37

C. Borgman, *Big Data, Little Data, No Data: Scholarship in The Networked World* (MIT, Cambridge, 2015)

S. Brier, *Cybersemiotics: Why Information Is Not Enough* (University of Toronto Press Inc., Toronto, 2008)

S. Brier, in *Theories of Information, Communication and Knowledge: A Multidisciplinary Approach*, ed. by F. Ibekwe-SanJuan, T. M. Dousa. The transdiciplinary view of information theory from a cybersemiotic perspective (Springer, New York, 2013), pp. 23–50

C.T. Chisita, and I. Abdullahi. *Rising Above the Grain Silo Mentality Through Collaboration: Creating Opportunities Between the Lis Educators and Prationners in Developing Countries.* World Library and Information Congress: 78th IFLA General Conference and Assembly. Helsinki: IFLA, 2012. 1–16.

Cisco, *The Zettabyte Era: Trends and Analysis* (Cisco Visual Networking Index, White Paper, San Jose, 2015)

D. Cohen, Defining the Digital Humanities. *Defining the Digital Humanities.* Panel presentation at Columbia University (2011).

R.J. Cox, E. Rasmussen, Reinventing the information professions and the argument for specialization in LIS education: Case studies in archives and information technology. J. Educ. Libr. Inf. Sci. **38**(4), 255–267 (1997)

L. Dechman, *Library of Congress to Cancel the Subject Heading "Illegal Aliens"* (Library of Congress, Memo, Washington D.C., 2016)

A.R. Diekama, A. Wesolek, C. Walters, The NSF/NIH effect: Surveying the effect of data management requirements on faculty, sponsored programs, and institutional repositories. J. Acad. Librariansh. **40**(3/4), 322–331 (2014)

K. Dill. The Best and Worst Master's Degrees for Jobs in 2015. (Forbes, July 15, 2015).

Q. Dombrowski. *Dirt: Digital Research Tools.* 2014. http://dirtdirectory.org/resources/pie-slice Accessed 4 Sept 2016

W.C. Dougherty, The Google books project: Will it make libraries obsolete? J. Acad. Librariansh. **36**(1), 86–89 (2010)

B. Franklin, Managing the electronic collection with cost per use data. IFLA J. **31**(3), 241–248 (2005)

J. Furner, Information science is neither. Library Trends **63**(3), 362–377 (2015)

J. Furner, Philosophy and information studies. Annu. Rev. Inf. Sci. Technol. **44**(1), 159–200 (2010)

R. Glanville Cybernetics: Thinking through the technology. In Traditions of Systems Theory: Major Figures and Contemporary Developments, by A Darrell, 45–83. New York: Routledge, 2014.

R. Guenther, S. McCallum, New metadata standards for digital resources: MODS and METS. Bull. Am. Soc. Inf. Sci. Technol. **29**(2), 12–15 (2003)

M.Y. Herring, *Are Libraries Obsolete? An Argument for Relevance in the Digital Age* (McFarland & Company, Inc., Jefferson, 2014)

T. Hey, and A. Trefethen. The data deluge: An E-science perspective. In Grid Computing: Making the Global Infrastucture a Reality, by F. Berman, G. Fox and T. Hey, 809–924. New York: Wiley, 2003.

F. Heylighen, C. Joslyn, V. Turchin, *What are Cybernetics and Systems Science?* (Principia Cybernetica Web, 1999).

B. Hjorland, Domain analysis in information science: Eleven approaches – Traditional as well as innovative. J. Doc. **58**(4), 422 (2002)

B. Hjørland, Library and information science: Practice, theory, and philosophical basis. Inf. Process. Manag. **36**(3), 501–531 (2000)

W. Hong, J.Y.L. Thong, K.-Y. Tam, W.-M. Wong, Determinants of user acceptance of digital libraries: An empirical examination of individual differences and system characteristics. J. Manag. Inf. Syst. **18**(3), 97–124 (2002)

J.B. Horrigan, M. Duggan, *Home Broadband 2015.* Washington D.C. (Pew Research Center, 2015)

A. Konrad. On Inquiry: Human concept formation and construction of meaning through library and information science intermediation (Doctoral dissertation), 2007.

S.D. Lee, Digitization: Is it worth it? Comput. Libr. **21**(5), 28–31 (2001)

A. Liu, The state of the digital humanities: A report and a critique. Arts Humanit. High. Educ. **11**(1/2), 8–41 (2012)

C.A. Lynch, Institutional repositories: Essential infrastructure for scholarship in the digital age. Portal Libr. Acad. **3**(2), 327–336 (2003)

S. Machlis, *IBM to shutter dataviz pioneer many eyes*. (Computer World, 2015).

P.F. Marty, M.B. Twidale, Museum informatics across the curriculum: Ten years of preparing LIS students for careers transcending libraries, archives, and museums. J. Educ. Libr. Inf. Sci. **52**(1), 9–16 (2011)

M. McLure, A.V. Level, C.L. Cranston, B. Oehlerts, M. Culbertson, Data curation: A study of researchers practices and needs. Portal: Libraries and the Academy **14**(2), 139–164 (2014)

D. Meadows, *Thinking in Systems: A Primer* (Chelsea Green Publishing, White River Junction, 2008)

M.D. Mesarovic, Views on general systems theory, in *Preface*, By M.D. Mesarovic, D.P. Eckman, (Wiley, New York, 1964), pp. xiii–xxvi.

V. Moniarou-Papaconstantinou, V. Evgenia, A. Tsatsaroni, Choice of library and information science in a rapidly changing information landscape: A systematic literature review. Libr. Manag. **36**(8/9), 584–608 (2015)

C.H. Montgomery, D.W. King, Comparing library and user related costs of print and electronic journal collections. D-Lib Mag. **8**(10), 1–14 (2002)

N.A., Digital Humanities Lab (2016). http://as.tufts.edu/csaios/digitalHumanities/. Accessed 30 Mar 2016.

S. Newbutt. What impressions do young people have of librarianship as a career? Thesis, Department of Information Studies, University of Sheffield, 2008.

J.E. Newhagen, S. Rafaeli, Why communication researchers should study the internet: A dialogue. J. Comput. Mediat. Commun. **1**(4) (1996)

NPR, *Before The Internet, Librarians Would 'Answer Everything'—And Still Do* (National Public Radio, 2014).

NYU Health Sciences Library, Data sharing and management snafu in 3 short acts. YouTube Video **4**, 40 (2012)

G. Oliver, in *Seventh International Conference on Conceptions of Library and Information Science*. Transcending silos, developing synergies: Libraries and archives (Information Research, London, 2010)

J. Oliver. *Last Week Tonight with John Oliver: Infrastructure*. New York, 2015.

Z. Papacharissi, A.M. Rubin, Predictors of internet use. J. Broadcast. Electron. Media **44**(2), 175–196 (2000)

J.-R. Park, Metadata quality in digital repositories: A survey of the current state of the art. Cat. Classif. Q. **47**(3/4), 213–228 (2009)

C. Prabha, L.S. Connaway, L. Olszewski, L.R. Jenkins, What is enough? Satisficing information needs. J. Doc. **63**(1), 74–89 (2007)

E. Ridge, M. Rogers, *Guerilla Analytics: A Practical Approach to Working with Data* (Morgan Kaufmann, Massachusetts, 2015)

L. Rosenfeld, P. Morville, *Information Architecture for the World Wide Web* (O'Reilly, Cambridge, 2002)

J. Smith. The Best and Worst Master's Degrees for Jobs. Forbes, 2012.

Southern Semiotic Review, *Peirce's Categories of Signs*. (Lowell, Massachusetts, 2013).

J. Teglovic, C. Jordan-Makely, L. Boyd, L. Hofschire, *What is the Value of an MLIS to You? Study* (Library Research Service, Denver, 2012)

C. Tenopir, *Use and Users of Electronic Library Resources: An Overview and Analysis of Recent Research Studis. White Paper* (Council on Library and Information Resources, Washington, DC, 2003)

L. Treaude, LIBREAS interview: Semiotics in information science. LIBREAS Libr. Ideas **19**, 70–77 (2011)

University of California, Los Angeles, Projects. UCLA Digital Humanities (N.D.), http://www.cdh.ucla.edu/projects/. Accessed 03 Feb 2016.

University Products, Inc, Archival Gold DVD-R: Lasts 100 Years! (02 Feb, 2010), http://www.universityproducts.com/cart.php?m=product_list&c=261 Accessed 03 Apr 2016.

R. Van Noorden, Open acess: The true cost of science publishing. Nature **495**(7442) (2013)

E. Vassilakaki, V. Moniarou-Papaconstantinou, Identifying the prevailing images in library and information science profession: Is the landscape changing? New Libr. World **115**(7/8), 355–375 (2014)

L. von Bertalanffy. The meaning of general system theory. In General System Theory: Foundations, Development, Application, by Ludwig von Bertalanffy, 30–53. New York: George Braziller, 1968.

C. Zins, Conceptual approaches for defining data, information, and knowledge. J. Am. Soc. Inf. Sci. Technol. **58**(4), 479–493 (2007)

Printed in the United States
By Bookmasters